Directory of Photographers in the United States 1888 & 1889 and Canada 1889

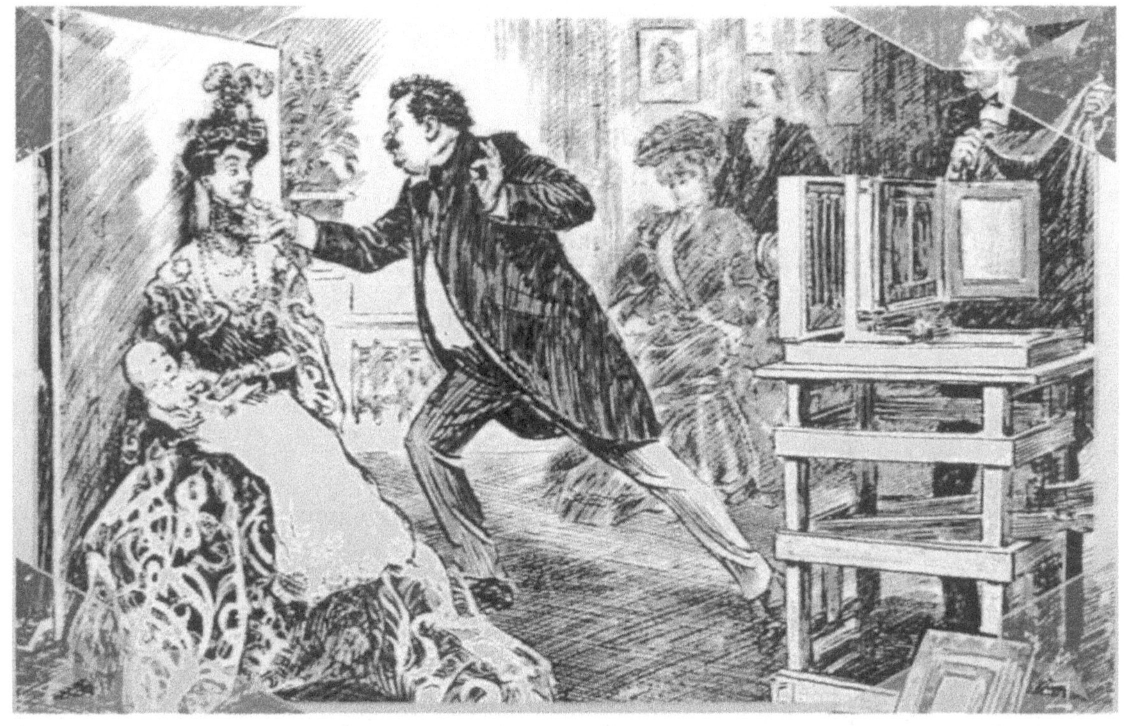

Compiled by
Diane VanSkiver Gagel

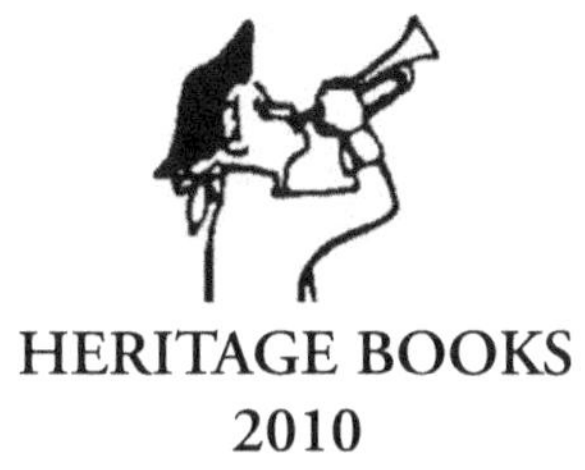

HERITAGE BOOKS
2010

HERITAGE BOOKS
AN IMPRINT OF HERITAGE BOOKS, INC.

Books, CDs, and more—Worldwide

For our listing of thousands of titles see our website
at
www.HeritageBooks.com

Published 2010 by
HERITAGE BOOKS, INC.
Publishing Division
100 Railroad Ave. #104
Westminster, Maryland 21157

Other books by the author:
Windows on the Past: Identifying, Dating, and Preserving Photographs

International Standard Book Numbers
Paperbound: 978-0-7884-2263-8
Clothbound: 978-0-7884-8347-9

Table of Contents

Introduction

This Directory was taken from the First and Second Annual Editions of the Lithographers' and Photographers' Directory: A Directory for Lithographers, Photographers and for all allied Arts and Trades in the United States and Canada, Mexico, Central and South America, published in 1888 and 1889. In the original format it was arranged by country, state and city. I have included a copy of this format in this publication. However, to make it easier to locate the name of a photographer in either the United States or Canada, I have also compiled an alphabetical listing by the surname and first name of the photographer.

For abbreviations for the states in the U. S. I have used the standard postal abbreviations. One must remember, however, that in 1889 the following states were then territories: Arizona and Washington. There were no photographers listed for New Mexico in 1889. The 1888 edition did not contain information on the Canadian photographers. For the Canadian provinces I have used the following abbreviations:

BC-British Columbia
MB—Manitoba
NB—New Brunswick
NWT—North-West Territories
NS—Nova Scotia
ON—Ontario
PQ—Quebec

The * after a photographer's name designates that the photographer's name appeared only in the 1888 edition of the Directory.

ALPHABETICAL LISTING OF PHOTOGRAPHERS IN THE U. S. IN 1888 & 1889

NAME		ADDRESS	CITY	STATE
Aaberg	John		Cooperstown	DK
Abbett	E. R.		Flora	IL
Abbey	L. C.		Kalamazoo	MI
Abbott	B.		Biddeford	ME
Abbott	C. A.	351 Lincoln	Chicago	IL
Abbott	C. E.		Henry	IL
Abbott	J. L.	91 N. Pearl	Albany	NY
Abbott	R. R.		Union Springs	NY
Abbott	S. C.		Morris	IL
Abbott	W. D.		Auburn	NE
Abbott	W. D.		Peru	NE
Abbott	W. H.		Little Falls	NY
Abbotts	D. E.		Huntington	WV
Abell & Son			Corvallis	OR
Abell & Son			Portland	OR
Aber	J. F.		Auburn	IN
Abernathy	Arthur		Champaign	IL
Abraham	A. W.		Detroit	MI
Abrahams	David	273 Fulton	Brooklyn	NY
Abrams & Son	J. R.		Brownsville	PA
Acker	Victor	159 6th	New York City	NY
Acme Copying Co.		302 W. VanBuren	Chicago	IL
Acme Portrait Co.*			Newton	IA
Adams	A. W.		Decorah	IA
Adams	C. A.		West Gardner	MA
Adams	C. W.		Whitehall	NY
Adams	E.	120 Main	Gloucester	MA
Adams	G. H.		Griswold	IA
Adams	J. A.		Sterling	IL
Adams	J. M.		Irwin	PA
Adams	John M.		Terre Haute	IN
Adams	Mrs. C. N.		El Dorado	KS
Adams	Mrs. T. E.		Davenport	IA
Adams	Mrs. T. E.		Davis City	IA
Adams	R. F.		East St. Louis	IL
Adams	S. M.		Elgin	IL
Adams	Charles H.	145 Canal	New Orleans	LA
Adams Bros.			Ogden City	UT
Adams Safford & Co		48 Bond	New York City	NY
Adams*	C. E.		Downs	KS
Adams*	Charles H.	111 Royal	New Orleans	LA

ALPHABETICAL LISTING OF PHOTOGRAPHERS IN THE U. S. IN 1888 & 1889

NAME		ADDRESS	CITY	STATE
Adams*	I. W.		Minneapolis	MN
Adamson	Samuel J.		Brownsville	PA
Addleman	B. T.		Athens	OH
Adlington & Chase			Viroqua	WI
Admire	C. A.		Cowles	NE
Adt	Alfred A.	63 Bank	Waterbury	CT
Adt & Brother			Waterbury	CT
Affolter	W. H.		Princeville	IL
Ahern	John	175 Milwaukee	Chicago	IL
Ahlbon*	W. J.	335 W. Madison	Chicago	IL
Ahlborn	W. H.	335 W. Madison	Chicago	IL
Ahrens	Frederick		Tarrytown	NY
Ahrens & Bro.	J.		Yonkers	NY
Aichberg	C.		Santa Cruz	CA
Aikin	Charles		Evanston	IL
Ainsworth	J. A.		Pleasant Hill	MO
Albee	M. H.		Marlborough	MA
Albert & Son	A.		Alexandria	LA
Albright	William H.		New Castle	IN
Albright & Bernard			Fort Burford	DK
Albritton & Ellison			Union City	TN
Alden	A. E.	63 Court	Boston	MA
Alden Photo Co..		62 Arcade	Providence	RI
Aldrich	George H.		Littleton	NH
Aldrich & Ludeke		600 McMillan	Walnut Hills	OH
Aldridge	George	1013 N. Kansas	Topeka	KS
Alexander	J. B.	1930 Carson	Pittsburgh	PA
Alexander	W. S.		Camden	SC
Alford	B. F.		Oswego	NY
Allderidge	F. W.		New Britain	CT
Allderidge	W.		Plainville	CT
Alldridge*	J. W.	42 Bank	Waterbury	CT
Allen	A. M.		Pottsville	PA
Allen	E. H.		Bradford	VT
Allen	F. L.		Norwich	CT
Allen	Frank		Catskill	NY
Allen	G. B.		Plainfield	NJ
Allen	H. S.		Manchester	VT
Allen	J. H.		Russell	KS
Allen	Jonathan	335 8th	New York City	NY
Allen	M. W.		Jamaica	VT

ALPHABETICAL LISTING OF PHOTOGRAPHERS IN THE U. S. IN 1888 & 1889

NAME		ADDRESS	CITY	STATE
Allen	N. E.		Leslie	MI
Allen	W. H.		Chippewa Falls	WI
Allen	A. T. H.		Townsend	MT
Allen	J. R.		Mansfield	MA
Allen	S. V.		Freeport	IL
Allen	W. R.		Cambridge	IL
Allen	Warren P.		Gardner	MA
Allen & Haines			La Plata	MO
Allen & Hay		342 Kearney	San Francisco	CA
Allen & Rowell		25 Winter	Boston	MA
Allen*	F. W.		Chanute	KS
Allen*	J. O.		Fort Wayne	IN
Allen*	O. T. H.		Buffalo	WY
Aller*	Charles		Detroit	MI
Allerton	W. H.		Port Jervis	NY
Alley	E. H.	91 Summit	Toledo	OH
Alley	Hiram F.		Beverly	MA
Alley & Bell		123 5th	New York City	NY
Allgier	F. X.	8 Syracuse House Bl.	Syracuse	NY
Allis	J. R.		Lansingburgh	NY
Allison*	James D.		Bloomington	IN
Alman	Louis	172 5th	New York City	NY
Alman	Louis		Newport	RI
Alter	David		Greencastle	PA
Alvord	C. E.	244 Woodward	Detroit	MI
Alvord	E. D.		Bushwell	IL
American Portrait Co.		13 Bible	New York City	NY
Ames	A. E.	214 State	Chicago	IL
Ames & Co.	A. E.	3035 Indiana	Chicago	IL
Anable	J. M.		Leland	IL
Anderson	A. W.		Haverhill	MA
Anderson	C. M.		Sioux City	IA
Anderson	Clarence		Hopkinsville	KY
Anderson	D. H.	785 Broadway	New York City	NY
Anderson	George		Norwich	CT
Anderson	J. T.		Rockford	IL
Anderson	J. T.		Warren	IL
Anderson	John		Cadillac	MI
Anderson	L. S.		Springfield	IL
Anderson	O. N.		Minneapolis	MN
Anderson	P. G.		Redfield	DK

ALPHABETICAL LISTING OF PHOTOGRAPHERS IN THE U. S. IN 1888 & 1889

NAME		ADDRESS	CITY	STATE
Anderson	U. J.		Wahoo	NE
Anderson & Cheaney			Hopkinsville	KY
Anderson*	Daniel	785 Broadway	New York City	NY
Anderson*	N. J.		Oakland	NE
Anderson*	W. A.		Ord	NE
Anderson's Studio		251 King	Charleston	SC
Andre & Dettra			Pottstown	PA
Andrews	A. F.		La Crosse	WI
Andrews	D. W.		Raleigh	NC
Andrews	H. L.		Lincoln	NE
Andrews	John D.	178 Washington	Boston	MA
Andrie	Charles	94 Chatham	New York City	NY
Angell	C. L.		Litchfield	MN
Angell	Daniel		East Saginaw	MI
Ansbach	J. S.		Pillow	PA
Anschultz	Leo		Boscobel	WI
Ansher	L.	57 W. Madison	Chicago	IL
Ansher*	Louis	835 S. Halsted	Chicago	IL
Anson	E.	46 W. Madison	Chicago	IL
Anthony	M.		Longview	TX
Anthony	William. H.	905 Pennsylvania	Washington	DC
Antle	Logan		Elk City	KS
Antrey	George		Hico	TX
Anundson	Olaf		Sheffield	PA
Apfel	Henry		Shell Rock	IA
Apgar	W. A.		Sommerville	NJ
Aplington	L. A.		Long Island	KS
Applegate	James R.	256 N. 8th	Philadelphia	PA
Applegate & Sons	J. R.		Atlantic City	NJ
Applequist	A. J.		Ellendale	DK
Appleton	J. M.	3rd & Jefferson	Dayton	OH
Araah	Antheonia		Monticello	IA
Araah	Athonia		Oxford Junction	IA
Archer	George W.		Baldwin	MS
Archer	William		Gaffney City	SC
Architectural Publishing Co.*		70 Kilby	Boston	MA
Arcouet	Casimer		Aurora	IL
Armand*	E. F.		Portland	ME
Armbrust	J. D.		Meyersdale	PA
Armor	A. H.	465 W. Indiana	Chicago	IL
Armsbury	Stiles P.		Adams	NY

ALPHABETICAL LISTING OF PHOTOGRAPHERS IN THE U. S. IN 1888 & 1889

NAME		ADDRESS	CITY	STATE
Armstead & Son*			South Bend	NE
Armstrong	J. W.		Virden	IL
Armstrong	Samuel		Washington	IA
Armstrong	W. A.	389 Broadway	Milwaukee	WI
Armstrong	W. E.		Nashville	TN
Arnold	A.		Greenwich	NY
Arnold	C. R.		Marseilles	IL
Arnold	Charles D.	25 E. 14th	New York City	NY
Arnold	S. C.		Ottawa	OH
Arnold	T. J.		Ballston	NY
Arnold	W.		San Luis Obispo	CA
Arnold & Co.*			Des Moines	IA
Arnold*	Charles D.	10 E. 14th	New York	NY
Arnout	J. M.	River co. 4th	Troy	NY
Arnow	Nathan	16 W. 14th	New York City	NY
Arrico	Frank	146 W. 5th	Cincinnati	OH
Arrington	F. P.		Millen	GA
Arthur & Philbric		204 Woodward	Detroit	MI
Arvin	A. J.		Mexia	TX
Asher	Julius	810 ½ J	Sacramento	CA
Ashforth*	G. H.		Shakopee	MN
Asnon	A. F.		Elizabeth	NJ
Asthoff	Herman	237 N. Clark	Chicago	IL
Astrom	Carl G.	7 State	Boston	MA
Atchley	A. S.		Rockford	IL
Atherton	F. P.		Reed City	MI
Atherton	H. M.		North Topeka	KS
Atherton	M. M.		Topeka	KS
Atherton	Mary		Concordia	KS
Atkins	Joseph		Warren	RI
Atkins	W. B.		Bunker Hill	IL
Atkinson	C. W.		Moline	IL
Atkinson	George		Kansas City	KS
Atkinson Bros.*			East Liverpool	OH
Atkinson*	A. T.		Thayer	KS
Atkinson*	George		Kansas City	MO
Atwood	B. L.		Petaluma	CA
Atwood	L. A.		Burlington	VT
Auberts	A. J.	305 North	Chicago	IL
Aubner	Calvin		Curllsville	PA
Auchmoody	D. J.		Rondout	NY

ALPHABETICAL LISTING OF PHOTOGRAPHERS IN THE U. S. IN 1888 & 1889

NAME		ADDRESS	CITY	STATE
Aufrecht	G.		Allegheny	PA
Aufrecht*	G.	66 Federal A.	Pittsburgh	PA
Augusta Photo C.			Augusta	GA
Ault & Clark			Unionville	MO
Aunspach	W. S.		Pine Grove	PA
Austin	A. C.		Nashua	NH
Austin	Americus	108 Wakeman	Toledo	OH
Austin	C. W.		Rockford	MI
Austin	Honoria		Shelbyville	IL
Austin	Samuel		Oswego	NY
Austin & Bowers*			St. Louis	MO
Avenarius	G. A.		Ellsworth	KS
Averill*	T.		Honey Grove	TX
Avery*	R. S.		Pulaski	NY
Ayer	E.		Norwich	CT
Ayer	G. O.		Augusta	ME
Ayer	George O.	74 Meridian	Boston	MA
Ayers	Edgar M.	269 Warren	Jersey City	NJ
Ayers	Ellis		Dodge Centre	MN
Aylesworth	John		East Greenwich	RI
Aylesworth	John		Phenix	RI
Ayres	J. T.		McConnelsville	OH
Baag	Peter	1536 3rd	New York City	NY
Babb	G. W.	Chapel St.	New Haven	CT
Babb & Root			Shelbyville	IL
Babbitt	J. P.		Wyandotte	KS
Babcock	W. R.	235 Summit	Toledo	OH
Bach	Frederick	507 8th	New York City	NY
Bachman	Rudolph	1437 Broadway	New York City	NY
Bachman*			Allentown	PA
Bachs & Bros.	G. W.		Cambridgeport	MA
Bacon	F. W. & G. W.	118 E. Main	Rochester	NY
Bacon	J. H.		Litchfield	MN
Bacon Bros.			San Jose	CA
Baer	Alfred		Baraboo	WI
Bagley	F. L.		Butler	PA
Bailer	S. J.		Mankato	MN
Bailey	A. F.		Tulare	CA
Bailey	David		Tamaqua	PA
Bailey	Elisha		Eden	NY
Bailey	H. C.		Concord	NH

ALPHABETICAL LISTING OF PHOTOGRAPHERS IN THE U. S. IN 1888 & 1889

NAME		ADDRESS	CITY	STATE
Bailey	J. W.		Dowagiac	MI
Bailey	Robert		Jackson	MI
Bailey	William		Columbia	PA
Bailey*	David C.	2566 Broadway	Cleveland	OH
Bailor	J. M.		Culbertson	NE
Bainbridge*	J. G.	291 Manhattan	Brooklyn	NY
Baird	J. A.		Rushville	IL
Baird	J. B.	22 S. Phelps	Youngstown	OH
Baird	J. H.	209 Wabash	Chicago	IL
Baird*	J. R.	22 S. Phelps	Youngstown	OH
Bairstow	J. R.		Warren	PA
Bairstow	W. A.		Warren	PA
Bairstow*	J. R.		Warren	PA
Bake	E. P.		Maple Rapids	MI
Baker	C. R.	39 Monroe	Detroit	MI
Baker	E. P.		Grand Haven	MI
Baker	E. W.		Placerville	CA
Baker	G. M.		Rutland	VT
Baker	G. W.		Johnson	VT
Baker	J. H.	406 Main	Worcester	MA
Baker	L. M.	Comstock's Opera House	Columbus	OH
Baker	Mrs.		Rapid City	DK
Baker	N. B.		Brockport	NY
Baker	Thomas		Burlington	NJ
Baker	W. H.		Saratoga Springs	NY
Baker	W. J.	390 Main	Buffalo	NY
Baker	W. W.		East Fairfield	VT
Baker & Co.	L.	10 Weybosset	Providence	RI
Baker & Johnson*			Detroit	MI
Baker & Johnson*			Chester	SC
Baker*	E. P.		Maple Rapids	MI
Baker*	H. J.		Chrisman	IL
Baker*	Miss C. E.		Galena	KS
Balatka Bros.		363 Division	Chicago	IL
Balcom	Abram		Stamford	CT
Balding	L. W.		Augusta	KS
Baldwin	A. A.		Torrington	CT
Baldwin	A. A.		Ludlow	VT
Baldwin	G. W.		Plattsburgh	NY
Baldwin	J. E. D.	421 J.	Sacramento	CA
Baldwin	J. E. D.		Stockton	CA

ALPHABETICAL LISTING OF PHOTOGRAPHERS IN THE U. S. IN 1888 & 1889

NAME		ADDRESS	CITY	STATE
Baldwin	W. D.		Superior	WI
Baldwin	J.		La Fayette	IN
Baldwin & Ames		55 Central Music Hall	Chicago	IL
Baldwin & Charles		2029 Wabash	Chicago	IL
Baldwin & Co.	O. N.		Clarksville	MO
Baldwin & Peck			Watertown	NY
Baldwin & Son			Wichita	KS
Baldwin*	O. K.		Amherst	WI
Ball	A. P.		Eaton Rapids	MI
Ball	H. A.		Park River	DK
Ball	J. A.		Albion	MI
Ball	J. D.		Grafton	DK
Ball	James		Fostoria	OH
Ball	W. B.		Hastings	MI
Ball*	H. A.	333 W. 14th	Chicago	IL
Ballard	G. E.		Appleton	WI
Ballard	M. O.		Nimrod	KS
Ballard*	M. T.		Appleton	WI
Baltes	Frank E.	329 Grove	Milwaukee	WI
Baltimore Photographic Co.		66 Lexington	Baltimore	MD
Bamgartem	H.		Charlotte	NC
Bancroft	George W.	6 City Hall Place	New York City	NY
Bangs	Dwight		Sleepy Eye	MN
Bangs	E. D.	86 Wisconsin	Milwaukee	WI
Bangs, Jr.	J. A.		Wells	MN
Banister	Frank		New Richmond	WI
Bankes	T. W.		Little Rock	AR
Bankins	Frank A.		Eugene City	OR
Banta	J. C.		Watertown	NY
Banthoux	Emil	2 First	New York City	NY
Barber	A.		Indianola	NE
Barber & Co.	A. J.		Auburn	NY
Barber & Son*			Lawson	MO
Barbour	J. S.		Williamstown	KY
Barbour	J. W.		Chambersburgh	PA
Barcalow & Co.	R. G.	76 Bowery	New York City	NY
Bardwell	Jex	115 Jefferson	Detroit	MI
Bardwell*	J. J.		Detroit	MI
Bare	M. E.		Hummelstown	PA
Barentzen Photographic Parlors		11 Park Sq	Boston	MA
Barge	John W.	249 Superior	Cleveland	OH

ALPHABETICAL LISTING OF PHOTOGRAPHERS IN THE U. S. IN 1888 & 1889

NAME		ADDRESS	CITY	STATE
Barker	George		Niagara Falls	NY
Barker	George B.		Granville	NY
Barker	J. F.		Galesburgh	IL
Barkman*	Charles G.	419 Broadway	New York	NY
Barler	Oliver K.		Granville	NY
Barling	Miss M.		Gordon	NE
Barnard	G. N.		Painesville	OH
Barnard	George C.	33 Goodrich	Springfield	MA
Barnard & Johnson			Conway Springs	KS
Barner	William		Galena	IL
Barnes	Chauncey		Mobile	AL
Barnes	G. W.		Rockford	IL
Barnes	Isaac		Chatfield	MN
Barnes	J. C.		New Bethlehem	PA
Barnes	J. H.		Ottawa	KS
Barnes	J. M.		Bloomington	IN
Barnes	John H.	2336 Carson	Pittsburgh	PA
Barnes	William H.		Barnesville	OH
Barnes	William L.		Winona	MN
Barnes*	John H.	2340 Carson	Pittsburgh	PA
Barnett	A. L.		Halstead	KS
Barnett	George W.	2 New Chambers	New York City	NY
Barney	J. R.		Champlain	NY
Barnhart*	James		Germantown	OH
Barnhouse	T. E.		Grand Junction	CO
Barr	D. P.		San Antonio	TX
Barr	H. A.		Grand Rapids	MI
Barr	Mike		Tompkinsville	KY
Barr & Hayter*			Battle Creek	MI
Barrett	Henry		E. Cambridgeport	MA
Barrett	James		Wenona	IL
Barrett	W. H.		Hyde Park	MA
Barrett*	J. H.		Waco	TX
Barrette	Thornton		Ironton	OH
Barrette*	T.		Clarksburg	WV
Barron	W. H.		Port Huron	MI
Barrows	F. R.		Ft. Wayne	IN
Barrows	J. G.		Grand Rapids	MI
Barry	A. L.		Port Deposit	MD
Barry	D. F.		Bismark	DK
Bartley*	F. H.		Salinas	CA

ALPHABETICAL LISTING OF PHOTOGRAPHERS IN THE U. S. IN 1888 & 1889

NAME		ADDRESS	CITY	STATE
Barton	C. J.		North Anson	ME
Barton	L. W.		Jackson	MI
Barton	M. B.		Alexandria	DK
Bass	E. A.		Brockton	MA
Bassett	F. J.		Erie	PA
Bassett & Payne			Augusta	GA
Bassett*	G. T.		Chicago	IL
Bassney	J. J.		Memphis	MI
Bastian	Z. T.		Olathe	KS
Batchelder	B. P.		Stockton	CA
Batchelder*			Georgetown	MA
Bates	W. L.		Denver	CO
Batterson	Lincoln S.	635 Third	Brooklyn	NY
Battle Creek View Co.*			Battle Creek	MI
Battles	B. F.	106 E. Market	Akron	OH
Batty	James		Utica	MI
Bauder	G. W.		Marinette	WI
Bauer & Son	S.		Leavenworth	KS
Baugh	George W.		Wilmington	DE
Baumgardner & Helbling		3915 Lancaster	Philadelphia	PA
Baurmann	G.		Macon	GA
Baxter	M. D.		Melton	IA
Baxter	Port C.		Carrollton	OH
Bayha	G. L.		Monongahela City	PA
Bayley*	F. L.		Butler	PA
Bayme	J. A.		Pulaski	NY
Bayne	James		Grand Rapids	MI
Bays	E. W.		Rushville	IL
Beach	A. W.		Nashua	IA
Beach	E. A.		Sparta	WI
Beach & Shaw		125 Fulton	New York City	NY
Beacham	James		Plymouth	PA
Beal	Joshua H.	278 Pearl	New York City	NY
Beal	W. A.		Ipswich	MA
Beal & Burt			Minneapolis	MN
Beals	Charles	654 Newark	Jersey City	NJ
Beals	Ferris		Evansville	WI
Beals	H. C.		Fulton	NY
Beals	H. S.	415 J.	Sacramento	CA
Beam	L. V.		Sioux Fall	DK
Bean	A. M.		Lawrence	MA

ALPHABETICAL LISTING OF PHOTOGRAPHERS IN THE U. S. IN 1888 & 1889

NAME		ADDRESS	CITY	STATE
Bean*	B. F.		New Kiowa	KS
Beane	C. E.	2180 Washington	Boston	MA
Beannor*	J.		West Bridgewater	PA
Beard	A. S.		Du Bois	PA
Beard	H. A.		Waukegan	IL
Bearden	W. L.		Princton	MO
Beardsley	J.		Ithaca	NY
Beatty	J. W.		Carrollton	IL
Beatty	Kate		Milford	MA
Beatty	William		Sigourney	IA
Beauchamp*	C. E.		Tallapoosa	GA
Bebby	Frederick		Pawtucket	RI
Bechtel	G. W.		Colfax	WA
Beck	A. A.		Sauk City	WI
Beck	G. F.	327 S. Sharp	Baltimore	MD
Beck	Hezekiah		Winfield	KS
Beck	John C.	35 First Ave.	Corry	PA
Beck & Fields		207 Summit	Toledo	OH
Beck & Reese			Worthington	IN
Beck*	E. H.		Parsons	KS
Beck*	John C.		Carry	PA
Becker & Co.		405 8th	New York City	NY
Becker Bros.		783 Lorain	Cleveland	OH
Beckett	C. J. H.		Wilmington	DE
Beckley	Eli		Jesup	IA
Beckwith & Brown			Helena	MT
Beckwith & Son	M. E.	261 Pearl	Cleveland	OH
Bedell	E.		Poughkeepsie	NY
Bedell	S. W.		Talmage	NE
Bedford	George O.		Haverstraw	NY
Beebe	John E.		Denver	CO
Beebe	W. S.		Owosso	MI
Beebe & Feighner			Nashville	MI
Beech*	Thomas J.	706 Chestnut	Philadelphia	PA
Beecher*	A. S.		Dover	DE
Beedy	F. N.		Postville	IA
Beekman	Fred.		Ottawa	KS
Beeles	H. M.		Troy	PA
Beels	H. M.		Hornellsville	NY
Beem	R. D.		Greenville	OH
Beenck	P. H.	3727 N. Broadway	St. Louis	MO

ALPHABETICAL LISTING OF PHOTOGRAPHERS IN THE U. S. IN 1888 & 1889

NAME		ADDRESS	CITY	STATE
Beer	A. G.		Trenton	NJ
Beers	W. A.	762 Chapel	New Haven	CT
Beery*	G. W.		Logan	OH
Beidle	H. F.		Shippensburgh	PA
Belbrough	J.		Dubuque	IA
Belden	A.		Albion	NY
Bell	A. S.		East Brady	PA
Bell	Charles M.	463 Pennsylvania	Washington	DC
Bell	E. H.	1427 Pine	St. Louis	MO
Bell	R. H.		Hodgensville	KY
Bell	William	2330 Montgomery	Philadelphia	PA
Bell	C. G.		Greenville	MS
Bell & Melton			Santa Ana	CA
Bell & Melton*			Santa Ana	CA
Belle Studio		716 Olive	St. Louis	MO
Bellis	Henry		Atlantic City	NJ
Bellis & Cummings			Chester	PA
Belts	J. W.		Neosho	MO
Bendann	D.	28 E. Baltimore	Baltimore	MD
Bender	J. F.		Towanda	PA
Bender	Louis	305 North	Chicago	IL
Bendixen*	E.		Weedport	NY
Bendixen*	Emil		Chittenango	NY
Benecke	Theodore	4th S. E. c. Market	St. Louis	MO
Benecke*	Robert		St. Louis	MO
Benedict	C. B.	70 Bank	Waterbury	CT
Benedict	Neal D.		Litchfield	CT
Benedict	W. W.		Barrington	IL
Benicsky	Sara	2 New Chambers	New York City	NY
Benjamin	De Forrest		De Ruyter	NY
Benjamin & Sons	W. C.		Orange	NJ
Bennett	A. J.		Woonsocket	RI
Bennett	Alexander	420 3rd	New York City	NY
Bennett	C. E.	3915 Cottage Grove	Chicago	IL
Bennett	H. H.		Kilbourn City	WI
Bennett	Jalet	793 Broad	Newark	NJ
Bennett	L. E.		McHenry	IL
Bennett & Co.		1311 Broadway	New York City	NY
Bennett*	A. C.		Worcester	MA
Benoit	A.		New Bedford	MA
Bensen	J. H.		Pontiac	MI

ALPHABETICAL LISTING OF PHOTOGRAPHERS IN THE U. S. IN 1888 & 1889

NAME		ADDRESS	CITY	STATE
Benson	Harvey		Bellaire	OH
Bentley*	A. L.		Pierce	NE
Benton	L. B.	155 Bank	Waterbury	CT
Benton*	W. E.		Valparaiso	NE
Berg	Jacob		Grand Forks	DK
Berger	Frederick		Anna	IL
Berger	J. N.		Elgin	IA
Berger	William A.		Frederick	MD
Bergerson	W. O.		Lake Park	MN
Berggren	P. A.		Hector	MN
Bergmann	Caroline	204 W. Market	Louisville	KY
Bergstresser	J. B.		Renova	PA
Berkely	George P.		Milton	VT
Berker*	H. F.		Savanna	IL
Berlin Photographic Studio*			Chicago	IL
Berry	E. M.		Bridgton	ME
Berry	Marion		Sturgeon	MO
Berry*	T. J.		Shelbyville	TN
Berryman	E. C.		Midland	MI
Bertlieb	William		Random Lake	WI
Bertrand	E. E.		Cresco	IA
Bertrand	S. A.	149 Chicago	Chicago	IL
Besker & Fell			Charleston	WV
Bestic & Logan			Fargo	DK
Bettison	N. Byron	323 4th	Louisville	KY
Betts	E. C.	356 Main	Bridgeport	CT
Betz & Richards			Lancaster	PA
Betz, Jr.	John	417 N. Washington	Baltimore	MD
Bevair			Elgin	IA
Beverage	M. C.		Marshalltown	IA
Bevington & Stutz			Upper Sandusky	OH
Beyer Portrait Co.		1713 Oak	Kansas City	MO
Bickelman	O. Conrad	397 Grand	Brooklyn	NY
Bickett	Hugh		Litchfield	IL
Bidde	Henry	75 Euclid	Cleveland	OH
Biddle	F. S.		Xenia	OH
Biddle*	Henry	75 Euclid	Cleveland	OH
Bidwell	G. W.		Farmersville	MO
Bidwill	William		Galt	MO
Bielefield	P. F.	169 Canalport	Chicago	IL
Bierstadt	C.		Niagara Falls	NY

ALPHABETICAL LISTING OF PHOTOGRAPHERS IN THE U. S. IN 1888 & 1889

NAME		ADDRESS	CITY	STATE
Biery	T.		Pleasant Lake	IN
Biffar	Bernard T.	516 Broadway	Brooklyn	NY
Biffar	Henry W.	109 Bedford	Brooklyn	NY
Bigden	F. A.	262 W. Madison	Chicago	IL
Bigden	C. W.	252 Main	Buffalo	NY
Bigelow	A. M.		Moorhead	MN
Bigelow	G. H.		Elysian	MN
Bigelow	H. S.		Dowagiac	MI
Bigelow	L. W.		Jackson	MI
Bigelow	W. A.		Plattsburgh	NY
Bigelow	W. H.		Port Henry	NY
Biggart Solar Printing	Co.	58 & 60 University Place	New York City	NY
Biggins	T. A.		Wheeling	WV
Bijou Photo Studio		235 Fulton	Brooklyn	NY
Billian	Benjamin		Doylestown	PA
Billings	E. T.	501 Main	Racine	WI
Billingsley	George W.		Grandview	IN
Billows	A. R.		Dallas	TX
Bingham & Hilliard			Memphis	TN
Birig	George		St. Louis	MO
Birtles	F. C.		Woonsocket	RI
Bischoff	C. S.		Wymore	NE
Bishop	C.		Indianapolis	IN
Bishop	Frank, Jr.	99 Wisconsin	Milwaukee	WI
Bishop	G. W.		Necedah	WI
Bishop	Giles		New London	CT
Bishop	Henry		Chambersburgh	PA
Bishop	S. J. & A. H.	380 Main	Springfield	MA
Bishop & Buckley			Peabody	KS
Bishop & Co.		Washington Row	Sandusky	OH
Bishop Bros.			Minneapolis	MN
Bishop Bros.			Altoona	PA
Bishop*	C. D.		Elwood	NE
Bissell	Edward		Milford	MI
Bissell	L. H.		Effingham	IL
Bittenbender	L. C.		Knoxville	IA
Bitter & Weston		148 State	Chicago	IL
Bixby	Hira L.		Chelsea	VT
Bixby	M. A.		Ludlow	VT
Bixby	M. J.		Castleton	VT
Bjorlund	Swamug		Paxton	IL

ALPHABETICAL LISTING OF PHOTOGRAPHERS IN THE U. S. IN 1888 & 1889

NAME		ADDRESS	CITY	STATE
Bjornson	S. J.		Mountain	DK
Black	A. C.		Washington	IA
Black	Isaiah		Franklin	PA
Black & Co.	J. W.	333 Washington	Boston	MA
Blackburn	G. F.		Grand Forks	DK
Blackburn	G. H.		Appleton	WI
Blackburn & Webb		120 W. Federal	Youngstown	OH
Blackburn*	G. H.		Seymour	WI
Blackemore	B. A.		Staunton	VA
Blackman	C. A.		Norwalk	CT
Blackmann	F. G.		Wauseon	OH
Blair	C. L.	44 Front	Worcester	MA
Blair*	J. E.		Fort Worth	TX
Blair	L. G.		Ida Grove	IA
Blair	W. E.		Sac City	IA
Blair*	W. F.		Randolph	IA
Blair & Son	R. H.	411 Main	Worcester	MA
Blake	E. F.		Chattanooga	TN
Blake	F. J.		Bellow's Falls	VT
Blake*	J. M.	1York Sq.	New Haven	CT
Blakeslee & Moore			Ashtabula	OH
Blanchard	A. N.		Montpelier	VT
Blanchard*	J. B.	57 W. Madison	Chicago	IL
Blanchard	W. T.		Braintree	VT
Bland	J. S.		Anoka	MN
Blanks	A. L.		Vicksburg	MS
Blanks	A. L.		Memphis	TN
Blatt	C. G.		Bernville	PA
Blaul	Louis	1937 Germantown	Philadelphia	PA
Blaul & Baumgardner*		3915 Lancaster	Philadelphia	PA
Blaylock	J. W.		Lyons	KS
Blessing	J. H.		Salamanca	NY
Blessing	Samuel P.		Galveston	TX
Blessing & Co.		214 N. Charles	Baltimore	MD
Blessing & Co.*		46 N. Charles	Baltimore	MD
Bline	J. W.		Hartsville	IN
Bliss	H. L.	368 Main	Buffalo	NY
Bliss	L. R.		Coudersport	PA
Block	Benoit	179 Myrtle	Brooklyn	NY
Blocksom*	H. H.		Hastings	MI
Blumenshein	George	2826 State	Chicago	IL

ALPHABETICAL LISTING OF PHOTOGRAPHERS IN THE U. S. IN 1888 & 1889

NAME		ADDRESS	CITY	STATE
Blunt	A. H.		Danville	VA
Blurton	W. F.		Beecher City	IL
Bock	Frederick	418 Fulton	Brooklyn	NY
Bodey	Kate		Sherman	MI
Bodge	E. R.	330 E. Division	Chicago	IL
Bodie	Joseph A.		Honesdale	PA
Bodurtha	Charles H.		Delaware	OH
Bodwell	Albert L.	37 Weybosset	Providence	RI
Body	W.		Hillman	MI
Boehl & Koenig		707 N. 4th	St. Louis	MO
Boepple	Charles		Erie	PA
Bogardus	Abraham	872 Broadway	New York City	NY
Bogardus		348 6th	New York City	NY
Bogardus*	Ed. W.	349 6th	New York City	NY
Bogardus*		349 6th	New York City	NY
Boggs	J. F.		Liberty	SC
Bogrand	Peter		Marshfield	WI
Bohner	J. A.		Carrol	IA
Bolles	Charles E.	242 Fulton	Brooklyn	NY
Bolton	George M.		Rockville	CT
Bonine*	Robert A.		Altoona	PA
Bonnell	Frederick		Eau Claire	WI
Bonney	A. F.		Marshalltown	IA
Bonney	James		South Bend	IN
Bonney & Roberts			Machias	ME
Boone & Co.	C. H.	185 Howard	Akron	OH
Booth	H. M.		Rich Hill	MO
Booth	James		St. George	UT
Booth	S. L.		Elmwood	IL
Borah	C. W.		Lancaster	OH
Borchers	A.	894 Sheffield	Chicago	IL
Border	Henry		East Liverpool	OH
Borlang	O. E.		Calmar	IA
Boroman	H. G.		New Lexington	OH
Borry & Co.*	J.		Minneapolis	MN
Bosch			St. Louis	MO
Boss	D. W.		Mechanicsburgh	PA
Bosshard*	Gebhard		Cobden	IL
Bostwick	H. L.	98 6th	New York City	NY
Bostwick	J. H.		Bristol	PA
Boswell	A. C.		Wayne City	IL

ALPHABETICAL LISTING OF PHOTOGRAPHERS IN THE U. S. IN 1888 & 1889

NAME		ADDRESS	CITY	STATE
Boswell	William		Flint	MI
Bottomly	Thomas F.		Franklin	KY
Bottomly	Thomas F.		Glasgow	KY
Bottorf	J. K.		Clearfield	PA
Bouffier	Charles	4 New Chambers	New York City	NY
Boulter	D. K.		Montgomery	AL
Bousley	Nathaniel C.		Salem	MA
Bouton	C. H.		Mason City	IA
Bovee	W. L.		Gibbon	NE
Bowdish & Hoagland		94 Arcade	Rochester	NY
Bowdle	C. M.		Nevada	OH
Bowdle*	E. T.		Lewistown	OH
Bowdoin	Gilbert T.	1115 Pennsylvania	Washington	DC
Bowen	G. M.		Elroy	WI
Bowen	J. C.		Carmi	IL
Bower	Charles	6201 Penn	Pittsburgh	PA
Bower*	Charles	100 Collins	Pittsburgh	PA
Bower*	Henry		East Liverpool	OH
Bower*	M. B.		Slater	MO
Bowerman & Becker		605 E. Baltimore	Baltimore	MD
Bowers	Berry F.	340 Fulton	Brooklyn	NY
Bowers	Sereno A.	110 E. 125th	New York City	NY
Bowers	W. T.		Lynn	MA
Bowers*	Rudolph		St. Louis	MO
Bowers*	William F.	340 Fulton	Brooklyn	NY
Bowersox	A. L.	2nd & Main	Dayton	OH
Bowman	D. A.		Mahanoy	PA
Bowman	R. M.	1075 Chapel	New Haven	CT
Bowman	W. E.		Ottawa	IL
Bowman*	H. M.		Indianapolis	IN
Bowring	T. D.		De Pere	WI
Boyce	D. N.		Tuscola	IL
Boyce	Washington		Danville	IL
Boyd	Cincinnatus		La Porte	IN
Boyd	J. D.		Pittsburgh	TX
Boyd	S.	2176 Archer	Chicago	IL
Boyd	W. T.		Des Moines	IA
Boyd & Orr			Rapid City	DK
Boyer	T. G.		Altamont	IL
Boyer	W. H.		Little Falls	NY
Boynton	J. J.		Clinton	MA

ALPHABETICAL LISTING OF PHOTOGRAPHERS IN THE U. S. IN 1888 & 1889

NAME		ADDRESS	CITY	STATE
Boysen	I.		Colusa	CA
Boysen*	T.		Colusa	CA
Bozen	H. & F.		St. Louis	MO
Brace	Frederick		Dundee	NY
Brace*	A. F.		Miltonvale	KS
Brach*	W. G.		Clay Centre	KS
Brachrach & Bros.		327 W. Lexington	Baltimore	MD
Bracy	C. F.		Wells River	VT
Bradbeer	A. D.		Charlevoix	MI
Bradfisch	Louis	227 Fulton	Brooklyn	NY
Bradford	G. W.		Smyrna	DE
Bradley	A. O.		Stockton	CA
Bradley	B.		Eden	ME
Bradley	G. W.		Menasha	WI
Bradley	H. E.		Kirwin	KS
Bradley	H. N.		Midland	MI
Bradley	Isaac	73 S. Terry	Dayton	OH
Bradley	W. L.	14 Hanover	Boston	MA
Bradley & Rulofson		14 Dupont	San Francisco	CA
Bradley*	Alvin F.	18 Blue Hill	Boston	MA
Bradshaw	A. J.		East Tawas	MI
Bradshaw	A. J.		Oscoda	MI
Bradway Bros.			Richmond	IN
Brady	H. J.		Orange	NJ
Brady	J. M.		Petersburgh	IN
Brainerd	J. M.		Rome	NY
Brainerd*	Emma		Wooster	OH
Bramblett	W. R.		St. Paul	MN
Brand	E. L.	212 Wabash	Chicago	IL
Brandmo & Lodgaard			Montevideo	MN
Branin	R. C.		Dixon	CA
Brannan	J. C.		Athens	OH
Brassart	A.		Naugatuck	CT
Brasseur	Charles	123 Chambers	New York City	NY
Braun	John		Two Rivers	WI
Braunberg*	M.		Indianapolis	IN
Brayton	J. G.		Napa City	CA
Breath	E. H.		Canton	IL
Breece	H. S.		Salem	NJ
Breeding	Walker		Willow	CA
Breiner	William	252 Washington	Hoboken	NJ

ALPHABETICAL LISTING OF PHOTOGRAPHERS IN THE U. S. IN 1888 & 1889

NAME		ADDRESS	CITY	STATE
Bremen	Frederick		Greenville	MI
Brendt Bros.			Avoca	IA
Brenner	Daniel		Bucyrus	OH
Breslow	B.		Clayton	NY
Bretz	George M.		Pottsville	PA
Bretz*	Gill		Pottsville	PA
Breuker	John C.	722 Chestnut	Philadelphia	PA
Brewer	W. H.		Shenandoah	IA
Brewster	J. C.		San Buenoventura	CA
Brewster & Rogers			Bethel	VT
Briber	Ed. L.		Johnstown	PA
Bricker	J. M.		Freeport	PA
Bricker & Corliss*			Allegheny	PA
Bricker & Corliss*		71 Federal A.	Pittsburgh	PA
Bride	Henry C.	1112 Hunter	Philadelphia	PA
Bridge	E. C.		Chariton	IA
Bridge	E. C.	Mechanic's Falls	Minot	ME
Bridge*	H. W.		St. Marys	PA
Briggs	F. H.		Bristol	NH
Briggs	J.		Friend	NE
Briggs	J. P.		Murdock	MN
Briggs	S. M.		S. Hanson	MA
Briggs & Co.	F. L.		Ottumwa	IA
Briggs & Davis		311 8th	New York City	NY
Briggs*	Charles W.	311 8th	New York City	NY
Brigham	E. T.		Dover	NH
Brigham	J. M.		Plainwell	MI
Brigham	Joseph T.		Northfield	MA
Brighton Photo Art. Co.		733 Fulton	Brooklyn	NY
Brimmer & Kalb		2 W. 4th	St. Louis	MO
Brinckman Bros.			Madison	NE
Brinkley & Fry			Keota	IA
Brisbois	Mrs. M. L.		Leadville	CO
Brissell	Mrs. E. C.		Fort Atkinson	WI
Britt	Peter		Jacksonville	OR
Brittingham*	J. G.		Springfield	IL
Broadaway	J. S.		Winston	NC
Broadbent Bros.		1415 Chestnut	Philadelphia	PA
Broadt	J. F.		Berwick	PA
Brockway	A.		Sheldon	IL
Brockway	S. B.		Winneconne	WI

ALPHABETICAL LISTING OF PHOTOGRAPHERS IN THE U. S. IN 1888 & 1889

NAME		ADDRESS	CITY	STATE
Brodeck	H. H.		Walla Walla	WA
Brodesser*	Charles		Milwaukee	WI
Broich	Hugo	116-118 Grand	Milwaukee	WI
Brokau	C. W.		Albion	NE
Bronson	C. R.	407 Main	Bridgeport	CT
Bronson	James	4646 Germantown	Philadelphia	PA
Brook & Co.	W. T.		Water Valley	MS
Brooklyn Photo-Enlarging co.		59 E. 9th	New York City	NY
Brooks	A. F.		Bath	NY
Brooks	Arthur J.		Hartford	CT
Brooks	E. A.		Morganfield	KY
Brooks	Walter W.	748 E. Market	Louisville	KY
Brooks & Hicks			Tecumseh	MI
Brookshire	W. C.		Meridian	MS
Browing	G. W.		Bloomington	IL
Brown	A. L.		Independence	KS
Brown	A. V.	380 Main	Springfield	MA
Brown	Albert		Indianapolis	IN
Brown	C. E.		Chelsea	MA
Brown	C. L.		Peacham	VT
Brown	Charles		Indianapolis	IN
Brown	Charles		Easton	PA
Brown	D. A.		North Branch	MI
Brown	E. C.		Ellsworth	KS
Brown	Eva		Beverly	OH
Brown	F. D.		Hudson	MI
Brown	F. M.		Troy	MO
Brown	G. A.		Fairfield	NE
Brown	G. E.	285 ½ Middle	Portland	ME
Brown	H. A.		Galesburgh	MI
Brown	H. G.		Whitehall	NY
Brown	H. M.		Girard	KS
Brown	H. R.		Missouri Valley	IA
Brown	H. V.		Clyde	OH
Brown	H. V.		Green Spring	OH
Brown	H. W.		Penfield	PA
Brown	Harman		Kansas City	MO
Brown	Harmon		Kansas City	KS
Brown	Hugh J.		Saratoga Springs	NY
Brown	J. M.		Milford	MI
Brown	J. P.		Cambridge	OH

ALPHABETICAL LISTING OF PHOTOGRAPHERS IN THE U. S. IN 1888 & 1889

NAME		ADDRESS	CITY	STATE
Brown	J. Paul		Wilmington	DE
Brown	John		Wheeling	WV
Brown	Joseph	136 Grand	Milwaukee	WI
Brown	L. P.		Michelville	IA
Brown	M. & C.E.		Howell	MI
Brown	M. P.		Tekonsha	MI
Brown	O. B.		Osceola	NE
Brown	S. B.	243 Westminster	Providence	RI
Brown	T. A.	606 Kearney	San Francisco	CA
Brown	T. A.		Marshalltown	IA
Brown	Theo.		Mount Gilead	OH
Brown	W. S.	123 S. Halsted	Chicago	IL
Brown	William		Marshall	TX
Brown	William J.		Burlington	VT
Brown	William		Modesto	CA
Brown	H. J.		Newport	NH
Brown & Co.	Samuel W.	915 Sansom	Philadelphia	PA
Brown & Eldridge			Winona	MN
Brown & Karras		18 3rd	San Francisco	CA
Brown & Sellick			Auburn	NY
Brown*	A. W.		Delmont	PA
Brown*	F. E.		Marion	IN
Brown*	H. E.		Mapleton	IA
Brown*	M. P.		Tecumseh	MI
Browne	E. E.		Asheville	NC
Brownell	Alexander C.	90 Westminster	Providence	RI
Brownell	C. A.	196 W. 5th	Cincinnati	OH
Brownell Mfg. Co.			Rochester	NY
Browning	G. W.		Atlanta	IL
Brua & Clark			Taylorville	IL
Bruce & Co.			Auburn	NY
Bruce & Fisher			Everett	PA
Brumfeld	John		Kingsley	KS
Brummit	W. H.		Pontiac	MI
Brummitt*	W. H.		Pontiac	MI
Brush	J. A.		Minneapolis	MN
Brush	L. N.		Bowling Green	KY
Bryan	C. H.		Mount Sterling	KY
Bryan	S. T.		Kirkwood	IL
Bryan	S. T.		Burlington	IA
Bryan	Stockton		Mound City	MO

ALPHABETICAL LISTING OF PHOTOGRAPHERS IN THE U. S. IN 1888 & 1889

NAME		ADDRESS	CITY	STATE
Bryant	D. C.		Indianapolis	IN
Bryant	John W.		La Porte	IN
Bryant	W. H.		King City	MO
Bryant & Chestnut			Monticello	AR
Bryant & Gilllingwater			Humboldt	KS
Bryant & Zimmerman			Plattsburgh	MO
Bryant & Zimmerman*			Edgerton	MO
Bryson	John		Houlton	ME
Buchan	E. F.		Worthington	MN
Buchanan	F. M.		Indianapolis	IN
Buchanan	H. N.		Indianapolis	IN
Buchannan	J. G.		Benton	IL
Bucher, Jr.	Herman	Box 116	College Point, L. I.	NY
Buchman			Tuscon	AZ
Buchmoody*	D. J.		Rondout	NY
Bucholz	Herman	365 Main	Springfield	MA
Buck	F .A.		Hopkins	MO
Buck	James W.		New Albany	IN
Buck & Glaser			Minneapolis	MN
Buck Bros.			Holden	MO
Buckingham	W.	127 ½ W. Main	Springfield	OH
Buckmyer	F. J.	69 S. High	Columbus	OH
Buckwater	Edward	618 Main	Kansas City	MO
Budd*	James		Lakota	DK
Buel*	J. W.		Craig	MO
Buell	J.		Geneseo	IL
Buell	O. W.		Osborne	KS
Buenschhoff	A.	151 Central	Albany	NY
Buffham	A. T.		Sedalia	MO
Buffham Bros.		5 W. Lexington	Baltimore	MD
Buffham Bros.*		116 S. Broadway	Baltimore	MD
Bugbee	F. E.		Wilton	NH
Buhler	Otto	1434 3rd	New York City	NY
Buker	M. S.		Oldtown	ME
Bulkley	Eli E.	2294 3rd	New York City	NY
Bulkley	J. A.		Oneida	IL
Bulkley	William M.	1132 N. 3rd	New York City	NY
Bulkley*	Eli E.	383 N. 3rd	New York	NY
Bullard	Mrs. S. G.	424 Main	Worcester	MA
Bullock	John		Lake Geneva	WI
Bullock	Seneca		East Durham	NY

ALPHABETICAL LISTING OF PHOTOGRAPHERS IN THE U. S. IN 1888 & 1889

NAME		ADDRESS	CITY	STATE
Bumgardner	J. A.	38 S. Market	Springfield	OH
Bunce	E. S.		Merrillon	WI
Bundy	Horace L.	368 Main	Hartford	CT
Bundy & Filley		838 Chapel	New Haven	CT
Bundy & Stoddard*		838 Chapel	New Haven	CT
Bundy & Train			Helena	MT
Bundy*	J. K.		New Haven	CT
Bunker	H. P.	Jefferson	Dayton	OH
Bunn	J. W.		Lawson	MO
Burbank	G. A.		Woodstock	IL
Burd	M. S.		Junction	NJ
Burdge	Robert		Appleton City	MO
Burdick	C. W.		East Saginaw	MI
Burdick	E. H.		Milton	WI
Burdick	H. R.		Malden	MA
Burdick	O. C.		Minneapolis	MN
Burgener	J. H.		Harper	KS
Burgert	P. P.		Jacksonville	FL
Burgess	A. M.		Holland	MI
Burgess	Charles F.	911 Broadway	Oakland	CA
Burgess	Frank H.		Hopkinton	MA
Burgoyne	G.		Manhattan	KS
Burke	Major	2514 Smallman	Pittsburgh	PA
Burkholder	C. C.		Tyrone	PA
Burkitt	C. W.	472 Pearl	Cleveland	OH
Burland	C. S.		Chester	PA
Burleigh	G. N.		Taylorville	IL
Burlington Photo Co.			Burlington	VT
Burneo	L.		Takamah	NE
Burnett	Dryett		Olney	IL
Burnett	J. F.		West Point	MS
Burnett & Slattery		6th c. Valencia	San Francisco	CA
Burnham	A. T.		Faribault	MN
Burnham	E. R.		Barry	IL
Burnham	T. R.	725 Washington	Boston	MA
Burnite	D. C.		Harrisburgh	PA
Burns	M. W.		Eau Claire	WI
Burns	W. F.		Ayer	MA
Burpee	C. L.		Beloit	WI
Burr	J. E.		Atlantic City	NJ
Burrell	David T.		Brockton	MA

ALPHABETICAL LISTING OF PHOTOGRAPHERS IN THE U. S. IN 1888 & 1889

NAME		ADDRESS	CITY	STATE
Burress & Morlan			Walnut	IL
Burt Studio		103 State	Chicago	IL
Busch	C. G.		Claremont	NH
Busche & Co.		901 N. 11th	St. Louis	MO
Busec	S. L.		Warren	IL
Buser	H. R.		Cedar Rapids	IA
Buser	J. S.		Mount Vernon	IA
Busey	N. H.	112 N. Charles	Baltimore	MD
Busey*	N. H.	24 N. Charles	Baltimore	MD
Bush	G. C.		Rio	WI
Bush & Kadgehn			Bloomington	IL
Bushby & McCurdy		521 Washington	Boston	MA
Bushnell	W. A.		Coffeyville	KS
Busier	J. S.		Mechanicsville	IA
Buskirk	C. V.		Theodore	DK
Buss	H. J.		Fond Du Lac	WI
Busse	Robert	165 W. Madison	Chicago	IL
Busse*	R.	113 N. Halsted	Chicago	IL
Busse*	William M.	1132 N. 3rd	New York	NY
Bussell	A. Frank		Quincy	MA
Butcher	S. D.		West Union	NE
Butkiewicz & Putrament		662 Noble	Chicago	IL
Butler	C.		Kingsley	IA
Butler	D. E.		Holyoke	MA
Butler	E. P.		Reno	NV
Butler	Elijah		Greenville	IL
Butler	G. W.		Westerly	RI
Butler	Henry		Vermillion	DK
Butler	Robert G.		Lexington	KY
Butler	W. S.	313 Main	Springfield	MA
Butler & Co.	A. C.	253 Woodward	Detroit	MI
Butler & Dorsez		715 Market	San Francisco	CA
Butler*	D. S.		Atchison	KS
Butt	George		Norwalk	OH
Butterfield	D. W.		Cambridgeport	MA
Butterfield	T. L.		Prairie du Chien	WI
Butterworth	Charles		New Vienna	OH
Butterworth	Charles		Wilmington	OH
Butterworth	J. T.		Saginaw	MI
Buttman	J. J.		Little Falls	NY
Buttoriff	Reuben H.		York	PA

ALPHABETICAL LISTING OF PHOTOGRAPHERS IN THE U. S. IN 1888 & 1889

NAME		ADDRESS	CITY	STATE
Butts & Co.		965 F	Washington	D.C.
Butts & Co.*		936 F.	Washington	D. C.
Buys	William		Heber	UT
Byarlay	L. A.		Maryville	MO
Byerly	J. Davis		Frederick	MD
Byerly	Orison		Parkersburg	IA
Byrne	T.		North Springfield	MO
Byron	J. N.	50 S. Pearl	Albany	NY
Cable	Jacob		Newport	PA
Cadawallader	J. D.		Marietta	OH
Cadwallader*	J. D.		Parkersburg	WV
Cadwallader & Fearnaught			Indianapolis	IN
Cady	H. B.		Waitsfield	VT
Cady	W. J.		Holyoke	MA
Cahoon	Clement A.		Harwich	MA
Cahoon	J. C.		Jackson	OH
Cain	C. T.		Owensboro	KY
Caldwell	F. M.		Berlin	WI
Caldwell	M.		Flatonia	TX
Caldwell	W. N.		Brockton	MA
Cale	William		Dalson	IL
Calendar	H. W.	23 S. Limestone	Springfield	OH
Calfee	H. B.		Missoula	MT
Calhoun	Mrs. Ross		Ness City	KS
Call	Miss Mary		Flushing	MI
Call	W. R.		Manchester	NH
Callihan			Grand Rapids	OH
Cammack	W. R.		Oskaloosa	IA
Camp	A. N.		Jamestown	NY
Campbell	A. R.		Beatrice	NE
Campbell	G. M.	38 S. 15th	Pittsburgh	PA
Campbell	H. S.		Hickman	KY
Campbell	J. A.		Ada	OH
Campbell	J. D.		Attica	IN
Campbell	S. W.		Detroit	MI
Campbell & Camp		8 ½ N. Main	Mansfield	OH
Campbell & Co.			Richmond	VA
Campbell & Co.*	C. R.		Wisner	NE
Canfield	E. H.		Wausau	WI
Canfield	H. A.		Braidwood	IL
Canfield Bros.			New Milford	CT

ALPHABETICAL LISTING OF PHOTOGRAPHERS IN THE U. S. IN 1888 & 1889

NAME		ADDRESS	CITY	STATE
Caniff*	T. H.		Cross Timbers	MO
Cannon & Hayes			Norborne	MO
Canova Studios		241 Wabash	Chicago	IL
Capital Gallery		222 S. High	Columbus	OH
Caradine	James N.		Sherman	TX
Carden*	C. H.		Fort Scott	KS
Cardon	Thomas B.		Logan	UT
Carew	G. A.		Sibley	IA
Carl	E.		West Burke	VT
Carlisle	C. J. H.		Fort Howard	WI
Carlisle	George M.	199 Westminster	Providence	RI
Carlson	G. A.		Willmar	MN
Carlton	C. G.		Waterville	ME
Carman	Charles		Andes	NY
Carman	J. D.		Shabbona	IL
Carman*	I. D.		Shabbona	IL
Carnahan	G. E.		Fairbury	NE
Carpenter	A. O.		Ukiah	CA
Carpenter	D. W.		Millville	NJ
Carpenter	Dyer H.		Minerva	OH
Carpenter	J. B.		Fonda	IA
Carpenter	Marcus		Tionesta	PA
Carpenter	Marion		Kansas City	KS
Carpenter	Marion		Kansas City	MO
Carpenter	Thomas H.		Sherman	TX
Carpenter	William		Weston	MO
Carpenter & Chase		846 W. Market	Louisville	KY
Carr	A. B.		Farmington	MN
Carr	E. S.		Webster	MA
Carr	W. R.		Wareham	MA
Carr & Brown			Putnam	CT
Carr*	E.		West Burke	VT
Carriere	P. F.		New Orleans	LA
Carroll	J. P.		New Haven	KY
Carroll	John		Wilmington	OH
Carroll	Joseph F.	192 E. 125th	New York City	NY
Carroll	L. A.		Sheffield	IL
Carroll	William		Cuba	NY
Carroll	William	2640 South	Philadelphia	PA
Carroll*	Lawrence	101 W. 21st	New York	NY
Carson	Arthur		Caldwell	OH

ALPHABETICAL LISTING OF PHOTOGRAPHERS IN THE U. S. IN 1888 & 1889

NAME		ADDRESS	CITY	STATE
Carson	C.		Gothenburg	NE
Carson	W. H.		Hillsdale	MI
Carter	C. W.		Salt Lake City	UT
Carter	G. W.		Lowville	NY
Carter	H. L.		Sand Lake	MI
Carter	J. L.		Union City	PA
Carter	R. R.		Basil	OH
Cartwright	C. A.		Marengo	IA
Carvalho	D. N.	291 Broadway	New York City	NY
Carver	E. M.		Tracy	MN
Cary	C. H.		Wilkesbarre	PA
Cary	Frank		Penn Yan	NY
Case	F. R.		Beatrice	NE
Casey	A. F.		Cisco	TX
Cashner	J. N.		Paris	IL
Cass	William		Grand Haven	MI
Casselman	S. R.		Greenfield	OH
Cassey & Whitney			Lansing	MI
Cassilly	Louisa	1266 S. Broadway	St. Louis	MO
Cassilly	C. W.	421 Franklin	St. Louis	MO
Cassilly*	G. E.		St. Louis	MO
Cassilly*	J. H.		St. Louis	MO
Castle*	F.		Charleston	WV
Castor & Bro.			Carthage	MO
Caswell	William.		Grand Forks	DK
Caswell Bros.			Gardner	MA
Cathcart	Marvin		Buchanan	MI
Cathcart	N. H.		Fowlerville	MI
Cathcart	W.	1073 ½ Market	San Francisco	CA
Catterlin	W. H.		Bolckow	MO
Cawker*	Victor		Manistee	MI
Chabiss & Co.	H.	189 ½ Bank	Waterbury	CT
Chadband	F. A.	320 Warren	Boston	MA
Chadband*	F. A.	330 Warren	Boston	MA
Chadbourne*	G.		Milwaukee	WI
Chalfant	A. B.		Beaver Falls	PA
Chamberlain	A. T.		Woonsocket	RI
Chamberlain	C. A.		Shawano	WI
Chamberlain	Ephraim		Medfield	MA
Chamberlain	W. G.		Denver	CO
Chamberlin	H. B.		Shullsburgh	WI

ALPHABETICAL LISTING OF PHOTOGRAPHERS IN THE U. S. IN 1888 & 1889

NAME		ADDRESS	CITY	STATE
Chambers	J. M.		Bloomington	WI
Chandler	E. C.		Walnut	IL
Chandler	Ellis		Quincy	IL
Chandler	J. W.		St. Albans	ME
Chandler	Martin		Marshfield	MA
Chandler	W. D.		St. Albans	VT
Chandler & Scheetz		828 Arch	Philadelphia	PA
Chandler & Sheetz			Atlantic City	NJ
Chandler*	J. H.		Madison	IN
Channell	R. F.		Phoenixville	PA
Chapin*	W. P.		Minneapolis	MN
Chaplin*	Joseph		Ontonagon	MI
Chapman	A.	756 Broadway	New York City	NY
Chapman	George L.		Montague	MA
Chapman	Henry		Hartland	WI
Chapman	I. O.		Stanton	MI
Chapman & Co.		115 Bedford	Brooklyn	NY
Chapman*	E. A.		Big Rapids	MI
Chappell	Mrs. E. B.		Sturgis	MI
Charles	Oliver		Knightstown	IN
Charles & Hultgren		2029 Wabash	Chicago	IL
Chase	D. B.		Trinidad	CO
Chase	Ezra B.		Newburyport	MA
Chase	G. W.		Newark	OH
Chase	Harvey E.	2550 Broadway	Cleveland	OH
Chase	J. K.		Oxford	ME
Chase	J. M.		Newburyport	MA
Chase	M. E.		Urbana	IL
Chase	O. W.		Middlebury	VT
Chase	Theodore F.	249 ½ Westminster	Providence	RI
Chase	W. H.		Minneapolis	MN
Chase	William M.	Eutaw	Baltimore	MD
Chatterton	H. D.		Villisca	IA
Cheetham*	Edgar		Kansas City	KS
Cheney	C. B.		Waterbury	VT
Cheney & Christmas			Charlotte	MI
Cheney & Langdon			Jonesville	MI
Chenoweth	D. W.		Kearney	NE
Cherrington	T. J.		Marysville	OH
Chesley	G. W.		Owatonna	MN
Chester & Handy		494 Maryland	Washington	DC

ALPHABETICAL LISTING OF PHOTOGRAPHERS IN THE U. S. IN 1888 & 1889

NAME		ADDRESS	CITY	STATE
Chicago Art Publishing Co.		134 VanBuren	Chicago	IL
Chickering	W. E.	467 Washington	Boston	MA
Chickering*	Elmer	21 West	Boston	MA
Chickering*	W. E.	467 & 627 Washington	Boston	MA
Chiesman	E. D.		Galt	MO
Child	A. L.		Grinnell	IA
Child	Frank H.		Newport	RI
Childs	B.		Ishpeming	MI
Childs	B. F.		Houghton	MI
Childs	H. A.		New Richmond	WI
Childs	H. F.		Marquette	MI
Childs	H. L.		Shell Lake	WI
Chillman	Philip E.	914 Arch	Philadelphia	PA
Choate	J. N.		Carlisle	PA
Chouinard	R. L.	775 S. Halsted	Chicago	IL
Chrisman	John		Adrian	MI
Christensen	H. P.		Emmetsburgh	IA
Christenson	Christ		Jamestown	KS
Christian	J.		Ava	IL
Christman	E. J.		Waterville	MN
Christopher*	C. E.		Cheyenne City	WY
Churchill	C. E.		Arcade	NY
Churchill	G. O.		Hastings	NE
Churchill	L. O.		Gloucester	MA
Churchill	Mrs. Susan		Three Oaks	MI
Churchman	Henry		Longton	KS
Churman	L. H.		Beloit	WI
City Art Gallery			Albany	MO
Claflin	C. R. B.	377 Main	Worcester	MA
Claflin	D. B.	183 Summit	Toledo	OH
Clark	A. W.		Cedartown	GA
Clark	Andrew		Dexter	MI
Clark	C. H.		Salida	CO
Clark	D. L.		Hannibal	MO
Clark	D. R.	2134 Michigan	Chicago	IL
Clark	Damon P.		Dunkirk	NY
Clark	Daniel R.		Indianapolis	IN
Clark	David		New Brunswick	NJ
Clark	David L.		High Point	NC
Clark	E. C.		Jamaica	VT
Clark	Forester		Pittsfield	MA

NAME		ADDRESS	CITY	STATE
Clark	G. W.		Ionia	MI
Clark	H.	352 Main	Worcester	MA
Clark	I. A.		Maple Rapids	MI
Clark	J. L.		Miamisburgh	OH
Clark	J. T.		El Dorado	MO
Clark	J. W.		Mendota	IL
Clark	J. W.		Vinton	OH
Clark	L. W.		Pittsfield	IL
Clark	L. W.		Streator	IL
Clark	L. W.		Olympia	WA
Clark	Lyman		Webster City	IA
Clark	R.		Bolivar	OH
Clark	Thomas B.		Indiana	PA
Clark	W. S.		Paw Paw	IL
Clark	William		Griggsville	IL
Clark & Lewis		14 ½ E. Main	Springfield	OH
Clark & Son*	L. H.		Mendota	IL
Clark*	A. S.		Grand Rapids	MI
Clark*	H. S.		Petoskey	MI
Clark*	W. H.		Litchfield	MI
Clarke	G. W.		Raymond	NH
Clarke	L. H.		Wakefield	RI
Clarke	John H.	161 Canal	New Orleans	LA
Clarke*	John H.	151 Canal	New Orleans	LA
Clary	James O. A.		Harrisonburgh	VA
Clauser	W. H.		Jacksonville	IL
Clauss	C. M.	61 Bond	New York City	NY
Clayton	J. F.		Groesbeck	TX
Clayton*	F. H.		Chattanooga	TN
Cleaver	John		Lovington	IL
Clegg	M. A.		Shullsburgh	WI
Clegg	Mrs. M. A.		Darlington	WI
Clegg & Parker*			Plymouth	MI
Clemens	Mathias J.	336 Market	Louisville	KY
Clement	E. L.	8-10 S. Peoria	Chicago	IL
Clement	F. M.		Berlin Falls	NH
Clement	F. M.		Haverhill	NH
Clements	C. F.		Milo	ME
Clements	E. G.		Lincoln	NE
Clements	Ed. N.		Leadville	CO
Clemons	John R.	915 Sansom	Philadelphia	PA

ALPHABETICAL LISTING OF PHOTOGRAPHERS IN THE U. S. IN 1888 & 1889

NAME		ADDRESS	CITY	STATE
Clendenon & Nichols			Jacksonville	IL
Click	M. E.		Columbia City	IN
Clifford	D. A.		St. Johnsbury	VT
Clifton	Y. B.		Athens	GA
Clinch	C. E.		Iowa City	IA
Clinch	W.		Grass Valley	CA
Clinedinst	B. M.	216 N. Charles	Baltimore	MD
Clinediust*	B. M.	20 N. Charles	Baltimore	MD
Close & Perkins			Elkton	DK
Cloud	A. P.		Moulton	IA
Clow	W. F.		Lisbon	DK
Clute	E. E.		Wyandotte	KS
Coates	Alfred		Benton Harbor	MI
Coates	James H.	82 Hudson	Albany	NY
Coats	T. D.		Merrimack	WI
Cobb	D.	1144 Market	San Francisco	CA
Cobb	George N.		Binghampton	NY
Cochran	J. H. & H. H.		Gardiner	ME
Cochran	Will		Wooster	OH
Cockrell	Thomas J.		Laredo	TX
Coe	E. V.		Coshocton	OH
Coe	Norman L.	681 Broadway	New York City	NY
Coe*	Theodore D.	331 Grand	Brooklyn	NY
Coerver	John		Staunton	IL
Coffee	D. G.		Freeport	PA
Coffin	Ira S.		Freeport	ME
Coffin	W. J.		Delano	MN
Coker	C. W.		Burlington	KS
Colburn	C. B.		Bay City	MI
Colburn	E. J.		Frankfort	MI
Colby	C. H.		Meredith Village	NH
Colby	James T.		Springfield	NH
Colby	L. W.		Manchester	NH
Cole	H. G.		Minneapolis	KS
Cole	H. H.		Pekin	IL
Cole	J. R.		Hillsdale	MI
Cole	James K.	34 W. 14th	New York City	NY
Cole	James K.	174 6th	New York City	NY
Cole*	James K.	832 Broadway	New York	NY
Colehase	William		Lewistown	OH
Coleman	M. O. T.		Westfield	MA

ALPHABETICAL LISTING OF PHOTOGRAPHERS IN THE U. S. IN 1888 & 1889

NAME		ADDRESS	CITY	STATE
Coley & Tatman			Connersville	IN
Collamer	G. W.		Wilkesbarre	PA
Collier	Charles T.		Riverside	CA
Collier	G. L.		New Haven	MO
Collins	D. C.		West Haven	CT
Collins	E. M.		Oswego	NY
Collins	I. A.		Rochester	NH
Collins	Ira F.		Huntsville	AL
Colman & Co.		283 Westminster	Providence	RI
Colson	Edgar A.		Searsport	ME
Columbus	Archibald C.	805 Market	Washington	DC
Columbus Excelsior Copying House*		405 N. High	Columbus	OH
Coman	G. S.		Storm Lake	IA
Coman	J. L.		North Grosvenor Dale	CT
Compton	Alma W.		Box Elder	UT
Comstock	A. B.		Waverly	NY
Conant	F. L.		Skowhegan	ME
Conat	C. W.		Manistee	MI
Conee	S. S.		Lake Linden	MI
Conkey	George W.		Glens Falls	NY
Conklin*	S. L.		Atchison	KS
Conley Bros.			Celina	OH
Conly	C. F.	465 Washington	Boston	MA
Connel & Murphy			Newark	OH
Connor	G. P.		Charles City	IA
Conrad	Jacob	398 National	Milwaukee	WI
Converse	J. O.		Morenci	MI
Cook*	A. I.		Cincinnatus	NY
Cook	A. L.		Cincinnatus	NY
Cook	C. C.		Little Rock	AR
Cook	C. F.		Wilkesbarre	PA
Cook*	F. E.		Corunna	MI
Cook	G. S.		Richmond	VA
Cook	George L. V.	265 King	Charleston	SC
Cook	J. N.		Santa Barbara	CA
Cook*	L. C.		Viola	WI
Cook	L. W.		Lynn	MA
Cook	N. G.		Ames	IA
Cook	O. H.		Portsmouth	NH
Cook	W. B.		Willow	CA

ALPHABETICAL LISTING OF PHOTOGRAPHERS IN THE U. S. IN 1888 & 1889

NAME		ADDRESS	CITY	STATE
Cook & Co.			Fairfield	ME
Cook & Knowles			Rockford	IL
Cookingham	J. B.		Jackson	MI
Cooledge	H. W.		De Smet	DK
Cooledge	H. W.		Zumbrota	MN
Cooley	Alfred		Cooperstown	NY
Coolidge	Baldwin	154 Tremont	Boston	MA
Cooper	B. S.		California	MO
Cooper	C. E.	631 W. Lake	Chicago	IL
Cooper	C. S.		Clyde	NY
Cooper	F. P.		Belton	TX
Cooper	Robert F.		Monongahela City	PA
Cooper	Thomas		Weir	KS
Cope & Day			Conshohocken	PA
Cope & Day*			Norristown	PA
Copeland	J. H.	586 Pearl	Cleveland	OH
Copeland & Greene			Monroe	WI
Copelin	A. J. W.	237 Deaborn	Chicago	IL
Copelin	T.		Winnetka	IL
Copelin Photographic	Studio	75 Madison	Chicago	IL
Copley	W. S.		Mobile	AL
Cordingly	John	2106 Wabash	Chicago	IL
Core	F. W.		Lincoln	IL
Core & Co.	F. B.	50 W. 5th	Cincinnati	OH
Core & Co.*	E. B.	56 W. 5th	Cincinnati	OH
Corell			Eldred	PA
Corey	A. S.		Clinton	MO
Corey & Roberts			Clinton	MO
Corliss	Edward J.		Allegheny	PA
Cormany	M. L.		Augusta	GA
Cornelius	J. W.		Lewisburgh	PA
Cornell	J. A.		Colon	MI
Cornell	Miss S. A.		Colden	NY
Cornell	S. S.		Stamford	NY
Cornell & Bothwell			Ligonier	IN
Cornell & Wick			Norwich	NY
Cornell*	J. A.		Colon	MI
Cornish	J. J.		Del Norte	CO
Cornwall	C. T.		Coldwater	MI
Correvont	Frank	1032 Central	Cincinnati	OH
Correvont*	Frank	1030 Central	Cincinnati	OH

ALPHABETICAL LISTING OF PHOTOGRAPHERS IN THE U. S. IN 1888 & 1889

NAME		ADDRESS	CITY	STATE
Corse	S. W.		Montpelier	VT
Corwin	E. H.		Ottawa	KS
Cosand & Mosser			Caldwell	KS
Costello	J. K.		Carthage	MO
Costello	Alfred B.	588 Newark	Jersey City	NJ
Cotton*	Enoch		Sterling	KS
Cottrell	D. H.		Seneca	KS
Cottrell	Frank		Freehold	NJ
Couch	H. E.		Danbury	CT
Couis & Finn*			Spearfish	DK
Coulter*	H. A.	134 E. Madison	Chicago	IL
Coumbe	J.		Rhinebeck	NY
Coup	J. B.		Bedford	IA
Courliss	William		Marine City	MI
Courtney	S. V.	43 S. Market	Canton	OH
Covelle	Mrs. F. A.		Middleville	MI
Cover	W. L.	754 W. Baltimore	Baltimore	MD
Cover*	W. L.	560 W. Baltimore	Baltimore	MD
Covey	E. J.		Stanberry	MO
Coville*	Mrs. F. A.		Middleville	MI
Cowan	Henry	181 8th	New York City	NY
Cowan*	Henry	577 8th	New York City	NY
Cowles	C. A.		Hamburg	IA
Cowley	D. J.	34 W. 14th	New York City	NY
Cox	W. A.		St. Augustine	FL
Cox	W. H.		Cynthiana	KY
Cox	William H.		Kendallville	IN
Cox & Co.	C. C.	59 E. 12th	New York City	NY
Cox*	George C.	826 Broadway	New York	NY
Coyle	F. A.		Monticello	IA
Coyle*	J. H.		Walker	IA
Craiq*	Charles E.	637 Preston	Louisville	KY
Cramer	Adon C.		Carbondale	PA
Cramer	C. L.	402 Kearney	San Francisco	CA
Cramer	Gustavus		St. Louis	MO
Cramer	J.		Rulo	NE
Cramer	Joseph		Grafton	WI
Cramer & King		818 Chapel	New Haven	CT
Cramer*	Elijah A.	818 Chapel	New Haven	CT
Crandall Bros.			Canandaigua	NY
Crane	F. M.		Ogdensburg	NY

ALPHABETICAL LISTING OF PHOTOGRAPHERS IN THE U. S. IN 1888 & 1889

NAME		ADDRESS	CITY	STATE
Crane	T. F.	156 First	Newark	NJ
Cranford	Charles		Brookville	KS
Crawford	E. L.		Georgetown	CA
Crawford	J. C.		Albany	OR
Crawford	Jno. W.	543 Fulton	Brooklyn	NY
Crawford & Davis			Morris	IL
Craycraft	A. B.		Mattoon	IL
Crayton	J. A.		Auburn	NY
Credlebaugh*	T. L.		Fremont	OH
Creech	A. S.		Sullivan	IL
Creese	M. P.		Burr Oak	KS
Creighton	J. M.		Winters	CA
Creighton & Mix		653 Broad	Newark	NJ
Crenshaw*	S. H.		Price	GA
Cress	Mell		East Palestine	OH
Crew	E.		Hempstead	TX
Cridland	F. W.	12 Main	Dayton	OH
Criley	N. J.		Butler	PA
Crim*	J. T.		Opelika	AL
Cripps	O. N.	35 ½ W. Main	Springfield	OH
Crissman	J.		Santa Ana	CA
Crobaugh	Samuel	Congress	Cleveland	OH
Crocker	Abel B.		Allegany	NY
Crocker	J. L.		Naples	NY
Crocker	M. N.		Perry	NY
Crockett	T. H.		Rockland	ME
Crofoot	J. E.		Kendallville	IN
Croft	C. H.		Huntsville	MO
Croley	W. A.		Valentine	NE
Cromwell	B. J.		Bowdoinhain	ME
Cromwell	Oscar		Adin	CA
Cronhardt & Son	Henry	1412 E. Madison	Baltimore	MD
Cronin & Critcherson		33 Hayward Pl	Boston	MA
Cronin & Critcherson*		32 Hayward	Boston	MA
Cronning	J. P.		Scipio	UT
Cropper	Samuel		Jamesport	MO
Crosby	George E.	920 W. Market	Louisville	KY
Crosier	Frank		Readsborough	VT
Crosier	George		West Richfield	OH
Cross	A. B.		Salem	MA
Cross	L. P.		Petrolia	PA

ALPHABETICAL LISTING OF PHOTOGRAPHERS IN THE U. S. IN 1888 & 1889

NAME		ADDRESS	CITY	STATE
Cross	M. F.		Batavia	NY
Cross	S. H.		Edwardsville	IL
Crossley	William	192 Hains	Germantown	PA
Crossman	B. P.	150 State	Rochester	NY
Crossman	C. L.		Alton	IL
Crossman*	C. L.		Athony	KS
Crouch	W. A.		East Saginaw	MI
Crouch	W. T.		Belleville	IL
Crow	J. W.		Knappa	OR
Crow	S. B.		Astoria	OR
Crowell	F. S.		Mount Vernon	OH
Crowell	E. S.		Rochester	MN
Crowell & Ellison*			El Paso	TX
Crowell & Son			Erie	PA
Crowley & Frey			Kensington	IL
Crowns	J. H.		Kaukauna	WI
Crozior & Linaweaver			Findlay	OH
Crum & Son	R. D.		Watkins	NY
Crus	J. H.		Lineville	IA
Crystal	David S.	21 School	Germantown	PA
Crystal*	D. S.		Harrisburgh	PA
Cudding	A. J.		Bolivar	NY
Cuddy	S. B.	1103 Franklin	St. Louis	MO
Culver	W. H.		Bay City	MI
Culver	W. H.		Maiden	MT
Culver*	W. A.	134 E. Madison	Chicago	IL
Cummingham	J. R.		Maquon	IL
Cummings	M.		Corsicana	TX
Cummings	Thomas		Lancaster	PA
Cummins	J. S.	106 N. Charles	Baltimore	MD
Cummins*	J. S.	7 N. Charles	Baltimore	MD
Cundill	W. M.		Maquoketa	IA
Cunningham	J. K.		Gouverneur	NY
Cunningham & Herbaugh*		57 W. Madison	Chicago	IL
Currier	Herman J.		New London	NH
Currier*	F. E.		Omaha	NE
Curtis	C. C.		Traver	CA
Curtis	C. L.		Oregon	IL
Curtis	George E.		Niagara Falls	NY
Curtis	M. E.	62 S. Salina	Syracuse	NY
Curtis	W. A.		Rabun Gap	GA

ALPHABETICAL LISTING OF PHOTOGRAPHERS IN THE U. S. IN 1888 & 1889

NAME		ADDRESS	CITY	STATE
Curtis	W. B.		Pomeroy	OH
Curtis & Rose			Lewiston	ME
Curtis & Thompson			Gallipolis	OH
Curtiss	E. R.		Madison	WI
Curtiss	Nathan S.		Syracuse	NY
Cushman	W. S.	1 Arcade	Springfield	OH
Cutting	Chauncey P.		Lee	MA
Dabb	R. I.		Le Mars	IA
Dabbs	B. L. H.	602 Liberty	Pittsburgh	PA
Dafoe	J. W.		Ann Arbor	MI
Dahlen	H. P.		Cambridge	MN
Dahlquist	A. T.		Duluth	MN
Dahms*	Gustav		Davenport	IA
Dailey	E. V.		Rockland	MA
Daily	John		Altoona	PA
Dake	J. R.		Centralia	WI
Dale	D. E.		Lucas	IA
Daley*	Jonas		Hart	MI
Daliet & Bro.		33 Frenchman	New Orleans	LA
Dall	John H.		San Francisco	CA
Dallinds	J. S.		Kennekuk	KS
Dalrymple	J. P.		Hightstown	NJ
Damelle	T. L.		Cumberland	MD
Dames	W. W.	911 Broadway	Oakland	CA
Dames & Butler		715 Market	San Francisco	CA
Dames*	W. W.		San Francisco	CA
Dammand	R. P.		Harlan	IA
Dampf	John H.		Corning	NY
Dana	Edward C.	63 W. 14th	New York City	NY
Daniel	J. E.		Fort Worth	TX
Daniels	A. F.	333 Main	Worcester	MA
Daniels	C. F.		Macon	GA
Daniels, Jr.	T. E.		Provo City	UT
Darwin	C. T.		Decatur	IN
Dassau	Emil		Fort Madison	IA
Datsman	P.		Blue Springs	NE
Davenport	B. F.		Waxahachie	TX
Davenport*	G. F.		Wellington	KS
Davenport*	S. M.		Salisbury	MO
Davidson	E. M.		Cloverdale	CA
Davidson	I. G.		Portland	OR

ALPHABETICAL LISTING OF PHOTOGRAPHERS IN THE U. S. IN 1888 & 1889

NAME		ADDRESS	CITY	STATE
Davidson	I. G.		Tacoma	WA
Davidson	J.		Linkville	OR
Davidson	J. E.		Alma	MI
Davidson	John N.		Sulphur Springs	TX
Davidson	L. S.		Los Angeles	CA
Davidson	N. R.		Santa Rosa	CA
Davidson	T. M.		Des Moines	IA
Davidson	W. W.		Cheboygan	MI
Davidson	William B.		Newport	RI
Davies	G. W.		Richmond	VA
Davies	George W.		Portland	OR
Davies & Son	John W.		Richmond	VA
Davis	A. E.	503 Main	Worcester	MA
Davis	Alonzo S.	180 Middle	Portland	ME
Davis	C. H.	138 E. Main	Rochester	NY
Davis	D. R.		Painesville	OH
Davis	G. W.	925 Pennsylvania	Washington	DC
Davis	Henry		Cadiz	OH
Davis	Josephine E.	180 6th	New York City	NY
Davis	Mrs. A.		East Corinth	ME
Davis	S.		Kenton	OH
Davis	S. P.		Danielsonville	CT
Davis	Samuel		Manchester	MI
Davis	W. S.		Ellenville	NY
Davis	William		Mankato	MN
Davis	William A.	180 6th	New York City	NY
Davis	G. S.		Knoxville	TN
Davis	G. W.		Jacksonville	FL
Davis	James P.	495 6th	New York City	NY
Davis	P. H.		Paris	IL
Davis & Douglass			Fall River	MA
Davis Bros.			Portsmouth	NH
Davis*	C. L.		Wyoming	IL
Davis*	Josephine E.	180 E. 121st	New York City	NY
Davis, Jr.	S. H.		Berne	NY
Davison	Albert J.		Hartford	CT
Davison	B.		Odin	IL
Davison	J. A.		Polo	IL
Dawdy	Andrew J.		Goshen	IN
Dawes	G. F.		Plainfield	WI
Dawes	G. W.		St. Louis	MI

ALPHABETICAL LISTING OF PHOTOGRAPHERS IN THE U. S. IN 1888 & 1889

NAME		ADDRESS	CITY	STATE
Dawson	J. C.		New London	WI
Dawson	R. W.		Little Rock	AR
Day	E. M.		Ogallala	NE
Day	F. O.		Wesley	ME
Day	George A.		Wesley	ME
Day	George W.	317 DeKalb	Norristown	PA
Day	M. E.		Wesley	ME
Dayton	C. S.		Towanda	PA
De Anguino & Son	Alex		Nashville	TN
De Camp	George W.	671 Broad	Newark	NJ
De Forest	D. A.		Menominee	MI
De Foro	Frank	19 Union Sq W.	New York City	NY
De Groot	H.		Corvallis	OR
De Grush	F. H.		Stillwater	MN
De Guire	I. J.		Appleton	WI
De Harradora	J. B.		Winnsborough	SC
De Lappotterie	Charles	140 Washington	Hoboken	NJ
De Lemas	Louis	134 Gratiot	Detroit	MI
De Morat*	Oliver B.	2 S. 8th	Philadelphia	PA
De Morte	Oliver B.	914 Chestnut	Philadelphia	PA
De Planque	Louis		Corpus Christi	TX
De Silva*	Abraham M.	69 Church	New Haven	CT
De Vaux	E. S.		Gooch's Mill	MO
De Voll & Co.			Utica	NY
De Witt	M. M.		Scranton	PA
Dean	Frank E.		Gunnison	CO
Dean	R. A.		Middlebury	VT
Dean	W. P.		Katahdin Iron Works	ME
Dean	C. C.		Houston	TX
Dean & Cornwell			Williamsport	PA
Dean & Gray			Mariposa	CA
Deane	R. J.		Griffin	GA
Dearborn	T. E.		Malvern	IA
Decker	E.	143 Euclid	Cleveland	OH
Decker	P. J. & J. P.		Newburgh	NY
Decker	Philip I.	365 8th	New York City	NY
Decker	William		Mount Vernon	MO
Decker & Wilber*		143 Euclid	Cleveland	OH
Decuir	J. A.	195 Canal	New Orleans	LA
Deibert	H. S.		Schuylkill Haven	PA
Delahunt	R. C.		Bertram	IA

ALPHABETICAL LISTING OF PHOTOGRAPHERS IN THE U. S. IN 1888 & 1889

NAME		ADDRESS	CITY	STATE
DeLamater	R. S.	15 Pratt	Hartford	CT
Deland	E. J.		Great Falls	NH
Delanoy	J. A.		Ainsworth	NE
Delglish Bros.*			Ord	NE
Delius	W.	100 Bank	Waterbury	CT
Dellac	Marcellin	54 W. 14th	New York City	NY
Delling	G. W.		Madelia	MN
Demarest & Staler*			Perth Amboy	NJ
Demers & Son			Holyoke	MA
Dengler	S. S.		Slatington	PA
Denison & Roberts		3907 Cottage Grove	Chicago	IL
Denman	M. H.		Defiance	OH
Denninger	Anson	93 E. Houston	New York City	NY
Dennington	C. J.		Meadville	PA
Dennison	William M.	647 Pearl	Cleveland	OH
Dennison & Hardy			Fergus Falls	MN
Dennison*	J. W.		Bedford	OH
Dennison*	John	136 Ontario	Cleveland	OH
Denny	T. W.		Momence	IL
Densmore	Jay		Niles	MI
Denton	B. F.		Newton	KS
Denton	J. W.		Jacksonville	IL
Derry	J. M.		Kingman	KS
DeSilva	Abraham M.	201 George	New Haven	CT
Desmarais	O.		Manchester	NH
Dessaar	Fernando	551 8th	New York City	NY
Detlor & Waddell			Bradford	PA
Detroit Viewing Co.			Detroit	MI
Dettmer	John	402 Freeman	Cincinnati	OH
Detwiler & Son			Canton	MO
Devenney	C. H.	267 W. Jefferson	Louisville	KY
Devenport*	B. F.		Waxahachie	TX
Devereaux	Albert		Olivet	MI
Devinney	B. F.		Moberly	MO
Devinney	William		Judsonia	AR
DeWaal	C. M.		Orlando	FL
Dewey	George N.	177 N. High	Columbus	OH
Dewhurst	O. T.		Lynn	MA
Dexter	George G.		Ipswich	MA
Dexter	J. C.		Ware	MA
Deyo	Phillip		Schoharie	NY

ALPHABETICAL LISTING OF PHOTOGRAPHERS IN THE U. S. IN 1888 & 1889

NAME		ADDRESS	CITY	STATE
Deyoung	Joseph B.	815 Broadway	New York City	NY
Dibble	H. E.		Clarksville	TN
Dickinson*	Wellington	96 W. 5th	Cincinnati	OH
Diehl	Albert	Wyoming	Pittsburgh	PA
Diehl & Co.	A. J.	246 Woodward	Detroit	MI
Dietrich	W. A.		Kutztown	PA
Dillinger	S. L.		Marietta	PA
Dillon	J. W.		Fond Du Lac	WI
Dimmers	Kuno	388 Bowery	New York City	NY
Dimmers	Theodore G.	105 4th	New York City	NY
Dimmick	J. E.		Augusta	WI
Dimmock	W. H.		Elizabeth	NJ
Dinmon*	Henry		Carlisle	PA
Dinsmore	Mrs. D. C.		Dover	ME
Dintruff	J. H.		Rushville	NY
Dippe	Henry	356 W. Chicago	Chicago	IL
Dippel	Louis A.	716 Olive	St. Louis	MO
Dittmar	C. F.		Kenosha	WI
D'Lamatter	J. H.		Earlville	IL
Doane	Robert N. B.		New Bedford	MA
Dober	Daniels	27 Ave. A	New York City	NY
Dobler Bros.			Beloit	KS
Dockweiler*	M.		Shenandoah	PA
Dodd*	L. N.		Sharon	PA
Dodge	George K.	646 Washington	Boston	MA
Dodge	S.		Assumption	IL
Dodges	A. H.		Indianapolis	IN
Doerr	H. A.		San Antonio	TX
Doerr	J. Henry	1202 W. Market	Louisville	KY
Dole	A. K.		Bangor	ME
Dolph	O. A.		Rock Creek	OH
Donaldson	Albert N.		Logansport	IN
Donaldson	George T.		Tiffin	OH
Donaldson	Sol. I.		Dexter City	OH
Donnelly	W. F.	851 Chapel	New Haven	CT
Donnelly*	B. M.		Palmyra	MO
Dooley	C. O.		Panora	IA
Doolittle	A. P.		Lanark	IL
Doolittle	George W.		Montrose	PA
Doolittle	H. G.		Sibley	IA
Doolittle	R. C.		Sabetha	KS

ALPHABETICAL LISTING OF PHOTOGRAPHERS IN THE U. S. IN 1888 & 1889

NAME		ADDRESS	CITY	STATE
Dopp	J. C.		Du Quoin	IL
Doremus	L. H.		Paterson	NJ
Dorey	Charles		Lock Haven	PA
Dorrance	C. E.		Vicksburgh	MI
Dorrance	Charles		Scotts	MI
Dorsey*	W. A.		Everton	MO
Dougherty	James		Bucyrus	OH
Dougherty*	Henry J.		Waterloo	NY
Douglas	Charles B.	55 Myrtle	Brooklyn	NY
Douglass	S. W.		Evansville	IN
Douglass*	W. H.		Cape Girardeau	MO
Doumet & De Ligarde		102 W. 18th	New York City	NY
Dousseau	A. J.		Butte City	MT
Doust	J. V.	24 E. Genesee	Syracuse	NY
Dow	J. M.		Ogdensburg	NY
Dow	James H.		Walden	VT
Dowe	L.	4th c. Market	San Francisco	CA
Dowe	O. W.		San Luis Obispo	CA
Dowe*	D. W.		San Francisco	CA
Downing	George		Topeka	KS
Downing	J. J.		Waynesville	OH
Downing	N. H.		Hillsborough	OH
Downs*	Dana		Riverhead	NY
Drake	B. W.		Belleville	OH
Drake	H. S.		S. Framingham	MA
Drake	W. H.		Waterloo	WI
Drake	J. L.		Centre Effingham	NH
Draper	Edmund	1313 Columbia	Philadelphia	PA
Draper*	Edward	1313 Columbia	Philadelphia	PA
Dressel	G. A.	179 West	Buffalo	NY
Dresser	G. H.		Arkansas City	KS
Drew	A. P.		Dover	NH
Drew	H. B.		Jefferson	WI
Drew	H. B.		Lake Mills	WI
Drummond	Alonzo J.	50 Fulton	New York City	NY
Drury	A. K.		Le Roy	NY
Dubbs*	J. H.		Geneseo	IL
Duboce	M. A.		Mount Pulaski	IL
Dubus	J.		New Iberia	LA
Duchochois	Peter C.	123 Chambers	New York City	NY
Duck & Carlson			Caro	MI

NAME		ADDRESS	CITY	STATE
Ducobu	Gustav		Pickneyville	IL
Duhem	Victor	1324 Polk	San Francisco	CA
Dulenbaugh	H. A.		Gordon	OH
Dumble	A. E.	44 State	Rochester	NY
Dummer	Oscar	433 6th	New York City	NY
Dummer	Thomas G.	105 4th	New York City	NY
Dunbar	Mrs. H. M.		Baldwinsville	NY
Duncan	D.		Adamsville	PA
Duncan	Joseph		Aurora Springs	MO
Duncan	W. A.		Oskaloosa	IA
Duncan	William		Pierce City	MO
Dunham	Ephraim		Owosso	MI
Dunham	M. M.		Minneapolis	MN
Dunham	O. W.		Susanville	CA
Dunham	S. E.		Waucoma	IA
Dunham & Kelsey			Reno	NV
Dunihue*	W. H.		Sinclairville	NY
Dunlap	F. A.		Bloomfield	IA
Dunlap	William		Chillicothe	MO
Dunlevy	J. M.		Waukon	IA
Dunn	F. P.		New Brunswick	NJ
Dunn	J. D.		Meadville	PA
Dunn	J. H.		Vincennes	IN
Dunne & Co.	A.	56 Reade	New York City	NY
Dunshee	Edward S.	1330 Chestnut	Philadelphia	PA
Dunshee & Co.	E. S.	3 Tremont Row	Boston	MA
Dunton	E. H.		Bristol	VT
Dunton	E. H.		Lyndonville	VT
Dunwick	W. H.		Pulaski	NY
Dupont Studio		110 E. 125th	New York City	NY
Dupree	H.	239 Front	Worcester	MA
Duque	Francis	760 Broadway	New York City	NY
Durfee	E. O.		Port Allegany	PA
Durgan	James O.		Norwich	CT
Duryea	S. B.	253 Fulton	Brooklyn	NY
Duryea	William C.	201 6th	New York City	NY
Duryea*	C. W.	39 Greenpoint	Brooklyn	NY
Dutton	William M.	1635 Atlantic	Brooklyn	NY
Duvall	J. H.		Lexington	MO
Dwight*	J. M.		Shelbina	MO
Dygert	George H.		Jordan	NY

ALPHABETICAL LISTING OF PHOTOGRAPHERS IN THE U. S. IN 1888 & 1889

NAME		ADDRESS	CITY	STATE
Dygert	S.		Canajoharie	NY
Eagle Gallery			Dover	NJ
Eagles	Joseph D.		Ithaca	NY
Earle	C. W.	53 & 55 Rowland	Detroit	MI
East	T.		North Loop	NE
Easterline	J. W.		Scranton	PA
Eastman	W. C.		Trempealeau	WI
Easton	J. H. & Mrs. L. J. B.		Rochester	MN
Eaton	A. B.		Potsdam	NY
Eaton	D. F.		Magnolia	IA
Eaton	E. F.		Lewistown	PA
Eaton	E. L.		Omaha	NE
Eaves	J. & M.		Mount Pleasant	TX
Ebert	Emery		Grind Stone City	MI
Echard*	A. C.		Cedartown	GA
Echard	W. C.		Columbus	MS
Ecker	J. M.		Evansville	IN
Eckert	Mrs. M. A.		Helena	MT
Eddington	C. G.		Pontiac	MI
Edgecomb	J. E.		Stoneham	MA
Edgeworth	A. D.	157 S. Paulina	Chicago	IL
Edgeworth	Reuben	167 Blue Island	Chicago	IL
Edick	E. L.		Parish	NY
Edinger	W. C.		Des Moines	IA
Edmiston	S. A.		Moberly	MO
Edmondson	G. W.		Norwalk	OH
Edny	James		Superior	NE
Edsall	Frank	487 8th Ave	New York City	NY
Edsall*	Frank	248 W. 125th	New York City	NY
Eduart	Alex	6 Turk	San Francisco	CA
Edwards	C. G.		Rushford	MN
Edwards	D. E.		Huntington	CT
Edwards	E. B.		Muscatine	IA
Edwards	John C.		Merced	CA
Edwards	O. D.		Boonville	MO
Edwards	P. S.		South Haven	MI
Edwards & Dorman			Atlanta	GA
Edwards*	John E.		Merced	CA
Egbert	W. P.		Atlantic	IA
Egerton	George		Goodell's	MI
Eggert	H. B.		Bethlehem	PA

ALPHABETICAL LISTING OF PHOTOGRAPHERS IN THE U. S. IN 1888 & 1889

NAME		ADDRESS	CITY	STATE
Ehm	Henry	566 Broadway	Brooklyn	NY
Ehrlich	Professor	160 E. 66th	New York City	NY
Ehrlicher, Jr.	Henry	833 Arch	Philadelphia	PA
Eichler	George	13 Ave. A	New York City	NY
Eisele	H.		Indianapolis	IN
Eisemann*	Charles	229 Bowery	New York City	NY
Eisenhardt	Constantine	204 Randolph	Detroit	MI
Eisenmann	Charles	18 W. 14th	New York City	NY
Eldredge	I. E.		Crescent City	CA
Eldredge*	J. E.		Crescent City	CA
Eldridge & Price			Mankato	MN
Elite Studio			Iowa City	IA
Elkin	L.	163 ½ Poydras	New Orleans	LA
Elkins*	Mrs. Lotta	195 Canal	New Orleans	LA
Ellinwood	J. G.		Manchester	NH
Elliot	H. I.		Marion	IA
Elliot	J. A.		Butte City	MT
Elliott	A. B.		Mount Vernon	OH
Elliott	George R.	High & Main	Columbus	OH
Elliott	H. G.		Hicksville	OH
Elliott	H. S.		Madrid	IA
Elliott	J. M.	95 S. High	Columbus	OH
Elliott	J. P.		Indianapolis	IN
Elliott	John		Madrid	IA
Elliott	Orman		Stockton	CA
Elliott	R. F.		Morris	MN
Elliott	S. D.		Perry	IL
Elliott*	John A.		Pueblo	CO
Ellis	M. D.		Dallas	OR
Ellis	T. W.	120 Court	Boston	MA
Ellis & Son			Los Angeles	CA
Elrod	J. C.	313 W. Jefferson	Louisville	KY
Elton	George M.		Palmyra	NY
Ely	William F.	756 Broadway	New York City	NY
Ely & Meddins			Neenah	WI
Emerling	F.	193 Genesee	Buffalo	NY
Emerson	M. W.		Lowell	MA
Emery	G. H.		Saxton's Rivert	VT
Emery	J. W.		Galva	IL
Emery	W. H.	Athol Centre	Athol	MA
Emhuff	Joseph	154 Hastings	Detroit	MI

ALPHABETICAL LISTING OF PHOTOGRAPHERS IN THE U. S. IN 1888 & 1889

NAME		ADDRESS	CITY	STATE
Emory & Bradbury		S. W. Harbor	Tremont	ME
Empire Photographic Studio		361 Canal	New York City	NY
Ender*	J. E.		Fort Gaines	GA
Engel	Christian		Spring Grove	MN
English	N. F.		Hartland	VT
Ennis	James W.		Trafalgar	IN
Ennis	John W.		Delphi	IN
Ennor	J. A.		Neillsville	WI
Enoch	A. C.		Mount Pleasant	OH
Enoch	Alexander C.		Martin's Ferry	OH
Enos & Co.	E. W.		Wichita	KS
Ensminger Bros.			Sanford	FL
Ensminger Bros.			Independence	IA
Enterekin Photographic Gallery			Atlantic City	NJ
Entrekin	William G.	4384 Main	Philadelphia	PA
Eoley*	Warren G.	6 Winter	Boston	MA
Eppert	Charles		Terre Haute	IN
Erickson	Erich		Rockford	IL
Erickson	Frank C.		Lynn	MA
Ericsson	William	614 Fifth	Brooklyn	NY
Ericuis	Emil A.	130 Broadway	Brooklyn	NY
Erler	Max		Peoria	IL
Ernsberger	John D.	419 E. Baltimore	Baltimore	MD
Ernsberger	W. H.		Auburn	NY
Erskine	Robert	138 N. 4th	Philadelphia	PA
Ersley	P.		Hillsborough	TX
Eruscan Art Co.			Pawtucket	RI
Eskill	J. J.		Florence	WI
Esmay	John		Sabula	IA
Essery	R. W.		St. Paul	MN
Estabrook	Charles B.	711 Market	Washington	DC
Estabrook	E. R.		Hoosick Falls	NY
Estabrook	J. S.		Houlton	ME
Estabrook	T. S.		Presque Isle	ME
Estabrook*	I. S.		Houlton	ME
Esteves	A.		Key West	FL
Ethelberry	William		Casey	IL
Eureka Copying House		10 6th	Pittsburgh	PA
Eureka Photo Copying House			Huntington	WV
Evans	Even		Ithaca	NY
Evans	G. E.		Collinsville	IL

ALPHABETICAL LISTING OF PHOTOGRAPHERS IN THE U. S. IN 1888 & 1889

NAME		ADDRESS	CITY	STATE
Evans	J. G.		Los Angeles	CA
Evans	L. R.		Binghampton	NY
Evans	T. A.		Samoth	IL
Evans	Z. W.		Centralia	IL
Evans		485 State	Chicago	IL
Evans	R.	207 S. Halsted	Chicago	IL
Evans	William M.		Houtzdale	PA
Even	Joseph		Peru	IL
Evens*	Winfield		New Brighton	PA
Everett	F. O.	393 Main	Worcester	MA
Everitt	E. F.		Grant's Pass	OR
Evick	Christ		Chillicothe	OH
Ewald & Bro .	J. E.		Atlantic City	NJ
Ewald Jr.	John A.	2145 Aramingo	Philadelphia	PA
Ewing	H. H.		Sycamore	IL
Excelsior Art Portrait Co.		Smithfield	Pittsburgh	PA
Excelsior Copying House*			St. Louis	MO
Excelsior Portrait Co.		508 Arch	Philadelphia	PA
Excelsior Portrait Co.*			St. Louis	MO
Faber	J. J.		Norfolk	VA
Fadner	Henry		Chilton	WI
Fagan*	J. K.		Watertown	WI
Fahnestock	J. A.		Glasford	IL
Fairbank	O. D.		Adrian	MI
Fairbanks	J. A.		Centre Point	IA
Fairfield	T. J.		Milledgeville	GA
Faist	C. G.	c. Market & 4th	San Francisco	CA
Faivre	L. H.		Wilmington	DE
Falk	Benjamin J.	949 Broadway	New York City	NY
Falk*	Benjamin J.	947 Broadway	New York City	NY
Fallert	Paul	1505 Carson	Pittsburgh	PA
Falor	A. C.		Berea	OH
Fancy	J. A.	43 Winter	Boston	MA
Faragher	T. J.		Adrian	MN
Faries	T. C.		Indianapolis	IN
Farley	A. D.		Nashua	NH
Farley*	W. H.		Gibson City	IL
Farmer	C. W.	399 4th	Detroit	MI
Farnsworth	W. E.		Buckhannon	WV
Farr	H. R.		Minneapolis	MN
Farr & Son			Minneapolis	MN

NAME		ADDRESS	CITY	STATE
Farrach	John	31 Myrtle	Brooklyn	NY
Farrar	Mrs. Adele	284 Tulane	New Orleans	LA
Farrell	J. F.		Waterbury	CT
Farrington	F. W.		Arcadia	WI
Farrington	Maurice		Delhi	NY
Farrington	Theodore		McGregor	IA
Farris	H. A.		Lancaster	MO
Farrow*	M. F.		Garnett	KS
Fassett	A. G.		Dexter	ME
Faucett	E. E.		Eau Claire	WI
Favre	Leon	236 W. 44th	New York City	NY
Fay	W. D.		Joliet	IL
Fay & Branling			Cuero	TX
Fearn	William R.	120 S. 2nd	Philadelphia	PA
Feay	A. J.		Evansville	IN
Feeley	James R.	58 W. 23rd	New York City	NY
Feiger	E. F.		Pomeroy	OH
Feiker & Raab		1102 Walnut	Milwaukee	WI
Feinberg & Koran		228 Bowery	New York City	NY
Fell	A. W.		Watsonville	CA
Fellison	O. F.	192 W. 5th	Cincinnati	OH
Fellows	E. G.		Vinton	IA
Felt	L. W.	215 Chicabo	Chicago	IL
Feltman	A. M.		Salem	IL
Fenner	W. J.		Gallipolis	OH
Fenwick	Richard		Bloomington	IL
Ferguson	J. H.		Leavenworth	KS
Ferguson	W. F.		Clinton	IA
Ferguson*	G. W.		Springfield	MO
Fermann	W. A.		Stoughton	WI
Ferrin	P. E.		Altoona	DK
Ferron	John		St. Clairsville	OH
Ferry & Holtzman		132 Bowery	New York City	NY
Ferry & Holtzmann*		132 Bowery	New York City	NY
Fest	Paul	Wyoming	Germantown	PA
Few	Wm. E.		Canon City	CO
Fichtl	Sigmund	46 Bloomfield	Hoboken	NJ
Ficken & Haines*			Baylis	IL
Fickes	John C.		Steubenville	OH
Fickhardt*	W. R.		Gaylord	KS
Field	J. C.		Tampa	FL

ALPHABETICAL LISTING OF PHOTOGRAPHERS IN THE U. S. IN 1888 & 1889

NAME		ADDRESS	CITY	STATE
Fielding	John H.	2196 Third	New York City	NY
Fielding	Paul		Allegheny	PA
Fields	George	57 Summit	Toledo	OH
Fields & Daviess			Harrisonville	MO
Fields & Son	William		Lyons	IA
Fike	G. W.		Wilber	NE
Filson & Son	D.		Steubenville	OH
Finch	P. F.		Lebanon	OH
Finch	W. B.		Billings	MO
Finkenberg	Philip	10 Ave. B.	New York City	NY
Finley	George W.		Jeffersonville	IN
Finley	Horace		Canandaigua	NY
Finley & Co.*	I. I.		St. Marys	KS
Finney	S. B.		Washington	IA
Firoe	J. W.	28 Emery Arcade	Cincinnati	OH
Fischer	J. W.	826 N. 9th	St. Louis	MO
Fischer*	J. W.		St. Louis	MO
Fisher	A. F.		Hindsdale	NH
Fisher	A. J.		Towanda	PA
Fisher	C. U.		Harlan	IA
Fisher	E. C.		Claremont	NH
Fisher	Jacob		Fayette	MO
Fisher	S. R.		Norristown	PA
Fiske	Charles		Riverside	RI
Fitch*	M. W.	SW c. Beacon	Toledo	OH
Fitton*	William H.		Worcester	MA
Fitzgerald	J. C.		Greenville	SC
Fitzsimmons*	E. D.		Lehigh	IA
Fitzsimons	E. D.		Lehigh	IA
Flagg	B. A.		Junction City	KS
Flagg	Charles		Ovid	NY
Flaglor	E. P.	SE c Market & 9th	San Francisco	CA
Flanagan	J. H.		Waterville	ME
Flanders	C. M.		Corydon	IA
Flanders	C. M.		Humeston	IA
Flannagan	H. H.		Woodstown	NJ
Flaten	O. E.		Moorhead	MN
Fleischer	P.	249 Chicago	Chicago	IL
Fleischer*	Paul	245 N. Clark	Chicago	IL
Fleming	E. G.		Wausau	WI
Fling	J.		Shelby	NE

ALPHABETICAL LISTING OF PHOTOGRAPHERS IN THE U. S. IN 1888 & 1889

NAME		ADDRESS	CITY	STATE
Flint	F. C.	100 S. Salina	Syracuse	NY
Flodin & Thyberg		411 Main	Worcester	MA
Flood*	G. W.		Minneapolis	MN
Florence	C. W.		Sioux City	IA
Flower	W. A.		Weeping Water	NE
Flower	W. B.		Petoskey	MI
Floyd	G. W.		Minneapolis	MN
Floyd	J. W.		Lock Haven	PA
Fluck	Samuel B.		Woodbury	PA
Flye	Winfeld W.		East Hiram	ME
Folsom	A. H.	48 Alleghany	Boston	MA
Folsom	Edward S.		Katonah	NY
Folsom	Mrs. J. H.		Danbury	CT
Foltz	F. H.		Bedford	PA
Foltz & Cochran*			Wooster	OH
Foot	David		Wolcott	NY
Foote	W. C.		Flint	MI
Foote	W. H.		Flint	MI
Forbes	John		Tecumseh	NE
Ford	B. A.		Braidwood	IL
Ford	E. A.		Grundy Centre	IA
Ford	Harry		Lyndon	KS
Forell	Carl		McPherson	KS
Foreman	Alexander		Grafton	WV
Foreman	C. R.		Osage Mission	KS
Foreman	Israel		Fairmont	WV
Forney	J. G.		Lacon	IL
Forney	S. P.		Albany	MO
Forrest	S. D.		Covington	PA
Forsberg	J. C.		Willmar	MN
Forshew	Frank		Hudson	NY
Forster	J. S.		Detroit	MI
Forster & Son	John	178 Gratiot	Detroit	MI
Forsythe & Hickok			Flint	MI
Fortin*	Joseph		Alton	IL
Fortune	E. W.		Fremont	MI
Fosnot	L. C.		Keosauqua	IA
Foss	F. H.		Dover	NH
Foss	Oscar		San Francisco	CA
Foster	C. E.		Nevada	MO
Foster	Charles H.	219 Hanover	Boston	MA

ALPHABETICAL LISTING OF PHOTOGRAPHERS IN THE U. S. IN 1888 & 1889

NAME		ADDRESS	CITY	STATE
Foster	F. D.		Norwalk	OH
Foster	Fred W.	115 Lewis	Union Hill	NJ
Foster	H. W.		Syracuse	NE
Foster	J. A.		Adrian	MI
Foster	J. C.		Pawnee City	NE
Foster	W. E.	542 State	Chicago	IL
Foster	H. C.		Shelby	IA
Foster & Creese			Cawker City	KS
Foucar & Co.	E. L.		El Paso	TX
Fouch	J. H.		Excelsior	MN
Foulk	J. Z.		Hillsborough	OH
Fowler	A.		Xenia	IN
Fowler	A. R.		Meadville	PA
Fowler	Ed. L.	3105 Prairie	Chicago	IL
Fowler	Edward P.		Haverhill	MA
Fowler	G. H.	S. Cochran	Charlotte	MI
Fowler	Harry		Indianapolis	IN
Fowler	I. D.		Rochester	MN
Fowler & Flower*			Charlotte	MI
Fox	A. J.	304 N. 6th	St. Louis	MO
Fox	A. R. P.		Rezar Falls	ME
Fox	Ed. H.		Danville	KY
Fox	G. S.	98 Congress	Troy	NY
Fox	J. M.		Rochester	NY
Fox & Symons			Salt Lake City	UT
Fox & Wiltse			Mitchell	DK
Fox*	A. H.		St. Louis	MO
Foy	C. W.		Brockton	MA
Foye	C. E.		Whitman	MA
Fragstein*	M. V.		St. Louis	MO
Frambo*	W. L.		Bennetsville	SC
Franck & Swett*			St. Louis	MO
Franklin*	Edwin		Niles	MI
Frayser*	W. G. R.		Danville	VA
Frazee	A. R.		Bethel	OH
Frazier & Wood			Chavis	AL
Frear	W.		Ithaca	NY
Freash	F. B.		Philo	OH
Frederichs	Charles	672 Broadway	Brooklyn	NY
Frederick	J. D.		Waynesboro	PA
Fredericks	M. T.		Vicksburg	MS

ALPHABETICAL LISTING OF PHOTOGRAPHERS IN THE U. S. IN 1888 & 1889

NAME		ADDRESS	CITY	STATE
Fredricks	Charles D.	770 Broadway	New York City	NY
Fredricks & Koester			St. Paul	MN
Freeborn	L. H.		Des Moines	IA
Freeburger	Alexander	709 Light	Baltimore	MD
Freedle & Bro.	J. W.	225 Superior	Cleveland	OH
Freehoefer	F.		Adamstown	PA
Freeland	G. W.		Milford	NJ
Freeman	Alfred		McKinney	TX
Freeman	B. F.		Somerville	MA
Freeman	D. G.		Blissfield	MI
Freeman	G. W.	82 Main	Boston	MA
Freeman	Josiah		Nantucket	MA
Freeman	W. H.		Rochelle	IL
Freeman	W. U.		Canandaigua	NY
Freeman*	D. W. G.		North Topeka	KS
Frees	O. P.		Tiffin	OH
Frees	J. H.		Newcomerstown	OH
Fregeau	Lawrence	1607 Washington	Boston	MA
French	D.		Meridian	CT
French	J. A.		Keene	NH
French	L. B.	405 Vine	Cincinnati	OH
French & Co.		102 S. High	Columbus	OH
French & Co.*	W. G.	19 E. Main	Springfield	OH
French & Hoagland			Auburn	NY
French*	Charles L.		Ravenna	OH
Frey	E.		Corsicana	TX
Frey	Henry		Hyde Park	PA
Frey	Henry		Scranton	PA
Fricke	William	50 Bowery	New York City	NY
Friederich	H.	163 Springfield	Newark	NJ
Friend	Ferdinand		Detroit	MI
Friesleben	L. W.	3922 State	Chicago	IL
Fritz	F. Z.		Lambertville	NJ
Fritz	M. J.		White Lake	DK
Frommeyer	David A.		Hanover	PA
Frost	G. B.		Independence	OR
Frovarp	C. R.		Grafton	DK
Frye	H. H.		Chico	CA
Fulker*	C.		Arcadia	KS
Fulkerson	Charles		Tuscumbia	MO
Fulkerson	W. W.		Someset	OH

NAME		ADDRESS	CITY	STATE
Fuller	A. W.	1150 Market	San Francisco	CA
Fuller	C. E.		Birch Cooley	MN
Fuller	F. E.		Merrill	WI
Fuller	J. A.		Albert Lea	MN
Fuller	William		New London	OH
Fullerton	R. W.		Bathgate	DK
Fullmer	J. A.	723 7th	Washington	DC
Fulsang	J.	2486 Archer	Chicago	IL
Fulton Fureman			Lancaster	OH
Fulton & Fureman*			Lancaster	OH
Fults & Lafayette			Waterloo	IL
Furman	Robert H.	62 State	Rochester	NY
Fyler	F. F.		Eureka Springs	AR
Gable	G.		Marietta	GA
Gabler	George		Batesville	IN
Gabriel	Herman C.	508 Arch	Philadelphia	PA
Gabriel*	Herman C.	1555 N. 4th	Philadelphia	PA
Gaertner	Sigmund		Tremont	PA
Gage	H. K.		Truckee	CA
Gagne	E.	913 Washington	Boston	MA
Gaines	F. H.		Red Bluff	CA
Gale	G. F.		Joliet	IL
Gale	H. N.		Bristol	CT
Gale	C. A.		Piqua	OH
Gallaher	J. B.		Chippewa Falls	WI
Galliker	Charles H.	509 8th	New York City	NY
Galloway & Co.		318-320 Fulton	Brooklyn	NY
Galloway*	Robert	779 Broadway	New York City	NY
Galloway*	Robert	318 Fulton	Brooklyn	NY
Gallup	C. H.		Poughkeepsie	NY
Gamble	G. R.		Frankfort	IN
Ganisford	Mrs. Minerva		Great Bend	KS
Gano	Richard M.	13 ½ E. Main	Springfield	OH
Ganvin & Bro.*	J. E.		Burlington	VT
Garber	Davis	747 Broadway	New York City	NY
Gardiner	R. G.		Kansas City	KS
Gardner	Edwin B.	200 W. 34th	New York City	NY
Gardner	J. C.		Brookfield	MO
Gardner	M. H. & W. H.		Atlanta	GA
Gardner	R. G.		Kansas City	MO
Gardner & Co.	A. C.		Milford	MA

ALPHABETICAL LISTING OF PHOTOGRAPHERS IN THE U. S. IN 1888 & 1889

NAME		ADDRESS	CITY	STATE
Gardner & Co.		276 Fulton	Brooklyn	NY
Gardner & Philbrick			Biddeford	ME
Gardner & Son	J. B.	147 Fulton	New York City	NY
Gardner & Son			Napoleon	OH
Gardner*	Levi		Kent	PA
Gardnier	C. W.		Springfield	IL
Garner	Joseph		Moline	KS
Garniere & Layton		3140 State	Chicago	IL
Garns & Co.	H. D.	526 S. 2nd	Philadelphia	PA
Garrett	M. & W.		Wilmington	DE
Garrett	T. P.		Bloomington	IL
Garrison	C. F.		Fort Dodge	IA
Garrity	Miss	307 4th	Louisville	KY
Garrity & Woollett*	Misses & Mr.	430 N. Clark	Chicago	IL
Garvin	J. F.	1546 Wabash	Chicago	IL
Garvin*	J. F.	1230 State	Chicago	IL
Gasberg	Jans C.		Brigham City	UT
Gaston & Co.*	J. B.		Coldwater	KS
Gates	A. P.		Charleston	WV
Gates	C. L.		Waverly	IL
Gates	C. W.		Wilmington	NC
Gates	Edwin R.		Woodstock	VT
Gates	Thomas	693 8th	New York City	NY
Gates	W. D.		Watkins	NY
Gaugler & Heal			Bellevue	OH
Gausemel	P. A.		Kenyon	MN
Gauthier	Joseph		Nashua	NH
Gauvin & Bro.			Burlington	VT
Gay	Anton		New Ulum	MN
Gay	Mrs. Edwin F.		Fall River	MA
Gaylord	P. B.		Duluth	MN
Gaynes	A. D.		Corning	NY
Gebhard	Julia	314 2nd	New York City	NY
Gebhard & Mendenhall*			Unadilla	NE
Gebhardt & Co.			Memphis	TN
Gebhart*	J. D.		Olathe	KS
Geer	L. H.		Orlando	FL
Geer	William F.	10 ½ Market	Canton	OH
Gegoux	Theodore		Watertown	NY
Gehrig	J. W.	337 W. Madison	Chicago	IL
Gellespie	S. M.		New Castle	PA

ALPHABETICAL LISTING OF PHOTOGRAPHERS IN THE U. S. IN 1888 & 1889

NAME		ADDRESS	CITY	STATE
Gellie	Charles		Kansas City	KS
Genelli, Hulbert Bros.		923 Olive	St. Louis	MO
Genelli*			St. Louis	MO
Genest	Gideon		Salem	MA
Gentile & Co.		81 State	Chicago	IL
Gentz*	A. H.	289 W. 12th	Chicago	IL
Gentzel	A. H.	659 Lincoln	Chicago	IL
George	Isaac		Lehigh	KS
George & Lelless			Parker's Landing	PA
Gerdom	H. E.		Lykens	PA
Gerhard*	W. P.		Keokuk	IA
Gerlach	C. S.		Elgin	IL
German	C. S.		Springfield	IL
Gerock	Edward		New Berne	NC
Gertz	E. R.	105 Dorchester	Boston	MA
Gesberger	Charles	264 ½ Bowery	New York City	NY
Gesel & Gerhard			Alma	WI
Gettie	John C.	2021 Frankfort	Philadelphia	PA
Getz	William	210 N. Charles	Baltimore	MD
Gibbon*	H. E		Negaunee	MI
Gibboney	H. E.		Columbus Junction	IA
Gibbs	George E.		Auburn	NY
Gibson	J. B.		Coatsville	PA
Gibson	J. J.		Ann Arbor	MI
Gifford	B. R.		Dunkirk	NY
Gifford	Fred A. H.		Provincetown	MA
Gifford	Noah		New Bedford	MA
Gilbert	M. V.		Ada	OH
Gilbert	Zallman		Mandan	DK
Gilbert & Bacon		820 Arch	Philadelphia	PA
Gilbert & Bacon		40 N. 8th	Philadelphia	PA
Gilchrist	G. K.		Cedar Falls	IA
Gilchrist	George C.		Lowell	MA
Gilchrist	George E.	24 Tremont Row	Boston	MA
Gilchrist	J. W.		Fairfield	IA
Gilhousen	W. H.		The Dalles	OR
Gili*	Charles		Kansas City	MO
Gill	W. L.		Lancaster	PA
Gillen	J. R.		Phillipsburgh	NJ
Gillett Copying Co.			Concord	NH
Gillingham	Chas. L.		Colorado Springs	CO

ALPHABETICAL LISTING OF PHOTOGRAPHERS IN THE U. S. IN 1888 & 1889

NAME		ADDRESS	CITY	STATE
Gillis	Frank E.	164 Leverett	Boston	MA
Gillmore	George W.	204 Main	Worcester	MA
Gills	F.		San Bernardino	CA
Gilman	J. Bryant		Canajoharie	NY
Gilmartin	F. J.		St. Paul	MN
Gilmore	Lowell		Binghampton	NY
Gilmore Bros.		204 Front	Worcester	MA
Gilson	A. S.		Wellington	OH
Ginter	David		Sunbury	PA
Ginter	W. M.		Lewisburgh	PA
Ginther	J.	329 Main	Buffalo	NY
Gist	John		New Sharon	IA
Gittings	J. H.	3432 Cottage Grove	Chicago	IL
Givens	W. D.		Seward	NE
Glancy	S. W.		Milford	CT
Glass	C. E.		Janesville	WI
Glass*	C. G.		Washington	KS
Glazener	J. R.		Easley	SC
Gleason	F. M.		Ware	MA
Gledhill	R. C.		Jerseyville	IL
Glenn	C. A.		Snow Shoe	PA
Glenney	S. W.	11 Exchange Pl	Waterbury	CT
Glenton	Frederick		Nashua	NH
Gline	Andrew	794 3rd	New York City	NY
Glines	Arthur A.	6 Winter	Boston	MA
Glines	W. B.		Eureka	KS
Glines*	Arthur A.		Newton	MA
Globe Novelty Co.		150 Dearborn	Chicago	IL
Globen & Son			Gainesville	TX
Goddard	Emmerson		Woonsocket	RI
Godfrey	G. W.	146 E. Main	Rochester	NY
Godfrey	Peter		Fulton	MO
Goding	C. G.		Old Orchard	ME
Godkin	W. R.		Long Pine	NE
Goe	B. F.		Camden	AR
Goebel*	Rudolph		St. Charles	MO
Goetchins	J. C.		Titusville	PA
Goettel*	Philip		White Water	WI
Goetz	John		West Bend	WI
Goff	F. L.		Wausau	WI
Goff	Frank L.		Elkhart	IN

ALPHABETICAL LISTING OF PHOTOGRAPHERS IN THE U. S. IN 1888 & 1889

NAME		ADDRESS	CITY	STATE
Goff*	George		Washburn	IL
Gogler	Louis	350 Bowery	New York City	NY
Goin	J. M.	101 W. Madison	Chicago	IL
Goins	J. M.	163 Race	Cincinnati	OH
Gokay	E. S.		Petersburgh	NY
Gokay	E. S.		Bennington	VT
Goldesman	Nachson	38 Bowery	New York City	NY
Goldesman*	Nachson	391 Canal	New York City	NY
Goldsberry	B. E.		Bedford	IA
Golsh	Arthur A. C.		Los Angeles	CA
Gomber	J. C.	229 Reed	Milwaukee	WI
Goodale*	C. M.		Hannibal	MO
Goodell	C. E.		Wilkesbarre	PA
Goodell & Ganiere		299 W. Indiana	Chicago	IL
Goodenough	G. C.		Farmington	IA
Goodhall	H. S.		New Hampton	IA
Gooding	Charles G.		Yarmouth	ME
Goodlander	M. D.		Muncie	IN
Goodloe	W.		Valdosta	GA
Goodman	H. P.		White Water	WI
Goodman	J. E.	69 Church	New Haven	CT
Goodman	R. A.	60 S. Salina	Syracuse	NY
Goodman*	J. W.		Apple River	IL
Goodrich	G. A.		Shelbyville	IN
Goodrich*	H.		Highland	WI
Goodridge Bros.			East Saginaw	MI
Goodwin	James W.	59-65 Arcade	Providence	RI
Goolsbay	J. W.		Rockville	MO
Goossen	N. B.		Grand Rapids	MI
Gordon	E. M.		Solon	ME
Gordon Bros.			Soldiers' Grove	WI
Gorgas	J. R.		Madison	IN
Gorham	Edwin L.	103 S. Portland	Brooklyn	NY
Gorham	J. A.		Council Bluffs	IA
Gorham	L. D.		Mount Kisco	NY
Gorham	T. P.		Wayne	MI
Gorham*	James E.		Covington	IN
Gorman	W. H.		Jersey Shore	PA
Gorrell*	S. C.		New Castle	PA
Goss	Albert		Auburn	NE
Goss	E. L.		E. Pepperell	MA

ALPHABETICAL LISTING OF PHOTOGRAPHERS IN THE U. S. IN 1888 & 1889

NAME		ADDRESS	CITY	STATE
Gosslee*	R. H.		Sullivan	IL
Gostin & Guerin			Strawberry Point	IA
Gosting	G. G.		Le Mars	IA
Gough	George		Brockway Centre	MI
Gould	A. R.		East Liverpool	OH
Gould	Robert		Rochester	IN
Gould*	J. W.		Carrollton	OH
Graeff	Adolph	679 W. Lake	Chicago	IL
Graeff & Gardner			Liberty	NY
Graham	F. P.		Urbana	OH
Graham	J. W.		St. Joseph	MO
Graham	Richard		Mexico	MO
Graites	H. W.		Macomb	IL
Granger	H. P.		Lebanon	NH
Granniss	C. N.	48 Bank	Waterbury	CT
Grant	W. P.		Mount Sterling	IL
Grant*	H. M.		Eureka	CA
Grasett & Boys			Los Angeles	CA
Gratch	W. M.		Xenia	OH
Graves	E. L.		Albion	MI
Graves	Jesse A.		Delaware Water Gap	PA
Graves	T. K.		East Troy	WI
Graves	W. B.		Shinglehouse	PA
Graves Bros.			Osceola	IA
Gray	Benjamin		Peoria	IL
Gray	G. E.	1070 Tremont	Boston	MA
Gray	H. E.		Omaha	NE
Gray	John C.		Centralia	IL
Gray	Warren A.		Salem	MA
Graybiel	Edwin		Alameda	CA
Greanleaf	C. J.		St. Paul	MN
Greany	John T.	770 S. Broad	Philadelphia	PA
Green	George M.		Blairsville	PA
Green	J. F.		Meriden	CT
Green	J. M.	209 Superior	Cleveland	OH
Green	Josiah H.	Harrison Pike	Cincinnati	OH
Green	Nathaniel		Marion	OH
Green	L. H.		Brighton	IA
Greene	P. B.	342 W. Adams	Chicago	IL
Greene	J. N.		Sterling	IL
Greening	Louis A.	1800 N. Front	Philadelphia	PA

NAME		ADDRESS	CITY	STATE
Greenwood	W. H.		Beloit	KS
Greeves & McFeeters*			Chaska	MN
Gregg	S.	94 State	Rochester	NY
Gregory	A. O.	502-504 J	Sacramento	CA
Gregory	J. M.	810 W. Market	Louisville	KY
Gregory	B. F.		Fullerton	NE
Gregory, Jr.	E. R.		Manchester	OH
Greisemer	S.		East Greenville	PA
Greismer	T. P.		Quakertown	PA
Gribble	Charles		Fostoria	OH
Grier Bros.		906 Arch	Philadelphia	PA
Griffin	William		Hebron	NE
Griffin	C. L.		Tunkhannock	PA
Griffin	M.	446 Main	Buffalo	NY
Griffing	W. W.		Morris	IL
Griffith	G. W.		Watertown	WI
Griffiths	P. W.		Marysville	CA
Griggs	C. T.		Pascoag	RI
Griggs	E. W.		Topeka	KS
Griggs Bros.			Topeka	KS
Grimsehl	Herman	227 Bleecker	New York City	NY
Grinton	D.	191 Seneca	Buffalo	NY
Gripe*	David		Logansport	IN
Griswold	T. F.		Braidwood	IL
Grobe	Jacob		Jacksonville	OR
Grobe	R.		Fremont	OH
Groeff	J. W.		Lebanon	PA
Groesel Bros.	Howard		Akron	OH
Groesel Bros.*	Howard	SW c Market	Akron	OH
Groh & Bro.	G. M.		Sheboygan	WI
Gronemann	F. C.		Fort Dodge	IA
Groomes	J. C.		Ripley	OH
Groomes	John W.	170 W. 5th	Cincinnati	OH
Gross	C. A.	232 Columbus	Sandusky	OH
Gross	P. L.		Bethlehem	PA
Gross & Co.	Julius	1001 S. Broadway	St. Louis	MO
Gross Bros.		176 Atlantic	Brooklyn	NY
Grossfield			Rushford	MN
Grotecloss	John H.	46 W. 14th	New York City	NY
Grotecloss	W. G.	138 E. 42nd	New York City	NY
Grove	Charles		Conway Springs	KS

ALPHABETICAL LISTING OF PHOTOGRAPHERS IN THE U. S. IN 1888 & 1889

NAME		ADDRESS	CITY	STATE
Grover	F. A.		Bennett	NE
Grover*	W. H.		Bridgeport	IL
Grubbs	J. A.		Waynesborough	GA
Gubelman	Theodore	79 Newark	Jersey City	NJ
Gubin	Oscar	190 Ontario	Cleveland	OH
Guenveur	S. F.		Selma	AL
Guerin	F. W.	1534 S. Broadway	St. Louis	MO
Guild	F. D.		Lebanon	MO
Guild	W. J.		Rolla	MO
Gulney	Caleb S.		Kennebunk	ME
Gumbiuski	Leon	196 Ontario	Cleveland	OH
Gunter	B. F.		Aiken	SC
Gurney	W. H.		Pawtucket	RI
Gurrad	J. L.		La Salle	IL
Gustin	J. E.		West Brook	ME
Gutekunst	Frederick	712 Arch	Philadelphia	PA
Guthrie*	J. A.		Nevada	MO
Gutley	G. W.		Utica	NY
Haag	Joseph		Leavenworth	KS
Haarer	John		Ann Arbor	MI
Haas	Albert		Petersburgh	IN
Hacker Photo Co.		2 Moulton	Providence	RI
Hadaway	Miss Julia		Prophetstown	IL
Hadden	James		Uniontown	PA
Haefer	F. C.		Calumet	MI
Haefer	F. C.		Hancock	MI
Hafer	E. E.		Reading	PA
Hagedorn	Charles		Butler	MO
Hagelstein Bros.		142 Bowery	New York City	NY
Hagenbuch	H. W.		Watsontown	PA
Hagendoff	Louis	436 Milwaukee	Milwaukee	WI
Hagenstab	William J.	713 Chouteau	St. Louis	MO
Hager	J. S.		Marlette	MI
Haight	E. M.		Fort Gratiot	MI
Haines	Charles B.		Warren	OH
Haines	Joseph		Phillipsburgh	PA
Haines	O. P.		Chadron	NE
Hakelier	Oscar		Rockford	IL
Halbach	C. H.		Sheboygan	WI
Hale	B. F.	150 State	Rochester	NY
Hale	Frank W.		E. Hartford	CT

ALPHABETICAL LISTING OF PHOTOGRAPHERS IN THE U. S. IN 1888 & 1889

NAME		ADDRESS	CITY	STATE
Hale	Herbert A.		Vergennes	VT
Hale	J. E.		Seneca Falls	NY
Hale	Mark L.		Winamac	IN
Hale	O. C.		Ripley	OH
Hale	J. W.		West Randolph	VT
Hale*	Frank W.		E. Hartford	CT
Hale*	J. A.		Malden	MO
Haley	John F.	229 Atlantic	Boston	MA
Haley	John F.	Dover	Boston	MA
Haley	Joseph	Hanover	Boston	MA
Haley	Joseph F.	249 Dover	Boston	MA
Hall	A. H.		Chatsworth	IL
Hall	B. L.		Sunbury	PA
Hall	C. H.		Amenia	NY
Hall	C. M.		Newport	VT
Hall	E. Clark		Brookville	PA
Hall	E. S.		Hoopeston	IL
Hall	G. S.		Lohrsville	IA
Hall	I. Wilton	21 School	Boston	MA
Hall	J. R.		Monroe	IA
Hall	John		Elizabeth	NJ
Hall	John L.		Monson	ME
Hall	Joseph	111 Fulton	Brooklyn	NY
Hall	R.		Millersburgh	OH
Hall	S. A.		Clarington	OH
Hall	W. W.		Smith Centre	KS
Hall & Priest			Littleton	NH
Hall & Son	George P.	157 Fulton	New York City	NY
Hall & Son*	H. M.		Detroit	MI
Hall*	H. G.		Schuyler	NE
Halliday & Kessberger			Springfield	IL
Halloran Bros.			Pawtucket	RI
Halsey*	I. S.		Vallejo	CA
Halstead	J. D.		Millard	MO
Halstead	Joseph		Dixon	IL
Halvorsen	J. R.		Albert Lea	MN
Ham*	B. N.	357 W. Madison	Chicago	IL
Hambelton & Potter			East Aurora	NY
Hamblin	Alpheus L.		Lovell	ME
Hamel	E. H.		Yankton	DK
Hamelton	G. C.		Nevada	IA

ALPHABETICAL LISTING OF PHOTOGRAPHERS IN THE U. S. IN 1888 & 1889

NAME		ADDRESS	CITY	STATE
Hamilton	A. C.		Lawrence	KS
Hamilton	J. B.		Shenandoah	IA
Hamilton	J. H.		Sioux City	IA
Hamilton & Co.	J. K.	5th & Plum	Cincinnati	OH
Hamilton*	J. K.		Frankfort	KY
Hamlin	J. R.		Casselton	DK
Hammaker	J. D.		Wamego	KS
Hammer	L. F.	1534 S .Broadway	St. Louis	MO
Hammerly	A. O.		Barnhart's Mills	PA
Hammers*	Fred		St. Louis	MO
Hammersley	Charles H.	109 8th	New York City	NY
Hammond	C. E.		Winthrop	ME
Hammond	C. E.		Hampden	OH
Hammond	H.		New Windsor	IL
Hamor	A. B.		Lawrence	MA
Hampton	A. W.		Pleasonton	KS
Hampton*	P. W.		Harper's Ferry	WV
Hamrich	Wesley		Minonk	IL
Handel	F. G.		Orange	NJ
Handsome	Pritchard		Louisiana	MO
Handy	Levin C.	494 Maryland	Washington	DC
Handy*	C. F.		White Bear	MN
Hanford*	J.		Ithaca	NY
Hang*	Robert R.	2443 Ktn.	Philadelphia	PA
Hanigan	John O.		Warsaw	NY
Hanlon	T. F.	405 Main	Worcester	MA
Hansbrough	J. A.		Abilene	KS
Hansen	C. G.		Manning	IA
Hansen	Neil		Ida Grove	IA
Hansen & Menke			Manistee	MI
Hanson	Jacob		Yreka	CA
Hanson	S. P.		Bridgewater	DK
Hanson	W. R.	884 Milwaukee	Chicago	IL
Harbers	Gunther	354 Grand	New York City	NY
Harcourt*	Myron		Baldwin	MI
Hardeman	L. E.		Madisonville	KY
Harden	A. B.		Emporia	KS
Harden	A. B.		Joplin	MO
Harden	A. W.		Wichita	KS
Harden	C. T.		Windsor	NC
Harding	A. D.		Susquehanna	PA

ALPHABETICAL LISTING OF PHOTOGRAPHERS IN THE U. S. IN 1888 & 1889

NAME		ADDRESS	CITY	STATE
Harding	Stephen T.	1666 Fulton	Brooklyn	NY
Hardman	J. F.		Greenville	KY
Hardy	A. N.	493 Washington	Boston	MA
Hardy	F. W.	310 Main	Springfield	MA
Hardy	W. H. B.		Wesson	MS
Hardy & Van Arnum		390 River	Troy	NY
Hare	T. H.		Hamilton	MO
Harens	C. V.		Sterling	KS
Harger*	G. L.	514 Market	Pittsburgh	PA
Hargrave	J. J.		Larned	KS
Hargrave & Gubelman		40 W. 23rd	New York City	NY
Hargrave & Gubelman*		38 W. 23rd	New York City	NY
Haring	Jacob C.		Massillon	OH
Harknep	F. M.	556 E. 12th	Oakland	CA
Harlan	C. C.		Eaton	OH
Harlow	A. C.		Montpelier	VT
Harman	H. J.		York Sulphur Springs	PA
Harman & Verner			Bay City	MI
Harmon	J. E.		Hiawatha	KS
Harna	E.		Boone	IA
Harnish	George A.		Bluffton	IN
Harnish	O. A.		Noblesville	IN
Harnish	T. H.		Kentland	IN
Harper	C. C.		Audubon	IA
Harper	C. L.		Mount Ayr	IA
Harper	J.		Greenville	OH
Harper	J. A.		Hutchinson	KS
Harper	T. J.		Camden	MI
Harriman	M. C.		Warner	NH
Harrington	J. H.		Sidney	NE
Harrington*	Neal P.		Orrville	OH
Harris	C. L.		Ottawa	KS
Harris	Charles H.		Blair	NE
Harris	F.		Lena	IL
Harris	G. W.		Lancaster	NY
Harris	George A.	150 State	Chicago	IL
Harris	H.		Chetek	WI
Harris	H. E.		Carver	MN
Harris	James		Rolfe	IA
Harris	Louis	124 Park Row	New York City	NY
Harris	N. J.		Meredosia	IL

ALPHABETICAL LISTING OF PHOTOGRAPHERS IN THE U. S. IN 1888 & 1889

NAME		ADDRESS	CITY	STATE
Harris	R.		Clarksville	AR
Harris	H. V.	16 Market Sq.	Portland	ME
Harris & Abell			Vermillion	OH
Harris & Co.	Frank		Skaneateles	NY
Harris & Co.*	George A.	148 State	Chicago	IL
Harris*	Daniel		Tyrone	PA
Harrison	Thomas		Galesburgh	IL
Harrison	Washington	22 W. 4th	New York City	NY
Harrling	J. C.		Ridgway	PA
Harrold*	W. H.		Hammonton	NJ
Harry	A. S.		Steubenville	OH
Hart	A. P.		Elmira	NY
Hart	C. S.		Watertown	NY
Hart	W. E.		Watertown	NY
Hart	Willie		Athony	KS
Harter	J. H.		Nevada	MO
Hartford	F. A.	376 W. Broadway	Boston	MA
Hartford	George		River Point	RI
Hartley	E. F.	309 W. Madison	Chicago	IL
Hartman	Jay J.	231 Grand	Brooklyn	NY
Hartshorn	J. G.		Corydon	IA
Hartwell	C. C.		North Vassalborough	ME
Hartwell & Son			Laramie	WY
Harvey	C. E.	3115 Indiana	Chicago	IL
Harvey	George		St. Joseph	MO
Harvey	L. L.		Greene	IA
Harvey	Mrs. H. P.		Maquoketa	IA
Harvey	S. H.		Berlin	MO
Harvey & Lyles		271 Wabash	Chicago	IL
Harwick	E. B.	229 State	Chicago	IL
Haseltine	J. P.		Lancaster	NH
Hasenbein	H.	876 W. 21st	Chicago	IL
Hasken	W. K.		Columbus	WI
Haskins	George		Osakis	MN
Haskins*	Nye		Ashton	MN
Hassal	A. J.		Toledo	IA
Hassal	George		Keokuk	IA
Hassan	Nelson		Glencoe	MN
Hastings	George H.	147 Tremont	Boston	MA
Hastings*	S. E.		Minneapolis	KS
Hatch	A.		Bath	ME

ALPHABETICAL LISTING OF PHOTOGRAPHERS IN THE U. S. IN 1888 & 1889

NAME		ADDRESS	CITY	STATE
Hatch	A. E.		Elkhorn	WI
Hatch	Henry F.		New Bedford	MA
Hathaway	John G.		Portsmouth	OH
Hathaway Bros.			Staplehurst	NE
Hatstat	A. J.	71 Cambridge	Boston	MA
Hatter	G. L.		Clark	DK
Hatton	Clarence R.	419 Broadway	New York City	NY
Hau	E. W.		Caribou	ME
Haug	Robert R.	2743 Kensington	Philadelphia	PA
Haupt			Butte City	MT
Haus	James		Mifflinburgh	PA
Hausard	J. W.		Fayetteville	AR
Hausen*	Jacob		Yrcka	CA
Hauser	Emil		Tell City	IN
Hauser	G. E.		Michigan City	IN
Haverly	P.		Rensselaervile	NY
Hawes	J. J.	19 Tremont Row	Boston	MA
Hawes	William		New Bedford	MA
Hawk*	P.		Hamilton	OH
Hawkes	A. T.	401 Canal	New York City	NY
Hawkes	M. E. H.		West Union	IA
Hawkes	N. S.		Skowhegan	ME
Hawkins	J. A.	3 ½ N. Park	Mansfield	OH
Hawkins	T. I.		Medina	OH
Hawley	N. D.		Scranton	PA
Haws	Mrs. Jennie		Decatur	IL
Hayden	J. A.		York	NE
Hayden	M. M.		Lowell	MA
Hayden	Mrs. Celia		Chelsea	MA
Hayes	P. M.		Coal Valley	WV
Haynes	Anson		Imlay City	MI
Haynes	Jay J.		Fargo	DK
Haynes	John		Sterling	IL
Haynes	T. C.		St. Johnsbury	VT
Haynes	T. W. B.		Barron	WI
Haynes*	F. J.		Fargo	DK
Hays	E. William	924 1st	Louisville	KY
Hays	J. N.		Kenton	OH
Hays*	I. N.		Kenton	OH
Hayward	W. H.		Crown Point	IN
Hazard	E. W.		Southington	CT

ALPHABETICAL LISTING OF PHOTOGRAPHERS IN THE U. S. IN 1888 & 1889

NAME		ADDRESS	CITY	STATE
Hazeltine	G. I.		Canyon City	OR
Hazer	W. H.		Johnstown	NY
Head	F. D.		Bloomfield	IA
Head	J. G.		Mexico	MO
Heald Co.		159 Westminster	Providence	RI
Healey	C. D.		Wells	ME
Healy	A. A.		Afton	IA
Heard & Delaney			Dalton	GA
Hearn	C. W.	514 Congress	Portland	ME
Hearn	J. P.		Union City	PA
Hearn*	Charles W.		Portland	ME
Heath	H. C.		La Crosse	WI
Heath	Harry		Plymouth	NH
Heath	L. F.		Lansing	MI
Heaton	H. F.		Lebanon	OH
Hebert	J. O.		Grand Rapids	WI
Hedley	G. H.		Medina	NY
Heeb	Adam	651 8th	Milwaukee	WI
Heffelman	O. B.		Doylestown	OH
Heffer	O. W.	872 Broadway	New York City	NY
Heffner	H. C.		Guide Rock	NE
Hegger	Frank	927 Broadway	New York City	NY
Hegger	Frank	1181 Broadway	New York City	NY
Heichert	L. V.		Frankfort	IN
Heidel	Miss E.		Carrollton	MO
Heighton	Miss Libby		Mound Valley	KS
Heim	A.	876 W. 21st	Chicago	IL
Heimberger & Son	C.		New Albany	IN
Heimburg	Charles H.	555 3rd	New York City	NY
Heising	Fred		Frankfort Station	IL
Helgeson	T. J.		Lake Mills	IA
Helmold	Adolar		Clinton	MA
Hemingway	E. B.		Cameron	MO
Hemming	T. M.		Charlottesville	VA
Hemmings	Edward		Whitesborough	TX
Hemple	Sarah M.	1003 Spring Garden	Philadelphia	PA
Hempsted	Charles		Coshocton	OH
Hendee	D. H.		East Portland	OR
Hendel	J. S.		Augusta	ME
Henderson	J. A.		Metropolis City	IL
Henderson & Patterson			Macon	MO

NAME		ADDRESS	CITY	STATE
Henderson Bros.			St. Paul	NE
Hending	Daniel		Texas	MI
Hendricks	William.		Stamford	CT
Hendrickson	C. E.		Niagara Falls	NY
Henigar	G. W.		Middletown	CT
Henigar	W. L.	437 Grand	Brooklyn	NY
Henit	John B.		Terre Haute	IN
Henkel	Charles A.	345 Palisade	Jersey City	NJ
Henney	John A.		Attica	IN
Hennie & Bircher			Columbia	SC
Hennigar	Charles L.	180 E. 121st	New York City	NY
Hennigar	John W.		New Rochelle	NY
Henninger	John H.		Johnstown	PA
Henri	J. R.	168 Bagg	Detroit	MI
Henrici	Henry	1157 S. Broad	Philadelphia	PA
Henrici & Brownworth		709 S. 2nd	Philadelphia	PA
Henry	E. E.		Leavenworth	KS
Henry	Frank	102 W. 5th	Cincinnati	OH
Henry	J. W.		Cedar Rapids	NE
Henry	Levi		Bonaparte	IA
Hensel	Londolph		Hawley	PA
Henshel	W. W.	3136 Cottage Grove	Chicago	IL
Henshel*	W. M.	3136 Cottage Grove	Chicago	IL
Hentscher & Klingholz			Manitowoc	WI
Henwood	A. R.		Aberdeen	MS
Hercher	Henry	365 3rd	Milwaukee	WI
Herks Photographic Gallery			Atlantic City	NJ
Herlocker & Schaad			Freeport	IL
Hermes, Jr.	A. J.		Savannah	GA
Heroff*	J. A.		Danielsville	GA
Herron & O'Donnell			Menominee	MI
Herschel	Gustav	611 Callowhill	Philadelphia	PA
Herstein	J.		Nashville	TN
Herstein & Mahon			Nashville	TN
Herves	George		Payson	IL
Herwick*	W. M.		St. Louis	MO
Hesler	Alexander	99 State	Chicago	IL
Hess	Godfrey		Williamsport	PA
Hess	Joseph		Mifflintown	PA
Hess	Louis		Cobleskill	NY
Hesse	Henry		Springfield	IL

ALPHABETICAL LISTING OF PHOTOGRAPHERS IN THE U. S. IN 1888 & 1889

NAME		ADDRESS	CITY	STATE
Hevy	L. N.		Spencer	MA
Hewitt	W. S.		Atlantic City	NJ
Hewitt & Hewitt			Salem	OH
Heyn	G.		Omaha	NE
Heyn	H.		Omaha	NE
Heyn	L.		Laramie	WY
Hibbard	Charles P.		Burlington	VT
Hickathier	A.		Drain	OR
Hickox	R. A.		Hiawatha	KS
Hicks	E. J.		Falls City	NE
Hicks	H. G.		Frankfort	IN
Hicks	J. T.		Liberty	MO
Hicks	Lemuel S.	191 Grand	Brooklyn	NY
Hicks*	A. G.		Franklin	IN
Hid	Henry I.		Hamilton	NY
Hiester*	H. T.		Chariton	IA
Higbee	E. R.		Chagrin Falls	OH
Higgins	B. P.		Holland	MI
Higgins	E. R.		Fresno	CA
Higgins	E. R.		Madera	CA
Higgins	J. C.		Bath	ME
Hilbert	James		Fairfield	IA
Hildahl	G. S.		Austin	MN
Hildreth*	T. J.		Slater	MO
Hile	William		Greenburgh	PA
Hill	C. G.	363 Washington	Boston	MA
Hill	E. S.		St. Cloud	MN
Hill	H. E.		Marinette	WI
Hill	J. G.		Monroe	MI
Hill	Joseph		St. Cloud	MN
Hill	Mrs. H. E.		Osage Mission	KS
Hill	Russell		Armstrong	KS
Hill	Samuel B.		Austin	TX
Hill	W. H.		Elizabeth	NJ
Hill		47 & 48 Monroe	Detroit	MI
Hill & Hazelton		24 Hanover	Boston	MA
Hill Bros.		1216 Broadway	New York City	NY
Hill Bros.*		50 W. 14th	New York	NY
Hill Photo. Co.		1227 Washington	New York City	NY
Hill*	E. T.		Abbeville	SC
Hill*	L. J.		Bird Island	MN

ALPHABETICAL LISTING OF PHOTOGRAPHERS IN THE U. S. IN 1888 & 1889

NAME		ADDRESS	CITY	STATE
Hiller	Milo		Lowell	MI
Hillerman	Leonard		Watkins	NY
Hillman	Adolph	539 Main	Buffalo	NY
Hillman	W. J.		Richland Center	WI
Hillman Bros.			Passaic	NJ
Hillmann	C. C.		Olewein	IA
HIlls	Martin T.		Attica	NY
Hillyer	Hamilton B.		Austin	TX
Hilton	W. H.	7 Blue Island	Chicago	IL
Hinckley	A. S.		Geneva	NY
Hinckley	Frank W.		Barre	MA
Hingtgen	T. J.		Wahpeton	DK
Hinkel	A.		Warrensburgh	MO
Hinkle	David	4673 Germantown	Philadelphia	PA
Hinman	Frank C.		Loudonville	OH
Hirsch	William	245 Blue Island	Chicago	IL
Hirshberg	Julius	150 2nd	New York City	NY
Hirst	Samuel		Hutchinson	KS
Hissong	G. W.		Lagrange	IN
Histed	E. W.	41 5th	Pittsburgh	PA
Hitchcock	George	185 S. Howard	Akron	OH
Hitchcock	J.		Canton	NY
Hitchcock	James		Mount Vernon	IL
Hitt	C. P.		Ironton	OH
Hixson	J. W.		Billings	MO
Hixson	J. W.		Marionville	MO
Hobart	C.	134 E. Madison	Chicago	IL
Hobart	J. A.		Rockford	IL
Hobart	M. E.		Big Rapids	MI
Hobbs	C. H.		Gorham	NH
Hobbs	J. S.		Bethel	ME
Hockett & Hartsook			Marion	IN
Hodge	Arthur M.	16 Mitchell	Providence	RI
Hodge	L. F.		Bement	IL
Hodge & Huston		622 Arch	Philadelphia	PA
Hodges	John		Paw Paw	MI
Hodges Art Gallery			Bristol	TN
Hodgman	Otis		Bedford	MA
Hodson	J. R.	521 J	Sacramento	CA
Hoff	C. A.		South Manchester	CT
Hoff	E. N.		Denison	IA

ALPHABETICAL LISTING OF PHOTOGRAPHERS IN THE U. S. IN 1888 & 1889

NAME		ADDRESS	CITY	STATE
Hoff	J. B.		Angola	IN
Hoff	W. H.		Carrol	IA
Hoff*	D. J.		Yorkville	IL
Hoffman	E.		Brookville	IN
Hoffman	G. W.		Auburn	NY
Hoffman	W. H.		Shenandoah	PA
Hoffmeir	S. B.		Easton	PA
Hoffmeister	E.		Fremont	NE
Hogan	J. H.		Oroville	CA
Hogle & Nims			Watseka	IL
Hohlweg	Louis		Naperville	IL
Hoiland	A. J.		Benson	MN
Hoit	W. C.		Wadena	MN
Holborn	Henry	1631 Franklin	St. Louis	MO
Holcomb	O.		Salina	KS
Holcomb*	G. W.		Union City	MI
Holcombe	B. J.	222 Woodward	Detroit	MI
Holcombe & Aloord*			Detroit	MI
Holden	Alfred	2603 S. Walnut	Philadelphia	PA
Holden	C. W.		Camp Point	IL
Holden & Brinkley*			Keota	IA
Holland	O. E.		Champaign	IL
Holland	T. G.		Wilmington	DE
Holland	H. F.	10 Temple Place	Boston	MA
Holler	Henry	149 Ewen	Brooklyn	NY
Hollis	C. R.		Pittsfield	MA
Holloway	Charles B.		Newport	RI
Holly	M. S.		Berlin	WI
Holman	Charles		Warren	OH
Holmes	A. S.	66 State	Albany	NY
Holmes	A. S.	282 River	Troy	NY
Holmes	A. T.		Odessa	MO
Holmes	C. D.		Maynard	MA
Holmes	R. C.		Dover	DE
Holmes	Russell		Milford	DE
Holmes & Davis			Du Bois	PA
Holmes Bros.		19 Main	Boston	MA
Holton	Eugene A.	8 Summer	Boston	MA
Holtzinger	J. H.		Tyrone	PA
Holyland	J.	3 W. Baltimore	Baltimore	MD
Holyland*	J.	229 W. Baltimore	Baltimore	MD

ALPHABETICAL LISTING OF PHOTOGRAPHERS IN THE U. S. IN 1888 & 1889

NAME		ADDRESS	CITY	STATE
Homan	Charles	858 Chapel	New Haven	CT
Homrig	C. P.		La Fayette	IN
Hook	R. W.		Waukegan	IL
Hook	W. E.		Marquette	MI
Hooker	A. E.		St. Paul	MN
Hooker	F. S.		Addison	NY
Hoop	S. W.		Manhattan	KS
Hoosier	Isaac		Boulder	CO
Hoot	H. S. & J. W.		Spring Valley	MN
Hoover	J. V.		Ft. Wayne	IN
Hope	J. D.		Watkins	NY
Hopkins	A. C.		Palmyra	NY
Hopkins	G. P.		Lockport	NY
Hopkins	T. E.		Salina	KS
Hopkins*	C. A.		Tecumseh	MI
Hopkins*	C. E.		Wetmore	KS
Hopp	H. H.		Neodesha	KS
Hoppe	E. D.		Holton	KS
Horn	M. U.		Newcomerstown	OH
Horner	Samuel		Onawa	IA
Horning	J. M.		Phoenixville	PA
Horning	Lewis	56-63 N. 8th	Philadelphia	PA
Horton	G. W.		Beaver Dam	WI
Horton	V. W.	15 N. Pearl	Albany	NY
Horton Bros.		87 Westminster	Providence	RI
Hoskings	J. M.		Mount Morris	IL
Hoskins	C. A.		Cheboygan	MI
Hotchkiss	A. E.		Norwich	NY
Hotchkiss	Eugene		Kankakee	IL
Hough	E. H.		Beatrice	NE
Hough	Edward B.	633 Arch	Philadelphia	PA
Hough	J.	135 Chicago	Chicago	IL
Hough*	Joshua	125 E. Chicago	Chicago	IL
Houghton	J. & E.		Joplin	MO
Houghton	R. R.		Felicity	OH
Houseknecht	P. B.		Batavia	NY
Houseman	J. H.		Grundy Centre	IA
Houser	J. K. P.		Clarksville	TX
Houser	Mrs. E. F.		Sterling	IL
Houseworth	Thomas	12 Montgomery	San Francisco	CA
Houston	J.		Clarksburgh	WV

ALPHABETICAL LISTING OF PHOTOGRAPHERS IN THE U. S. IN 1888 & 1889

NAME		ADDRESS	CITY	STATE
Hover	H. S.		Marysville	KS
Hover	W. M.		Tecumseh	NE
Hovey	Alvin		Burr Oak	KS
Hovey	J. S.		Rome	NY
Hovey's Sons	D.	74 Asylum	Rochester	NY
Howar*	J. S.		Pelican Rapids	MN
Howard	C. R.		Clay Centre	KS
Howard	E. J.	32 Arcade	Akron	OH
Howard	E. P.		Eldon	IA
Howard	George		Greenport	NY
Howard	James		Plattsburgh	NY
Howard	N. W.		Eureka	KS
Howard	S. H.		Connellsville	PA
Howard	W. A.		Clay Centre	KS
Howard	W. M.		Mulvane	KS
Howard	W. S.		Paolo	KS
Howard	E. E.		Fitchburg	MA
Howard & Miller*			Harrisburgh	PA
Howard & Son	A.		West Gardner	MA
Howard Bros.*			Westminster	SC
Howard*	J. B.		Bush Creek	IA
Howard*	J. B.		Port Washington	WI
Howd	D. H.		Paterson	NJ
Howe	C. J.		Elmira	NY
Howe	Frederick L.	58 W. 23rd	New York City	NY
Howe	J. M.	6 Eddy	San Francisco	CA
Howe	Randolph		Fryeburg	ME
Howe	T.		New Canaan	CT
Howe	W. H.		Pittsfield	ME
Howe & Co.		1557 Broadway	New York City	NY
Howe & Son	C. L.		Brattleboro	VT
Howell	Frank A.	249 King	Charleston	SC
Hower	William H.		Goshen	IN
Hower & Hawes			Butte City	MT
Howie	G. W.	145 Randolph	Detroit	MI
Howland	B. F.		Napa City	CA
Howland*	B. F.		San Francisco	CA
Howland*	C. W.	176 W. Fourth	Cincinnati	OH
Howland	E. A.	427 Kemper	Cincinnati	OH
Howland	E. H.		Streator	IL
Howland*	S. P.		Belton	MO

ALPHABETICAL LISTING OF PHOTOGRAPHERS IN THE U. S. IN 1888 & 1889

NAME		ADDRESS	CITY	STATE
Howson	William S.	957 Fulton	Brooklyn	NY
Hoyer	H. C.		Covington	KY
Hoyt	J. S.		Fort Recovery	OH
Hubbard	E. E.		Milford	NH
Hubbard & Keys			Nora Springs	IA
Hubbard*	A. L.		Ashland	OH
Hubbel	O. C.	649 Pearl	Cleveland	OH
Hubbell	R. M.		Norwich	CT
Hubbell	R. W.		Red Wing	MN
Hubley	J. W.		Lancaster	PA
Huckel	Joseph		Cawker City	KS
Huddleston*	F. M.		Newton	KS
Hudson	Alinzar		Carbondale	IL
Hudson	Edward		Eldora	IA
Hudson & Gard			Valley Centre	KS
Hudson*	J. L.		Denver	CO
Huebinger Bros.			Davenport	IA
Huebschmann	L. C. F.		Sparta	IL
Huey	B. W.		Windsor	MO
Huff	F. L.	707 Broad	Newark	NJ
Huff	W. C.		Stevens' Point	WI
Huffman	J. B.		Chillicothe	MO
Huffman*	L. A.		Miles City	MT
Huffmann & Barnard*			Waverly	IA
Hughes	A. A.		Humboldt	NE
Hughes	B. E.		Omaha	NE
Hughes	R. F.	32 Chamber of Commerce	Toledo	OH
Hughes	T. J.		Evansville	AR
Hughes	W. F.		Colorado	TX
Hughes Bros.			Blanchard	IA
Hughes*	F. N. B.		Memphis	TN
Hulbert Bros.	923 Olive		St. Louis	MO
Hull	A. C.		Fremont	NE
Hull	H. B.		Portsmouth	OH
Hull	Huber H.	381 Canal	New York City	NY
Hull	O. S.		Thomaston	CT
Hull	V. N.	823 Chapel	New Haven	CT
Hull & Son*			Battle Creek	MI
Hull*	O. N.	823 Chapel	New Haven	CT
Hummel & Hoerger			Faribault	MN
Humphrey	W. R.		Jacksonville	IL

ALPHABETICAL LISTING OF PHOTOGRAPHERS IN THE U. S. IN 1888 & 1889

NAME		ADDRESS	CITY	STATE
Humphreys	A. H.		Camden	NJ
Hunold	Frank	4th Ave.	College Point, L. I.	NY
Hunster	Louie P.	13 ½ E. Main	Springfield	OH
Hunt	C. L.		Franklin Falls	NH
Hunt	E. J.		Camden	NJ
Hunt	M.		Lisbon	NH
Hunt	William		Rockville	IN
Hunt & Fisher			Plainfield	NJ
Hunter	John B.	229 Greenwich	New York City	NY
Hunter	John E.	551 N. 3rd	New York City	NY
Hunter	P. C.		Martinsburg	WV
Hunter	Thomas		Young	DK
Hunter	William F.	243 Fulton	Brooklyn	NY
Hunter & Co.*			Lockwood	MO
Hunter Bros.			Taunton	MA
Hunter's Art Gallery		227 Jefferson	Detroit	MI
Huntington	H. H.		Blairstown	IA
Hunton	F. D.		Hallowell	ME
Hunton	F. N.		Henderson	KY
Hunton	Frank N.		Evansville	IN
Huntoon	R. C.		Pontiac	IL
Hupp	Phillips		Louisburgh	KS
Hurd	Gustine L.	257 Westminster	Providence	RI
Hurd	William E.		South Shaftsbury	VT
Hurd & Son*	W. P.		Clarinda	IA
Hurd*	Ernest W.		North Adams	MA
Hurlburt*	G. H.		Beloit	WI
Hurst	John A.	1738 Ridge	Philadelphia	PA
Hurst*	John A.	1800 Ridge	Philadelphia	PA
Husband	Harvey	613 W. Market	Louisville	KY
Husbands	S.		Hood River	OR
Hussey	William A.		Salem	MA
Husted	Joseph F.	1344 Ridge	Philadelphia	PA
Huston*	J. A.		Marion	KS
Huszah	O. H.	163 S. Halsted	Chicago	IL
Huszah	W. O.	1553 Wabash	Chicago	IL
Hutchins	C. S.		Auburn	NY
Hutchinson	H. S.	149 22nd	Chicago	IL
Hyde	M. F.		Chamberlain	DK
Hyder	Charles		Havana	IL
Hyder	Ed.		Winterset	IA

ALPHABETICAL LISTING OF PHOTOGRAPHERS IN THE U. S. IN 1888 & 1889

NAME		ADDRESS	CITY	STATE
Ide	D. T.		Pawtucket	RI
Iler	F. M.		Amboy	MN
Illingworth	W. H.		St. Paul	MN
Immke	H. W.		Princeton	IL
Imrie	H. N.	59 Monroe	Detroit	MI
Imus	C. W.		Alton	KS
Ingall	Z.		Madison	ME
Ingalls	F. M.		Le Sueur	MN
Ingalls	Z. D.		New Vineyard	ME
Ingersoll	T. W.		St. Paul	MN
Ingersoll	William. B.	1069 Broadway	Oakland	CA
Ingle	Mrs. Elizabeth		Gainesville	TX
Inglis	J. S.		Montgomery City	MO
Inman	William M.		Lancaster	PA
Insley	Henry A.		Nyack	NY
Interguglielmi	Louis	227 Royal	New Orleans	LA
Iron City Photo Co.		99 5th	Pittsburgh	PA
Irvin	George. C.		Stockton	CA
Irwing	J.	13 2nd	Troy	NY
Isaacs	A. C.		Madison	WI
Ish	J. W.		Gaylord	MI
Israel	S. G. & R. B.		Chicago	IL
Iverson*	H.	2176 Archer	Chicago	IL
Ives	E. B.		Niles	MI
Ivie	Theodore L.		Atlanta	GA
Izard & Co.		229 State	Chicago	IL
Jackson	B. D.		Grand Rapids	MI
Jackson	Calvin		Hannibal	MO
Jackson	Dwight N.	823 Washington	Boston	MA
Jackson	G. M.		Brunswick	GA
Jackson	J. O.		Franklin	PA
Jackson	John		Oswego	NY
Jackson	W. D.		Waco	TX
Jackson	W. P.		Tacoma	WA
Jackson & Clower			Newman	GA
Jackson & Co.	W. H.		Denver	CO
Jackson & Kenny		478 ½ Congress	Portland	ME
Jackson*	John		Owego	NY
Jacobs	Alfred W.	204 Atlantic	Brooklyn	NY
Jacobs	J. M.		Auburn	CA
Jacobs	W. H.		Eagle Grove	IA

ALPHABETICAL LISTING OF PHOTOGRAPHERS IN THE U. S. IN 1888 & 1889

NAME		ADDRESS	CITY	STATE
Jacobs*	F. M.		Auburn	CA
Jacobs*	W. L.		Logan	IA
Jacobsen*	J.		Hooper	NE
Jacobson	O. C.	488 Milwaukee	Chicago	IL
Jacoby	H. J.		St. Peter	MN
Jacoby	W. H.		Minneapolis	MN
Jacques	Joseph		Garden	MI
Jaeger	G. J.	202 2nd	New York City	NY
Jaeger	George	811 Arch	Philadelphia	PA
Jaeger	Henry	302 S. Halsted	Chicago	IL
Jaeger	Josephine	18 Ave. B.	New York City	NY
Jaeger*	H. J.	86 S. Halsted	Chicago	IL
Jahn Bros.		760 Broadway	New York City	NY
Jaison	D.	237 Clark	Chicago	IL
Jalass	H. V.	301 Prairie	Milwaukee	WI
James*	Caroline B.	407 8th	New York City	NY
James	Caroline B.	583 8th	New York City	NY
James	Charles H.	624 Arch	Philadelphia	PA
James	E. N.		Northfield	MN
James	N. W.		Iowa City	IA
James	Thomas		Des Moines	IA
James, Jr.	Thomas		Carlyle	IL
Jameson	J. W.		Stamping Ground	KY
Janousek	L.		Niobrara	NE
Jaquith	E. C.		Sedan	KS
Jarvis	J. W.		Canton	GA
Jarvis	John F.	135 Pennsylvania	Washington	DC
Jauchler*	Stephen	211 Orleans	New Orleans	LA
Jaynes	E. L.		Spencer	MA
Jaynes & Bristol*			Corning	NY
Jeanes	E. D.		Allentown	PA
Jeans	Joseph		Chester	PA
Jeffers	J. E.		Norfolk	VA
Jeffers	William. H.	1202 Mission	San Francisco	CA
Jefferson	R.		Clarendon	TX
Jellotson*	Nelson		Hawley	PA
Jenkins & Hasking			Mineral Point	WI
Jenkins Bros.		1059 Green	Brooklyn	NY
Jenks*	J. M.		Marseilles	IL
Jennings	Joseph		Scandia	KS
Jensen	George		Ephraim	UT

ALPHABETICAL LISTING OF PHOTOGRAPHERS IN THE U. S. IN 1888 & 1889

NAME		ADDRESS	CITY	STATE
Jensen	Martin		Ephraim	UT
Jensen	N. P.		Howell	MI
Jenson*	E. M.		Kerkhoven	MN
Jerauld & Co.	P. W.		Niagara Falls	NY
Jessen	William	41 5th	Pittsburgh	PA
Jessup	Edward		Middletown	NY
Jestram	Henry	393 Blue Island	Chicago	IL
Jette	Joseph		Fall River	MA
Jeush	W.	695 Broad	Newark	NJ
Jewell	Frank		Scranton	PA
Jewell*	Daniel		Flint	MI
Joas & Parker			Kingman	KS
Johles	Robert	477 Milwaukee	Chicago	IL
Johns	W. E.		Lexington	KY
Johns & Son			Marshall	MO
Johns*	H. C.		Plattsmouth	NE
Johnson	A. A.		Cazenovia	NY
Johnson	A. M.		Greenville	OH
Johnson	A. S.		Brandon	WI
Johnson	A. S.		Waupun	WI
Johnson	Adelaide		Adams	NY
Johnson	C. F.		Kalamazoo	MI
Johnson	C. W. J.		Monterey	CA
Johnson	E.		Hicksville	OH
Johnson	E. M.		Crown Point	NY
Johnson	Ed		Ladonia	TX
Johnson	Ed		Savoy	TX
Johnson	George G.	99 Euclid	Cleveland	OH
Johnson	H. Worthley	395 8th	New York City	NY
Johnson	J. B.		Los Gatos	CA
Johnson	J. M.		Columbus	KS
Johnson	J. Scott	R 17, 134 Madison	Chicago	IL
Johnson	L. D.		Vineland	NJ
Johnson	L. K.		Mill Village	PA
Johnson	L. M.		Joplin	MO
Johnson	L. W.		Maysville	MO
Johnson	Loren		Crookston	MN
Johnson	Newton G.	1211 3rd	Washington	DC
Johnson	P. A.		Cumberland	WI
Johnson	P. P.		Glenwood	MN
Johnson	W. W.		Sullivan	IN

ALPHABETICAL LISTING OF PHOTOGRAPHERS IN THE U. S. IN 1888 & 1889

NAME		ADDRESS	CITY	STATE
Johnson	William		Abingdon	IL
Johnson	William P.		Salem	OR
Johnson & Co.		717 S. Halsted	Chicago	IL
Johnson & Lacombe		384 Bowery	New York City	NY
Johnson & Wilson			Kewanee	IL
Johnson Bros.		469 Pennsylvania	Washington	DC
Johnson Bros.			Watertown	NY
Johnson*	Edward J.	4209 Lancaster	Philadelphia	PA
Johnson*	H. Worthley	205 Sixth	New York City	NY
Johnston	James	218 Michigan	Detroit	MI
Jones	A. C.		Winona	MN
Jones	F. R.	357 Westminster	Providence	RI
Jones	J. H.		Hillsborough	IL
Jones	J. N.		Marshalltown	IA
Jones	J. W.		Hammonton	NJ
Jones	Jacob	3313 Woodland	Philadelphia	PA
Jones*	Jacob	3311 Woodland	Philadelphia	PA
Jones	L. M.		Columbia City	IN
Jones*	L. M.		Markesan	WI
Jones	L. P.		Elkhart	IN
Jones	L. W.		Mount Vernon	IN
Jones	Maurice L.		Ft. Wayne	IN
Jones	N. P.		Madison	WI
Jones	R. H.		Clarence	MO
Jones	T. M.		Moline	IL
Jones	W. H.		Cedar Springs	MI
Jones	William	40 Newark	Jersey City	NJ
Jones & Bower			Greencastle	IN
Jones & Lotz		838 Market	San Francisco	CA
Jones Bros.			Union	OR
Jordan	Ella G.	1227 Pennsylvania	Washington	DC
Jordan	H. A.		Dubuque	IA
Jordan	James J.		Wilmington	DE
Jordan Photo-Art Gallery		419 Broadway	New York City	NY
Jordon*	John T.		Augusta	GA
Jornes	F. W.		Girard	IL
Jorns	G. W.		Springfield	IL
Joseph	C. A.		Farley	IA
Joseph	Dideron		Lorain	OH
Joseph	L. W.		Fordland	MO
Joung*	E. S.		Leon	IA

NAME		ADDRESS	CITY	STATE
Joy	B. F.		Ellsworth	ME
Judd	A. W.		Chattanooga	TN
Judd	C. L.		Jamestown	DK
Judd	C. S.		Columbia	TN
Judd	H. M.		Chicopee Falls	MA
Judd	W. H. E.		Kalkaska	MI
Judd	W. H. E.		Mancelona	MI
Judd*	J. E.		Holly	MI
Judkins	L. D.		Bismark	DK
Judkins	S. B.		Portland	OR
Julian	C. H.		Fredericksburgh	IN
Jull	R. W.		Jamestown	NY
Kabley	Charles A.		Clinton	MA
Kahn	Leopald		Livingston	MT
Kail*	W. H.		Beaver Falls	PA
Kale	Mrs. L. R.		Sarcoxie	MO
Kamber	F. J.		Alton	IA
Kammer	Joseph H.	118 Pleasant	New Orleans	LA
Kanberg	J. J.	433 Division	Chicago	IL
Kane*	Thomas	459 Grand	Brooklyn	NY
Karras	M.	18 3rd	San Francisco	CA
Kasten	William		Freeport	IL
Kastenholz*	John		Milwaukee	WI
Katell	S. M.		Gloucester	MA
Kaufman*	Peter	Wayne & McLain	Dayton	OH
Kay	Wallace		Jackson	CA
Keck	Calvin	W. Federal	Youngstown	OH
Keefe	Richard		Somerville	MA
Keeler	E. C.		Salt Lake City	UT
Keeler	H. L.	37 Main	Mount Holly	NJ
Keeley	H. C.	1 Blue Island	Chicago	IL
Keely*	H. C.	174 S. Halsted	Chicago	IL
Keen	George		Mankato	MN
Keen	L. W.		Jonesborough	TN
Keenan	N. E.	238 ½ Elm	Cincinnati	OH
Keeran	J. W.		Bloomington	IL
Keesler	J. J.		Marathon	NY
Keil	Ed. A.	715 Market	San Francisco	CA
Keim	John H.	40 Newark	Jersey City	NJ
Keim & Co.	G. W.	260 Bowery	New York City	NY
Keis*	G.		Batavia	NY

ALPHABETICAL LISTING OF PHOTOGRAPHERS IN THE U. S. IN 1888 & 1889

NAME		ADDRESS	CITY	STATE
Keith	Justin W.		Pelham	MA
Keith	S. F.		Alta	IA
Keith	W. S.		Erie	PA
Keller	H. D.		Wapello	IA
Keller	Henry S.	1431 Ridge	Philadelphia	PA
Keller & Jarvis			Little Falls	NY
Kellett & Wife*	T. A.		La Porte City	IA
Kelley	E. T.		Sommerville	NJ
Kelley	James H.	832 Broadway	New York City	NY
Kelley*	I. P.		Broken Bow	NE
Kellmer	Peter		Hazelton	PA
Kellog	W. F.		River Falls	WI
Kellogg	C. H.		Norwalk	OH
Kellogg	D. R.		Reedsburgh	WI
Kellogg	Edwin P.	265 Main	Hartford	CT
Kellogg	H. W.		Fall River	MA
Kellogg	J. D.		Red Wing	MN
Kellum	John		Connersville	IN
Kelly	E. T.	767 Broadway	New York City	NY
Kelly	I. P.		Broken Bow	NE
Kelly	J. C.		Freeburgh	IL
Kelly	John		Perry	ME
Kelly	M. F.		Winfield	KS
Kelly	R. L.		Pierre	DK
Kelly & Co.			Lincoln	NE
Kelly & Sobieski			Los Angeles	CA
Kelly Bros.			Chenoa	IL
Kelman & Spate*		305 E. Division	Chicago	IL
Kelsey	Orrin		Hutchinson	MN
Kelsey	Will. H.		St. Marys	OH
Kemp	Carl		El Dorado	KS
Kemp	J. M.		Paterson	NJ
Kemp*	H.		Fredricksburgh	PA
Kempf	Charles L.	185 Myrtle	Brooklyn	NY
Kempf	Charles L.	627 Myrtle	Brooklyn	NY
Kempvanee	Henry		Santa Rosa	CA
Kendall	O.		East Hardwick	VT
Kendall	R. A.		Modesto	CA
Kendig	A. C.		Naperville	IL
Kendig	J. D.		Burlington Junction	MO
Kenefick	Owen A.		Lawrence	MA

ALPHABETICAL LISTING OF PHOTOGRAPHERS IN THE U. S. IN 1888 & 1889

NAME		ADDRESS	CITY	STATE
Kennedy	James. F.		Hot Springs	AR
Kennedy	W. H.		Poplar Bluff	MO
Kenney	A. L.		Newton	IA
Kenney	C. C.		Hackettstown	NJ
Kenney	H. J.		West Fairlee	VT
Kent	Eugene		Sparta	OH
Kent	John H.	243-247 State	Rochester	NY
Kent & Amburn*			Attumwa	KS
Kent*	John H.	24 State	Rochester	NY
Kenyon	A. J.		Port Leyden	NY
Kenyon	F. H.		Claremont	NH
Kenyon & Son	F. P.		New London	CT
Keon & Miller			Ashland	PA
Kerberg	J. F.		Hull	IA
Kerlin	T. J.	318-320 J	Sacramento	CA
Kerman*	B. H.		Montgomery	MN
Kerns	N. A.		Girard	OH
Kerr	C. E.		Buchanan	MI
Kersting	H. C.	730 Milwaukee	Chicago	IL
Kersting			Deadwood	DK
Kertson	H. J.		Crookston	MN
Kertson & Curteau			Sank Centre	MN
Kester	C. M.		Oregon City	OR
Kester*	Elias		Grampian Hill	PA
Ketchledge	P. D.		Belvidere	NJ
Ketchum	M. D.		Springfield	IL
Ketchum	W. G.		Augusta	IL
Kets	Kennethy M.	1109 Pennsylvania	Washington	DC
Kett	T. H.		Fairhaven	VT
Keyce	J. M.		Alamo	TN
Keystone Gallery			Braddock	PA
Kibbe	W. H.		Johnstown	NY
Kibble	George		Amsterdam	NY
Kiddle	Thomas	252 Michigan	Detroit	MI
Kidney	W. F.		Adrian	MI
Kientzle	Alexander	733 Girard	Philadelphia	PA
Kilborn & Co.	W. F.		Cedar Rapids	IA
Kilbourn	J. E.		Tipton	IA
Kilgore	H. L.		Belfast	ME
Killam*	A.	37 Asylum	Hartford	CT
Kimball	A. W.		Richmond	ME

ALPHABETICAL LISTING OF PHOTOGRAPHERS IN THE U. S. IN 1888 & 1889

NAME		ADDRESS	CITY	STATE
Kimball	C.	140 Court	Boston	MA
Kimball	W. G. C.		Concord	NH
Kimball Bros.			Fitchburg	MA
Kimball Photographic Art Studio			Lowell	MA
Kindmark	E.		Galion	OH
King	C. H.	767 Washington	Boston	MA
King	E. C.		Tacoma	WA
King	J. R.		Clyde	KS
King	M. F.	482 Congress	Portland	ME
King	T. L.		Ponce de Leon	MO
Kingsbury	William E.		Centralia	MO
Kingsley	Lewis H.		Hatfield	MA
Kinkade Bros.*			Collins	IA
Kinney	S. C.		Salem	NY
Kinsman	W. E.		Sparta Centre	MI
Kirby	Frank		Eldora	IA
Kirchhoff	Arthur	527-529 Chestnut	Milwaukee	WI
Kirk	F. J.		Allegheny	PA
Kirk	George W.		Huntington	WV
Kirk	H. P.		Mason City	IA
Kirk	Joseph	661 Broad	Newark	NJ
Kirk*	F. J.	196 Beaver	Pittsburgh	PA
Kirkham*	Reuben		Logan	UT
Kirkland	C. D.		Cheyenne City	WY
Kirklank & Schuster			Neillsville	WI
Kirkpatrick	W. L.		Geneseo	IL
Kiser	J. B.		New Albany	IN
Kitchen	William		Warren	PA
Kittell	Charles		Springfield	MA
Kittle	H. M.		Pontiac	MI
Kittredge	F. K.		Danville	VT
Klain	J. J.	921 McAllister	San Francisco	CA
Klauber	Edward	332 4th	Louisville	KY
Kleckner	M. A.		Atchison	KS
Klein	Charles	481 1st	New York City	NY
Klein	George J.	206 N. Clark	Chicago	IL
Klein	Jacob	324 Grand	New York City	NY
Kleindinst	David		Coldwater	MI
Kline	J. A.		Batavia	OH
Kline	Luther B.		Huntingdon	PA
Kline Bros.	Exchange		Akron	OH

ALPHABETICAL LISTING OF PHOTOGRAPHERS IN THE U. S. IN 1888 & 1889

NAME		ADDRESS	CITY	STATE
Klotter	Charles	906-912 N. 6th	St. Louis	MO
Klotter & Scherer*			St. Louis	MO
Klugherz	Samuel		Shenandoah	PA
Knaffe & Bros.			Knoxville	TN
Knecht	Charles F. A.	Ridge & Montgomery	Philadelphia	PA
Knecht	Frank		Easton	PA
Knecht*	Charles F. A.	Ridge & N. 25th	Philadelphia	PA
Kneeland	Charles		Allegheny	PA
Kneeland*	C.	143 Federal A.	Pittsburgh	PA
Knight	George. H.	19 6th	San Francisco	CA
Knight	J. H.	23 Washington Sq	Worcester	MA
Knight	W. M.	321 Main	Buffalo	NY
Knight*	O. P.		Batavia	NY
Knoder	H. F.		Cardington	OH
Knowles	Joseph C.		New Bedford	MA
Knowlton	Charles		Kankakee	IL
Knowlton	G. E.		Windsor	VT
Knowlton	Willis	335 4th	New York City	NY
Knowlton Bros.			Northampton	MA
Knox	Herbert		Hartford	CT
Knudtson	J. O.		Northwood	IA
Koehler	Gottfried		Indianapolis	IN
Koella	John	Division	Toledo	OH
Koester & Sievers		279 6th	New York City	NY
Koestle Bros.		629 Lorain	Cleveland	OH
Kohn	Arnold		Centralia	IL
Kohnen	Arnold		Frazee City	MN
Kolb	F. J.		Elizabeth	IL
Koogle	Milton		Bellefontaine	OH
Koonz	J. L.		Appleton	WI
Koonz & Son	J.		Greeley	CO
Koopman	H. R.		Roseland	IL
Kooy	P.	90 N. Clark	Chicago	IL
Kopke	John	407 Fulton	Brooklyn	NY
Korn	Bernhardt	897 Pearl	Cleveland	OH
Kortwright			Wayne	NE
Kosel*	W. E.	181 Myrtle	Brooklyn	NY
Kraeling*	B.	4016 Butler	Pittsburgh	PA
Kraft	John F.	216 3rd	New York City	NY
Kraft	L. A.	634 N. Clark	Chicago	IL
Kraft Bros.		390 Bowery	New York City	NY

ALPHABETICAL LISTING OF PHOTOGRAPHERS IN THE U. S. IN 1888 & 1889

NAME		ADDRESS	CITY	STATE
Kraft*	L. A.	150 State	Chicago	IL
Kratzer	J. W.		Blanchester	OH
Krogman*	Charles H.	Spring Grove	Cincinnati	OH
Krogmann	Charles	2245 Spring Grove	Cumminsville	OH
Kromer	Nicholas		Connellsville	PA
Krone*	Charles		Delavan	IL
Kroneberger	F. A.		Chester	PA
Krug	Simon	531 Vine	Cincinnati	OH
Krug*	Simon	Vine & 15th	Cincinnati	OH
Krumhar & Co.	R. F.	548-550 Pearl	Cleveland	OH
Kruse	August	255 North	Chicago	IL
Kuebler, Jr.	William	1204 Chestnut	Philadelphia	PA
Kuehner	Fred W.	High & Main	Columbus	OH
Kuhlmann	Bruno	55 3rd	New York City	NY
Kuhn	J. M.		Stillwater	MN
Kuhn	W. J.		Marlborough	MA
Kuhn Bros.		1628 Olive	St. Louis	MO
Kuhns	W. T.		Atlanta	GA
Kundler*	Gustav		Milwaukee	WI
Kunkle*	Isaac		Liberty	PA
Kunkler	B. P.		Canal Dover	OH
Kurtz	William	6 E. 23rd	New York City	NY
Kurtz*	William	233 Broadway	New York City	NY
Kuser	William W.	1520 Market	Philadelphia	PA
Kyle	Alexander	1316 3rd	New York City	NY
La Marsh	Bernard		Kenosha	WI
La Tour*	A. E.	249 Chicago	Chicago	IL
Labelle	E.		Holyoke	MA
Labonte	Soloman A.		Southbridge	MA
Lacey	Frank M.	Vance Block	Indianapolis	IN
Lachman	I. S.		Pottstown	PA
Laighton Bros.			Norwich	CT
Lainer	C. & Co.	31 3rd	San Francisco	CA
Lakin	J. H.		Montgomery	AL
Lalonrette	Mrs. H.	214 E. 5th	Dayton	OH
Lamb*	R. B.		Passaic	NJ
Lambder	J. S.	95 E. Chicago	Chicago	IL
Lamont	Frank		Pottsville	PA
Lamphere	E. C.		South Ryegate	VT
Lamprey	M. S.		Penacook	NH
Lamson	George L.		La Fargeville	NY

NAME		ADDRESS	CITY	STATE
Lamson	Josiah		Lynn	MA
Lamson & Co.			Somerville	MA
Lamson Studio		5 Temple	Portland	ME
Lamson*	J. H.		Portland	ME
Lancaster Bros.			Cedar Falls	IA
Landis	L. K.		Richland Station	PA
Landy	James	208 W. 4th	Cincinnati	OH
Lane	A. H.		Lee	ME
Lane	Alonzo		Pike	NY
Lane	Amos	186 ½ Summit	Toledo	OH
Lane	E. S.		Hope	DK
Lane	Frank P.		Clinton	CT
Lane	O. R.		Chattanooga	TN
Lane	W. V.		Camden	ME
Lane*	W. H.		Mount Horeb	WI
Lang	C.		Fond Du Lac	WI
Lang	Charles		Duluth	MN
Langan Bros.			Richmond	MO
Langan*	W. E.		Marshall	MO
Langdell	Gillis	1831 Lombard	Philadelphia	PA
Lange	O. V.	1025 Market	San Francisco	CA
Langer	H.		West Point	NE
Langhorne	F. C.		Plainfield	NJ
Langill & Darling		10 E. 14th	New York City	NY
Langley	Josiah T.		Manchester	NH
Langlois	E. T.		Winooski	VT
Langston	T. J.		Johnston	SC
Lansil	George		Bangor	ME
Laplant	Octave	Oak, I. O.	Springfield	MA
Laplante*	O.		Springfield	MA
Lardner & Barr		927 Pennsylvania	Washington	DC
Larkin	John E.		Elmira	NY
Larrabee	F. H.		Hillsborough	IL
Larrabee	George A.		Carroll	ME
Larrock	H.		Lewiston	ME
Larsen	Nicholas	465 W. Indiana	Chicago	IL
Larson	Anton		Minneapolis	MN
Lasseson	P. E.		Sioux Fall	DK
Lasswell	G. F.		Peoria	IL
Latham	Charles		Bradford	PA
Latour	William		Sedalia	MO

ALPHABETICAL LISTING OF PHOTOGRAPHERS IN THE U. S. IN 1888 & 1889

NAME		ADDRESS	CITY	STATE
Latto	J. C.	202 W. Broadway	Boston	MA
Lauck	J. A.	112 Main	Zanesville	OH
Laue*	O. R.		Chattanooga	TN
Laughlin	John R.	3518 Market	Philadelphia	PA
Launey	A. R.		Shelbyville	IL
Launey & Goebel			Savannah	GA
Law	F.		Boulder	CO
Lawhead	O. W.		Onarga	IL
Lawrence	Frank	492 Main	Worcester	MA
Lawrence	O. J.		Arlington	TX
Lawrence	C. A.		Lawrence	MA
Lawrence & Son			Los Angeles	CA
Lawrence*	S. A.	1293 Lorain	Cleveland	OH
Lawson	A. J.		Alpena	MI
Lawson	Elisha		Troy	OH
Lawson	N. B.		Muskegon	MI
Lawton	D. G.		Corinth	NY
Lawyer	R.	Smithfield	Pittsburgh	PA
Lawyer*	J. H.	Smithfield	Pittsburgh	PA
Lawyer, Jr.	R.	6 6th	Pittsburgh	PA
Lay	H. E.	181 Main	Hartford	CT
Lay	Herman N.	204 Washington	Hoboken	NJ
Lazelle	Edward J.	358 Main	Springfield	MA
Le Bau	J. S.	167 Blue Island	Chicago	IL
Le Clear	A. A.		Jackson	MI
Leach	A. L.		Dwight	IL
Leach	C.	19 E. Baltimore	Baltimore	MD
Leach	E. A.		McCook	NE
Leach*	C.	207 W. Biddle	Baltimore	MD
Leach*	J. H.		Logan	IA
Lean	Mrs. E. L.		Fort Scott	KS
Leas	J. O.		Peru	IN
Leavitt	A. L.		Newport	RI
Leavitt & Sherman		145 A. Tremont	Boston	MA
Leavitt & Sherman		535 Washington	Boston	MA
Lecher	Paul	296 W. Water	Milwaukee	WI
Leck	George H.		Lawrence	MA
Leddy	T. J.	1157 Tremont	Boston	MA
Lednare	A. J.	249 6th	New York City	NY
Lee	F. W.		Florence	KS
Lee	James H.	4223 Frankford	Philadelphia	PA

NAME		ADDRESS	CITY	STATE
Lee	John		Reading	PA
Lee	M. W.		Oconto	WI
Lee*	James H.	North 7th	Philadelphia	PA
Leeds	G. W.	262 Columbia	Brooklyn	NY
Lefavour	John S.		Salem	MA
Leffler*	Frank		Odessa	MO
Leggett*	A. W.		Lamar	MO
Lehnkering	A. L.	208 E. Main	Rochester	NY
Leidloff	H.	269 King	Charleston	SC
Leisenring Bros.			Mount Pleasant	IA
Leisenring*	H. H.		?	PA
Leiter	Elmer E.		Hamilton	OH
Leitz	Mrs. Louisa	606 Magazine	New Orleans	LA
Lelonard*	C. W.		Lansing	MI
Lemer	Le Rue		Harrisburgh	PA
Lemire	Henri		Westfield	MA
Lemke	Carl		Wausau	WI
Lemon	G. R.		Leon	KS
Lenhart Bros.		330 Broadway	Toledo	OH
Lentwiler*	John	937 S. Second	Philadelphia	PA
Lentz Bros.			Peru	IN
Lenz Bros.			Green Bay	WI
Lenzi	George A.		Norristown	PA
Leon & Chapman			Aurora	NE
Leon*	Thomas		Springfield	NE
Leonard	J. H.	613 Kansas	Topeka	KS
Leonard	P. F.	333 Main	Racine	WI
Leonard	V. V.		Plattsmouth	NE
Leonard & Martin			Topeka	KS
Leonard*	C. W.		Detroit	MI
Leroy & Terrill		45 N. Phelps	Youngstown	OH
Leruez*	Arthur		St. Louis	MO
Leschinsky	J.		Harvard	NE
Lesser	W. F.		St. Joseph	MI
Lester	J. J.		Paynesville	MN
Lesure	H. A.		Danbury	CT
Letton	J. A.		Jacksonville	IL
Leutwiler	John	937 S. 2nd	Philadelphia	PA
Levi*	Mrs. C. H.		Abilene	KS
Levilly	L.	515 Main	Buffalo	NY
Levin	Henry	430 N. Clark	Chicago	IL

ALPHABETICAL LISTING OF PHOTOGRAPHERS IN THE U. S. IN 1888 & 1889

NAME		ADDRESS	CITY	STATE
Levoy	L. T.		Webster	DK
Levy	Charles	232 Woodward	Detroit	MI
Lewin	Otto	1296 3rd	New York City	NY
Lewis	A. C.		Minneapolis	MN
Lewis	Augustus B.	306 Ogden	Chicago	IL
Lewis	C. E.		Lebanon	NH
Lewis	David		Logan	UT
Lewis	F. M.		Clarion	PA
Lewis	G. C.	1427 F	Washington	DC
Lewis	G. F.		Carthage	NY
Lewis	G. H.		Sumter	SC
Lewis	German		Amboy	IL
Lewis	H. C.		Worthington	OH
Lewis	H. H.		North Troy	VT
Lewis	Harriet H.	1216 Broadway	New York City	NY
Lewis	J. A.		New Britain	CT
Lewis	Mrs. J. B.		Greenwich	CT
Lewis	T. C.		Kingston	NY
Lewis	T. R.		New Market	NH
Lewis	J. H.		Foxborough	MA
Lewis*	Richard A.	160 Chatham	New York City	NY
Lewis	Russell B.		Hudson	MA
Lewis & Gibson			Ypsilanti	MI
Ley	T. A.		Woodland	CA
Libby	E. P.		La Harpe	IL
Libby	Minnie		Norway	ME
Lichtenberger & Co.		183 Essex	New York City	NY
Lidberg	Andrew		Ishpeming	MI
Liebich's Photographic Art Gallery		344 Ontario	Cleveland	OH
Lien	C. K.		Mayville	DK
Lighty Bros.			Monticello	IN
Lilienthal	Theodore	137 Canal	New Orleans	LA
Lilienthal*	Theodore	32 Chartres	New Orleans	LA
Lillard	L.		Dixon	CA
Lilly	T.		Mitchie	IL
Lincoln	George W.		Hillsborough Bridge	NH
Lind	C. A.		Kaukauna	WI
Lind	H. C.		Fond Du Lac	WI
Lind & Dittmar			Fond Du Lac	WI
Lindahl	A. O.		Norwood	MN
Linder	C. W.		South Chicago	IL

ALPHABETICAL LISTING OF PHOTOGRAPHERS IN THE U. S. IN 1888 & 1889

NAME		ADDRESS	CITY	STATE
Linder	James A.	1747 N. Broadway	St. Louis	MO
Lindgreen	J. A.		Cleburne	TX
Lindquist*	A. V.		Dayton	IA
Lindsay	S. T.		Robinson	IL
Lindsay & Leighton*			Lewistown	OH
Lindsey	Charles H.		Nashua	NH
Lindsey & Hodges			Knoxville	TN
Lindsey & Leighton*		Gilbert Ave.	Cincinnati	OH
Lindsley	H. B.		Auburn	NY
Linenschmidt	H. E.		Wellsville	MO
Lingo	E. A.		Uniontown	PA
Linkskog & McCoy			Sutton	NE
Linnenschmidt*	H. E.		Port Byron	IL
Linney & Tooley			Concordia	KS
Litchfield	Charles M.	352 Washington	Boston	MA
Litchfield	Edward C.		Arlington	MA
Little	H. N.		Des Moines	IA
Littlefield	C. E.		Anamosa	IA
Lively	W. S.		McMinnville	TN
Lloyd	J. H.	44 3rd	Troy	NY
Lloyd	J. H.		Wyalusing	PA
Lloyd	J. M.		Sandusky	OH
Lobbrecht	G. J.		Keokuk	IA
Lobenthal	Lewis		Galion	OH
Lochman	W. J.		Hamburgh	PA
Lock	William K.	602 ½ Poplar	Philadelphia	PA
Locke	J. T.		Canaan	NH
Locke	Robert		Canton	DK
Locke	W. A.		La Salle	IL
Lockhart	William H.		Bryan	OH
Lockman	Benjamin		Allentown	PA
Lockman	C. L.		Bethlehem	PA
Lockwood	F. C.		Freehold	NJ
Lockwood	Mrs. E. N.		Ripon	WI
Lockwood*	Miss M. S.		Lisbon	DK
Loder	W. R.	773 Broad	Newark	NJ
Lodge	S. H.		Gilmanton	NH
Lofland	D. R.		Watsonville	CA
Logan	Charles W.		Ashland	OR
Lollin	Miss Mary		Weyauwega	WI
Lone	J. B.		Flint	MI

ALPHABETICAL LISTING OF PHOTOGRAPHERS IN THE U. S. IN 1888 & 1889

NAME		ADDRESS	CITY	STATE
Lonergan	M. B.	3 N. Clark	Chicago	IL
Long	J. H.		Longville	PA
Long	J. T.		Menomonee	WI
Long	William		Cape May	NJ
Long	William	1632 N. 13th	Philadelphia	PA
Long & Son	George		Quincy	IL
Longcor	Levi		Newton	NJ
Longlin	J. W.		Rowlesburg	WV
Lonsbury	G. W.		Allegan	MI
Lonsbury*	H. E.		Mendon	MI
Loomis	D. A.		Fredonia	KS
Loomis	F. C.		Cherry Vale	KS
Loomis	J. R.		Plymouth	CT
Loomis	Milo A.		Jefferson	OH
Loomis	S. C.	357 W. Madison	Chicago	IL
Loomis & Thompson			Parkersburg	WV
Loops	Charles	758 12th	Milwaukee	WI
Lopez	Jose	16 W. 14th	New York City	NY
Loquist Bros.			Peoria	IL
Loring	Davis		Eastport	ME
Loryea Bros			San Jose	CA
Losch*	D. W.		Viola	WI
Lothrop	David	54 N. 9th	Philadelphia	PA
Loud & Bros.*		508 N. 2nd	Philadelphia	PA
Loud Bros.		301 Market	Philadelphia	PA
Loud*	George W.	397 Bedford	Brooklyn	NY
Lounsbery	J. B.		Des Moines	IA
Loupret	N. J.		Lowell	MA
Lovejoy	Charles J.		Glens Falls	NY
Lovejoy	H. C.		Trenton	NJ
Lovejoy	Howard E.	500 S. 2nd	Philadelphia	PA
Lovejoy*	Charles I.		Glens Falls	NY
Lovell	Charles O.		Northampton	MA
Lovell	George M.		Southbridge	MA
Lovell	J. L.		Amherst	MA
Low	Michael E.		Greenburgh	PA
Lower	G. W.		Roseville	IL
Lowers	M.		Wood's Run	PA
Lown	C. H.		Sterling	IL
Lozo	Alexander		St. Joseph	MO
Lucas	C. W.		Brodhead	WI

ALPHABETICAL LISTING OF PHOTOGRAPHERS IN THE U. S. IN 1888 & 1889

NAME		ADDRESS	CITY	STATE
Lucas	G. L.		Sank Centre	MN
Lucas	J. H.		St. Paul	MN
Lucas*	W. J.		Farmington	IA
Lucas*	W. P.		Larimore	MN
Luccock	C. D.		Council Bluffs	IA
Luce	E. B.		Hinckley	IL
Luchtemey	Louis		Blue Island	IL
Ludewig	W. H.		Keystone	IA
Ludovici	Julius	254 5th	New York City	NY
Ludovici	Julius		Newport	RI
Ludovici*	Julius	152 5th	New York City	NY
Ludwig	Frank		Chicopee	MA
Luke	W. O.		Leadville	CO
Lundelius	August	184 Pike	Port Jervis	NY
Lundy	H. R.		Columbus	NE
Luplan	L.	169 Canakport	Chicago	IL
Lupton	John		Lebanon	IL
Lupton	O. L.		Burlington	IA
Lusby	C. P.	403 E. Baltimore	Baltimore	MD
Lusby*	C. P.	91 W. Baltimore	Baltimore	MD
Lutes	C. M.		Stewardson	IL
Lutes Bros			Danville	IL
Lutge	F. C.	53 Monroe	Detroit	MI
Lutz	J. N.		Portsmouth	OH
Lydston	A. F.		San Jose	CA
Lyman	Mrs.		Corry	PA
Lyman & Son			Pomona	KS
Lynch	H.		Flovilla	GA
Lynd	J. A.		Perry	NY
Lynn	E. A.		Hawarden	IA
Lynn	Samuel		Paris	TX
Lyon	E. W.		Ithaca	MI
Lyon	T. D.		Gloucester	MA
Lytte	A. D.		Baton Rouge	LA
Macaulay	J. W.		San Jose	CA
MacDonald & Co.	C. F.	2228 Washington	Boston	MA
Macintosh	H. P.		Newburyport	MA
Mackenzie	A. H.		Dubuque	IA
Mackey	Lawrence J.	418 Grand	New York City	NY
Mackey	Thomas M.		Cambridge	OH
Macomber	A. D.		East Saginaw	MI

ALPHABETICAL LISTING OF PHOTOGRAPHERS IN THE U. S. IN 1888 & 1889

NAME		ADDRESS	CITY	STATE
Macorquodale	Hugh	171 Tremont	Boston	MA
Macurdy	J. C.		Boonville	MO
Macurdy	J. C.		Fayette	MO
Macy	O. W.		Vinton	IA
Madden	T. H.		Ashland	NE
Madison	Charles		Oshkosh	WI
Madsen*	Andrew		South Chicago	IL
Magee	W. E.		Tuscaloosa	AL
Magill	Z. F.	17 Keenan Bldg.	Troy	NY
Magras	John	196 Washington	Boston	MA
Magras	John	796 Washington	Boston	MA
Mahan	Davis	43 5th	Pittsburgh	PA
Mahan	W. H.		Pawnee City	NE
Mahler	Henry	547 8th	New York City	NY
Mahoney	C. C.		Ellenorah	MO
Maier	Jacob		Cass City	MI
Main	John F.	304 Lenox	New York City	NY
Malcolm*	Hugh		Kansas City	KS
Mallory	J. H.	68 James	Springfield	MA
Malloy*	John W.	109 E. Market	Akron	OH
Malousek & Rubicek*		635 Blue Island	Chicago	IL
Mancel	Henry		Pensacola	FL
Manchester Bros.		216 Fountain	Providence	RI
Manderfeld	Hubert		Waseca	MN
Mangold	E. E.		Moline	IL
Mangold	J. G.		Palatka	FL
Mangold	J. D.		Eufaula	AL
Mangrum & Moran			Canton	IL
Manly	George W.	19 E. 8th	Canton	OH
Mann	R. H.		Virginia	IL
Mann	S. M.		Mechanicsburgh	OH
Mann	W. G.		Waukesha	WI
Manning	A. W.		Edina	MO
Manning	E. J.		McPherson	KS
Manville & McDonald			Ahnapee	WI
Manzer	O. H.		Oshkosh	WI
Marable & Caldwell			Henrietta	TX
Marcellus	P.		Fairbury	NE
Marean	W. C.		Hubbardston	MA
Margo	J. C.		Sprague	WA
Margo & Wunderlich			Spokane Falls	WA

ALPHABETICAL LISTING OF PHOTOGRAPHERS IN THE U. S. IN 1888 & 1889

NAME		ADDRESS	CITY	STATE
Marian & Holmes			Stewartsville	MO
Marion	John S.		Lowell	MA
Marken	J. R.		Frederick	MD
Markhain	John		Bellevue	MI
Markham & Johnson		335 Washington	Brooklyn	NY
Markley & Son	T.	870 W. Madison	Chicago	IL
Marks	Harvey R.		Austin	TX
Marks	Robert		Mount Vernon	NY
Marratt*	William		Detroit	MI
Marratt, Jr.	William		St. Johns	MI
Marratt, Jr. & Co.	William	274 Woodward	Detroit	MI
Marsh	B. F.		Greeley	CO
Marsh	Daniel		Bozeman	MO
Marsh	Levi		Adams	MA
Marsh	W. C.		Quincy	MI
Marsh & Co.	T. I.	829 Arch	Philadelphia	PA
Marsh Bros.			Greeley	CO
Marshall	Augustus	44 Boylston	Boston	MA
Marshall	E. S.		West Chester	PA
Marshall	L. P.	1833 Ridge	Philadelphia	PA
Marshall	Samuel		Ladonia	TX
Marshall	T.		Fort Plain	NY
Marshall	W.		Meriden	CT
Marshall & Gilling		816 Market	Washington	DC
Marshall*	W. E.		Montague	MI
Marston	C. A.		Carson City	NV
Marston	C. L.		Bangor	ME
Martin	A.		Georgetown	CO
Martin	Allis		Greenville	NH
Martin	E. R.	296 S. Clark	Chicago	IL
Martin	H. T.	721 Kansas	Topeka	KS
Martin	J. P.		Boone	IA
Martin	Jay		Paris	IL
Martin	W. J.		Greensburg	KS
Martin	Charles W.	195 W. 5th	Cincinnati	OH
Martin	J. J.		North Manchester	IN
Martin Bros.			Ashland	KS
Martin*	A. A.		Meadville	PA
Martin*	J. R.		Mount Vernon	IN
Martland	T. C.		Lexington	MO
Martyr	C. J. J.		Norborne	MO

ALPHABETICAL LISTING OF PHOTOGRAPHERS IN THE U. S. IN 1888 & 1889

NAME		ADDRESS	CITY	STATE
Marvaise*	Andrew		Dallas	TX
Marvin	E. A.		Grand Ledge	MI
Marvin	Henry R.	99 Montgomery	Jersey City	NJ
Marvin*	E. D.		Milwaukee	WI
Mason	J. S.		Medina	OH
Mason	J. T.		Leavenworth	KS
Mason	L. E.		La Crosse	WI
Mason	S. Rufus		Purple Crane	NE
Mason	A. F.		Porter	ME
Mason & Co.	H. M.	1519 E. Pratt	Baltimore	MD
Masse	Theodore		Woonsocket	RI
Massey	Arthur G.	1109 Market	Philadelphia	PA
Massicot	Eugene	Magazine	New Orleans	LA
Massnick	O. H.	199 St. Aubin	Detroit	MI
Mast	J. E.		Marshall	MI
Masters	C. H.		Princeton	IL
Masters	W. H.		Blue Mounds	KS
Masterson*	E. P.		Port Jervis	NY
Mater	D. P.		Columbus	KS
Mather	H. S.		Clear Lake	IA
Mathers	Miss E. L.		North Springfield	MO
Mathes	J. A.		Titusville	PA
Mathew	Thomas	18 E. Broad	Columbus	OH
Mathews	E. W.		Coshocton	OH
Mathews	W. C.		Kewaskum	WI
Mathews & Reed			Ottawa	KS
Mathewson	T. C.		North Platte	NE
Mathis	E. R.		Delphos	OH
Mathis	George W.		Owensboro	KY
Matousek	M.	635 Blue Island	Chicago	IL
Matsen	S. C.		Sleepy Eye	MN
Matson*	G. C.		Lapeer	MI
Matter	William		Minneapolis	MN
Mattern	H. G.		Frankfort	KY
Matthews	Thomas R.	50 W. 14th	New York City	NY
Mauer	Max	305 Division	Chicago	IL
Mauer*	Max	379 State	Chicago	IL
Maul	Jacob	439 Milwaukee	Chicago	IL
Maury	C. O.		Newton	IL
Maury	Charles L.		Salem	VA
Maxon	E. H.		Ballston	NY

ALPHABETICAL LISTING OF PHOTOGRAPHERS IN THE U. S. IN 1888 & 1889

NAME		ADDRESS	CITY	STATE
Maxwell	Augustus	104 Chatham	New York City	NY
Maxwell	J. D.		Dayton	WA
Maxwell	James A.	21 ½ S. Market	Springfield	OH
Maxwell	Joseph E.	202 Bowery	New York City	NY
Maxwell & Hobby*		136 Bowery	New York City	NY
Maxwell & Mansfield		186 Bowery	New York City	NY
Maxwell Bros.			Spokane Falls	WA
May	George W.		Lebanon	OR
May	J. B.		Watertown	WI
Maybin	Joseph A.		Wilmington	DE
Mayers	Joseph M.		Ft. Wayne	IN
Mays*	Jacob		Blissfield	MI
Mazee	M. D.		Monticello	IA
McAdam Bros.			Mount Pleasant	IA
McAdams	T. T.		Galesville	WI
McAhron	C. O.		Golden City	MO
McAllister	J. S.		Columbus	NE
McArthur	W. E.		Shelby	NC
McAtee*	P. H.		Marshall	MO
McCabe Bros.			Rock Island	IL
McCaffrey	Patrick H.	139 E. 59th	New York City	NY
McCahon	J.		Upper Sandusky	OH
McCall	A. F.		Bethel	OH
McCandless	W. H.	5th & Wayne	Dayton	OH
McClain	J. W.		Columbia	KY
McClannahan	W. H.		Shawnee	OH
McClannahan*	W. H.		Shawnee	OH
McClellan*	W.		Dallas	TX
McClelland	G. B.		La Crosse	WI
McClintock & Harper			Jackson	TN
McClure	Marstela E.	192 ½ Camp	New Orleans	LA
McClure	W.		Toms River	NJ
McColl	J. A.		Brainerd	MN
McCollin	A. W. T.		Williamsport	PA
McComb	William		Muskegon	MI
McCombe	Robert		Berrien Springs	MI
McConnell	F. B.		Albion	IL
McCormack	Alexander		Oxford	PA
McCormick	J. L.	22 Winter	Boston	MA
McCormick	W. S.		Clarksville	TN
McCosker	T.	51 Washington	Boston	MA

ALPHABETICAL LISTING OF PHOTOGRAPHERS IN THE U. S. IN 1888 & 1889

NAME		ADDRESS	CITY	STATE
McCrary & Branson			Knoxville	TN
McCullough	C. S.		Petersburgh	IL
McCullough	R. L.		Virden	IL
McCune	Miles		Dixon	IL
McCutchin*	S. L.		Scottdale	PA
McDaniel & Weathers*			Centralia	MO
McDermott*	J. W.		Salem	OH
McDonald	Albert		South Bend	IN
McDonald	G. H.	289 W. Madison	Chicago	IL
McDonald	J. N.	520 Broadway	Albany	NY
McDonald	L. E.		Minneapolis	KS
McDonnell	C. A.		Wattsburgh	PA
McDonnell	C. P.		Cambridgeborough	PA
McDougall	F. H.		Booth Bay	ME
McDowell	Alexander	46 Broadway Extension	Boston	MA
McDowell	Lee		Nelsonville	OH
McElhiney	H.		Nebraska City	NE
McElhose	E. H.		Dodgeville	WI
McElrose	R. D.		Humbird	WI
McElroy	J. W.	67 S. Pearl	Albany	NY
McFadden	A.		Bath	ME
McFadden	J. J.		Salineville	OH
McFarlin & Speck*			Moravia	NY
McGandy	Joseph		Marshall	MN
McGarry	Charles		Cohoes	NY
McGary	H. C.		Norwalk	WI
McGaughey	C. O.		Indianapolis	IN
McGilvray	Joseph	175 Dover	Boston	MA
McGilvray*	Joseph	175 & 218 Dover	Boston	MA
McGowan	Maurice		Fond Du Lac	WI
McInnis	H. C.		Petoskey	MI
McIntire	J. H.		Crestline	OH
McIntire			Troy	AL
McIntire & Steele*			Cairo	IL
McIntire Bros.		1528 Ridge	Philadelphia	PA
McIntosh	C. F.		Colchester	CT
McIntosh	George F.		Gardiner	ME
McIntosh	R. M.		Northfield	VT
McIntosh	W. H.		Oswego	NY
McInturff	Andrew		Hutchinson	KS
McIntyre	D. J.		East Saginaw	MI

NAME		ADDRESS	CITY	STATE
McIntyre	S. H.		Sandy Lake	PA
McIntyre	William		Maple Valley	WI
McIntyre & Co.	A. C.		Alexandria Bay	NY
McIntyre*	William		Lexington	MI
McKay	A. L.		Cresco	IA
McKay & Co.	H. D.		Calais	ME
McKean	James		Anderson	IN
McKechnye	E.		Sangerville	ME
McKecknie & Oswald		197 Summit	Toledo	OH
McKee	C. L.		Lucas	OH
McKenna	D. W.		Fond Du Lac	WI
McKenney	A. S.		Marlborough	MA
McKenzie	Daniel N.	964 Kinnickinnie	Milwaukee	WI
McKenzie & Co.		19 Westminster	Providence	RI
McKeon	J. T.		Ennis	TX
McKeon*	James		Anderson	IN
McKinnon & Kenneth			Jacksonville	IL
McKinzie & Mertins			Neosho	MO
McKnight	Frank		Centralia	IL
McKown	George		Kingston	NY
McLain	J. D.		Logan	OH
McLain	T. B.		Yorkville	SC
McLain	William		Garnett	KS
McLaughlin	James		Woburn	MA
McLaughlin	Miss P.		Muir	MI
McLaughlin	T. C.		Nickerson	KS
McLaughlin	T. C.		Breckinridge	MO
McLeisch	William		Des Moines	IA
McLellan	J. W.		Valparaiso	IN
McLellan	R. R.		Biddeford	ME
McLellan*	W. E .	363 E. Division	Chicago	IL
McLeod	D. M.		Atchison	KS
McLeod	N. E. A.	262 Pearl	Cleveland	OH
McMahon	M. F.		Wabash	IN
McMahon	Mrs. F. V.		Paolo	KS
McMahon & Ireland*			?	PA
McManus	F. P.		Oxford	IA
McManus	J. H.		Litchfield	IL
McManus Bros.			Traverse City	MI
McMichael	A. G.	152 Woodward	Detroit	MI
McMichael	H.	246 Main	Buffalo	NY

ALPHABETICAL LISTING OF PHOTOGRAPHERS IN THE U. S. IN 1888 & 1889

NAME		ADDRESS	CITY	STATE
McMillan	G. A.		Council Grove	KS
McMillan & Co.	Q. A.	28 W. 4th	Cincinnati	OH
McMillan Bros			Santa Maria	CA
McMillan Bros.		8 6th	San Francisco	CA
McMillan Bros.			Marshfield	OR
McMillan*	F. H.		Sioux City	DK
McMillen	Ephraim		Flushing	MI
McMullen	C.		Greenville	AL
McMullen	J. F.		Atlantic	IA
McMullen	Samuel	1610 Page	Philadelphia	PA
McMurray	J. M.		Port Townsend	WA
McNab	Francis P.	813 Broadway	New York City	NY
McNaught	John		Lothron	IA
McNeill	Henry		Fredonia	NY
McNicoll	John	SE c 15th & Mission	San Francisco	CA
McNutty	Finley		Springfield	IL
McPeek	John		Cambridge	OH
McPeek & Dutcher			Plainfield	OH
McPhee*	Mrs. Catherine		Minneapolis	MN
McPherson	J. G.		McKeesport	PA
McQueen	Alfred G.	275 6th	New York City	NY
Meacham	C. T.		Greenville	PA
Mead	Edwin		Janesville	WI
Mead	Edwin	506 6th	Racine	WI
Meadler	John W.		Poughkeepsie	NY
Mealy	E. W.		Monroe	LA
Mealy	M. W.		Pueblo	CO
Medcalf	E. B.		Monroe City	MO
Medlar	J. B.		Rockford	IL
Medlicott	T. S.		Rochester	PA
Mehrle*	F. W.	315 W. Indiana	Chicago	IL
Meidlar	J. S.		Woodstock	IL
Meier	C. F.	1406 S. Broadway	St. Louis	MO
Meinerth Bros.			Cohoes	NY
Mekels*	E.		Hooper	NE
Melander	S. P.	659 Sedgwick	Chicago	IL
Melander & Bro.	L. M.	208 E. Ohio	Chicago	IL
Melendy & Packard			Manitowoc	WI
Melven	L. B.		Westfield	NY
Mendenhall	D. D.		Maryville	MO
Mendenhall	F. M.		Elmwood	IL

NAME		ADDRESS	CITY	STATE
Mendenhall	J. B.		Roodhouse	IL
Mendenhall	T. B.		Audubon	IA
Mendenhall*	J. H.		Allerton	IA
Menkee	Horace		Howard City	MI
Menkee	L. E.		Barnesville	GA
Mercantile Photograph & Photo-Engraving Co.		218 Fulton	New York City	NY
Meredith & Swap			Boonville	MO
Mering	J. S.	505 5th	Pittsburgh	PA
Mernnan & Engle*			Cosby	MO
Merrill	J. C.		Geneseo	NY
Merrill	N. L.		Johnson	VT
Merrill	Stephen		Lexington	IL
Merrill	Stuart	659 Clay	San Francisco	CA
Merrill	W. E.		Ovid	MI
Merrill & Co.	C. L.		Grand Rapids	MI
Merriman	A. G.		Allegheny	PA
Merriman	F. S.		Baker's Landing	PA
Merriman	O. G.		Eau Claire	WI
Merriman*	A. R.	Smithfield	Pittsburgh	PA
Merritt & Wood		925 Pennsylvania	Washington	DC
Merritt*	George		Winchester	IL
Messmore	Isom		Jasper	IN
Metcalf	Franklin	503 Washington	Boston	MA
Mettner	F. F.		Lawrence	KS
Metzung	F. J.	472 W. Baltimore	Baltimore	MD
Meuer	Max	252 Bowery	New York City	NY
Meuro & Co.		361 6th	New York City	NY
Meyer	Adolph	c. Milwaukee & Ashland	Chicago	IL
Meyer	J. H.	465 Vine	Cincinnati	OH
Meyer*	Mrs. L. M.		Milwaukee	WI
Meyer	Max	38 Bowery	New York City	NY
Meyers*	A.		Omaha	NE
Meynen & Co.		540 Franklin	Philadelphia	PA
Micciullo & Co.		64 S. Washington	New York City	NY
Michaelis	Fred		Frankfort Station	IL
Michell*	A. D.		Kansas City	KS
Miles	W. B.		Holyoke	MA
Miles & Greenlee			Belle Plaine	IA
Miley	J. H.		Eaton	OH
Miley	M.		Lexington	VA

NAME		ADDRESS	CITY	STATE
Millan	William		Poughkeepsie	NY
Millar	H. C.		Madison	IN
Millard	C. A.	224 Woodward	Detroit	MI
Millard	Charles		Clifton	KS
Millard	D. B.		Scranton	PA
Miller*	A. C. D.		Dallas	TX
Miller*	C. C.		Loup City	NE
Miller	C. C.		Moline	IL
Miller	Charles	60 Nassau	New York City	NY
Miller	Charles H.	34 S. Main	Dayton	OH
Miller	G. W.		Paris	TN
Miller	J. C.		Appleton	WI
Miller*	J. E.		Indianapolis	IN
Miller	J. Q.		Aberdeen	DK
Miller	J. W.		Anamosa	IA
Miller	John W.		Pittstown	PA
Miller*	L. T.		Lykens	PA
Miller	Louis E.		Alliance	OH
Miller	Mrs. Jennie	157 Wabash	Chicago	IL
Miller	N. H.		Cherokee	IA
Miller	R. E.		Waterville	MN
Miller	R. R.	276 5th	Milwaukee	WI
Miller	R. W.		Cherokee	KS
Miller	S. M.		Mason City	IL
Miller	W. D.		Tiffin	OH
Miller	W. D.		Manheim	PA
Miller	W. E.		Birmingham	CT
Miller	W. R.		Minneapolis	MN
Miller	W. R.		St. Cloud	MN
Miller	Walter M.		Springfield	MA
Miller	E. P.		Waverly	OH
Miller	J. F.		Battle Creek	MI
Miller	S.	156 State	Rochester	NY
Miller & Co.	Albert	1725 Germantown	Philadelphia	PA
Miller & Jones			Paris	TN
Miller & King			Green Bay	WI
Miller & Nichols*		1 Cedar	Newark	NJ
Miller & Sprague*			Walton	NY
Miller & Williams			Jackson	OH
Miller Bros.			Bay City	MI
Milleson	H. E.		Shelbyville	IN

ALPHABETICAL LISTING OF PHOTOGRAPHERS IN THE U. S. IN 1888 & 1889

NAME		ADDRESS	CITY	STATE
Millice	H. C.		Warsaw	IN
Milliken	J. J.		Bellefontaine	OH
Milliken	William		Monticello	NY
Mills	C. B.		Greensboro	GA
Mills	C. B.		Manchester	IA
Mills	H. A.		Camden	ME
Mills	Thomas		Peoria	IL
Mills*	W. H.		Saugatuck	MI
Mills & Cole			Torrington	CT
Mills & Son	William		Olneyville	RI
Milner	Alonzo W.	355 Reed	Milwaukee	WI
Mimper	Levi		Gettysburg	PA
Mims	R. H.		Edgefield	SC
Minard	William E.		Marathon	NY
Miner & Guivits			Richfield Springs	NY
Minor & Guievits*			Waterville	NY
Mink	B. A.	715 S.Halsted	Chicago	IL
Minner & Son	J. W.		Sparta	IL
Minor	Guievits		Waterville	NY
Minor	T. L. R.		Waterville	NY
Mintonye	John		Mount Clemens	MI
Misick	G. W.		Doniphan	MO
Misick*	W. A.		Bancroft	MI
Mitchell	J. S.		Jacksonville	FL
Mitchell	Mrs. G. W.		Bowling Green	MO
Mitchell	W. H.		Wilmington	IL
Moberly	L.		Greensburgh	IN
Mock*	J. W.		Lewistown	OH
Modder*	C. A.		Columbus	GA
Moe	E. J.		Millbank	DK
Moelk	C. F.		Edina	MO
Moeller	J. R.		Grand Island	NE
Moerk	Albert	1838 Callowhill	Philadelphia	PA
Moffatt Bros.			Key West	FL
Moffet & Co.		174 6th	New York City	NY
Moffitt	A. L.		New Britain	CT
Mohler	J. W.		Wichita	KS
Moler	George B.	Wayne & Van Buren	Dayton	OH
Moloney	M.	35 Hanover	Boston	MA
Moloney*	M.	35 Hanover & Columbus	Boston	MA
Moltz	T. M.		West Fairview	PA

ALPHABETICAL LISTING OF PHOTOGRAPHERS IN THE U. S. IN 1888 & 1889

NAME		ADDRESS	CITY	STATE
Momeyer	W. P. & M. B.		McKeesport	PA
Monaco	Louis		Eureka	NV
Monaco Bros			Stockton	CA
Monfort & Hill			Burlington	IA
Monroe	C. H.		Jamestown	NY
Monroe	Harry D. T.	180 E. 121st	New York City	NY
Monroe*	Harry D. S.	220 Bowery	New York City	NY
Montgomery	Joseph		Lockport	NY
Montignani	F. M.	304 Main	Bridgeport	CT
Monty	John B. L.		Holyoke	MA
Moody	H. W.		Red Oak	IA
Moon	T. C.		Laconia	NH
Mooney	Arthur		Charles City	IA
Moor	M. V.		Carson City	MI
Moore	A. C.		Arcola	IL
Moore	Arthur K.		Gilroy	CA
Moore	B. L.		Eureka	IL
Moore	Charles B.		Rochester	IN
Moore	F. J.		Middletown	CT
Moore	G. W.		Athol	MA
Moore	George N.		Seattle	WA
Moore	George S.		New Lisbon	OH
Moore	H. C.	Gill's Art Bldg	Springfield	MA
Moore	H. L.		Elizabeth	NJ
Moore	H. P.		Concord	NH
Moore	J. R.		Jamestown	NY
Moore	J. S.		Toledo	IA
Moore	J. W.		Bellefonte	PA
Moore	W. H.		Marion	OH
Moore	W. H.		Uniontown	PA
Moore	F.		Baker City	OR
Moore & Bros.			Rochester	IN
Moore & Co.	C.		Pembina	DK
Moore & Co.	Chauncey L.	Republican Block	Springfield	MA
Moore & Duffey			Curwensville	PA
Moore & Friffiths*			Minneapolis	MN
Moore Bros.			Owosso	MI
Mora Jose M.		707 Broadway	New York City	NY
Morano	W. A.		Erie	PA
More, Jr.	A. R.		Blue Earth City	MN
Morehouse	N. J.		Greenville	MI

ALPHABETICAL LISTING OF PHOTOGRAPHERS IN THE U. S. IN 1888 & 1889

NAME		ADDRESS	CITY	STATE
Moreno & Lopez		4 E. 14th	New York City	NY
Morey	L. F.		Edmore	MI
Morgan	G. W.		Viroqua	WI
Morgan	W.		Paris	KY
Morgan Bros.			Antigo	WI
Morgeneier	J. W.		Sheboygan	WI
Morgeneier	Robert		Winona	MN
Morhiser	W. H.		Dubuque	IA
Moriarty	J. M.		Helena	MT
Morin	I. Noel		Amesburg	MA
Morphis*	L. A.		Millsap	TX
Morrell Bros.			Pent Water	MI
Morrill	F. A.		Malden	MA
Morrill	Frank L.		Lowell	MA
Morris	J. H.		Queen City	MO
Morris	Mrs. E. M.		Santa Cruz	CA
Morris	S. D.	N. Canal & 11th	Pittsburgh	PA
Morris	George W.		Cornishville	KY
Morris*	Joseph G.	16 Sixth	Pittsburgh	PA
Morrison*	F. P.		Nashville	MI
Morrison	Hugh		Harrisonburgh	VA
Morrison	J. A.	505 5th	Pittsburgh	PA
Morrison	J. T.		Dover	ME
Morrison	Martin		Ames	IA
Morrison	R. P.		Bowling Green	OH
Morrow	O. A.		White Hall	IL
Morse	Andrew		Irving Park	IL
Morse	C. C.		Portland	OR
Morse	E. T.		Cambridgeport	MA
Morse	Gardner S.		W. Boxford	MA
Morse	George D.	826 Market	San Francisco	CA
Morse	Levi		Thomaston	ME
Morse	S. G.		Exeter	NH
Morse	W. H.		Sheffield	IL
Mortensen	C. A.	173 W. Indiana	Chicago	IL
Morton	A. C.		Monona	IA
Morton	H. Q.		Block Island	RI
Morton	H. Q.	75 Westminster	Providence	RI
Mortonson	Peter		Corning	OH
Moses	Bernard	369 Dryades	New Orleans	LA
Moses	Charles		Smethport	PA

ALPHABETICAL LISTING OF PHOTOGRAPHERS IN THE U. S. IN 1888 & 1889

NAME		ADDRESS	CITY	STATE
Moses	Gustave	92 Canal	New Orleans	LA
Moses*	J. S.		Anderson	IN
Mosher	C. D.	125 State	Chicago	IL
Mosher	G. A.	444 Broadway	Albany	NY
Mosher	J. W.	22 Kearny	San Francisco	CA
Moss	J. T.		Paris	MO
Moss	T. F.		Hudson	WI
Mote	E. V.		Greenville	OH
Motes	C. W.		Atlanta	GA
Mott	M. M.		Anamosa	IA
Motzbanes	Joseph		Brillion	WI
Mould	F. W.		La Crosse	WI
Mould	T. J.		Baraboo	WI
Moulthrop*	M.	818 Chapel	New Haven	CT
Moulton	F. J.		Tilton	NH
Moulton	H. D.		Fitchburg	MA
Moulton	Joseph C.		Fitchburg	MA
Mouzon	S. C.		Spartanburgh	SC
Movies	S. D.		Sharpsburgh	PA
Mowack	Michael		Minneapolis	MN
Mowrey	W. C.	51 Boardman Bldg.	Troy	NY
Mowry	C.		Wyanet	IL
Mowry	Cornelius		Fontanelle	IA
Mowry*	E. L.		Muncy	PA
Moye	J. C.		Uhrichsville	OH
Moyer	D. C.		Plainwell	MI
Moyer*	R. D.		Bucyrus	OH
Moyston	J. H.		Memphis	TN
Mudge	M. M.		Valparaiso	IN
Mueller	H.	627 Central	Cincinnati	OH
Mueller	H. J.	720 3rd	Milwaukee	WI
Mueller	John G.	28 Ave. C.	New York City	NY
Mueller & Co.		515 Broadway	Baltimore	MD
Mueller & Co.*		166 S. Broadway	Baltimore	MD
Mueller & Franklin			Owatonna	MN
Mueller*	Franklin		Owatonna	MN
Mueller*	John G.	20 Ave. C	New York City	NY
Muench	William	147 3rd	New York City	NY
Mulit	H. S.		Concordia	KS
Mullen	James		Lexington	KY
Muma	Charles		Holstein	IA

ALPHABETICAL LISTING OF PHOTOGRAPHERS IN THE U. S. IN 1888 & 1889

NAME		ADDRESS	CITY	STATE
Mumbrauer	R. C.		Hermann	MO
Mummy	Mrs. K. F.		Argonia	KS
Mundy	L. C.		Utica	NY
Munger*	D. G.		Oconomowoc	WI
Munich	C.	756 Broadway	New York City	NY
Munroe & Van Doorn			Taunton	MA
Munson	J. M.		Madison	DK
Murdock	W. N.		Woodstock	NH
Murdock*	W. S.	359 Main	Buffalo	NY
Murphy	E.		Binghampton	NY
Murphy	J. W.		Potsdam	NY
Murphy	M.		Grand Island	NE
Murphy			Ipava	IL
Murr	Charles		Joliet	IL
Muth	J. R.		Clyde	NY
Myer	William	650 Milwaukee	Chicago	IL
Myers	Abraham	2700 Palethrop	Philadelphia	PA
Myers	Benjamin		Hancock	NY
Myers	G. W.		Marcellus	MI
Myers	J. B.		Peoria	IL
Myers	J. S.		New Hartford	CT
Myers	Mrs. E. W.		La Crosse	WI
Myers*	Abraham	Lehigh & Palethorp	Philadelphia	PA
Myles & Son			Wheeling	WV
Naegeli	William A.	46 E. 14th	New York City	NY
Nagel	Louis	192 Washington	Hoboken	NJ
Nagely	Albert		Richfield	UT
Nagle	J. R.		Oswego	NY
Nallen	C. H.		Montgomery	AL
Naramore	W. S.		Easton	PA
Nash	C. S.		Westborough	MA
Nason & Son*	J. H.		Portland	ME
Nast	J. E.		Pueblo	CO
Nast*	J. E.		Denver	CO
National Crayon Portrait Co.		50 W. 14th	New York City	NY
National Ferrotype Co.			Hartford	CT
National View Co.		1420 Pennsylvania	Washington	DC
Naughton	Thomas		Champaign	IL
Neal	C. C.		Little Falls	MN
Neale	William A.	102 W. 18th	New York City	NY
Needham	F. J.	22 Tremont Row	Boston	MA

ALPHABETICAL LISTING OF PHOTOGRAPHERS IN THE U. S. IN 1888 & 1889

NAME		ADDRESS	CITY	STATE
Needham	J. H.		Grant City	MO
Neel	J. C.		Salem	MO
Neel*	J. C.		Madison	MO
Neff	Joseph	6 E 3rd	Dayton	OH
Neff*	Joseph	7 E. 3rd	Dayton	OH
Neibergall	Frederick	346 Larrabee	Chicago	IL
Neick	Henry J.	3rd and North	Milwaukee	WI
Neidhardt*	G. E.	403 Larabee	Chicago	IL
Neidhardt	George E.	403 North	Chicago	IL
Neidhardt*	H. F.	361 Milwaukee	Chicago	IL
Neidhardt	H. F.	357 Milwaukee	Chicago	IL
Neidhardt	W.	984 Milwaukee	Chicago	IL
Neihart	A. W.		Fairmont	NE
Neihart & Co.			Nebraska City	NE
Neilson & Brundage			Niagara Falls	NY
Nelson	C. A.	444 ½ 3rd	San Francisco	CA
Nelson	Elinor		Neenah	WI
Nelson	O. R.		Omaha	NE
Nelson	William B.		Mattapoisett	MA
Nesbit & Frew			Dillon	MT
Nesbitt & Co.	H. R.		Oswego	NY
Neville	David S.	60 N. High	Columbus	OH
New	John H.		Cohoes	NY
New England Engraving Co.			Middletown	CT
New Photo Art Co.		905 Pennsylvania	Washington	DC
New York Photo Co.		174 Westminster	Providence	RI
New York Photograph Gallery			Birmingham	CT
New York Portrait Co.		1428 Franklin	St. Louis	MO
Newberg	P. A.		Galesburgh	IL
Newcomb	C. H.		Huron	DK
Newcomb	C. H.		Watertown	DK
Newcomb	Marion W.		Salt Lake City	UT
Newcomer	W. S.		Codorus	PA
Newell*	A.		Cadillac	MI
Newell	A. R.		Rockville	CT
Newell	L. V.		Portsmouth	NH
Newell & Son	R.	626 Arch	Philadelphia	PA
Newkam	F.		Carrollton	MO
Newman	Adolph	228 N. 9th	Philadelphia	PA
Newman & Co.		181 Essex	New York City	NY
Newton	Samuel	451 Grand	Brooklyn	NY

ALPHABETICAL LISTING OF PHOTOGRAPHERS IN THE U. S. IN 1888 & 1889

NAME		ADDRESS	CITY	STATE
Newton	W. M.		Port Clinton	OH
Ney	Augustus		Galesburgh	IL
Nicaulin	J. F.		Algona	IA
Nice	R. Y.		Williamsport	PA
Nicholas	J. K.		Louisville	NE
Nicholas*	N. E.		Emporium	PA
Nichols	A. H.		Findlay	OH
Nichols	C. W.		Saxton's Rivert	VT
Nichols	E. P.		Hastings	NE
Nichols	F. N.		Elkader	IA
Nichols	G. B.		Clinton	IA
Nichols	J. D.		Eclectic	AL
Nichols	John W.	840 Bowery	New York City	NY
Nichols & Handy		229 Mercer	New York City	NY
Nicholson	John		Crawfordsville	IN
Nickerson	G. H.		Provincetown	MA
Nicol	John		Monmouth	IL
Nidy & Zellar			Hutsonville	IL
Nightengale & Son		69 Carroll	Brooklyn	NY
Nikodem*	A. M.	701 W. Madison	Chicago	IL
Nikodeur	Miss A. M.	701 Madison	Chicago	IL
Nims	C.	372 Genesee	Buffalo	NY
Nims	F. A.		Colorado Springs	CO
Nims	William		Fort Edward	NY
Nix	F. H.		Reed City	MI
Nix	T. F.		Evart	MI
Nix & De Vogt			Clare	MI
Nix*	W. M.		Licking	MO
Noble	H. E.		Lincoln	NE
Noble	O. D.		Paxton	IL
Nock	E. B.	148 Ontario	Cleveland	OH
Noe	J. S.		Virginia City	NV
Noe*	M.		Santa Rosa	CA
Noel	C.		Grape Creek	IL
Noll	Charles	597 Fifth	Brooklyn	NY
Noll	Lawrence	232 Bleecker	New York City	NY
Noll*	Charles	232 Bleecker	New York City	NY
Norman	H. C.		Natchez	MS
Norris	Joseph E.	2343 Olive	St. Louis	MO
North	A. M.		Bainbridge	NY
North	C. S.		S. Norwalk	CT

ALPHABETICAL LISTING OF PHOTOGRAPHERS IN THE U. S. IN 1888 & 1889

NAME		ADDRESS	CITY	STATE
North	F. E.		Watertown	MA
North	W. C.		Utica	NY
North American Photo-Copying Co.			Jamestown	NY
Northrup	L. L.		Bangor	MI
Norton	E. B.		Shelbyville	IL
Norton	H. M.		Vermontville	MI
Norton	H. Q.	276 Middle	Portland	ME
Norton & Hawley			Beatrice	NE
Noss	Henry		New Brighton	PA
Notman Photograph Co.		48 N. Pearl	Albany	NY
Notman Photographic Co.		3 Park	Boston	MA
Notman*	James	99 Boylston	Boston	MA
Nott	Charles		Rice Lake	WI
Nott	Edward S.		Hamburgh	NY
Nott	W. S.		Lodi	WI
Noyes	A. K.		Jefferson	WI
Nulf	O. E.	299 Beaver	Allegheny	PA
Nute	C. N.		Bloomington	IL
Nutter	T. S.		Lancaster	OH
Nye	B. A.		Monticello	MN
Nye	D. B.		Minneapolis	MN
Nye	J. L.		Platteville	WI
Nye	W. A.	2228 Indiana	Chicago	IL
Oakes	Omega		Roseburgh	OR
Oakes & Ireland			Holton	KS
Oakley	F. M.	PO Box 2718	Denver	CO
Oakley	John H.		Ravenna	OH
Oberdallhoff*	W. H. S.	125 W. Baltimore	Baltimore	MD
Oberlin	G. W.		Mecosta	MI
Obst	C. L.		Pittsfield	IL
O'Connor & Balcom			Lyons	IA
O'Connor*	H. P.		Wetumka	AL
O'Donohue	J. B.		Jefferson	IA
O'Donohue	Mrs. J. B.		Grand Junction	IA
O'Dwyer	Joseph	413 Canal	New York City	NY
O'Dwyer*	Joseph	283 Eighth	New York City	NY
O'Flynn	T. F.		Weymouth	MA
O'Hara	A.		Bowensburgh	IL
Ohlwiler	E. H.		Erie	PA
O'Keefe	C. F.		Fort Madison	IA
O'Kelley	James F.		Athens	GA

ALPHABETICAL LISTING OF PHOTOGRAPHERS IN THE U. S. IN 1888 & 1889

NAME		ADDRESS	CITY	STATE
Oldarshaw	T. S.		Middletown	CT
Older & Turner*			Barnesville	MN
Oldfield*	T. M.		Sand Beach	MI
Oldroyd	L. K.		Falls City	NE
Olds	F. A.		Covington	IN
Oleson	Mrs. J. H.		Minneapolis	MN
Oleson*	J. O.		De Kalb	IL
Olin	Mrs. R. A.		Fall River	KS
Oliver	E. W.		Coumbus Junction	IA
Ollivier	Horace M.	1162 Broadway	New York City	NY
Olsen	Johann	449 Main	Hartford	CT
Olson & Anderson			Montevideo	MN
Olson*	Charles	165 W. Madison	Chicago	IL
O'Neil	Hugh	31 Union Sq.	New York City	NY
O'Neil	James	177 E. 127th	New York City	NY
Oppenheimer*	Ben		West Union	OH
Orem	A. R.	717 S. Halsted	Chicago	IL
Orem*	A. R.	179 E. Chicago	Chicago	IL
Orgill	John	281 Main	Hartford	CT
Ormsby	E. D.	1055 Broadway	Oakland	CA
Ormsby	William		Independence	MO
Orr	C. E.		Plano	IL
Orr	C. E.		Sandwich	IL
Orsborne*	O. W.		Oswego	KS
Ortiz	P. N.	253 N. 9th	Philadelphia	PA
Orvis	J. R.		Fayette	IA
Osborn	Emerson		Binghampton	NY
Osborn	L.		St. Albans	ME
Osborn*	A. T.		Orion	IL
Osborne	G. B.		Grand Rapids	MI
Osborne & May			Lancaster	OH
Osgood	Henry W.		Pittsfield	NH
Osgood	Irving		Ellsworth	ME
Osgood	T. B.		Damariscotta	ME
Oswald Bros.			Minneapolis	MN
Oswalt	M. E.		Tuscaloosa	AL
Overland	Holand		Fergus Falls	MN
Overland & Holand*			Fergus Falls	MN
Overpeck	L. C.		Hamilton	OH
Overstreet	Miss C. E.		Galena	KS
Overstreet	W. S.		Belle Plaine	KS

NAME		ADDRESS	CITY	STATE
Owen	W. H.		Scranton	PA
Owens	H. A.		Marysville	IA
Owens	M. W.		Muscatine	IA
Owens Photo. Copy Co.			Mount Vernon	IA
Oxford	A. C.		Birmingham	AL
Oyloe	G. G.		Ossian	IA
Pacetti	Gabriel N.		St. Augustine	FL
Pach	G. W.		Princeton	NJ
Pach & Bros.	G. W.	1002 Chapel	New Haven	CT
Pach Bros.		841 Broadway	New York City	NY
Pachs & Bros.*	G. W.		Cambridgeport	MA
Packard	C. C.		Kalamazoo	MI
Packard	W. D.		Frazeyburgh	OH
Page	F. R.		Malden	MA
Page	L. S.		Emporia	KS
Page	W. F.		Ansonia	CT
Page	Mary J.		Ackerman	MS
Paige	E. H.	53 Arcade Bldg.	Buffalo	NY
Paige	E. H.		Waukesha	WI
Paine	J. W.		Jackson	MI
Palethrope	Thomas		Greenville	MI
Pallnoke	L.		Alma	KS
Palmer	C. A.	207 S. Halsted	Chicago	IL
Palmer	E. H.		Waupaca	WI
Palmer	E. N.		Tomah	WI
Palmer	Frederick		Minneapolis	MN
Palmer	J. A.		Aiken	SC
Palmer	J. W.		St. James	MN
Palmer	Mrs. W. H.		Edon	OH
Palmer	W. H.		Shakopee	MN
Palmer	W. H.	208 S. 4th	St. Louis	MO
Palmeri	A.	691 Myrtle	Brooklyn	NY
Palmiter & Warrant			Kalamazoo	MI
Palmquist & Jurgens			St. Paul	MN
Pancoast	B. F.		Iola	KS
Panneberg	Amandus	219 North	Chicago	IL
Papineau	Frank		Bethany	MO
Parcell	H. G.		Kirksville	MO
Pardee	D.		Phelps	NY
Pardee	Phineas	746 Chapel	New Haven	CT
Pardoe	H. W.		Keithsburgh	IL

ALPHABETICAL LISTING OF PHOTOGRAPHERS IN THE U. S. IN 1888 & 1889

NAME		ADDRESS	CITY	STATE
Pardoe	H. W.		New Sharon	IA
Parfitt	William		Parker	DK
Paris	R. A.		Dongola	IL
Park	O. H.		Clarinda	IA
Park & Lee			Elyria	OH
Parker	A. H.	46 N. Salina	Syracuse	NY
Parker	C. W.		Bay City	MI
Parker	Charles	477 Pennsylvania	Washington	DC
Parker	Damascus		Humboldt	IA
Parker	Francis		El Paso	TX
Parker	H. R.		Sherburne	NY
Parker	J. C.		San Diego	CA
Parker	J. T.		Kansas City	MO
Parker	J. T.		Bowling Green	OH
Parker	J. W.		St. Charles	IL
Parker	John J.	245 E. Orthodox	Frankford	PA
Parker	Orne		Perry	IA
Parker	W. L.		Morrison	IL
Parker	J. & G. L.		Brandon	VT
Parker & Co.*			Kansas City	KS
Parker & Son*			San Diego	CA
Parker*	John J.	Meadow & Cherry	Philadelphia	PA
Parkinson	H. B.		Tecumseh	NE
Parkinson	L.		Fox Lake	WI
Parkinson & Co.		29 W. 26th	New York City	NY
Parkinson*	Maurice D.	29 W. 26th	New York City	NY
Parks	G. C.		Washington	MO
Parks	J. B.		Salem	OH
Parlow	George F.		New Bedford	MA
Parmley	C. H.		Harvard	IL
Parr & Varney*		299 W. Indiana	Chicago	IL
Parr*	J. S.	299 W. Indiana	Chicago	IL
Parrott	W. S.		Portland	OR
Parry	G. R.		Dodgeville	WI
Parshale	R. R.		Westfield	PA
Parshley	Frank	308 Fulton	Brooklyn	NY
Parsons	W. D.		Adams	MA
Parsons	F. R.	1407 Market	St. Louis	MO
Parsons	J. A. H.		Wheeling	WV
Parsons*	W. H.		Waterborough	ME
Partch	R. N.		Davenport	NE

ALPHABETICAL LISTING OF PHOTOGRAPHERS IN THE U. S. IN 1888 & 1889

NAME		ADDRESS	CITY	STATE
Partidge			The Dalles	OR
Partlon*	Mrs. L. A.		Toronto	KS
Partman	Herman	337 Hayes	San Francisco	CA
Partridge	S. C.	529 Commercial	San Francisco	CA
Partridge	W. H.	2832 Washington	Boston	MA
Pascoe	C. J.		Fremont	OH
Pasel	O. C.		St. Paul	MN
Patch	Jonas K.		Shelburne Falls	MA
Patrick*	John C.		Batavia	NY
Patridge	E. J. & W. H.		Portland	OR
Patten	J. D.	47 Hanover	Boston	MA
Patterson	Edgar		Macomb	IL
Patterson	George P.		Lebanon	OH
Patton & Dietrich			Reading	PA
Paul	J. P.		North Springfield	MO
Paullin	William T.	244 N. 8th	Philadelphia	PA
Paulus	Miss Annie		Fredonia	WI
Pausch	O. M.		Newark	OH
Paxson	J.	65 E. 9th	New York City	NY
Paye*	C. M.		Cortland	NY
Payne*	C. S.	9 N. Pearl	Albany	NY
Payne*	D. R.		Los Angeles	CA
Paynter	William		Atlantic City	NJ
Paynter	William E.	Lehigh	Philadelphia	PA
Peabody	Edwin N.		Salem	MA
Peabody	Henry G.	52 Boylston	Boston	MA
Peacock	E. R.		Colton	CA
Peaker	Thomas		Springfield	IL
Pearsall	Alva	615 Fulton	Brooklyn	NY
Pearsall	G. Frank E.	298 Fulton	Brooklyn	NY
Pearson	J. R.		Allegheny	PA
Pearson	S. M.		Cochran	GA
Pearson	W. B.		Mercer	PA
Pearson	James R.	96 5th	Pittsburgh	PA
Pearson & Nebit			Des Moines	IA
Pearson*	James R.	43 Federal A.	Pittsburgh	PA
Peart	F. T.	112 E. Main	Rochester	NY
Pease	A. H.		Schuylersville	NY
Pease	Mrs.		Bucksport	ME
Pease	Nathan W.		North Conway	NH
Peavey	Louis		Faribault	MN

ALPHABETICAL LISTING OF PHOTOGRAPHERS IN THE U. S. IN 1888 & 1889

NAME		ADDRESS	CITY	STATE
Peck	Abel		Newburgh	NY
Peck	G. G.		Zumbrota	MN
Peck	John M.		Portland	ME
Peckham	C. E.		Trenton	MO
Peckham	Leander A.		Newport	RI
Peeples	L. W.		Dawson	GA
Peiser	Theodore E.		Seattle	WA
Pellegrin	A. L.		Anaheim	CA
Pelot & Cole			Augusta	GA
Pendleton	W. S.	336 Fulton	Brooklyn	NY
Penfield	D. E.		Warren	MA
Penndorf	August	509 E. Water	Milwaukee	WI
Pennelle	R. W.		Glasgow	MO
Pennepacker	C.		Nanticoke	PA
Pennington	Barclay		Tiffin	OH
Penton	C. E.		East Aurora	NY
Pentz	B. C.		York	PA
Pepper	A. F.	1051 Tremont	Boston	MA
Peppet	William		Homer	MI
Percival	J. P.		Waltham	MA
Perkins	A. D.		Saxton's Rivert	VT
Perkins	A. J.		Vienna	IL
Perkins	A. J.	1217 Polk	San Francisco	CA
Perkins*	H. L.	103 W. Baltimore	Baltimore	MD
Perkins	John W.		Andover	ME
Perkins	John W.	1316 Pennsylvania	Baltimore	MD
Perkins	O. R.		Portage	WI
Perkins	T. B.		Grand Rapids	MI
Perkins	V. H.		Medicine Lodge	KS
Perkins	W. C.		Cuba	MO
Perkins*	W. C.		St. Clair	MO
Perkins	W. C.		Pacific	MO
Perkins	W. S.		Colfax	CA
Perkins & Baley			Lodi	CA
Perkinson	L. C.	176 E. 125th	New York City	NY
Perkinson	L. C.	2308 3rd	New York City	NY
Perky	Lenore		Wahoo	NE
Pernot	H. C.		Van Buren	AR
Perrin	G. B.		Springfield	VT
Perronington & Son*			Bee	KS
Perry*	E. F.		Windsor	MN

ALPHABETICAL LISTING OF PHOTOGRAPHERS IN THE U. S. IN 1888 & 1889

NAME		ADDRESS	CITY	STATE
Perry	Frank	607 Franklin	St. Louis	MO
Perry	Henry B.	3800 Cottage Grove	Chicago	IL
Perry	I. C.		Mendocino	CA
Perry	O. H.		De Witt	NE
Perry	W. E.		Canton	PA
Perry & Son	E. H.		Battle Creek	MI
Perry & Varney*		3800 Cottage Grove	Chicago	IL
Peters & Co.	J. H.	25 3rd	San Francisco	CA
Peters	L. H.		Patten	ME
Peters	M. G.	3509 S. Halsted	Chicago	IL
Peters	W. H.		Higginsville	MO
Peterson	C.		Randolph	KS
Peterson	C.		La Grange	TX
Peterson	C.		Byron	MN
Peterson	C. E.		Carson City	NV
Petterson	A. W.		Minneapolis	MN
Pfaff	Henry		Allegheny	PA
Pfaff*	H.	82 Ohio A.	Pittsburgh	PA
Pfeiffer	John A.	228 S. High	Columbus	OH
Phelps	A. O.		Cairo	IL
Phelps	G. C.	942 Chapel	New Haven	CT
Phelps	J. P.		Muscatine	IA
Phelps & Phelps			Muscatine	IA
Philadelphia Gallery			Burlington	NJ
Philips	Chauncey		Williamstown	MI
Phillipi & Bro.	William	825 Arch	Philadelphia	PA
Phillips	A.		Natick	MA
Phillips	C. W.		Nebraska City	NE
Phillips	E. M.		Danville	IL
Phillips	Henry		Atlantic City	NJ
Phillips	Henry	2608 Frankford	Philadelphia	PA
Phillips	Henry C.	1206 Chestnut	Philadelphia	PA
Phillips	J.		Ridgeway	MO
Phillips	John		Red Wing	MN
Phillips*	J. H.		Kirksville	MO
Phillips	L. H.		Independence	IA
Phillips	M. F.		Hamburg	IA
Phillips	S. D.		La Fayette	IN
Phillips	T. L.		Lowellville	OH
Phillips*	W. C.		Bordentown	NJ
Phillips & Bergstresser			Danville	IL

ALPHABETICAL LISTING OF PHOTOGRAPHERS IN THE U. S. IN 1888 & 1889

NAME		ADDRESS	CITY	STATE
Philpot	Fred. C.		Limerick	ME
Philpot	Thomas		Macomb	IL
Phinisey	T. W.		Howell	MI
Phipps	J. H.		Fentonville	MI
Phipps	William	708 7th	Washington	DC
Phipps & Johnson			New Castle	PA
Photo-Etching Co.		299 Washington	Boston	MA
Photo-Gravure Co.		853 Broadway	New York City	NY
Piatt	C. E.		Healsburg	CA
Piatt	J. A.		Mattoon	IL
Pickels	J. W.		Stella	NE
Picken & Co.		79 Greenwich	New York City	NY
Pickerell	P.		Indianapolis	IN
Pickerill	F. A.		Salem	OR
Pickerill	F. M.		Homer	IL
Pickett	J. M.		Hollister	CA
Pickett	J. M.		Willow	CA
Pier	F. B.		Erie	PA
Pierce	D. C.		Rockford	IA
Pierce*	E. W.		Greeley	CO
Pierce	H. C.		Bushwell	IL
Pierce*	L. V.		Collinsville	CT
Pierce	Miss Ann		Springville	NY
Pierce	N. E.		Waverly	IA
Pierce	A.		Cavendish	VT
Pierce & Bushnell			New Bedford	MA
Pierce & Co	William H.	352 Washington	Boston	MA
Pierre	L. V.		Collinsville	CT
Pierron	G.		St. Augustine	FL
Pietz & Houchens			Springfield	IL
Pigeon	Thomas		Belmond	IA
Pine	George		Trenton	NJ
Pinner	J. C.		Dyersburgh	TN
Pinter & Bro.	J.		Hancock	MI
Piper	E. R.		Decatur	IL
Piper*	Simeon	939 Pennsylvania	Washington	D. C.
Piper	Stephen		Manchester	NH
Piper & Marcus		270 S. 2nd	Philadelphia	PA
Pirrong & Son		322 N. 2nd	Philadelphia	PA
Pitcher	Gideon		Waterville	ME
Pitcher	H. P.		Conneaut	OH

ALPHABETICAL LISTING OF PHOTOGRAPHERS IN THE U. S. IN 1888 & 1889

NAME		ADDRESS	CITY	STATE
Pittman	J. A. W.		Springfield	IL
Pittsburgh Bromide Co.		Smithfield	Pittsburgh	PA
Pixley*	S. E.		Hallock	MN
Place	Frank		Warsaw	IN
Plank	Thomas J.		Canastota	NY
Plate	F.		Millstadt	IL
Platt	A. C.	Water & Columbus	Sandusky	OH
Platt	H. M.		Oberlin	OH
Platt	L. L.		Elgin	IL
Platts & Son	G. W.	36 & 65 5th	Pittsburgh	PA
Platts & Son*	G. W.	34 Fifth	Pittsburgh	PA
Platz	Max	88 N. Clark	Chicago	IL
Plauk*	Thomas J.		Canastota	NY
Pleasants	Bazil B.	735 Broadway	New York City	NY
Plecker	A. H.		Lynchburg	VA
Plimpton	Arthur L.	7 Hawthorne	Boston	MA
Ploetz	Julius		Kansas City	MO
Ploetz*	Julius		Kansas City	KS
Plumb	S. L.		Portage	WI
Plumlee & Burkhard*			Brownsville	MO
Plummer	F. W.		Wheeling	WV
Podoll	Gustav	333 3rd	Milwaukee	WI
Poff	J. H.		Loudonville	OH
Poister	F. E.		Kent	OH
Polder & Beck*			Corry	PA
Pollock	Albert		Deadwood	DK
Pollock	David		Cobden	IL
Pollock	H.	9 E. Lexington	Baltimore	MD
Pollock*	H.	44 Lexington	Baltimore	MD
Pollock	W. E.	196 Worth	New York City	NY
Pomeroy	C. T.	30 E. Main	Rochester	NY
Pomeroy	Charles T.		Kansas City	MO
Poock	C.		Essex	IA
Pool	E. E.		South Bend	IN
Poole	R.		Nashville	TN
Pooley	J. H.		Galena	IL
Poor	C. G.		Brownfield	ME
Popkins	Benjamin F.		Greenfield	MA
Popp	E.		Vincennes	IN
Portenus	J. E.		Bremen	IN
Porter	A. W.		Farmer Village	NY

ALPHABETICAL LISTING OF PHOTOGRAPHERS IN THE U. S. IN 1888 & 1889

NAME		ADDRESS	CITY	STATE
Porter	Byron		Connellsville	PA
Porter	M. H.		Allegan	MI
Porter	Mrs. M. A.		Madison	KS
Porter*	Perez		Moline	IL
Porter	Robert		Birmingham	IA
Portmess	J. R.		Keyser	WV
Portser	W. J.		Saltsburgh	PA
Post	A. B.		Ottumwa	IA
Post	H. F.		Paterson	NJ
Post	J. E.		Denver	CO
Pott*	Emil		Wright's Grove	IL
Potter	J. R.	323 Main	Buffalo	NY
Potter	W. H.		Indianapolis	IN
Potter	William E.		Wapakoneta	OH
Potter	William E.	171 Westminster	Providence	RI
Potter & Co.	G. C.	2 N. 13th	Philadelphia	PA
Potts	William B.		Indianapolis	IN
Potts*	W. B.		Springfield	MO
Powe	T. W.		Muskegon	MI
Powell	J. E.		Menomonee	WI
Powell	J. W.		Charlestown	IN
Powelson	G. A.	17 Chester	Cleveland	OH
Powers	M. J.		Richmond	VA
Powers	Peter		Deer Isle (Green's Landing)	ME
Powers	T. C.		Perryville	MO
Prater	J. H.		Paw Paw	MI
Prather*	W. E.		Augusta	GA
Pratt	A. S.		Phillips	ME
Pratt	Charles H.	727 S. Broad	Philadelphia	PA
Pratt	De W. C.		Aurora	IL
Pratt	H. E.		Marlborough	MA
Pray	Fred H.	26 Montgomery	San Francisco	CA
Prebinson	Peter		Neenah	WI
Prentice & Vail			Marion	OH
Presler	Hiram		Forest	OH
Preston	H. C.		Seward	NE
Preston	N. A.		Eau Claire	WI
Preston	W. C.	282 River	Troy	NY
Price	Andrew		Healsburg	CA
Price*	D. A.		St. Joseph	MO

ALPHABETICAL LISTING OF PHOTOGRAPHERS IN THE U. S. IN 1888 & 1889

NAME		ADDRESS	CITY	STATE
Price	E. J.		Greenfield	OH
Price	Frank H.	925 Broad	Newark	NJ
Price	W. A.	180 N. High	Columbus	OH
Price	W. S.		La Fayette	IL
Price	W. V.		McMinnville	OR
Prichard	C. F.		Decatur	MI
Primrose	George M.		East Stroudsburgh	PA
Prince	George	403 11th	Washington	DC
Prince	John H.	18 E. Tuscarawas	Canton	OH
Pringle	Charles		Fredonia	NY
Prior	John H.	81 Westminster	Providence	RI
Pritchard	D. W.		Tolona	MO
Proctor	E. C.		Hollidaysburgh	PA
Proctor	J. B.		Batchtown	IL
Proctor	J. H.		Girard	KS
Proctor	J. H.	409 N. Gay	Baltimore	MD
Proctor	Jefferson		Corning	IA
Protzman	Ed. C.		Morgantown	WV
Proutty	Jason W.		Brattleboro	VT
Prudden & Dunihue			Jamestown	NY
Prudden*	D. E.		Jamestown	NY
Pruden & Jones			Cortland	NY
Pruitt	G. H.		Iuka	MS
Prye*	Thomas	131 Poydras	New Orleans	LA
Pryor	W. A.		La Crosse	WI
Pugh	C. A.		Blacksburgh	VA
Pugh	James A.		Macon	GA
Pullman	Charles		Waterloo	NY
Pullman	Edgar J.	935 Pennsylvania	Washington	DC
Pummer	Monte		Pleasantville	IA
Punnett*	Milton B.		Rochester	NY
Purivance	William E.	115 Christopher	New York City	NY
Pusley			Wetmore	KS
Putnam	Franklin	481 Canal	New York City	NY
Putnam	George T.		Middleborough	MA
Putnam	S. A.	Hyannis	Baltimore	MA
Putnam	S. A.		Hyannis	MA
Pye	Thomas	131 Poydras	New Orleans	LA
Quantrell	M. L. & E.	101 W. 15th	New York City	NY
Quarterly*	C.	217 W. Baltimore	Baltimore	MD
Quiggle	H. F.		Doland	DK

ALPHABETICAL LISTING OF PHOTOGRAPHERS IN THE U. S. IN 1888 & 1889

NAME		ADDRESS	CITY	STATE
Quinby*	F. J.		Lebanon	PA
Quint	S. D.		Manchester	NH
Rabinoau	C. S.	9 N. Pearl	Albany	NY
Race	C. O.		Pleasant Hill	MO
Racer	William		Bolivar	MO
Rache	Thomas J.	94 Washington	Newark	NJ
Radobaugh	E. D.		Huntington	IN
Raffell*	T.	28 Arcade	Cincinnati	OH
Ragan*	W. O.		Kansas City	MO
Ragsdale	M. C.		San Angelo	TX
Raimfield	Henry		Warren	MN
Rainwater*	Terrel		Montrose	MO
Raitt	T. G.		Ashland	WI
Ralston	S. A.		Albia	IA
Rambo	R. L. C.	4080 Lancaster	Philadelphia	PA
Ramsdell	D. P.	817 Chapel	New Haven	CT
Ramsdell	John	162 Court	Brooklyn	NY
Ramsey	J. F.		New Lisbon	WI
Randall	A. R.		Jericho	MO
Randall	C. C.	Madison	Detroit	MI
Randall*	S. G.		Big Rapids	MI
Randall	W. F.		Newtown	PA
Ranger	W. V.	43 S. Salina	Syracuse	NY
Rank & Co.	J. F.		Van Wert	OH
Rankin	G. W.		College City	CA
Rankin	R. J.		Martinsburg	WV
Ranney	O. N.		Lockport	NY
Rase	E. R.		Osborne	KS
Rasmussen	Charles		Rock Island	IL
Ratelle	Charles	Worcester, I. O.	Springfield	MA
Ratornez	G. A.		Farmington	MO
Rau	George	930 Girard	Philadelphia	PA
Rau	William H.	1324 Chestnut	Philadelphia	PA
Rau & Kidd			Atlantic City	NJ
Rauscher	H.		Fresno	CA
Ravell	C. H.		Lyons	NY
Rawlins	W. J.		Vincennes	IN
Rawson	Charles S.	257 Fulton	Brooklyn	NY
Rayan	W. O.		Kansas City	MO
Rea	W. J.		Santa Barbara	CA
Read	W. F.		Vandalia	IL

ALPHABETICAL LISTING OF PHOTOGRAPHERS IN THE U. S. IN 1888 & 1889

NAME		ADDRESS	CITY	STATE
Readman	F. E.		Norwalk	CT
Reagan	G. C.		Hampton	IA
Ream Bros.			Delphos	OH
Reck	L. M.		Galion	OH
Reckling	W. A.		Columbia	SC
Record & Epler			Saratoga Springs	NY
Redheffer & Koch		419 N. Broadway	St. Louis	MO
Redman	George H.		Webster	MA
Redmon	E. C.		Pine Knot	KY
Redmond*	James	162 Court	Brooklyn	NY
Reed	Byron		Kokomo	IN
Reed*	F. H.		Omro	WI
Reed	H. C.		Forest City	IA
Reed	H. J.	581 Main	Worcester	MA
Reed	J. H.		Clinton	IA
Reed	J. Q.		Petaluma	CA
Reed	Mrs. W. A.		Quincy	IL
Reed	N. H.		Pontiac	IL
Reed	R. A.		Franklin	MA
Reed	Selwin C.		Newburyport	MA
Reed	W. H.	628 Pennsylvania	Washington	DC
Reed & Bock			Circleville	OH
Reed & Preble			Brunswick	ME
Reed & Wallace			Mobile	AL
Reeder	James		Knoxville	IA
Reef	J. T.		Decorah	IA
Rees	C. R.		Richmond	VA
Reese	C. S.		Westminster	MD
Reese	M. A.		Santa Cruz	CA
Reeves	Henry H.	1594 Hough	Cleveland	OH
Reeves	M. R.		Grenola	KS
Rehn & Clark		141 S. 5th	Philadelphia	PA
Reid	John		Paterson	NJ
Reid	W. R.		Licking	MO
Reiff	J. F.		Aurora	IL
Reilly	Thomas F.	249 6th	New York City	NY
Reiman	Joseph	842 Central	Cincinnati	OH
Reimer	Benjamin F.	613 N. 2nd	Philadelphia	PA
Reimer & Katz		406 Milwaukee	Milwaukee	WI
Reinhold	J. H.	449 Vine	Cincinnati	OH
Reis	F. L.		Marietta	OH

ALPHABETICAL LISTING OF PHOTOGRAPHERS IN THE U. S. IN 1888 & 1889

NAME		ADDRESS	CITY	STATE
Reiterman	William		Burr Oak	MI
Relfs	W. E.		Neligh	NE
Remmillard	A. B. E.		Newburgh	NY
Renshaw*	R.		Palatka	FL
Renvers & Gesman			Pella	IA
Retallick	Chester		Battle Lake	MN
Revenaugh*	S. B.		Ann Arbor	MI
Rey	Miss Josie		Baker City	OR
Reynders, Jr.	P. C.		Grand Rapids	MI
Reynold	H. J.		Jefferson	IA
Reynolds	A. C.		Griswold	IA
Reynolds	Charles C.	403 Grand	Brooklyn	NY
Reynolds	D. A.		Chatham Village	NY
Reynolds	E. E.		Fairhaven	VT
Reynolds	J. A.		Cresco	IA
Reynolds	J. H.		Burlington	IA
Reynolds	J. J.		Bigler	PA
Reynolds*	M. B.		Richmond	IN
Reyton	Miss Ada	147 Canal	New Orleans	LA
Rhine	G. C.		Gallatin	TN
Rhine	G. C.		Fort Worth	TX
Rhine & Co.	Ithamar L.		Hartford City	IN
Rhoades	D. C.		Verndale	MN
Rhoades		1800 Frankford	Philadelphia	PA
Rhodes	A. S.		Gouverneur	NY
Rhodes	Bert		Milan	MO
Rhodes	J.		Fredericktown	MO
Rhodes	J. P.		Reading	MI
Rice	B. T.		Frankford	KS
Rice	F. H.	311 Main	Worcester	MA
Rice	George M.	419 Main	Worcester	MA
Rice	Moses P.	1219 Pennsylvania	Washington	DC
Rice	T. J.		Rockport	MO
Rice	Luther M.		Warren	OH
Rice	Phillip J.	87 Montgomery	Jersey City	NJ
Rice*	S. A.		Brighton	IL
Rich	C. P.		Guthrie	IA
Rich	J. A.	95 Blue Island	Chicago	IL
Rich	J. E.		Minneapolis	MN
Rich	Mrs. S. A.	13 N. 5th	Zanesville	OH
Rich	S. A.	101 Main	Zanesville	OH

NAME		ADDRESS	CITY	STATE
Rich & Co.	Miss D. B.		Emporia	KS
Richards	L. Y.		Pittstown	PA
Richards	R. B.	2826 State	Chicago	IL
Richards	B. B.		Lockport	IL
Richards	S. S.		Newark	NY
Richardson	George		Logan	KS
Richardson	H. W.		Stevens' Point	WI
Richardson	J. C.		Marlborough	MA
Richardson	L. A.		Leominster	MA
Richardson	W. P.		Easthampton	MA
Richardson	W. T.		Oneida	NY
Richardson & Speh*		131 Broadway	Brooklyn	NY
Richardson Bros.		107 Broadway	Brooklyn	NY
Richardson Bros.			Sparta	WI
Richter	M. L.		Madison	GA
Richter & Co.	F. C.	1118 Passy'k	Philadelphia	PA
Riddle	A. J.		Columbus	GA
Rider	J. A.		Wellsville	NY
Rider	B. L.	339 W. Madison	Chicago	IL
Ridgway	I. A.		Portage	WI
Rieman & Pray		26 Montgomery	San Francisco	CA
Rifenburg	A. G.		Salinas	CA
Rile & Co.		406 N. 10th	Philadelphia	PA
Rile & Kearns*		233 N. 8th	Philadelphia	PA
Riley	J. J.		Marysville	CA
Riley	J. P.		New Cambria	MO
Rineberger	L.		Dunkirk	OH
Rinehart	A. F.		Denver	CO
Rinehart	F. A.		Omaha	NE
Ring	S. T.		Marshall	IL
Ringgold	Mrs. J. H.		Quincy	IL
Rino	Mrs. August	801 Franklin	St. Louis	MO
Rino*	August		St. Louis	MO
Ripple Bros.			Milton	PA
Ripple Bros.			Sunbury	PA
Risberg	J. O. P.		Rockford	IL
Riser	A. M.		Columbia	SC
Rising	Herman		La Fayette	IN
Ritter	J. F.		Parkersburg	WV
Ritton	E. D.		Danbury	CT
Ritz	Ernest F.	58 Temple	Boston	MA

NAME		ADDRESS	CITY	STATE
Robaart	Jacob		Prairie City	IA
Robbins	Frank		Bradford	PA
Robbins	Frank		Oil City	PA
Robbins	N. L.		Muncie	IN
Roberts	A. C.		Lake Benton	MN
Roberts	A. G.		Henderson	KY
Roberts	Benjamin W.	824 3rd	New York City	NY
Roberts	C. C.		Le Roy	IL
Roberts	H. H.		Wesley	ME
Roberts	J. E.		New Bedford	MA
Roberts	Martin	1943 Germantown	Philadelphia	PA
Roberts	W. M.		Mankato	KS
Roberts & Betts			Calais	ME
Roberts & Brooks		130 Ontario	Cleveland	OH
Roberts & Fellows*		1125 Chestnut	Philadelphia	PA
Roberts & Vanderwarker			Minneapolis	MN
Robertson	L. D.		Franklin	KY
Robertson	W. N.		Ennis	TX
Robinson	A. M.		Jackson	MS
Robinson	Edgar G.		Michigan City	IN
Robinson	F. N.		Howard	DK
Robinson	F. P.		Morrisville	VT
Robinson	G.		Oakland	ME
Robinson	H. F.		Phoenix	AZ
Robinson	H. N.		Bridgewater	MA
Robinson*	M. L.	Eutaw & Lexington	Baltimore	MD
Robinson	Martin L.	Eutaw	Baltimore	MD
Robinson	S. M.	2-4 6th	Pittsburgh	PA
Robinson	W. A.	631 W. Lake	Chicago	IL
Robinson	W. H. H.		Oshkosh	WI
Robinson	W. J.		Wyandotte	KS
Robinson*	W. J.		Maryville	MO
Robinson & Co.	J. T.		Holly Springs	MS
Robinson & Co.	J. T.		Oxford	MS
Robinson & Hopper			Brainerd	MN
Robinson & Roe		79 Clark	Chicago	IL
Robinson & Roe*		77 Clark	Chicago	IL
Robira	Louis	243 Royal	New Orleans	LA
Roblin	F. F.		Spirit Lake	IA
Robotham	Bedford		Brooklyn	NY
Roche	John L.	731 W. Market	Louisville	KY

ALPHABETICAL LISTING OF PHOTOGRAPHERS IN THE U. S. IN 1888 & 1889

NAME		ADDRESS	CITY	STATE
Rochelle	C. W.		Durham	NC
Rocher	Henry	241 Wabash	Chicago	IL
Rock	Robert		Morenci	MI
Rockstead*	Andrew		Mt. Carmel	IL
Rockwell	J. E.		Petersburgh	VA
Rockwood	George C.	17 Union Sq. W.	New York City	NY
Rockwood	J. M.	Cherry	Toledo	OH
Rodbird	James A.	305 7th	Washington	DC
Rodecker	L. M.		Cumberland	OH
Rodgers	Hart J.	471 Main	Hartford	CT
Rodocker	David		Winfield	KS
Roe	Sylvester		Flushing	NY
Roeder	T.		Smith	AR
Roessler	E. E.		Carthage	MO
Rogers	C. H.		Plymouth	MA
Rogers	Charles F.		Manchester	NH
Rogers	E. A.		Coon Rapids	IA
Rogers	Frank		Colebrook	NH
Rogers	G. E.		Fond Du Lac	WI
Rogers	J. A.		Bedford	IN
Rogers	S.		Tarrytown	NY
Rogers	W. B.		Hattonia	OH
Rogers	W. C.		Vincennes	IN
Rogers	W. S.		Wichita	KS
Rogers	W. S.		Garden City	KS
Rogers & Guiher*			Waynesborough	PA
Rogers & Son	J. H.	Wilson Bldg.	Washington	PA
Rogers & Son	J. H.		Waynesburgh	PA
Rogers*	Samuel G.		Washington	PA
Roloson	S. G.		Delphos	OH
Rombach & Groene		476 W. 4th	Cincinnati	OH
Rood	Frank M.		Poultney	VT
Rood	W. J.		Spencer	IA
Rood, Jr.	W. D.		Quincy	IL
Rooney	J. H.	417 E. Baltimore	Baltimore	MD
Rooney*	F. A.	19 E. Baltimore	Baltimore	MD
Rooney*	J. H.	73 W. Baltimore	Baltimore	MD
Roosevelt & Frantz			Ackley	IA
Root	D. O.		Woonsocket	DK
Root	Emerson		Monmouth	IL
Root	W. H.		Aledo	IL

ALPHABETICAL LISTING OF PHOTOGRAPHERS IN THE U. S. IN 1888 & 1889

NAME		ADDRESS	CITY	STATE
Root*	Samuel		Dubuque	IA
Rosberry	R. L.		Talladega	AL
Rosch	J. E. & A. J.	1513-1515 Olive	St. Louis	MO
Rose	P. H.	297 Westminster	Providence	RI
Rose	P. H.		Galveston	TX
Rose	R. H.		Princeton	NJ
Rose	T. H.		Indianapolis	IN
Rose & Bassett*		103 State	Chicago	IL
Rose & Co.			Denver	CO
Rosedale	A. S.		De Soto	MO
Rosenberger	G. L.		Selma	AL
Rosenger	Otto B.	55 Myrtle	Brooklyn	NY
Rosenstock	H.		Bloomsburgh	PA
Roshon	C. S.		Harrisburgh	PA
Roshon	C. S.		Lebanon	PA
Rosmussen	J. C.		Davenport	IA
Ross	A. J.		Chadron	NE
Ross	C. L.		Willimantic	CT
Ross	George		Petaluma	CA
Ross	J. B.		Linneus	MO
Ross	P. F.		Tipton	MO
Roswall	F. A.		Macon	MO
Rote	J. E.		Lancaster	PA
Roth	Andrew	11 Frenchman	New Orleans	LA
Rothengatter & Dillon		912 Arch	Philadelphia	PA
Rothwell	J. W.		Washington	PA
Rounds	A. A.		Yankton	DK
Rounds	Benjamin H.		Cannelton	IN
Rowe	C. G.		Waverly	MN
Rowe	Jesse		Cuba	IL
Rowland & Co.		2120 Callowhill	Philadelphia	PA
Rowley	C. W.		Elmira	NY
Rowley Bros.			Kearney	NE
Rowley Bros.*			Janesville	WI
Rowsey	W. H.		Corinth	MS
Rubin	H.		Ithaca	NY
Rubin	Levy		Ithaca	NY
Rudolph	A.		Williamstown	MA
Rudolph	Ernest B.	646 W. Baltimore	Baltimore	MD
Rudolph	Mrs. J. F.	627 J	Sacramento	CA
Rue	A. B.	341 4th	Louisville	KY

ALPHABETICAL LISTING OF PHOTOGRAPHERS IN THE U. S. IN 1888 & 1889

NAME		ADDRESS	CITY	STATE
Rugg	A. B.		Minneapolis	MN
Rummel	A.		Waynesburgh	OH
Rundle*	Edward		Edwardsville	IL
Rundlett	C. W.		Watertown	WI
Runions	L. F.		New York Mills	MN
Runkel	J. P.	469 3rd	Milwaukee	WI
Runnels	J. L.		Middleport	OH
Runnels & Stateler		957 Market	San Francisco	CA
Rupp	Christian	24 Ave. A	New York City	NY
Ruschle	F. C.		Lanark	IL
Rush	E. W.		Glen Gardner	NJ
Rush	Mrs. M. B.		Olney	IL
Russ	H. M.		Portland	OR
Russ	J. G.	104 5th	Pittsburgh	PA
Russ*	J. G.	204 5th	Pittsburgh	PA
Russell	Edward L.		Blossburgh	PA
Russell	Frank		Lawrence	MA
Russell	R. U.		Oxanna	AL
Russell	S. A.		Oxanna	AL
Russell	William		Jeffersonville	IN
Russell & Co.		17 & 203 W. Lexington	Baltimore	MD
Rust	C. B.		Hastings	MN
Rutherford	J.		Sault de St. Marie	MI
Rutter	T. H.		Butte City	MT
Ryan	D. J.		Shelbyville	IL
Ryan	D. J.		Springfield	IL
Ryan	W. A.		Blunt	DK
Ryder	D.		Richmond	IN
Ryder	John H.	211 Superio	Cleveland	OH
Ryder	P. S.	72 S. Salina	Syracuse	NY
Ryder*	J. F.	239 Superior	Cleveland	OH
Ryerson	R. D.		Detroit City	MN
Sabin	J. B.		Hammond	WI
Saettele	M. Lena	701 Franklin	St. Louis	MO
Saettele	Max Estate of		St. Louis	MO
Saettele & Son*	F.		St. Louis	MO
Salen	Peter	131 Fulton	Cleveland	OH
Salisbury	Arnold F.		Pawtucket	RI
Salter	J. Z.		Newberry	SC
Salzmann	W.		Ft. Wayne	IN
Salzmann*	William		Detroit	MI

ALPHABETICAL LISTING OF PHOTOGRAPHERS IN THE U. S. IN 1888 & 1889

NAME		ADDRESS	CITY	STATE
Sampson	Edward		Morrison	IL
Samson & Corning			Osage	IA
Samuels	M. A.	10th & Clay	Oakland	CA
Sanborn	Amos H.		Lowell	MA
Sander	F. W.		Cedarburgh	WI
Sanders	A. M.		Valley City	DK
Sandford	Gould		Garden Grove	IA
Sandifer	J. M.		Somerset	KY
Sandoz	Albert		Mobile	AL
Sandquist	J. J.		Dassel	MN
Sands, Jr.	J. A.		White Bear Falls	MN
Sansom	J. B.		Kahoka	MO
Santman	Conly T.	301 Girard	Philadelphia	PA
Sargent	A. J.		Rushville	IN
Sargent	F. V.		Hubbardson	MA
Sargent	M.		Pekin	IL
Sargent	S. C.		Taylor's Falls	MN
Sarnblad	Charles		St. Peter	MN
Sarony	Napoleon	37 Union Sq. W.	New York City	NY
Saterbo	Hans		Canton	DK
Satterlee	A.		Sandwich	IL
Sauer	Albert		Cedarburgh	WI
Saul	William H.	214 Bowery	New York City	NY
Saul & Wareham			Freeport	IL
Saunders	A. Tresize	210 Fir	Akron	OH
Saunders	Irving		Alfred Centre	NY
Saunders	Irving		Friendship	NY
Saunders	J. H.		Algona	IA
Saunders & Son			Lexington	MO
Saunders Bros.*		141-143 S. Howard	Akron	OH
Saurman	J. S.		St. Joseph	MO
Saurman	O. S.		Norristown	PA
Saurman	T. W.		Pottstown	PA
Savage	C. H.		San Antonio	TX
Savage	Charles R.		Salt Lake City	UT
Sawtell	E. E.		Biddeford	ME
Sawyer	G. L.		Central City	IA
Sawyer	Jesse		Peoria	IL
Sawyer	Llewellyn A.	159 N. 8th	Philadelphia	PA
Saxe	Theodore		Caledonia	MN
Saxe	Theodore		Plainview	MN

ALPHABETICAL LISTING OF PHOTOGRAPHERS IN THE U. S. IN 1888 & 1889

NAME		ADDRESS	CITY	STATE
Saxton	W.		Neligh	NE
Saylor	B. F.		Lancaster	PA
Scanland	J. F.		Frankford	MO
Scanlon	Mrs. J. B.		Wyandotte	KS
Scannell & Co.	David	814 Arch	Philadelphia	PA
Schaddle	P. J.		Sauk City	WI
Schadee	Ferdinand Florence		Northampton	MA
Schaefer	A. L.	1630 Franklin	St. Louis	MO
Schaefer	Henry C.	740 S. 4th	St. Louis	MO
Schaefer	J. H.	887 W. Baltimore	Baltimore	MD
Schaefer*	J. H.	643 W. Baltimore	Baltimore	MD
Schaeffer	C. E.		Poughkeepsie	NY
Schaeffer	W. L.		Beardstown	IL
Schaeffer*	H. C.		St. Louis	MO
Schaidner	Charles B.	186 E. 124th	New York City	NY
Schaub	J. L.		La Grange	GA
Schaub	J. T.		Hope	IN
Schelhous	Losen		Grand Rapids	MI
Schell	George		Myerstown	PA
Schellhous*	Losen		Grand Rapids	MI
Schenck	Philip	R21, Saxton Blk, 8th	Canton	OH
Scherer	Martin	816 N. 6th	St. Louis	MO
Schertzer	Leavitt L.		Massillon	OH
Schill	Ludwig	839 Broad	Newark	NJ
Schillare	A. J.		Northampton	MA
Schilling	W. P.		Duluth	MN
Schlattman Bros.			St. Paul	MN
Schlegel	Louis		Richmond	KY
Schlier	T. M		Nashville	TN
Schmedling	Marcus E.		Chattanooga	TN
Schmidt	Harry		Council Bluffs	IA
Schmidt	L. N.	302 Milwaukee	Chicago	IL
Schmidt	Oscar	148 W. Randolph	Chicago	IL
Schneider	Peter	2135 Archer	Chicago	IL
Schneider	T. W.		Green Bay	WI
Schneider*	Phillip		Olewein	IA
Schneidt & Dippel			St. Louis	MO
Schnell	C. A.		Troy	OH
Schoene	H.	504 Kearny	San Francisco	CA
Schoerry	Henry	143 E. 3rd	New York City	NY
Schofield	John	4442 Frankford	Philadelphia	PA

ALPHABETICAL LISTING OF PHOTOGRAPHERS IN THE U. S. IN 1888 & 1889

NAME		ADDRESS	CITY	STATE
Schofield Bros.			Westerly	RI
Scholl	Emil	1632 Chestnut	Philadelphia	PA
Scholl	J. B.	547 S. Halsted	Chicago	IL
Scholten	J. A.	920-922 Olive	St. Louis	MO
Scholze	H.		Birmingham	AL
Schooley	L. H.		Indianola	IA
Schooley*	Mrs. L. H.		Indianola	IA
Schoolof	William B.	415 E. 79th	New York City	NY
Schoreder & Bargen			Mountain Lake	MN
Schramm	Mathew		Oakland	CA
Schramm	Matthew		San Diego	CA
Schreiber & Sons		819 Arch	Philadelphia	PA
Schreiver	J. B.		Emporium	PA
Schriver	C. C.		Harrisburgh	PA
Schroder	J. D.	308 River	Troy	NY
Schroeder	Hugo	359 3rd	Milwaukee	WI
Schroeder	J. H.		Evansville	IN
Schubert	Joseph		Madison	WI
Schueler	John		Davenport	IA
Schueller	Frederick		Mount Pleasant	MI
Schultze	Carl	17 Chatham Sq	New York City	NY
Schultze*	Carl	5 Chatham Square	New York City	NY
Schulze	Carl W. F.	101 High	New Haven	CT
Schulze*	Carl F. W.	25 Crown	New Haven	CT
Schumacher	Frank G.		Los Angeles	CA
Schumacher	H.	186 William	Newark	NJ
Schurr*	Theodore P.		Lockport	NY
Schuster	George	489-491 W. 6th	Cincinnati	OH
Schutte	Henry B.	423 N. Washington	Baltimore	MD
Schutter	E. D. H.	142 State	Rochester	NY
Schuwirth	George		Austin	TX
Schwabe	H.		Omaha	NE
Schwarzer*	H. G.	11 Union	Brooklyn	NY
Schwind	William	1422 2nd	New York City	NY
Schwind*	William	27 Ave A	New York City	NY
Schwind, Jr.	William	27 Ave. A	New York City	NY
Scidmore	D.		Gloversville	NY
Scofield	C. H.		Utica	NY
Scoggins	James H.	163 Poydras	New Orleans	LA
Scotford & Co.	J. H.	715 Main	Kansas City	MO
Scotford & Co.			Kansas City	KS

ALPHABETICAL LISTING OF PHOTOGRAPHERS IN THE U. S. IN 1888 & 1889

NAME		ADDRESS	CITY	STATE
Scott	A. A.		Hastings	MN
Scott	A. B.		Xenia	KS
Scott	G. W.		Deadwood	DK
Scott	J. C.		New Brunswick	NJ
Scott	O. P.	2220 Indiana	Chicago	IL
Scott	O. P.		Quincy	IL
Scott	S. W.		Ashby	MN
Scott	William H.		La Porte	IN
Scott & Co.		602 N. Kansas	Topeka	KS
Scott*	J. P.		Osage Mission	KS
Scrimminger	Mrs. W.		Pomona	CA
Seails	E. T.		Auburn	NY
Searles	George W.		Amsterdam	NY
Searles	H. C.	303 King	Charleston	SC
Sears	C. L.		San Bernardino	CA
Seavey	William		Canton	IL
Seavy	H. P.		Columbia	TN
Sedgwick	H. M.	133 Main	Zanesville	OH
Sedgwick & Vannerson*			St. Augustine	FL
Seed	William		Jennings	MO
Seeley & Warnock		320 Main	Bridgeport	CT
Seeverts	A.		Fremont	IA
Seibert & Wolff			Oshkosh	WI
Seidmore	A.		Appleton	WI
Seiler	J. C.	59 ½ N. Main	Mansfield	OH
Seiter	E. E.		New Ulum	MN
Selander	Julius	1710 Eastern	Baltimore	MD
Selden	Harris	134 Park Row	New York City	NY
Seldner	Maurice	415 J	Sacramento	CA
Sellars	James W.		Bellaire	OH
Sellers*	J. M.		Ludell	KS
Sellers	M. J.		Hubble	NE
Selorer & Schutt			Cortland	NY
Senhart	R. D.		Brookfield	MO
Serdinko	J.		New Braunfels	TX
Service	W. E.		Bridgeton	NJ
Sessions	J. W.		Wayland	MI
Sessions & Kohne			Toledo	OH
Setter	C.		Clermont	IA
Setzer & Roth		1633 S. Broadway	St. Louis	MO
Seutter & Co.	F.		Jackson	MS

ALPHABETICAL LISTING OF PHOTOGRAPHERS IN THE U. S. IN 1888 & 1889

NAME		ADDRESS	CITY	STATE
Severn	Thomas		Joliet	IL
Severson	T. C.		Sioux Rapids	IA
Sewell D. & Co.		25 3rd	San Francisco	CA
Sexton	J. B.		Abilene	KS
Seymour	H. A.		Jackson	MI
Shaal	Robert	202 Westminster	Providence	RI
Shackell & Clauss		828 3rd	New York City	NY
Shackford	A. W.		Farmington	NH
Shadick	M. F.		Shunk	PA
Shadle	Amos		Latrobe	PA
Shadle	C. C.		Kittanning	PA
Shadle	Edwin J.		Latrobe	PA
Shadle	Isaac		Greenburgh	PA
Shaff	J. S.		Seneca	KS
Shanafeld	J. D.		Lyons	KS
Shanafelt*	J. D.		Lyons	KS
Shane	J. B.		Lawrence	KS
Shane	William	1316 Girard	Philadelphia	PA
Shange	H. L.		Pomona	CA
Shanks	J. W.		Pomeroy	WA
Shanswood	John		Adam	OR
Shanswool*	John		Adam	OR
Sharer	John		Brunswick	MO
Shares*	O. P.		Union Star	MO
Sharp*	W. O.		Washington	IL
Sharpnack	T.		Rice's Landing	PA
Sharpsteen	Elmer		St. Louis	MI
Sharpsteen	S. A.		Ionia	MI
Shartle	H.		Bowling Green	KY
Shattock	N. J.	175 Woodward	Detroit	MI
Shaver	E. E.		Chelsea	MI
Shaw	Arthur L.		Biddeford	ME
Shaw*	G. S.	8th & Race	Cincinnati	OH
Shaw	G. S.	7th & Race	Cincinnati	OH
Shaw*	J. R.		Olmstead	OH
Shaw*	Thomas		Chagrin Falls	OH
Shaw	Walter	749 Chapel	New Haven	CT
Shawd	J. R.		Kenton	OH
Shea	M. A.	194 ½ Hanover	Boston	MA
Sheahan	James		Astoria	IL
Shearer	G. W.		Humphreys	MO

NAME		ADDRESS	CITY	STATE
Sheets	Frederick		Wellsville	OH
Sheid	H.	401 7th	Washington	DC
Sheldon	Alfred	640 St. Clair	Cleveland	OH
Shellaberger	G. G.		Valley Falls	KS
Shelton	George B.		Peru	IN
Shepard	Charles		Melvin Village	NH
Shepherd	C. F.		St. Johnsbury	VT
Shepherd & Sweeny			Birmingham	AL
Sheppard	Arthur	61 Myrtle	Brooklyn	NY
Sherburne	F. H.		Monson	ME
Sheriff	J. A.		San Diego	CA
Sherman	G. H.		Elgin	IL
Sherman	Levi	40 State	Rochester	NY
Sherman	Littleton		Cadott	WI
Sherman*	O. G.		Marengo	IL
Sherman	Wilson S.	535 Washington	Boston	MA
Shettle	William M.	279 6th	New York City	NY
Shew	William	523 Kearny	San Francisco	CA
Shewaden	C. H.		Council Bluffs	IA
Shields	H. H.		Greenville	IL
Shinn	H. A.		Pine Bluff	AR
Shipler & Co.		65 5th	Pittsburgh	PA
Shipley & Ladd		210-212 Woodward	Detroit	MI
Shirley	Johnson O.		Chanute	KS
Shirley	S. R.		Yates Centre	KS
Shiveley	E. W.		Decatur	IL
Shively	S. L.		Erie	KS
Shoaff	John A.		Ft. Wayne	IN
Shoemaker	J. F.		Warsaw	IN
Shoemaker	W. L.		Phoenixville	PA
Shoemaker	William C.	602 ½ Poplar	Philadelphia	PA
Shomber	A. J.		State Centre	IA
Shook	C. W.	196 Beaver	Allegheny	PA
Shorey	C. E.		Augusta	ME
Shorey	W. F.	131 E. Baltimore	Baltimore	MD
Shorrock	Ralph	19 Centre	New York City	NY
Short	Lorenzo		Kingston	NY
Showman	L. K.		Portland	MI
Shroy	J. A.		Lebanon	IN
Shull	L. T.		Tyler	TX
Shultz	W. B.		Stromsburg	NE

NAME		ADDRESS	CITY	STATE
Shultz*	Mr. & Mrs.		Belvidere	IL
Shumway	H. L.		Cuyahoga Falls	OH
Shumway	J. D.	902 Chapel	New Haven	CT
Shurtleff	Henry		Amboy	IL
Shuster	H. S.		Salem	OR
Shute & Co.			Astoria	OR
Sickler	H. O.	39 Seneca	Buffalo	NY
Sidey	Thomas		Marysville	OH
Siebert	A. Z.	74 University Pl.	New York City	NY
Sifrit & Coover			London	OH
Sigmund	John		Rock Island	IL
Silkworth	Amos W.	261 Manhattan	Brooklyn	NY
Silva	Joseph T.		San Francisco	CA
Silver	F. C.		Ludington	MI
Silver	Joseph P.	57 N. 8th	Philadelphia	PA
Silver	W. W.	102 Fulton	New York City	NY
Silver*	William W.	102 Fulton	New York City	NY
Silvernail	E. W.		Bayfield	WI
Simington	J. N.		Memphis	MO
Simmer	Mathias		Henderson	MN
Simmons	L. D.		Natchez	MS
Simmons	E. A.	74 North, Wollison Block	Pittsfield	MA
Simmons, Latier & King			Waterloo	IA
Simms	Nicholas		Central City	KY
Simon	A. W.	215 W. Tupper	Buffalo	NY
Simon	Eugene	183 Canal	New Orleans	LA
Simonds	J. S.	214 Woodward	Detroit	MI
Simpson	Crit		Carthage	IL
Simpson	W. P.		Paterson	NJ
Simpson & Wright			Mayfield	KY
Sims	Andrew		Camden	NJ
Sims & Sons		700 Arch	Philadelphia	PA
Sims & Sons*		203 Race	Philadelphia	PA
Simson	A.	456 Main	Buffalo	NY
Singhi	John F.		Rockland	ME
Singhi	W. G.	Fairfield Ave.	Bridgeport	CT
Sink	D. P.		Calvert	TX
Sipperly	W. H.		Bennington	VT
Sipple	A. B.		Parsons	KS
Sires	J. W.		Oil City	PA
Sittler*	G. W.		Springfield	MO

ALPHABETICAL LISTING OF PHOTOGRAPHERS IN THE U. S. IN 1888 & 1889

NAME		ADDRESS	CITY	STATE
Siveet	Charles A.		Wellsboro	PA
Skervis*	B. P.		Spring Green	WI
Skewes	J. D.	222 W. 5th	Cincinnati	OH
Skinner	F. A.		Plymouth	MA
Skinner	J. A.		Woodsfield	OH
Skinner	N. C.		White Pigeon	MI
Skinner	T.		Kinston	NC
Skinner	Miss L. A.		Laingsburgh	MI
Skrivseth	J. L.		Hillsboro	DK
Slack & Berry			Wilmington	OH
Slater	A. C.		East Douglas	MA
Slater	E.		Edgerton	OH
Slater	E. B.		Osage City	KS
Slater	Joseph		Franklin	OH
Slater	W. F.		Middletown	OH
Slaugenhaupt	H. T.		Littlestown	PA
Slemmons	J. F.		Atlanta	GA
Sleyster	A. L.		Preston	MN
Sloan	F. J.		Eau Claire	PA
Sloan	Mrs. W. W.		Jefferson	TX
Slocum	A. T.	160 W. 5th	Cincinnati	OH
Slocum	D.		Hudsonville	MI
Slocum	Orville		Austin	MN
Smales	Thomas		Washington Depot	CT
Smalling	J. J.		Lancaster	PA
Smart	O. M.		Auburn	NY
Smedley	F. S.		Berea	OH
Smedley	J. E.		Belvidere	IL
Smith	A.		Crete	NE
Smith	Aaron	8 Bowery	New York City	NY
Smith	Aaron A.	402 Freeman	Cincinnati	OH
Smith	Abram		St. Joseph	MO
Smith	Arthur H.		Avon	NY
Smith	B. F.		Cleburne	TX
Smith	C. A. N.	397 Bedford	Brooklyn	NY
Smith	C. E.		Peoria	IL
Smith	C. E.		Bristol	VT
Smith	C. F.		Sterling	IL
Smith	C. H.		Detroit	MI
Smith	C. O.		Saybrook	IL
Smith	C. W.		Dalmatia	PA

NAME		ADDRESS	CITY	STATE
Smith	Catharine A.	N.840 Broadway	New York City	NY
Smith	Charles A.		Webster	MA
Smith*	Charles B.		Holyoke	MA
Smith*	Charles H.	303 Broadway	New York City	NY
Smith	Charles H.	302 Broadway	New York City	NY
Smith*	D.		Indianapolis	IN
Smith*	D. J.		Detroit	MI
Smith	D. W.		Saginaw	MI
Smith*	Mrs. D. W.		Saginaw	MI
Smith	David H.	531 Fulton	Brooklyn	NY
Smith	E. A. G.		Uxbridge	MA
Smith*	Edward		Woonsocket	RI
Smith*	Edward F.	22 Milk	Boston	MA
Smith	E. J.		West Bay City	MI
Smith	E. W.		Pittsburgh	KS
Smith	F. H.		Shelby	OH
Smith	F. M.		Mount Pleasant	MI
Smith	F. Wheaton	33 Westminster	Providence	RI
Smith	G.		South Bend	IN
Smith	G. B.		Bristol	TN
Smith	George M.		Lockport	NY
Smith*	H. G.	90 Studio Building	Boston	MA
Smith	H. L.		St. Clair	MI
Smith*	H. N.		Penn Yan	NY
Smith	Hazen A.		Winchendon	MA
Smith	Henry		New Bedford	MA
Smith	Henry F.	1800 Frankford	Philadelphia	PA
Smith*	Isaiah		Van Wert	OH
Smith	J. A.		Penn Yan	NY
Smith	J. E.		Bordentown	NJ
Smith	J. E.	26 ½ S. Market	Springfield	OH
Smith*	J. F.		Minneapolis	MN
Smith	J. F.		Jacksonville	FL
Smith	J. G.		Vallejo	CA
Smith	J. Henry	769 Broad	Newark	NJ
Smith	J. Rennie	727 Broad	Newark	NJ
Smith	J. W.		Lewistown	PA
Smith	James G.		Jamestown	NY
Smith	James W.	145 8th	New York City	NY
Smith	Jason	1716 7th	Oakland	CA
Smith	Joseph K.		Milton	VT

NAME		ADDRESS	CITY	STATE
Smith	Joshua	206 N. Clark	Chicago	IL
Smith	L. F.		El Paso	IL
Smith	L. W.		Enterprise	KS
Smith	Lewis		Mishawaka	IN
Smith	Luke		Greenleaf	KS
Smith	M. L.		Long Prairie	MN
Smith	M. O.		Lowell	MI
Smith	Miss Costillia D.		Lowell	MA
Smith	Morris W. (Estate of)		New Bedford	MA
Smith	Mrs. Belle		Ida Grove	IA
Smith	N. W.		Sioux Rapids	IA
Smith	N. W.		Leetonia	OH
Smith	P.	Bank	Waterbury	CT
Smith	Rollin H.		St. Albans	VT
Smith*	R. G.		Leavenworth	KS
Smith	S. B.		Marshall	MI
Smith	S. B.		Honeoye	NY
Smith	S. S.		Chester	VT
Smith*	S. S.		Brandon	VT
Smith	Sylvester		De Witt	IA
Smith	Thomas		Chester	IL
Smith	W. A.		Rockland	ME
Smith	W. G.		Cooperstown	NY
Smith	W. L.		East Saginaw	MI
Smith	W. M.		Engelwood	IL
Smith	W. T.		Liberty	VA
Smith	Walter		Wappinger's Falls	NY
Smith	Walter A.		Newark	OH
Smith	William W.		Minersville	PA
Smith*		148 W. 5th	Cincinnati	OH
Smith*			Lawrence	KS
Smith*			Portland	ME
Smith*			Ortonville	MN
Smith & Ayers			Odell	NE
Smith & Bechtel*			Frankfort	IN
Smith & Co.*	E. C.	374 Main	Springfield	MA
Smith & Dryer			Indianapolis	IN
Smith & Miller		436 Walnut	Philadelphia	PA
Smith & Palmer			Romeo	MI
Smith & Robinson*		260 Bowery	New York City	NY
Smith Bros.*			Chicago	IL

NAME		ADDRESS	CITY	STATE
Smythe	James		Guttenberg	IA
Snedeker	T. H. B.		Martinsville	IL
Snell	E. B.		Wellington	KS
Snider	B. F.		Salem	MO
Snodgrass	G. M.		Mulberry Grove	IL
Snook	George J.	186 S. Howard	Akron	OH
Snook	V. H.		Aurora	IL
Snow	Frank		Elgin	IL
Snyder	Adam W.	104 E. Girard	Philadelphia	PA
Snyder	B. Russell	1223 Woodbine	Philadelphia	PA
Snyder	C. S.		Washington Court House	OH
Snyder	C. W.		Kutztown	PA
Snyder	F. H. F.		Gloucester	NJ
Snyder*	George		Coldwater	KS
Snyder	R.	527 Kansas	Topeka	KS
Snyder	Ralph F.	829 N. 5th	Philadelphia	PA
Snyder	C. J.		Topeka	KS
Snyder & Walton		227 Girard	Philadelphia	PA
Soderburg	P.		Sutton	NE
Sodreberg	Pont.		Geneva	NE
Soffer	F. F.		Ogden	IA
Sollitt	Thomas S.	2897 Archer	Chicago	IL
Sommer	C.	3810 State	Chicago	IL
Sommer	Carl		Ft. Wayne	IN
Sommer*	Charles	3922 State	Chicago	IL
Sonders*	F. A.		Chambersburgh	PA
Sonnenberg	H.	52 Federal	Allegheny	PA
Sonnenberg	J. E.		Allegheny	PA
Sonnenberg*	J. E.	120 Ohio A.	Pittsburgh	PA
Sonnenberg*	H.	52 Federal A.	Pittsburgh	PA
Soper*	Allen		St Ignace	MI
Sorensen	Claus		Cedar Falls	IA
Souby	Edward J.	113 Canal	New Orleans	LA
Souder*	J. W.		Vincennes	IN
Souders	F. A.		Chambersburgh	PA
Sours Bros.			St. Joseph	MO
Spalt*	F. R.		Wahpeton	DK
Sparhawk	L. T.		West Randolph	VT
Sparks	Oliver		Rockport	MO
Spatt*	F. R.		Minneapolis	MN
Spaulding	S. E.		Springville	NY

ALPHABETICAL LISTING OF PHOTOGRAPHERS IN THE U. S. IN 1888 & 1889

NAME		ADDRESS	CITY	STATE
Speaker	E. R.		Beach City	OH
Speakers	I. G.		Paterson	NJ
Speck	Col.		Moravia	NY
Spedden	W. L.	723 7th	Washington	DC
Speechly	Miss S. T.		Ann Arbor	MI
Spencer	Francis A.		Georgetown	OH
Spencer	Frank M.		Mansfield	PA
Spencer	G. B.		Waterbury	CT
Spencer	H. S.		North Port	MI
Spencer	K. W.		Union	NY
Spencer	O. H.		Circleville	OH
Spencer	T. W.		Circleville	OH
Spencer*	John T.	616 E. Girard	Philadelphia	PA
Sperber	John		Allegheny	PA
Sperber*	J. E.	90-92 Federal A.	Pittsburgh	PA
Spettel	Clement		La Crosse	WI
Spettel	Clement		Onalaska	WI
Spicer	C. A.		Clintonville	WI
Spieler	Jacob M.	722 Chestnut	Philadelphia	PA
Spiess	William	13 Ave. A	New York City	NY
Spillman	B. F.		Harrodsburg	KY
Spooner	E.		Onslow	IA
Spooner	J. P.		Stockton	CA
Sprague	E. D.	374 Ontario	Cleveland	OH
Sprague	F. L.		Walton	NY
Sprague & Hathaway			Somerville	MA
Springfield	A. M.		Santa Barbara	CA
Sproul	J. J.		Waterville	KS
Spurgin	J. S.		Greencastle	IN
Spurr	A. H.		Cresco	IA
Spurr*	E. W.		Dysart	IA
Spuyer	H. S.		Auburn	NY
St. Clair	Alexander		Des Moines	IA
St. John	Henry	368 Main	Hartford	CT
St. John	Henry		Wallingford	CT
Stacy	C. A.		Medina	NY
Stacy	J. G.		Rahway	NJ
Stadon*	J. E.		Minneapolis	MN
Stafford	Charles	3140 State	Chicago	IL
Stahmer	A. J.		Waterbury	CT
Stahn	M.	229 N. Gay	Baltimore	MD

ALPHABETICAL LISTING OF PHOTOGRAPHERS IN THE U. S. IN 1888 & 1889

NAME		ADDRESS	CITY	STATE
Stahn*	M.	87 N. Clay	Baltimore	MD
Stair	L. E.		Florence	CO
Staley	J. M.		Watertown	DK
Stallings	W. F.		Grinnell	IA
Stamford	George E.		Salem	MA
Stamm	A. N.		Sioux City	IA
Standard Copying Agency		36 6th	Pittsburgh	PA
Standbrook	William		Nashville	IL
Standiford	J. F.		Parsons	KS
Staniford*	George E.		Salem	MA
Stanley	F. E.		Lewiston	ME
Stanley	G. C.		Ithaca	NY
Stanton	T. E.		Los Angeles	CA
Stanton Bros.		505 Forbes	Pittsburgh	PA
Stanton*	T. J. & D. W.	503 Forbes	Pittsburgh	PA
Staples	W. F.		Terre Haute	IN
Stapleton	Richard		East Lynne	MO
Starbird			Farmington	ME
Stark	N. P.		Rosalie	TX
Stark	W. L.		Tekonsha	MI
Starke	W. G.	5th S. E. c. Main	Zanesville	OH
Starke & Thrall		60 Cass	Chicago	IL
Starr*	T. C.		Evansville	IN
Starr	Jesse	1320 Chestnut	Philadelphia	PA
Statler	George		Johnstown	PA
Stauffer & Co.	A. N.		Mount Pleasant	PA
Staunton*	C. K.		Reinbeck	IA
Staynor & Dahling			Edgar	NE
Stead	James U.	383 6th	New York City	NY
Stearns	E. E.		Wabasha	MN
Stearns	Lee		Wilkesbarre	PA
Stearns	O. H.		Columbus	NE
Stebbins	A. B.		Canisteo	NY
Stebbins	A. W.		St. Charles	MN
Stebbins	N. L.	521 Washington	Boston	MA
Steel	B. R.		Nokomis	IL
Steele	Frank		Blue Hill	NE
Steele	H. A.		Jackson	MI
Steele	W. A.		Williamstown	MI
Steeley	W. R.		Cochran	GA
Steffens	M. J.	2249 Cottage Grove	Chicago	IL

ALPHABETICAL LISTING OF PHOTOGRAPHERS IN THE U. S. IN 1888 & 1889

NAME		ADDRESS	CITY	STATE
Steffey	J. H.		Alliance	OH
Stein	S. L.	310 State	Milwaukee	WI
Steinbauer	Henry		Groton	DK
Steinberg	Louis	216 W. Market	Louisville	KY
Steiner	Julius H.	77 Newark	Jersey City	NJ
Steinhardt	Theodore	145 8th	New York City	NY
Steinhardt*	Theodore	183 Eighth	New York City	NY
Steinman	Jacob C.	504 S. 2nd	Philadelphia	PA
Stempel	V. C.		Steelville	MO
Stenberg	O. L.		Evansville	MN
Stengel	H.	710 Broadway	New York City	NY
Stephan & Co.	George	1226-1232 Larimer	Denver	CO
Stephens	H. H.		Waynesborough	GA
Stephens	J. O.		Ogden City	UT
Stephens	W. J.		Palmyra	MO
Stephenson	C. A.		Greenfield	MO
Stephenson	J. J.		Ypsilanti	MI
Sterling	G. F.		Bay City	MI
Sterry	E. S.	520 Broadway	Albany	NY
Stetter*	C.		Clermont	IA
Stevens	A.	64 3rd	San Francisco	CA
Stevens	B.		Auburn	NY
Stevens	C. H.		Logansport	IN
Stevens	Caleb A.		Foxborough	MA
Stevens	G. L.		Richmond	MI
Stevens	H. N.		North Craftsbury	VT
Stevens	H. S.		Rushville	IN
Stevens	H. S.	30 Central Sq.	Keene	NH
Stevens*	H. S. & G. E.		Keene	NH
Stevens	J. A.		Spring Valley	MN
Stevens	J. K.	55 McVicker's Theatre	Chicago	IL
Stevens*	J. K.	108 Dearborn	Chicago	IL
Stevens & Trapp*			Maysville	KY
Stevenson	Edward		El Dorado	KS
Stevenson	John	200 E. 34th	New York City	NY
Stevenson	Joshua	271 Broadway	Brooklyn	NY
Stevenson*	R.		Atchison	KS
Stever	Miss Lizzie		Marshfield	MO
Steward	C. A.		Granite Falls	MN
Stewart	E. J.		Murphysborough	IL
Stewart	Frank		Millbury	MA

ALPHABETICAL LISTING OF PHOTOGRAPHERS IN THE U. S. IN 1888 & 1889

NAME		ADDRESS	CITY	STATE
Stewart	H. F.		Evanston	IL
Stewart	J. G.		Carlinville	IL
Stewart	J. R.		Williamsburgh	MS
Stewart	James L.		Mannington	WV
Stewart	John B.		Carrollton	GA
Stewart	Peter		Ogden	IA
Stewart*	Robert		Richmond	MI
Stewart & Phear			North East	PA
Stewart & Toast			Oneida	NY
Stickney	L.		Morris	NY
Stiff	Thomas P.		Brockton	MA
Stiffler	G. W.		Longmont	CO
Stigleman	G. W.		Richmond	IN
Stiles	A. J.	533 Pearl	Cleveland	OH
Stiltz	D. R.		Williamsport	PA
Stimson	J. E. H.		Appleton	WI
Stirrat*	Robert		Braceville	IL
Stivers	J. A.		Mount Vernon	NY
Stoakes	T. A.		Sturgeon Bay	WI
Stockton & Pitcher			Linesville	PA
Stoddard	F. A.		Calais	ME
Stoddard	H. H.		Granville	NY
Stoddard	S. R.		Glens Falls	NY
Stoffregen	Alfred	133 Montrose	Brooklyn	NY
Stokes	D. S.		Chattanooga	TN
Stone	Elbridge G.	652 St. Clair	Cleveland	OH
Stone	M. T.		Danville	IL
Stone & Brooks		195 W. Indiana	Chicago	IL
Stone & Needles			South Pueblo	CO
Stone & Sons	N. L.	58-60 Market	Potsdam	NY
Stone*	N. L.		Potsdam	NY
Stonebrook & Brand*			Rockville	MO
Stoops	L. M.		Perry	IA
Stopp	William		Ottumwa	IA
Storm	F. D.		Denver	CO
Story	Augustus	3 Lewis	E. Boston	MA
Story	D. D.		Ann Arbor	MI
Stout	J. V.		Easton	PA
Stout	Thomas		Unionville	MO
Strauch	H. W.		Rock	PA
Strauss	Julius C.	1245-1247 Franklin	St. Louis	MO

ALPHABETICAL LISTING OF PHOTOGRAPHERS IN THE U. S. IN 1888 & 1889

NAME		ADDRESS	CITY	STATE
Strauss Bros.*			St. Louis	MO
Strebeck	W. M.	216 ½ O'Farrell	San Francisco	CA
Street	Frank W.	1634 Chestnut	Philadelphia	PA
Streit	F. W.	30 Juneau	Milwaukee	WI
Streuser	J. J.		Cascade	IA
Streuser	M. J.		Bellevue	IA
Strickmaker	John		Canal Dover	OH
Strickmaker	Joseph N.		New Philadelphia	OH
Strickmaker	Philip		New Philadelphia	OH
Strode	J. M.		Kokomo	IN
Strong	L.		Kewanee	IL
Strong	N. P.		Eureka	CA
Strong*	N. F.		Whitehall	MI
Stroud	J. T.		Burlington Junction	MO
Strout	Howard E.		Woburn	MA
Strunk	J. D.		Reading	PA
Stuart	C. A.	186 Seneca	Buffalo	NY
Stuart	Charles T.	368 Main	Hartford	CT
Stuart	Eugene		Williamsport	PA
Stuber	W. G.	434 E. Market	Louisville	KY
Studley*	G. D.	46 W. Madison	Chicago	IL
Stumm & Co.*	A. Y.		Farmingham	PA
Stump	W. H.		Eagleville	MO
Sturdevant	A. T.		Wilkesbarre	PA
Sturdevant	E. K.		Wilkesbarre	PA
Sturdivant	J. B.		Atkinson	NE
Sturgeon	William J.	200 Main	Zanesville	OH
Sturtevant*	E. E.		Skowhegan	ME
Sturtevant	E. F.		Skowhegan	ME
Stutsman	W. G.		Central City	NE
Suddad	John F.		Fall River	MA
Suden	Gustav		Jefferson City	MO
Suessmmilch	F. V.	71 Washington	Chicago	IL
Sullivan	Charles M.	1705 South	Philadelphia	PA
Sullivan	Jeremiah F.		Greenbush	NY
Sullivan	Mrs. M. J.		Shubuta	MS
Sullivan Bros.			Decatur	MS
Summerhags	William.	612 Clay	San Francisco	CA
Summers	A. J.		Bloomington	IN
Summers	A. Y.		Winamac	IN
Summerville*	M. L.		Minneapolis	MN

ALPHABETICAL LISTING OF PHOTOGRAPHERS IN THE U. S. IN 1888 & 1889

NAME		ADDRESS	CITY	STATE
Sumner	Charles		Foxcraft	ME
Sumner	I. E.		Northfield	MN
Sunderland	J. C.		Girard	KS
Sunderland	J. C.		Hartford	WI
Sunderland	W. F.		Mayville	WI
Sunderlin	J. C.		Flemington	NJ
Sunderlins*	August		Port Jervis	NY
Suplau	Ludwig		Wheaton	IL
Sutter	H. S.	128 Wisconsin	Milwaukee	WI
Suttlerley	Clement		Ione	CA
Sutton	W. L.		Hornellsville	NY
Swain	A. C.		Constantine	MI
Swain	Allen		St. Paul	MN
Swain	S.		Rochester	NH
Swaine	H. J.		Richmond	IN
Swan	Harry		Lamar	MO
Swan & Cobb			Norway	ME
Swanell	Charles R.	483 Fulton	Brooklyn	NY
Swank	William		Osborne	KS
Swank*	William		Oswego	KS
Swanson	C.		Mead	NE
Swanson	Harvey		Detroit	KS
Swart	John S.		Nevada City	CA
Swartz	Adam		Stuart	IA
Swartz & Bro.	D. H.		Fort Worth	TX
Swasey	B.		Shasta	CA
Swearingen & Zachariah			Adel	IA
Sweeney	Thomas T.	R13, 307 Superior	Cleveland	OH
Sweet	J. A.	518 ½ Congress	Portland	ME
Sweet	J. L.		Framingham	MA
Sweet	P. W.		Lansing	MI
Sweetman	F.		Pioneer	OH
Sweetser	C. A.		Lynn	MA
Swem	Mrs. Emeline		Cedar Rapids	IA
Swem	T. M.		St. Paul	MN
Swett & Co.	A. G.	1406 Franklin	St. Louis	MO
Swift	G. W.		Raleigh	NC
Swift	Jno. M.	480 Broad	Newark	NJ
Swindells	Arthur	1078 High	Providence	RI
Swords & Pentz*			York	PA
Sybarger	Noah		Ash Grove	MO

ALPHABETICAL LISTING OF PHOTOGRAPHERS IN THE U. S. IN 1888 & 1889

NAME		ADDRESS	CITY	STATE
Tabbetts	G. H.		Laconia	NH
Taber	I. W.	8 Montgomery	San Francisco	CA
Taber & Co.	Charles		New Bedford	MA
Taft	O. A.	272 Main	Buffalo	NY
Taft	P. W.		Saxton's Rivert	VT
Taggard	F. E.		Lynn	MA
Tainter	E. E.		Cassopolis	MI
Talbot	F. T.		West Winfield	NY
Talbot	J. Warren		Norwood	MA
Talbot	N. H.		Evans	CO
Talbot	Walter E.		Montrose	PA
Tallman	C. W.		Batavia	NY
Talmadge	Frank		Edgerton	WI
Tankersley	J. R.		Bloomington	IL
Tanley	W. S.		Lincoln	IL
Tanner	C. C.		Pipestone	MN
Tansey	E. J.		Mendota	IL
Tapley	Isaac S.		Lewiston	ME
Tappan	T. S.		Bellaire	OH
Tappan & Co.			Wheeling	WV
Tarter	G. W.		Linn	MO
Tatman	J. R.		Shelbyville	IN
Tatman & Son			Shelbyville	IN
Tatum	C. E.		Shelbyville	IN
Taylor	A. B.	41 Monroe	Detroit	MI
Taylor	A. Sylvester		Great Falls	NH
Taylor	B. C.		Warsaw	IL
Taylor	B. F.		Clear Water	KS
Taylor	Benjamin F.	624 Arch	Philadelphia	PA
Taylor	C. H.		Lewistown	IL
Taylor	C. R.		Lamar	MO
Taylor	C. W.		Morristown	NJ
Taylor	Charles A.		Reading	PA
Taylor	D. D.	304 N. 7th	St. Louis	MO
Taylor	F. J.		Cambridgeport	MA
Taylor	Harry Morton		New Albany	IN
Taylor	J. H.		Republic	MI
Taylor	J. W.		Randolph	NY
Taylor	J. W.	152 E. Main	Rochester	NY
Taylor	S. B.		Aurora	IL
Taylor	S. M.		St. Paul	MN

ALPHABETICAL LISTING OF PHOTOGRAPHERS IN THE U. S. IN 1888 & 1889

NAME		ADDRESS	CITY	STATE
Taylor	Sanford A.	453 Fulton	Brooklyn	NY
Taylor	T. W.		West Chester	PA
Taylor	Thomas	24 Union PL	Hartford	CT
Taylor	Thomas		Pottstown	PA
Taylor & Blair			Chelsea	MA
Taylor & Co.	W. Curtis	101 S. 13th	Philadelphia	PA
Taylor & Co.*	W. Curtis	1328 Chestnut	Philadelphia	PA
Taylor & Martin		81 State	Chicago	IL
Taylor & Morgan			Reading	PA
Taylor & Preston			Salem	MA
Taylor*	B. H.		Ashland	WI
Taylor*	Mrs. Richard		Coney Island	NY
Tebbetts*	G. H.		Laconia	NH
Teeple	Mrs. J. S.		Wooster	OH
Teeple	T.		Ashland	OH
Tegarden	G. A.		Tyler	TX
Telfer	James	120 ½ Hackensack Plank Rd	Union Hill	NJ
Temple & Co.	G. L.		Clinton	IA
Templeman	J. N.		Miller	DK
Templeton	A. J.		Tower City	DK
Ten Eyck & Co.			Auburn	NY
Tennat	P. W.		Haverhill	MA
Tenney	C. A.		Winona	MN
Terreforte	Juan M.	2148 3rd	New York City	NY
Terry	William	826 Broadway	New York City	NY
Terry	William A.		Bristol	CT
Tewkesbury	J. R.		Fort Madison	IA
Thackeray & Kraeling		99 5th	Pittsburgh	PA
Tharling	J. W.		Evansville	IN
Thatcher	H.		Wakefield	MA
Thaver	A. A.		Otsego	MI
Thayer*	A. A.		Otsego	MI
Thayer*	G. D.		Lake City	IA
Thayer	L. E.		North Craftsbury	VT
Thayer	L. R.		Tonica	IL
Thayer	O. B.		Freeport	IL
Theilkuhl	G.	927 Pennsylvania	Washington	DC
Thein	Henry	476 Broad	Newark	NJ
Thibautt	Louis		Fall River	MA
Thiel	Charles		Duluth	MN
Thielemann	J.	82 Springfield	Newark	NJ

ALPHABETICAL LISTING OF PHOTOGRAPHERS IN THE U. S. IN 1888 & 1889

NAME		ADDRESS	CITY	STATE
Thomas	A. S.	166 W. 5th	Cincinnati	OH
Thomas	Frank		Columbia	MO
Thomas	Frank		Sedalia	MO
Thomas	George C.	1219 College	Racine	WI
Thomas	J. A.		Edmore	MI
Thomas	J. K.		Madison	WI
Thomas	M.		Shamokin	PA
Thomas	Samuel A.	717 6th	New York City	NY
Thomas & Co.		791 Broad	Newark	NJ
Thomason & Cook			Ball Ground	GA
Thomason & Leffler			Louisiana	MO
Thomlinson*	A.		Fort Wayne	IN
Thompson	A. D.		La Crosse	WI
Thompson	A. M.		Brownsville	PA
Thompson	A. R.		Oxford Junction	IA
Thompson	Ada A.		Ravenna	OH
Thompson	C. C.		Nora Springs	IA
Thompson	C. P.		Orange	MA
Thompson	G. H.		Orange	MA
Thompson*	J. H.		Ellicottsville	NY
Thompson	J. R.		Dongola	IL
Thompson	Mrs. Catherine		Waukegan	IL
Thompson	Orville		Glenwood	MO
Thompson	R. R.		Drayton	DK
Thompson	Scott		Merom	IN
Thompson	W. S.		Schell City	MO
Thompson	William C.		Amesburg	MA
Thompson*	W. W.		Atlanta	GA
Thompson & Co.	D. P.		Kansas City	KS
Thompson & Grier			Hamilton	DK
Thomsen & Co.	B. E.	515 Locust	St. Louis	MO
Thomson			Hatton	DK
Thomson & Co.	D. P.	610 Main	Kansas City	MO
Thorn	G.		Plainfield	NJ
Thorn	J. R.		Piqua	OH
Thornbladh	O. L.		Cannon River Falls	MN
Thornton	J. M. & S.		Skaneateles	NY
Thornton	L. W.		Manistee	MI
Thorpe	R. L.		Garwin	IA
Thors	F.		San Francisco	CA
Thors	Louis	1205 Larkin	San Francisco	CA

ALPHABETICAL LISTING OF PHOTOGRAPHERS IN THE U. S. IN 1888 & 1889

NAME		ADDRESS	CITY	STATE
Thorsen	John		Dundee	IL
Throckmorton	Franklyn	363 Bowery	New York City	NY
Thune & Folkedahl			Ada	MN
Thurston	A. R.		Coopersville	MI
Thuss, Koelein & Giers			Nashville	TN
Thwaites	Joseph	1 Chambers	New York City	NY
Thwaites	Joseph		Portland	OR
Tibbals	Fred B.		Millersburgh	OH
Tibbals	Lawrence J.		Niles	OH
Tibbels	J. C.		Lambertville	NJ
Tibbitts	H. B.		Vassar	MI
Tibbs	N. J.		Eureka Springs	AR
Tice	A. W.		Ellenville	NY
Tice	A. W.		Corry	PA
Tice	C. E.		Minonk	IL
Tice	N. J.		Redfield	IA
Tice & Donner			Janesville	WI
Tichenor	G. W.		Burlington	NJ
Tierney	J. J.	775 Chapel	New Haven	CT
Tiffany	B. B.		Indiana	PA
Tiffany	C. E.		Coldwater	MI
Tillett	James M.		Tullahoma	TN
Tilley	E. P.		Morrisonville	IL
Tillotson*	Nelson		Scranton	PA
Tilton	G. W.		Dickinson	DK
Tinkbinder	J. A.		Williamsport	PA
Tinsman	John		Kirksville	MO
Tipton	W. H.		Gettysburg	PA
Tirrell	G. W.		E. Weymouth	MA
Titus	Frank M.	228 W. 5th	Cincinnati	OH
Tobias	Henry		Columbia	MO
Tobin & Evans		725 Sansom	Philadelphia	PA
Tohey	F. D.	145 22nd	Chicago	IL
Toler	J. C.		Ottawa	OH
Tollman	T. W.		Glenwood	IA
Tollman & Co.			Omaha	NE
Tolman	T. W.		Sidney	IA
Tomlinson	Anson	20 Claybourn	Chicago	IL
Tomlinson	F. N.	236 Woodward	Detroit	MI
Tomlinson*	Isaac		Allegheny	PA
Tomlinson	Moses		Plainfield	IN

ALPHABETICAL LISTING OF PHOTOGRAPHERS IN THE U. S. IN 1888 & 1889

NAME		ADDRESS	CITY	STATE
Tompkins	E. P.		Holden	MO
Tonndorff	Charles H.	Choteau	St. Louis	MO
Torney & Co.		448 Mitchell	Milwaukee	WI
Torp	A. N.		Story City	IA
Torrey*	W. H.	154 Broadway	Buffalo	NY
Tounsend	Lill.		West Liberty	IA
Towle & Co.	H. R.		Cadillac	MI
Towle*	S. M.		Warsaw	NY
Towne	Anna F.		Athol	MA
Towne	W. L.	425 Washington	Boston	MA
Towne & Moore			Portland	OR
Townley	A. C.		Newton	NJ
Townsend	C. H.		Willimantic	CT
Townsend	H. L.		Fairmount	MN
Townsend	J. A.		Iowa Falls	IA
Townsend	T. W.		Iowa City	IA
Townsend	William		Covington	OH
Townsends Bros.			Hastings	NE
Towson & Proctor		163 N. Gay	Baltimore	MD
Tracy	C. B.		Pana	IL
Tracy*	C. B.		Moweaqua	IL
Trader	F. A.		Burlingame	KS
Trainor	J. M. D.	731 W. Baltimore	Baltimore	MD
Tralles	P.	309 9th	Washington	DC
Trapp	J. B.	95 5th	Pittsburgh	PA
Trapp*	J. B.	20 5th	Pittsburgh	PA
Trask	Albion K. F.	1210 Chestnut	Philadelphia	PA
Trauss & Ebersole*			Lewistown	OH
Trayser	W. G. R.		Danville	VA
Treadwell	Albert		Medford	MA
Treganowan	Thomas	150 Wylie	Pittsburgh	PA
Trellon	Oscar		New Haven	CT
Trenham	N. J.		Alexandria	MN
Tresize	W. F.		Fairbury	IL
Tresize*	Samuel P.		Logan	OH
Tresselt	R.	984 Milwaukee	Chicago	IL
Tressler	E. P.		Fort Scott	KS
Tressler	S. P.		Fort Scott	KS
Tretault	Edward		Centreville	RI
Trimble	J. H.		Blair	NE
Tripp	F. D.		Newton	KS

NAME		ADDRESS	CITY	STATE
Tripplett	W. A.		Bluffton	OH
Tritz*	M. J.		White Lake	DK
Trone	A. F.		Denison	IA
Trost	F. J.	49 Summit	Toledo	OH
Trostle	W. F.		Milford	IL
Truax	John		Hazelton	IA
Truax	L. B.		Swanton	VT
Truesdell	W. F.		Springfield	IL
Trumbull	L. J.		Harbor Springs	MI
Truscott	Charles	907 Filbert	Philadelphia	PA
Truxell	J. H.	12 5th	Pittsburgh	PA
Tryson	Harrison	1617 Spring Garden	Philadelphia	PA
Tucker	E. N.		Oxford	CT
Tucker	G. H.		Mauston	WI
Tucker	H. B.	397 Main	Worcester	MA
Tull	B. H.		Lena	IL
Tull	G. W.		Kirksville	MO
Tunison & Son			Tiffin	OH
Turnbull & Newton			Fairfield	IL
Turnell	Joseph		Silver Spring	RI
Turner	A. V.		Creighton	NE
Turner	C. F.		Janesville	WI
Turner	Charles F.	506 6th	Racine	WI
Turner	J. C.		Isle Au Haut	ME
Turner	M.		Tuscaloosa	AL
Turton	George W.		Pensacola	FL
Tusdale	H. H.		Blooming Prairie	MN
Tussey	J. C.		Clinton	MO
Tuttle	W. C.		Belfast	ME
Twist	Nathan H.		Lynn	MA
Tyner	O. N.		Kinmundy	IL
Tyson	S. E.		Onago	KS
Udell	A. A.		Three Rivers	MI
Udell	M. M.	13 Euclid	Cleveland	OH
Uhlman	Rudolph		St. Joseph	MO
Uleson	J. O.		DeKalb	IL
Ulrey	W.		Delaware	OH
Ulrich	Frederick	156 Bowery	New York City	NY
Ulrich	R. L.		Selin's Grove	PA
Umber*	Udlemor		Terre Haute	IN
Underwood	Clarence		Jackson	MI

ALPHABETICAL LISTING OF PHOTOGRAPHERS IN THE U. S. IN 1888 & 1889

NAME		ADDRESS	CITY	STATE
Underwood	George A.	326 Main	Worcester	MA
United States Portrait Co.		311 Fulton	Brooklyn	NY
Upson	D. D.		Hampton	IA
Upton	L. W.		Oberlin	OH
Urbano	Salvatore	1726 State	Chicago	IL
Urlin	George C.	216 S. High	Columbus	OH
Usher, Jr.	J.		Augusta	GA
Vahheich*	J.	292 North	Chicago	IL
Vahlteich	Julius	290 North	Chicago	IL
Vail	K.		Auburn	NY
Vail	William F.	46 Vesey	New York City	NY
Vail Bros.			Poughkeepsie	NY
Vale & Pellegrin			Riverside	CA
Vale & Pellegrin			San Bernardino	CA
Van Aken	E. M.		Elmira	NY
Van Alstine	C. W.		Red Oak	IA
Van Blarcom	H.		Tower	MN
Van Buskirk*	Charles		Columbia	DK
Van Buskirk	M. L. & H.		Savannah	MO
Van Court	J. E.		Redwood City	CA
Van De Grift	C. W.		Sidney	OH
Van de Wall	W. B.		Lancaster	WI
Van Doelzen	J. A.		Peoria	IL
Van Dyke	Valentine	1234 3rd	New York City	NY
Van Dyke	W. H.		Edinborough	PA
Van Gorden	C. E.		Catskill	NY
Van Gricken	Samuel		Keokuk	IA
Van Houten	Arthur	461 Fulton	Brooklyn	NY
Van Loo	Leon	148 W. 4th	Cincinnati	OH
Van Loo	W. F.	149 Summit	Toledo	OH
Van Ness	James H.		Charlotte	NC
Van Norman	George H.		Waltham	MA
Van Orsdells	C. M.		Orangeburgh	SC
Van Osdell	G. C.		Toulon	IL
Van Patten	Emerson		Elmwood	IL
Van Patten	W. H.		Great Barrington	MA
Van Riper	D. W.		Americus	GA
Van Schaick	C. J.		Black River Falls	WI
Van Sickle & Adolphus			Kalamazoo	MI
Van Slyke	C. W.		Mason	MI
Van Stavoren			Atlanta	GA

ALPHABETICAL LISTING OF PHOTOGRAPHERS IN THE U. S. IN 1888 & 1889

NAME		ADDRESS	CITY	STATE
Van Syckel	J. W.		Vermont	IL
Van Valkenburg	Charles E.		Auburn	NY
Van Wagoner*	I. M.		Nyack	NY
Van Wagoner	J. M.		Nyack	NY
Vanakin*	E. M.		Elmira	NY
Vance	Handel		Barnesville	OH
Vance*	M. C.		Leonardville	KS
Vancil & McDonald			Dodge City	KS
Vander May	John S.	1409 ½ W. Market	Louisville	KY
Vandersweep*	J.		San Francisco	CA
Vanderwarker & Nally			Minneapolis	MN
Vandyke	Ferdinand	509 8th	New York City	NY
Vane	J. H.		Dover	DE
Vanlieu*	A. J.		Aurora	NE
Vansickle	A. H.	40 E. Main	Springfield	OH
Vantersell	A. S.		Portland	OR
Variel	J. S.		Gardiner	ME
Varnal	Mahabel B.	738 Spring Garden	Philadelphia	PA
Varnal*	Mahabel B.	788 Spring Garden	Philadelphia	PA
Vaughan	Mrs. H. W.	724 ½ Market	San Francisco	CA
Vaupel	Herman M.	989 3rd	New York City	NY
Veazie	J. H.		Sherman	ME
Veedor	A.	32 N. Pearl	Albany	NY
Veling	P.		Beaver Dam	WI
Venner	J. F.		Brownsville	OR
Ver Lee	Isaac		Zeeland	MI
Vernon	C. D.		Minto	DK
Vetter	W. H.		Cottonwood Falls	KS
Vickery*	D. B.		Haverhill	MA
Vickey & Reed			Haverhill	MA
Victor & Co.	George	189 N. Clark	Chicago	IL
Vivian	N. J.		Iron Mountain	MI
Voigt	C. F.	224 Grand	Milwaukee	WI
Vollert*	W. P.		Milwaukee	WI
Volquarto	C. H.		Plymouth	WI
Von	Fielitz	297 Bowery	New York City	NY
Von der Herd	F. D.	7 Blue Island	Chicago	IL
Voorhees	S. M.	519 S. 4th	St. Louis	MO
Voorhees	S. M.		St. Louis	MO
Vosburgh	B. D.		Des Plaines	IL
Vose	E.		Machias	ME

ALPHABETICAL LISTING OF PHOTOGRAPHERS IN THE U. S. IN 1888 & 1889

NAME		ADDRESS	CITY	STATE
Vose & Son	S. S.		Waterville	ME
Voss	Charles		Kankakee	IL
Voss	N. A.		Hays City	KS
Vredenburg	Kelly	1013 W. Lake	Chicago	IL
Vreeland & Bank			Westmoreland	KS
Waddell & Johnson			Warrensburgh	MO
Waegen	O. F.		Horicon	WI
Wager	S. D.		Orlando	FL
Wager	S. D.		Indianapolis	IN
Wagner	A. H.		Oregon	IL
Wagner	C. A.	65 W. Baltimore	Baltimore	MD
Wagner	Hermann		Iron Mountain	MI
Wagner	J. A.		Burlington	WI
Wagner*	M. C.		McKeesport	PA
Wagner & Son*	F.	63 W. Baltimore	Baltimore	MD
Wagner & Sons	F.	427 E. Baltimore	Baltimore	MD
Wagoner	J. H.		Hagerstown	MD
Wahlstedt	Matilda	1 Blue Island	Chicago	IL
Waide	H. M.		Quincy	IL
Waite	C. B.		Plymouth	OH
Waite	S. H.		Emporia	KS
Waiteley	E. B.		Dunlap	IA
Walcott	F. B.		Berlin	WI
Waldack	Mrs. Charles	Vine & Liberty	Cincinnati	OH
Waldbillig	A. F.	394 2nd	Albany	NY
Waldbillig*	A. F.	30 N. Pearl	Albany	NY
Waldron & Wilson			Marion	IA
Wales	T. L.		Centre Ville	IA
Walfrid*	Jonas		Dwight	IL
Walker	Chas. H.		Oakland	CA
Walker	G. H.		Altamont	IL
Walker	J. W.		Golden	CO
Walker	John A.		Pensacola	FL
Walker	O. A.		Delta	OH
Walker	Stephen J.	818 Arch	Philadelphia	PA
Walker	W. C.		Uxbridge	MA
Walker	W. W.		Titusville	PA
Walker & Loofbourow			Hillsboro	DK
Walker*	J. S.		Mt. Holly	NJ
Wallace	J. H.		Fort Fairfield	ME
Wallace	Henry C.		Manchester	NH

NAME		ADDRESS	CITY	STATE
Wallace*	R. A.	154 Claybourn	Chicago	IL
Waller	Frederick	135 S. 5th	New York City	NY
Wallermire	P. C.		Lincoln	NE
Wallick	Joe		Hagerstown	IN
Wallin	C. E.		Montgomery	AL
Wallis	C. W.		Glenwood	IA
Walrath	G. A.		Norwood	NY
Walter	H. L.		Manchester	IA
Walter	Thomas		Norfolk	VA
Walter	J. P.	742 N. Clinton	Rochester	NY
Walthers*	C. B.		Knox	PA
Waltmire	N. J.		Ashland	NE
Walton	J. E.		Veray	IN
Walton	James N.		Aurora	IN
Walton	D.		Rising Sun	IN
Walz	George		St. Cloud	MN
Walz	R.	477 Pennsylvania	Washington	DC
Walzi*	Richard	205 W. Baltimore	Baltimore	MD
Walzl	L.	157 S. Broadway	Baltimore	MD
Walzl	Richard	21 E. Baltimore	Baltimore	MD
Wampler	J. T.		Charlottesville	VA
Wantz	James		White Sulphur Springs	MT
Ward	C. E.		North Attleborough	MA
Ward	E. D.		Lake Village	NH
Ward*	G. A.		Greenfield	IA
Ward*	H. D.		North Adams	MA
Ward	T. C.		Roseburgh	OR
Ward	W. H.		Burr Oak	IA
Ward Bros.			Laporte City	IA
Wardlaw*	Samuel	16 State	Rochester	NY
Wardwell	W. H.	7143 Washington	Boston	MA
Wardwell*	W. H.	1743 Washington	Boston	MA
Ware	G. A.		Winterset	IA
Ware	Leonard		Glasgow	MO
Wark	James		Kent	OH
Warner	A. M.		Quincy	IL
Warner	A. W.		Greene	NY
Warner*	Gustav		Waupaca	WI
Warnky	F. C.		Independence	MO
Warnock	J.	58 State	Bridgeport	CT
Warren	Joseph W.		Cottage City	MA

ALPHABETICAL LISTING OF PHOTOGRAPHERS IN THE U. S. IN 1888 & 1889

NAME		ADDRESS	CITY	STATE
Warren	O. H.		Lowell	MA
Warren	W. Shaw	41 Winter	Boston	MA
Warrington	E. W.		Oskaloosa	IA
Wartleg	E. B.		Gallatin	MO
Wasburn	G. L.		Castile	NY
Washburn*	A. L.		Houston	TX
Washburn	W. W.	109 Canal	New Orleans	LA
Wassum	O. O.		Slatington	PA
Wastermann	Otto		Lemont	IL
Waterman	G. E.		Ypsilanti	MI
Waters	R. J.		Virginia City	NJ
Waters	S. E.		Union	IA
Watkins	C. E.	427 Montgomery	San Francisco	CA
Watkins	Mr.	43 North	Pittsfield	MA
Watkins & Simmons*			Pittsfield	MA
Watrous	S. W.		Visalia	CA
Watson	A.		Richwood	OH
Watson	C. H.		Chariton	IA
Watson	G. C.		Lapeer	MI
Watson	H. W.		Denver	CO
Watson	J. E.		Detroit	MI
Watson	J. W.		Raleigh	NC
Watson	J. W.		Eufaula	AL
Watson	S. A.		Seneca	IL
Watson's		156 W. 4th	Cincinnati	OH
Watters*	S. E.		Union	IA
Watts	D. B.		Montrose	MO
Watts	L. H.		Ironton	MO
Waurzyniakowiski*	M. J.		Milwaukee	WI
Way	F. B.		Ashtabula	OH
Way	Fletcher	154 Claybourn	Chicago	IL
Wealthy	John E.		Angola	NY
Weatherby	C. C.		St. Paul	MN
Weatherby & Denison			Rock Valley	IA
Weatherington & Freeman			Decatur	TX
Weaver	O. F.		Beaver Dam	WI
Weaver	Peter S.		Hanover	PA
Weaver	W. H.		Watseka	IL
Webb	Henry A.	112 N. 9th	Philadelphia	PA
Webb	J. F.		Strawberry Point	IA
Webb	Marion		Franklin	KY

ALPHABETICAL LISTING OF PHOTOGRAPHERS IN THE U. S. IN 1888 & 1889

NAME		ADDRESS	CITY	STATE
Webb	W. J.		Red Bud	IL
Webb & Co.	John M.		Columbiana	OH
Webb*	Wilson T.		Greenfield	IN
Webber	W. L.		Saco	ME
Weber	F. J.		Gowanda	NY
Weber Bros.			Erie	PA
Webster	E. Z.		Norwich	CT
Webster	H. D.		Lapeer	MI
Webster	J. C.		St. Johns	MI
Webster	J. F.		Centre Harbor	NH
Webster	J. H.		Dallas	TX
Webster	W. A.	111 Moody	Waltham	MA
Webster	W. F.		Oshkosh	WI
Webster & Albee		175 Front	Rochester	NY
Weckman	J. P.	128 W. 5th	Cincinnati	OH
Weed	C. L.	120 Michigan	Detroit	MI
Weehler	R. S.		What Cheer	IA
Weelpe	Nicholas		Yankton	DK
Weemink & Bros.*	H. D.		Campbellsport	WI
Weenink	H. D.		Orange City	IA
Wehe	L. E.		Carbondale	KS
Weible	E. T.		Columbia	IL
Weick*	H. J.		Milwaukee	WI
Weigel	Miss Mary		Dyersville	IA
Weingartner	Leo	6th & Central	Cincinnati	OH
Weinig & Schmidt	G.	388 Bowery	New York City	NY
Weismantel	William	242 4th	New York City	NY
Weittle	Charles		Denver	CO
Weitz	Hugo	34 3rd	San Francisco	CA
Weitz & Dijean*			San Francisco	CA
Weld	D. S.		Mound City	KS
Welfley	W. H.		Somerset	PA
Weller	L. A.		Austin	NV
Weller*	L. P.		Oconomowoc	WI
Wells	A. F.		Bristol	IN
Wells	Ernest G.		Canton	NY
Wells	George		Franklin	NY
Wells	H. M.		Cambridge	NY
Wells	T. M.		Clinton	IL
Wells	W. H.		Danville	IL
Wels*	Ernest G.		Canton	NY

ALPHABETICAL LISTING OF PHOTOGRAPHERS IN THE U. S. IN 1888 & 1889

NAME		ADDRESS	CITY	STATE
Welsh	J. O.		Redding	CA
Welsh	William		Ashton	IL
Welton	C. W.		Willow Springs	MO
Wendel	William	91 Court	Brooklyn	NY
Wendell	H.		Hampton	IL
Wendorer	T. J.	51 State	Albany	NY
Wentworth	H.		Sharon Springs	NY
Wentworth	W. D.		Fort Plain	NY
Werner	J. A.		Tyrone	PA
Werner	Otto	680 Broadway	Brooklyn	NY
Werner & Co.		522 N. 2nd	Philadelphia	PA
Wertz	E. S.		Allentown	PA
Wertz	J. C.		Chanute	KS
Wesner	H. B.		San Bernardino	CA
West	F. E.		Odebolt	IA
West	J. S.	96 Blue Island	Chicago	IL
West	Jacob		Bradford	PA
West	Redfield		Guilford	CT
West	W. E.		Derby Line	VT
Westcott & Cummings			Wilmington	DE
Westervelt	J. D.		Los Angeles	CA
Westman	O. R.		Joliet	IL
Weston*	B.		Galva	IL
Weston	F. C.		Bangor	ME
Weston	H.		Red Bluff	CA
Weston	Henry		Anderson	CA
Westphal	Hermann		Mankato	MN
Westrick	J. C.		St. Clair	MI
Wetherell	Edwin		McConnelsville	OH
Wetherell*	M. L.	224 Columbus	Sandusky	OH
Wetzel	Conrad		Barnesville	MN
Wetzel, Jr.	Conrad		Perham	MN
Weyland	Jacob		Joplin	MO
Whalen*	A. J.		Saranac	MI
Whealdon	Joshua		Texarkana	TX
Wheatley	E. S.		Du Quoin	IL
Wheeland	Mrs. Ross		McPherson	KS
Wheeland*	Mrs. Rosa		McPherson	KS
Wheeland	W. P.		Milton	PA
Wheelden	G. R.		Winterport	ME
Wheeler	C. M.		Junction City	KS

ALPHABETICAL LISTING OF PHOTOGRAPHERS IN THE U. S. IN 1888 & 1889

NAME		ADDRESS	CITY	STATE
Wheeler	D. N.		Larned	KS
Wheeler	F. W.		Richford	VT
Wheeler	Frank		Meriden	CT
Wheeler*	R. S.		What Cheer	IA
Wheeler	S. S.		Bainbridge	NY
Wheeler	W. D.		Sterling	NE
Wheeler	W. S.		Ottawa	IL
Wheeler	W. W.		Meriden	CT
Whiddit	W. W.		Newburgh	NY
Whipple	Floyd M.		Valparaiso	IN
Whipple	Mrs. Galon		Valparaiso	IN
Whipple	S. M.		Mount Carmel	IL
Whitcomb	D. W.		Kellogg	IA
White & Donnel*			St. Louis	MO
White	A. D.		Ogden City	UT
White	A. H.		Red Bank	NJ
White	Augustus A.		Gloucester	MA
White	E. F.		Hollidaysburgh	PA
White	E. M.		Keene	NH
White	Ed. N.		Belfast	ME
White	Etta P.		Emporium	PA
White*	G. William	475 Beech	Cincinnati	OH
White	G. William		Pasadena	CA
White*	H. J.		Montello	WI
White	J. N.		Port Huron	MI
White	N. C.		Gainesville	GA
White	W. A.		Wilson	KS
White*	W. S.		Douglas	KS
White*	W. S.		Jackson	MI
White	W. W.	374 Seneca	Buffalo	NY
White*			Eagle Rock	ID
White & Fischer*			Davenport	IA
White & Hughes			Ottumwa	IA
White			Farmer City	IL
Whitehead	W. H.		McKeesport	PA
Whiteman	H. W.	232 Westminster	Providence	RI
Whitesides	William		Ashland	WI
Whiting	G. W.	7 Tremont Row	Boston	MA
Whiting	Warren		Clitherall	MN
Whiting's Art Gallery			Carrollton	MO
Whitley	J. H.		Elmira	NY

ALPHABETICAL LISTING OF PHOTOGRAPHERS IN THE U. S. IN 1888 & 1889

NAME		ADDRESS	CITY	STATE
Whitman	Mrs. M. E.		Chester	VT
Whitmore	J. W.		Waldoborough	ME
Whitney	A. B.		Hartford	MI
Whitney	E. T.		Wilton	CT
Whitney	L. M.		Batavia	IL
Whitney	W. H.		Ouray	CO
Whitney & Son			Cambridgeport	MA
Whittaker	R. B.		Liberty	NY
Whittemore	A. J.		Old Orchard	ME
Whittling	Louis		Cochranton	PA
Whitton	J. W.		Fort Fairfield	ME
Wickenden	J. N.		East Toledo	OH
Wickenden*	J. W.		Upper Sandusky	OH
Widner	A. W.		Sidney	OH
Wieland	William D.	491 N. 3rd	Philadelphia	PA
Wiggins	S. T.		Cedar Rapids	IA
Wigness & Foseide			Fargo	DK
Wiker	T. J.		Cortland	NE
Wiklund	Lamentz		Stillwater	MN
Wikoff	A. W.		Rising City	NE
Wilbur	Henry	46 W. 14th	New York City	NY
Wilcox	G. W.		Palmer	MA
Wilcox	G. W.		Oconto	WI
Wilcox Bros		R45, 75 Madison	Chicago	IL
Wilde	J. F.		Piedmont	WV
Wilder	Edwin A.		Durango	CO
Wilder	W. W.		Marion	IL
Wilder*	G. E.		Chardon	OH
Wilder*	W. W.		Harrisburg	IL
Wildey	O. H.		Homer	NY
Wildman	A. H.		Monticello	IL
Wiles	A. W.		Clyde	OH
Wilhelm	Rudolph	1000 3rd	New York City	NY
Wilhelmi	F. G.		Urbana	OH
Wilkens	C. E.		Delavan	WI
Wilkes	D. J.	211 E. Baltimore	Baltimore	MD
Wilkes*	D. J.	125 W. Baltimore	Baltimore	MD
Wilkie	James	163 8th	New York City	NY
Wilkie	Sarah	165 8th	New York City	NY
Wilkins	C. E.		Waterloo	IA
Wilkins	G. T.		Fort Collins	CO

ALPHABETICAL LISTING OF PHOTOGRAPHERS IN THE U. S. IN 1888 & 1889

NAME		ADDRESS	CITY	STATE
Wilkins	H. O.		Brazil	IN
Wilkins	Joseph W.		Suncook	NH
Wilkinson	J. F.		Adair	IA
Willard & Van Horn			Lake City	IA
Willet	W. F.		Washington Court House	OH
William & Butz*			Little Rock	AR
Williams	A. A.		Columbus	GA
Williams	B. S.		Manson	IA
Williams*	C. D.		Sanborn	IA
Williams	C. D. M.		Sheldon	IA
Williams*	F. L.		Seneca	MO
Williams	Giles T.		Columbus	GA
Williams	J. A.		Hackensack	NJ
Williams	J. B.		Ettrick	WI
Williams	J. C.		Woodland	CA
Williams	J. E.		Fergus Falls	MN
Williams	J. W.		Rome	NY
Williams	James H.		S. Scituate	MA
Williams	L. B.		Utica	NY
Williams	O. H.		Memphis	MO
Williams	S. H.		Elyria	OH
Williams	T. B.		New Boston	IL
Williams	W. L.		Alamosa	CO
Williams	B. L.		Doylestown	OH
Williams	C. C.		Somerville	TN
Williams	De Witt C.	914 Arch	Philadelphia	PA
Williams	G. H.		Pleasantville	NJ
Williams	J. C.		Reynoldsville	PA
Williams	M. F.		North Easton	MA
Williams	W. C.		Clayton	IL
Williams & Co.	F. H.	985 Broadway	New York City	NY
Williams & Co.*	F. H.	683 Broadway	New York City	NY
Williams & Norton		914 Market	San Francisco	CA
Williamson	E. H.		Rome	NY
Williamson	E. R.	102 State	Rochester	NY
Willis	Abner		Carmi	IL
Willis	E. L.		Milford	MA
Willis	S.		Beattie	KS
Willis	William		Heber	UT
Wilson	A. B.	22 ½ E. 4th	Cincinnati	OH
Wilson	B. A.		Plum Creek	NE

ALPHABETICAL LISTING OF PHOTOGRAPHERS IN THE U. S. IN 1888 & 1889

NAME		ADDRESS	CITY	STATE
Wilson	C. D.	2407 S. Broadway	St. Louis	MO
Wilson	E. T.		Barton	VT
Wilson	F.		Kokomo	IN
Wilson	G.		Indianapolis	IN
Wilson	G. A.		Janesville	MN
Wilson	J. A.		Ottawa	IL
Wilson	J. C.		Cherokee	IA
Wilson	Jeremiah F.	322 South	Philadelphia	PA
Wilson	Jerome U.		Savannah	GA
Wilson	L. E.		Peterborough	NH
Wilson	M. C.	76 Pleasant	Malden	MA
Wilson	W. E.		Savannah	GA
Wilson	J. B.	389 State	Chicago	IL
Wilson & Son James A.			New Albany	IN
Wilson & Vaughn			Savannah	GA
Wilson*	J. A.		Harper	KS
Wilt & Son			Franklin	PA
Wimermark	Mrs. A. H.	179 Chicago	Chicago	IL
Wimermark & Field*			Cambridge	IL
Winans	E. R.		Oneonta	NY
Winans	Solomon		Jefferson City	MO
Winchester	F. E.		Walla Walla	WA
Winder	Gustav	118 Myrtle	Brooklyn	NY
Windmayer & Co.*			New Kiowa	KS
Wing & Allen			San Francisco	CA
Wing & Co.	S.	120 Cambridge	Boston	MA
Wing & Co.	S.	478 Washington	Boston	MA
Wingard	Frederick	173 W. Indiana	Chicago	IL
Winkle	Joseph		Wild Rose	WI
Winkler	Otto M.	1114 Salisbury	St. Louis	MO
Winn	J. M.		Ottumwa	IA
Winney	M. A.	216 Kansas	Topeka	KS
Winslow	Nathan	294 Bowery	New York City	NY
Winslow	Nathan	381 Canal	New York City	NY
Winslow	Nathan	274 Grand	New York City	NY
Winslow*	Nathan	228 Bowery	New York City	NY
Winsor & Whipple			Olean	NY
Winstead	F. M.		Wilson	NC
Winter	J. W.	Washington c. Salina	Syracuse	NY
Winters	C. L.		Eugene City	OR
Winters	C. L.		Prineville	OR

ALPHABETICAL LISTING OF PHOTOGRAPHERS IN THE U. S. IN 1888 & 1889

NAME		ADDRESS	CITY	STATE
Winters Bros.			Kenton	OH
Wires	William H.		Lynn	MA
Wise	S. H.		Wilton Junction	IA
Wismer	Christian		Santa Rosa	CA
Wiston	Samuel C.		Salem	MA
Withers	E. H.		Streator	IL
Withers	William C.	2037 N. Front	Philadelphia	PA
Withington	A. E.		Danielsonville	CT
Witter	A. L.		Pecatonica	IL
Wittkins	Bernard	116 Bowery	New York City	NY
Wixson	G. S.		Cheboygan	MI
Wixson & McCourt			Escanabo	MI
Wolbach	T. D.		Wadsworth	OH
Wolcott	C. S.		Coldwater	MI
Wolcott	N. E.		Escanabo	MI
Wolcott	U. E.		Marinette	WI
Wolcott & Hendricks			Nashville	MI
Wolcott & Hendricks*			Negaunee	MI
Wolever	A.		Delphi	IN
Wolever	P. W.		La Fayette	IN
Wolfe*	H. F.		Newaygog	MI
Wolf	J. P.	224 State	Chicago	IL
Wolf	S. A.	428 J	Sacramento	CA
Wolfe	A. S.		Apollo	PA
Wolfe	J. J.		Lancaster	OH
Wolfe	M.	106 S. Main	Dayton	OH
Wolfenstein*	V.		New Bedford	MA
Wollensak	William	450 National	Milwaukee	WI
Wolsenstein	V.		New Bedford	MA
Wolt	Jacob	615 Broadway	Brooklyn	NY
Wonders	Lafe		Alliance	OH
Wood	D. H.		Henderson	TX
Wood	Fred J.	237 W. Canton	Boston	MA
Wood	Henry T.	615 Broad	Newark	NJ
Wood	J. G.		Towanda	PA
Wood	J. M.	496 Broadway	Albany	NY
Wood	J. W.		Lake City	MN
Wood	John	208 Bowery	New York City	NY
Wood	Richard L.	401 Canal	New York City	NY
Wood	T. H.		Geneva	NY
Wood	T. W.		Lower Lake	CA

ALPHABETICAL LISTING OF PHOTOGRAPHERS IN THE U. S. IN 1888 & 1889

NAME		ADDRESS	CITY	STATE
Wood	W. W.	56 State	Albany	NY
Wood & Co.	T. E.		Newburgh	NY
Woodbury	Mrs.		San Buenoventura	CA
Woodhill	J. W.		Natick	MA
Woodin	F. H.	831 Chapel	New Haven	CT
Woodruff	L.		Camden	NJ
Woodruff	W. C.		Pioneer	OH
Woods	A.		Oakland	CA
Woods	D. H.		Chico	CA
Woods	T. W.		Lock Haven	PA
Woodside	W. E.		Lowell	MA
Woodward*	George T.		Chillicothe	OH
Woodward	J. A.		Taunton	MA
Woodward*	L. F.		Schoolcraft	MI
Woodward	W. M.	180 N. High	Columbus	OH
Woodward & Co.	Clark		Portland	OR
Woodworth	H. S.		Chapman	NE
Woodworth	J. P.		Geneva	OH
Woolley	H. M.		Traer	IA
Wooster	Jno.		Jonesport	ME
Worden	N. R.	48 Winter	Boston	MA
Work	Frank P.		North Brookfield	MA
Workey	W. A.		Wakeeney	KS
Works	W. R.		Selma	AL
Wormell	E. O.		Burlington	VT
Wortham	J. D.		Winchester	VA
Worthley	W. E. G.		Lewiston	ME
Wright	C. B.		Argyle	WI
Wright	C. C.		Denver	CO
Wright	Charles J.		Houston	TX
Wright	D. H.		Terre Haute	IN
Wright	Elias		Henry	IL
Wright	G. Wallace		Rockville	CT
Wright	George B.		Worcester	NY
Wright	James	89 Fulton	New York City	NY
Wright	James L.		Comanche	TX
Wright	John		Clifford	MI
Wright	O. S.		Wellsville	NY
Wright	R. L.		Williamsport	PA
Wright	W. P.		Utica	NY

NAME		ADDRESS	CITY	STATE
Wright	W. W.		Corydon	IA
Wright	W. W.		San Jose	CA
Wright	William		Independence	KS
Wright & Co.			Richmond	VA
Wright Studio		518 ½ Congress	Portland	ME
Wrightson	Francis		Chesaning	MI
Wunder	H.	722 Fulton	Brooklyn	NY
Wunder	Mary A.	217 N Eutaw	Baltimore	MD
Wurst	Otto	180 6th	New York City	NY
Wyatt	Arthur B.		Brattleboro	VT
Wyatt	Mrs. M. J.		Holdredge	NE
Wybrandt	Frank	418 W. Market	Louisville	KY
Wyer	Henry S.		Yonkers	NY
Wykes	Warren		Grand Rapids	MI
Wyld	Frederick W.	1210 Columbia	Philadelphia	PA
Yager	Leroy		Paulding	OH
Yarrington & Rappertte			Williamsport	PA
Yeager, Jr.	L.		Decatur	IN
Yenni	C. T.	113 Canal	New Orleans	LA
Yeomans	O. L.		Gladbrook	IA
Yocum	A. M.		East Portland	OR
Yocum*	J. W.		Milo	IA
Yont	Alexander		Oshkosh	WI
Youndt	N. M.		Belvidere	IL
Young	C. P.		Utica	NY
Young	E. S.		Leon	IA
Young	Frank		Waterbury	CT
Young	G. A.		Hornellsville	NY
Young*	G. H.	136 Milwaukee	Chicago	IL
Young	G. W.		Princeton	WI
Young	George	220 Milwaukee	Chicago	IL
Young	J. A.		La Cygne	KS
Young	Mrs. M. J.		Fayetteville	AR
Young	P. R.		Oneonta	NY
Young	R. W.		Mattoon	IL
Young	Samuel		Willard	UT
Young	W. K.		Richmond	IN
Young	D. W.		Terre Haute	IN
Zay	F. B.		Findlay	OH
Zeit	Robert		Medford	WI
Zeleny	A. L.	417 Woodland	Cleveland	OH

ALPHABETICAL LISTING OF PHOTOGRAPHERS IN THE U. S. IN 1888 & 1889

NAME		ADDRESS	CITY	STATE
Zeller	F. M.		Richfield Springs	NY
Zeller	W. E.		Wellington	KS
Zelner	James		Mauch Chunk	PA
Zert	William		Medford	MA
Ziesik	Felix S.	365 Bowery	New York City	NY
Zieverink	A.	Colerain & Marshall	Camp Washington	OH
Zimmerman	C. A.		St. Paul	MN
Zimmerman	J. F.		Carey	OH
Zimmerman	William		Unionville	MI
Zook*	P. M.		Oregon	MO
Zorn	Philip	730 Spring Garden	Philadelphia	PA
Zundel	Adolph	405 Broadway	Brooklyn	NY
Zutterling	Peter	503 Vine	Cincinnati	OH

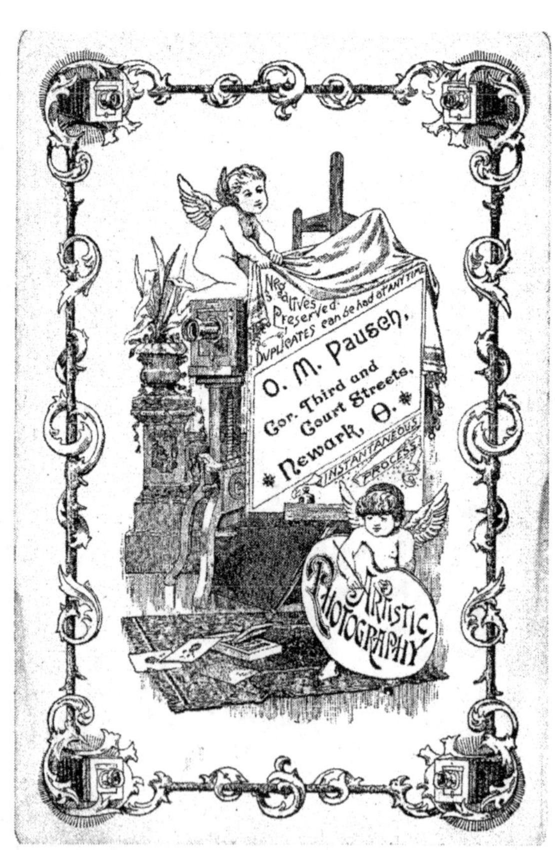

PHOTOGRAPHERS LISTED BY CITY/STATE IN THE UNITED STATES 1888-1889

NAME		ADDRESS	CITY	STATE
Oxford	A. C.		Birmingham	AL
Scholze	H.		Birmingham	AL
Shepherd & Sweeny			Birmingham	AL
Frazier & Wood			Chavis	AL
Nichols	J. D.		Eclectic	AL
Mangold	J. D.		Eufaula	AL
Watson	J. W.		Eufaula	AL
McMullen	C.		Greenville	AL
Collins	Ira F.		Huntsville	AL
Barnes	Chauncey		Mobile	AL
Copley	W. S.		Mobile	AL
Reed & Wallace			Mobile	AL
Sandoz	Albert		Mobile	AL
Boulter	D. K.		Montgomery	AL
Lakin	J. H.		Montgomery	AL
Nallen	C. H.		Montgomery	AL
Wallin	C. E.		Montgomery	AL
Crim*	J. T.		Opelinka	AL
Russell	S. A.		Oxanna	AL
Russell	R. U.		Oxanna	AL
Guenveur	S. F.		Selma	AL
Rosenberger	G. L.		Selma	AL
Works	W. R.		Selma	AL
Rosberry	R. L.		Talladega	AL
McIntire			Troy	AL
Magee	W. E.		Tuscaloosa	AL
Oswalt	M. E.		Tuscaloosa	AL
Turner	M.		Tuscaloosa	AL
O'Connor*	H. P.		Wetumka	AL
Robinson	H. F.		Phoenix	AZ
Buchman			Tucson	AZ
Goe	B. F.		Camden	AR
Harris	R.		Clarksville	AR
Fyler	F. F.		Eureka Springs	AR
Tibbs	N. J.		Eureka Springs	AR
Hughes	T. J.		Evansville	AR
Hausard	J. W.		Fayetteville	AR
Young	Mrs. M. J.		Fayetteville	AR
Roeder	T.		Fort Smith	AR
Kennedy	Jas. F.		Hot Springs	AR

PHOTOGRAPHERS LISTED BY CITY/STATE IN THE UNITED STATES 1888-1889

NAME		ADDRESS	CITY	STATE
Devinney	William		Judsonia	AR
Bankes	T. W.		Little Rock	AR
Cook	C. C.		Little Rock	AR
Dawson	R. W.		Little Rock	AR
William & Butz*			Little Rock	AR
Bryant & Chestnut			Monticello	AR
Shinn	H. A.		Pine Bluff	AR
Pernot	H. C.		Van Buren	AR
Cromwell	Oscar		Adin	CA
Graybiel	Edwin		Alameda	CA
Pellegrin	A. L.		Anaheim	CA
Weston	Henry		Anderson	CA
Jacobs	J. M.		Auburn	CA
Jacobs*	F. M.		Auburn	CA
Frye	H. H.		Chico	CA
Woods	D. H.		Chico	CA
Davidson	E. M.		Cloverdale	CA
Perkins	W. S.		Colfax	CA
Rankin	G. W.		College City	CA
Peacock	E. R.		Colton	CA
Boysen	I.		Colusa	CA
Boysen*	T.		Colusa	CA
Eldredge	I. E.		Crescent City	CA
Eldredge*	J. E.		Crescent City	CA
Branin	R. C.		Dixon	CA
Lillard	L.		Dixon	CA
Strong	N. P.		Eureka	CA
Grant*	H. M.		Eureka	CA
Higgins	E. R.		Fresno	CA
Rauscher	H.		Fresno	CA
Crawford	E. L.		Georgetown	CA
Moore	Arthur K.		Gilroy	CA
Clinch	W.		Grass Valley	CA
Piatt	C. E.		Healsburg	CA
Price	Andrew		Healsburg	CA
Pickett	J. M.		Hollister	CA
Suttlerley	Clement		Ione	CA
Kay	Wallace		Jackson	CA
Perkins & Baley			Lodi	CA
Davidson	L. S.		Los Angeles	CA

PHOTOGRAPHERS LISTED BY CITY/STATE IN THE UNITED STATES 1888-1889

NAME		ADDRESS	CITY	STATE
Ellis & Son			Los Angeles	CA
Evans	J. G.		Los Angeles	CA
Golsh	Arthur A. C.		Los Angeles	CA
Grasett & Boys			Los Angeles	CA
Kelly & Sobieski			Los Angeles	CA
Lawrence & Son			Los Angeles	CA
Payne*	D. R.		Los Angeles	CA
Schumacher	Frank G.		Los Angeles	CA
Stanton	T. E.		Los Angeles	CA
Westervelt	J. D.		Los Angeles	CA
Johnson	J. B.		Los Gatos	CA
Wood	T. W.		Lower Lake	CA
Higgins	E. R.		Madera	CA
Dean & Gray			Mariposa	CA
Griffiths	P. W.		Marysville	CA
Riley	J. J.		Marysville	CA
Perry	I. C.		Mendocino	CA
Edwards	John C.		Merced	CA
Edwards*	John E.		Merced	CA
Brown	William		Modesto	CA
Kendall	R. A.		Modesto	CA
Johnson	C. W. J.		Monterey	CA
Brayton	J. G.		Napa City	CA
Howland	B. F.		Napa City	CA
Swart	John S.		Nevada City	CA
Burgess	Charles F.	911 Broadway	Oakland	CA
Dames	W. W.	911 Broadway	Oakland	CA
Harknep	F. M.	556 E. 12th	Oakland	CA
Ingersoll	William B.	1069 Broadway	Oakland	CA
Ormsby	E. D.	1055 Broadway	Oakland	CA
Samuels	M. A.	10th & Clay	Oakland	CA
Schramm	Mathew		Oakland	CA
Smith	Jason	1716 7th	Oakland	CA
Walker	Charles. H.		Oakland	CA
Woods	A.		Oakland	CA
Hogan	J. H.		Oroville	CA
White	G. William		Pasadena	CA
Atwood	B. L.		Petaluma	CA
Reed	J. Q.		Petaluma	CA
Ross	George		Petaluma	CA

PHOTOGRAPHERS LISTED BY CITY/STATE IN THE UNITED STATES 1888-1889

NAME		ADDRESS	CITY	STATE
Baker	E. W.		Placerville	CA
Scrimminger	Mrs. W.		Pomona	CA
Shange	H. L.		Pomona	CA
Gaines	F. H.		Red Bluff	CA
Weston	H.		Red Bluff	CA
Welsh	J. O.		Redding	CA
Van Court	J. E.		Redwood City	CA
Collier	Charles T.		Riverside	CA
Vale & Pellegrin			Riverside	CA
Asher	Julius	810 ½ J	Sacramento	CA
Baldwin	J. E. D.	421 J.	Sacramento	CA
Beals	H. S.	415 J.	Sacramento	CA
Gregory	A. O.	502-504 J	Sacramento	CA
Hodson	J. R.	521 J	Sacramento	CA
Kerlin	T. J.	318-320 J	Sacramento	CA
Rudolph	Mrs. J. F.	627 J	Sacramento	CA
Seldner	Maurice	415 J	Sacramento	CA
Wolf	S. A.	428 J	Sacramento	CA
Bartley*	F. H.		Salinas	CA
Rifenburg	A. G.		Salinas	CA
Gills	F.		San Bernardino	CA
Sears	C. L.		San Bernardino	CA
Vale & Pellegrin			San Bernardino	CA
Wesner	H. B.		San Bernardino	CA
Brewster	J. C.		San Buenoventura	CA
Woodbury	Mrs.		San Buenoventura	CA
Parker	J. C.		San Diego	CA
Parker & Son*			San Diego	CA
Schramm	Matthew		San Diego	CA
Sheriff	J. A.		San Diego	CA
Allen & Hay		342 Kearney	San Francisco	CA
Bradley & Rulofson		14 Dupont	San Francisco	CA
Brown	T. A.	606 Kearney	San Francisco	CA
Brown & Karras		18 3rd	San Francisco	CA
Burnett & Slattery		6th c. Valencia	San Francisco	CA
Butler & Dorsez		715 Market	San Francisco	CA
Cathcart	W.	1073 ½ Market	San Francisco	CA
Cobb	D.	1144 Market	San Francisco	CA
Cramer	C. L.	402 Kearney	San Francisco	CA
Dall	John H.		San Francisco	CA

PHOTOGRAPHERS LISTED BY CITY/STATE IN THE UNITED STATES 1888-1889

NAME		ADDRESS	CITY	STATE
Dames & Butler		715 Market	San Francisco	CA
Dames*	W. W.		San Francisco	CA
Dowe	L.	4th c. Market	San Francisco	CA
Dowe	D. W.		San Francisco	CA
Duhem	Victor	1324 Polk	San Francisco	CA
Eduart	Alex	6 Turk	San Francisco	CA
Faist	C. G.	c. Market & 4th	San Francisco	CA
Flaglor	E. P.	SE c Market & 9th	San Francisco	CA
Foss	Oscar		San Francisco	CA
Fuller	A. W.	1150 Market	San Francisco	CA
Houseworth	Thomas	12 Montgomery	San Francisco	CA
Howe	J. M.	6 Eddy	San Francisco	CA
Howland*	B. F.		San Francisco	CA
Jeffers	William. H.	1202 Mission	San Francisco	CA
Jones & Lotz		838 Market	San Francisco	CA
Karras	M.	18 3rd	San Francisco	CA
Keil	Ed. A.	715 Market	San Francisco	CA
Klain	J. J.	921 McAllister	San Francisco	CA
Knight	George H.	19 6th	San Francisco	CA
Lainer & Co.	C.	31 3rd	San Francisco	CA
Lange	O. V.	1025 Market	San Francisco	CA
McMillan Bros.		8 6th	San Francisco	CA
McNicoll	John	SE c 15th & Mission	San Francisco	CA
Merrill	Stuart	659 Clay	San Francisco	CA
Morse	George D.	826 Market	San Francisco	CA
Mosher	J. W.	22 Kearny	San Francisco	CA
Nelson	C. A.	444 ½ 3rd	San Francisco	CA
Partman	Herman	337 Hayes	San Francisco	CA
Partridge	S. C.	529 Commercial	San Francisco	CA
Perkins	A. J.	1217 Polk	San Francisco	CA
Peters. & Co.	J. H.	25 3rd	San Francisco	CA
Pray	Fred H.	26 Montgomery	San Francisco	CA
Rieman & Pray		26 Montgomery	San Francisco	CA
Runnels & Stateler		957 Market	San Francisco	CA
Schoene	H.	504 Kearny	San Francisco	CA
Sewell & Co.	D.	25 3rd	San Francisco	CA
Shew	William	523 Kearny	San Francisco	CA
Silva	Joseph T.		San Francisco	CA
Stevens	A.	64 3rd	San Francisco	CA
Strebeck	W. M.	216 ½ O'Farrell	San Francisco	CA

PHOTOGRAPHERS LISTED BY CITY/STATE IN THE UNITED STATES 1888-1889

NAME		ADDRESS	CITY	STATE
Summerhags	William.	612 Clay	San Francisco	CA
Taber	I. W.	8 Montgomery	San Francisco	CA
Thors	F.		San Francisco	CA
Thors	Louis	1205 Larkin	San Francisco	CA
Vandersweep	J.		San Francisco	CA
Vaughan	Mrs. H. W.	724 ½ Market	San Francisco	CA
Watkins	C. E.	427 Montgomery	San Francisco	CA
Weitz	Hugo	34 3rd	San Francisco	CA
Weitz & Dijean*		34 3rd	San Francisco	CA
Williams & Norton		914 Market	San Francisco	CA
Wing & Allen			San Francisco	CA
Bacon Bros.			San Jose	CA
Loryea Bros			San Jose	CA
Lydston	A. F.		San Jose	CA
Macaulay	J. W.		San Jose	CA
Wright	W. W.		San Jose	CA
Arnold	W.		San Luis Obispo	CA
Dowe	O. W.		San Luis Obispo	CA
Bell & Melton			Santa Ana	CA
Crissman	J.		Santa Ana	CA
Cook	J. N.		Santa Barbara	CA
Rea	W. J.		Santa Barbara	CA
Springfield	A. M.		Santa Barbara	CA
Aichberg	C.		Santa Cruz	CA
Morris	Mrs. E. M.		Santa Cruz	CA
Reese	M. A.		Santa Cruz	CA
McMillan Bros			Santa Maria	CA
Davidson	N. R.		Santa Rosa	CA
Kempvanee	Henry		Santa Rosa	CA
Noe*	M.		Santa Rosa	CA
Wismer	Christian		Santa Rosa	CA
Swasey	B.		Shasta	CA
Baldwin	J. E. D.		Stockton	CA
Batchelder	B. P.		Stockton	CA
Bradley	A. O.		Stockton	CA
Elliott	Orman		Stockton	CA
Irvin	George C.		Stockton	CA
Monaco Bros			Stockton	CA
Spooner	J. P.		Stockton	CA
Dunham	O. W.		Susanville	CA

PHOTOGRAPHERS LISTED BY CITY/STATE IN THE UNITED STATES 1888-1889

NAME		ADDRESS	CITY	STATE
Curtis	C. C.		Traver	CA
Gage	H. K.		Truckee	CA
Bailey	A. F.		Tulare	CA
Carpenter	A. O.		Ukiah	CA
Halsey*	I. S.		Vallejo	CA
Smith	J. G.		Vallejo	CA
Watrous	S. W.		Visalia	CA
Fell	A. W.		Watsonville	CA
Lofland	D. R.		Watsonville	CA
Breeding	Walker		Willow	CA
Cook	W. B.		Willow	CA
Pickett	J. M.		Willow	CA
Creighton	J. M.		Winters	CA
Ley	T. A.		Woodland	CA
Williams	J. C.		Woodland	CA
Hanson	Jacob		Yreka	CA
Hausen*	Jacob		Yreka	CA
Williams	W. L.		Alamosa	CO
Hoosier	Isaac		Boulder	CO
Law	F.		Boulder	CO
Few	William E.		Canon City	CO
Gillingham	Charles L.		Colorado Springs	CO
Nims	F. A.		Colorado Springs	CO
Cornish	J. J.		Del Norte	CO
Bates	W. L.		Denver	CO
Beebe	John E.		Denver	CO
Chamberlain	W. G.		Denver	CO
Hudson*	J. L.		Denver	CO
Jackson & Co.	W. H.		Denver	CO
Nast*	J. E.		Denver	CO
Oakley	F. M.	PO Box 2718	Denver	CO
Post	J. E.		Denver	CO
Rinehart	A. F.		Denver	CO
Rose & Co.			Denver	CO
Stephan & Co.	George	1226-1232 Larimer	Denver	CO
Storm	F. D.		Denver	CO
Watson	H. W.		Denver	CO
Weittle	Charles		Denver	CO
Wright	C. C.		Denver	CO
Wilder	Edwin A.		Durango	CO

PHOTOGRAPHERS LISTED BY CITY/STATE IN THE UNITED STATES 1888-1889

NAME		ADDRESS	CITY	STATE
Talbot	N. H.		Evans	CO
Stair	L. E.		Florence	CO
Wilkins	G. T.		Fort Collins	CO
Martin	A.		Georgetown	CO
Walker	J. W.		Golden	CO
Barnhouse	T. E.		Grand Junction	CO
Koonz & Son	J.		Greeley	CO
Marsh	B. F.		Greeley	CO
Marsh Bros.			Greeley	CO
Pierce*	E. W.		Greeley	CO
Dean	Frank E.		Gunnison	CO
Brisbois	Mrs. M. L.		Leadville	CO
Clements	Ed. N.		Leadville	CO
Luke	W. O.		Leadville	CO
Stiffler	G. W.		Longmont	CO
Whitney	W. H.		Ouray	CO
Elliott*	John A.		Pueblo	CO
Mealy	M. W.		Pueblo	CO
Nast	J. E.		Pueblo	CO
Clark	C. H.		Salida	CO
Stone & Needles			South Pueblo	CO
Chase	D. B.		Trinidad	CO
Page	W. F.		Ansonia	CT
Miller	W. E.		Birmingham	CT
New York Photograph Gallery			Birmingham	CT
Betts	E. C.	356 Main	Bridgeport	CT
Bronson	C. R.	407 Main	Bridgeport	CT
Montignani	F. M.	304 Main	Bridgeport	CT
Seeley & Warnock		320 Main	Bridgeport	CT
Singhi	W. G.	Fairfield Ave.	Bridgeport	CT
Warnock	J.	58 State	Bridgeport	CT
Gale	H. N.		Bristol	CT
Terry	William A.		Bristol	CT
Lane	Frank P.		Clinton	CT
McIntosh	C. F.		Colchester	CT
Pierre	L. V.		Collinsville	CT
Pierce*	L. V.		Collinsville	CT
Couch	H. E.		Danbury	CT
Folsom	Mrs. J. H.		Danbury	CT
Lesure	H. A.		Danbury	CT

PHOTOGRAPHERS LISTED BY CITY/STATE IN THE UNITED STATES 1888-1889

NAME		ADDRESS	CITY	STATE
Ritton	E. D.		Danbury	CT
Davis	S. P.		Danielsonville	CT
Withington	A. E.		Danielsonville	CT
Hale	Frank W.		E. Hartford	CT
Lewis	Mrs. J. B.		Greenwich	CT
West	Redfield		Guilford	CT
Brooks	Arthur J.		Hartford	CT
Bundy	Horace L.	368 Main	Hartford	CT
Davison	Albert J.		Hartford	CT
DeLamater	R. S.	15 Pratt	Hartford	CT
Kellogg	Edwin P.	265 Main	Hartford	CT
Killam*	A.	37 Asylum	Hartford	CT
Knox	Herbert		Hartford	CT
Lay	H. E.	181 Main	Hartford	CT
National Ferrotype Co.			Hartford	CT
Olsen	Johann	449 Main	Hartford	CT
Orgill	John	281 Main	Hartford	CT
Rodgers	Hart J.	471 Main	Hartford	CT
St. John	Henry	368 Main	Hartford	CT
Stuart	Charles T.	368 Main	Hartford	CT
Taylor	Thomas	24 Union PL	Hartford	CT
Edwards	D. E.		Huntington	CT
Benedict	Neal D.		Litchfield	CT
French	D.		Meriden	CT
Green	J. F.		Meriden	CT
Marshall	W.		Meriden	CT
Wheeler	Frank		Meriden	CT
Wheeler	W. W.		Meriden	CT
Henigar	G. W.		Middletown	CT
Moore	F. J.		Middletown	CT
New England Engraving Co.			Middletown	CT
Oldarshaw	T. S.		Middletown	CT
Glancy	S. W.		Milford	CT
Brassart	A.		Naugatuck	CT
Allderidge	F. W.		New Britain	CT
Lewis	J. A.		New Britain	CT
Moffitt	A. L.		New Britain	CT
Howe	T.		New Canaan	CT
Myers	J. S.		New Hartford	CT
Babb	G. W.	Chapel St.	New Haven	CT

PHOTOGRAPHERS LISTED BY CITY/STATE IN THE UNITED STATES 1888-1889

NAME		ADDRESS	CITY	STATE
Beers	W. A.	762 Chapel	New Haven	CT
Blake*	J. M.	1 York Square	New Haven	CT
Bowman	R. M.	1075 Chapel	New Haven	CT
Bundy & Filley		838 Chapel	New Haven	CT
Bundy*	J. K.		New Haven	CT
Bundy & Stoddard*		838 Chapel	New Haven	CT
Cramer*	Elijah A.	818 Chapel	New Haven	CT
Cramer & King		818 Chapel	New Haven	CT
DeSilva	Abraham M.	201 George	New Haven	CT
DeSilva*	Abraham M.	69 Church	New Haven	CT
Donnelly	W. F.	851 Chapel	New Haven	CT
Goodman	J. E.	69 Church	New Haven	CT
Guyer*	B. F.	110 Church	New Haven	CT
Homan	Charles.	858 Chapel	New Haven	CT
Hull	V. N.	823 Chapel	New Haven	CT
Hull*	O. N.	823 Chapel	New Haven	CT
Moulthrop*	M.	818 Chapel	New Haven	CT
Pach & Bros.	G. W.	1002 Chapel	New Haven	CT
Pardee	Phineas	746 Chapel	New Haven	CT
Phelps	G. C.	942 Chapel	New Haven	CT
Ramsdell	D. P.	817 Chapel	New Haven	CT
Schulze	Carl W. F.	101 High	New Haven	CT
Schulze*	Carl F. W.	25 Crown	New Haven	CT
Shaw	Walter	749 Chapel	New Haven	CT
Shumway	J. D.	902 Chapel	New Haven	CT
Tierney	J. J.	775 Chapel	New Haven	CT
Trellon	Oscar		New Haven	CT
Woodin	F. H.	831 Chapel	New Haven	CT
Bishop	Giles		New London	CT
Kenyon & Son	F. P.		New London	CT
Canfield Bros.			New Milford	CT
Coman	J. L.		N. Grosvenor Dale	CT
Blackman	C. A.		Norwalk	CT
North	C. S.		S. Norwalk	CT
Readman	F. E.		Norwalk	CT
Allen	F. L.		Norwich	CT
Anderson	George		Norwich	CT
Ayer	E.		Norwich	CT
Durgan	James O.		Norwich	CT
Hubbell	R. M.		Norwich	CT

PHOTOGRAPHERS LISTED BY CITY/STATE IN THE UNITED STATES 1888-1889

NAME		ADDRESS	CITY	STATE
Laighton Bros.			Norwich	CT
Webster	E. Z.		Norwich	CT
Tucker	E. N.		Oxford	CT
Allderidge	W.		Plainville	CT
Loomis	J. R.		Plymouth	CT
Carr & Brown			Putnam	CT
Bolton	George M.		Rockville	CT
Newell	A. R.		Rockville	CT
Wright	G. Wallace		Rockville	CT
Hoff	C. A.		South Manchester	CT
Hazard	E. W.		Southington	CT
Balcom	Abram		Stamford	CT
Hendricks	William.		Stamford	CT
Hull	O. S.		Thomaston	CT
Baldwin	A. A.		Torrington	CT
Mills & Cole			Torrington	CT
St. John	Henry		Wallingford	CT
Smales	Thomas		Washington Depot	CT
Adt	Alfred A.	63 Bank	Waterbury	CT
Adt & Brother			Waterbury	CT
Alldridge*	J. W.	42 Bank	Waterbury	CT
Benedict	C. B.	70 Bank	Waterbury	CT
Benton	L. B.	155 Bank	Waterbury	CT
Chabiss & Co.	H.	189 ½ Bank	Waterbury	CT
Delius	W.	100 Bank	Waterbury	CT
Farrell	J. F.		Waterbury	CT
Glenney	S. W.	11 Exchange Pl	Waterbury	CT
Granniss	C. N.	48 Bank	Waterbury	CT
Smith	P.	Bank	Waterbury	CT
Spencer	G. B.		Waterbury	CT
Stahmer	A. J.		Waterbury	CT
Young	Frank		Waterbury	CT
Collins	D. C.		West Haven	CT
Ross	C. L.		Willimantic	CT
Townsend	C. H.		Willimantic	CT
Whitney	E. T.		Wilton	CT
Miller	J. Q.		Aberdeen	DK
Barton	M. B.		Alexandria	DK
Ferrin	P. E.		Altoona	DK
Fullerton	R. W.		Bathgate	DK

PHOTOGRAPHERS LISTED BY CITY/STATE IN THE UNITED STATES 1888-1889

NAME		ADDRESS	CITY	STATE
Barry	D. F.		Bismark	DK
Judkins	L. D.		Bismark	DK
Ryan	W. A.		Blunt	DK
Hanson	S. P.		Bridgewater	DK
Locke	Robert		Canton	DK
Saterbo	Hans		Canton	DK
Hamlin	J. R.		Casselton	DK
Hyde	M. F.		Chamberlain	DK
Hatter	G. L.		Clark	DK
Van Buskirk*	Charles		Columbia	DK
Aaberg	John		Cooperstown	DK
Kersting			Deadwood	DK
Pollock	Albert		Deadwood	DK
Scott	G. W.		Deadwood	DK
Cooledge	H. W.		De Smet	DK
Tilton	G. W.		Dickinson	DK
Quiggle	H. F.		Doland	DK
Thompson	R. R.		Drayton	DK
Close & Perkins			Elkton	DK
Applequist	A. J.		Ellendale	DK
Bestic & Logan			Fargo	DK
Haynes*	F. J.		Fargo	DK
Haynes	Jay J.		Fargo	DK
Wigness & Foseide			Fargo	DK
Albright & Bernard			Fort Burford	DK
Ball	J. D.		Grafton	DK
Frovarp	C. R.		Grafton	DK
Berg	Jacob		Grand Forks	DK
Blackburn	G. F.		Grand Forks	DK
Caswell	William		Grand Forks	DK
Steinbauer	Henry		Groton	DK
Thompson & Grier			Hamilton	DK
Thomson			Hatton	DK
Skrivseth	J. L.		Hillsboro	DK
Walker & Loofbourow			Hillsboro	DK
Lane	E. S.		Hope	DK
Robinson	F. N.		Howard	DK
Newcomb	C. H.		Huron	DK
Judd	C. L.		Jamestown	DK
Budd*	James		Lakota	DK

NAME		ADDRESS	CITY	STATE
Clow	W. F.		Lisbon	DK
Lockwood*	Miss M. S.		Lisbon	DK
Munson	J. M.		Madison	DK
Gilbert	Zallman		Mandan	DK
Lien	C. K.		Mayville	DK
Moe	E. J.		Millbank	DK
Templeman	J. N.		Miller	DK
Vernon	C. D.		Minto	DK
Fox & Wiltse			Mitchell	DK
Bjornson	S. J.		Mountain	DK
Ball	H. A.		Park River	DK
Parfitt	William		Parker	DK
Moore & Co.	C.		Pembina	DK
Kelly	R. L.		Pierre	DK
Baker	Mrs.		Rapid City	DK
Boyd & Orr			Rapid City	DK
Anderson	P. G.		Redfield	DK
Beam	L. V.		Sioux Fall	DK
Lasseson	P. E.		Sioux Fall	DK
McMillan*	F. H.		Sioux Fall	DK
Couis & Finn			Spearfish	DK
Buskirk	C. V.		Theodore	DK
Templeton	A. J.		Tower City	DK
Sanders	A. M.		Valley City	DK
Butler	Henry		Vermillion	DK
Hingtgen	T. J.		Wahpeton	DK
Spalt*	F. R.		Wahpeton	DK
Newcomb	C. H.		Watertown	DK
Staley	J. M.		Watertown	DK
Levoy	L. T.		Webster	DK
Fritz	M. J.		White Lake	DK
Tritz*	M. J.		White Lake	DK
Root	D. O.		Woonsocket	DK
Hamel	E. H.		Yankton	DK
Rounds	A. A.		Yankton	DK
Weelpe	Nicholas		Yankton	DK
Hunter	Thomas		Young	DK
Beecher*	A. S.		Dover	DE
Holmes	R. C.		Dover	DE
Vane	J. H.		Dover	DE

PHOTOGRAPHERS LISTED BY CITY/STATE IN THE UNITED STATES 1888-1889

NAME		ADDRESS	CITY	STATE
Holmes	Russell		Milford	DE
Bradford	G. W.		Smyrna	DE
Baugh	George W.		Wilmington	DE
Beckett	C. J. H.		Wilmington	DE
Brown	J. Paul		Wilmington	DE
Faivre	L. H.		Wilmington	DE
Garrett	M. & W.		Wilmington	DE
Holland	T. G.		Wilmington	DE
Jordan	James J.		Wilmington	DE
Maybin	Joseph A.		Wilmington	DE
Westcott & Cummings			Wilmington	DE
Anthony	William H.	905 Pennsylvania	Washington	DC
Bell	Charles M.	463 Pennsylvania	Washington	DC
Bowdoin	Gilbert T.	1115 Pennsylvania	Washington	DC
Butts & Co.*		936 F	Washington	DC
Butts & Co.		965 F	Washington	DC
Chester & Handy		494 Maryland	Washington	DC
Columbus	Archibald C.	805 Market	Washington	DC
Davis	G. W.	925 Pennsylvania	Washington	DC
Estabrook	Charles B.	711 Market	Washington	DC
Fullmer	J. A.	723 7th	Washington	DC
Handy	Levin C.	494 Maryland	Washington	DC
Jarvis	John F.	135 Pennsylvania	Washington	DC
Johnson Bros.		469 Pennsylvania	Washington	DC
Johnson	Newton G.	1211 3rd	Washington	DC
Jordan	Ella G.	1227 Pennsylvania	Washington	DC
Kets	Kennethy M.	1109 Pennsylvania	Washington	DC
Lardner & Barr		927 Pennsylvania	Washington	DC
Lewis	G. C.	1427 F	Washington	DC
Marshall & Gilling		816 Market	Washington	DC
Merritt & Wood		925 Pennsylvania	Washington	DC
National View Co.		1420 Pennsylvania	Washington	DC
New Photo Art Co.		905 Pennsylvania	Washington	DC
Parker	Charles	477 Pennsylvania	Washington	DC
Phipps	William	708 7th	Washington	DC
Piper*	Simeon	939 Pennsylvania	Washington	DC
Prince	George	403 11th	Washington	DC
Pullman	Edgar J.	935 Pennsylvania	Washington	DC
Reed	W. H.	628 Pennsylvania	Washington	DC
Rice	Moses P.	1219 Pennsylvania	Washington	DC

PHOTOGRAPHERS LISTED BY CITY/STATE IN THE UNITED STATES 1888-1889

NAME		ADDRESS	CITY	STATE
Rodbird	James A.	305 7th	Washington	DC
Sheid	H.	401 7th	Washington	DC
Spedden	W. L.	723 7th	Washington	DC
Theilkuhl	G.	927 Pennsylvania	Washington	DC
Tralles	P.	309 9th	Washington	DC
Walz	R.	477 Pennsylvania	Washington	DC
Burgert	P. P.		Jacksonville	FL
Davis	G. W.		Jacksonville	FL
Mitchell	J. S.		Jacksonville	FL
Smith	J. F.		Jacksonville	FL
Esteves	A.		Key West	FL
Moffatt Bros.			Key West	FL
DeWaal	C. M.		Orlando	FL
Geer	L. H.		Orlando	FL
Wager	S. D.		Orlando	FL
Mangold	J. G.		Palatka	FL
Renshaw*	R.		Palatka	FL
Mancel	Henry		Pensacola	FL
Turton	George W.		Pensacola	FL
Walker	John A.		Pensacola	FL
Cox	W. A.		St. Augustine	FL
Pacetti	Gabriel N.		St. Augustine	FL
Pierron	G.		St. Augustine	FL
Sedgwick & Vannerson*			St. Augustine	FL
Ensminger Bros.			Sanford	FL
Field	J. C.		Tampa	FL
Van Riper	D. W.		Americus	GA
Clifton	Y. B.		Athens	GA
O'Kelley	James F.		Athens	GA
Edwards & Dorman			Atlanta	GA
Gardner	M. H. & W. H.		Atlanta	GA
Ivie	Theodore L.		Atlanta	GA
Kuhns	W. T.		Atlanta	GA
Motes	C. W.		Atlanta	GA
Slemmons	J. F.		Atlanta	GA
Thompson*	W. W.		Atlanta	GA
Van Stavoren			Atlanta	GA
Augusta Photo C.			Augusta	GA
Bassett & Payne			Augusta	GA
Cormany	M. L.		Augusta	GA

PHOTOGRAPHERS LISTED BY CITY/STATE IN THE UNITED STATES 1888-1889

NAME		ADDRESS	CITY	STATE
Jordan*	John T.		Augusta	GA
Pelot & Cole			Augusta	GA
Prather*	W. E.		Augusta	GA
Usher, Jr.	J.		Augusta	GA
Thomason & Cook			Ball Ground	GA
Menkee	L. E.		Barnesville	GA
Jackson	G. M.		Brunswick	GA
Jarvis	J. W.		Canton	GA
Stewart	John B.		Carrollton	GA
Clark	A. W.		Cedartown	GA
Echard*	A. C.		Cedartown	GA
Pearson	S. M.		Cochran	GA
Steeley	W. R.		Cochran	GA
Modder*	C. A.		Columbus	GA
Riddle	A. J.		Columbus	GA
Williams	A. A.		Columbus	GA
Williams	Giles T.		Columbus	GA
Heard & Delaney			Dalton	GA
Heroff*	J. A.		Danielsville	GA
Peeples	L. W.		Dawson	GA
Lynch	H.		Flovilla	GA
Ender*	J. E.		Fort Gaines	GA
White	N. C.		Gainesville	GA
Mills	C. B.		Greensboro	GA
Deane	R. J.		Griffin	GA
Schaub	J. L.		La Grange	GA
Baurmann	G.		Macon	GA
Daniels	C. F.		Macon	GA
Pugh	James A.		Macon	GA
Richter	M. L.		Madison	GA
Gable	G.		Marietta	GA
Fairfield	T. J.		Milledgeville	GA
Arrington	F. P.		Millen	GA
Jackson & Clower			Newman	GA
Crenshaw*	S. H.		Price	GA
Curtis	W. A.		Rabun Gap	GA
Hermes, Jr.	A. J.		Savannah	GA
Launey & Goebel			Savannah	GA
Wilson	Jerome U.		Savannah	GA
Wilson	W. E.		Savannah	GA

PHOTOGRAPHERS LISTED BY CITY/STATE IN THE UNITED STATES 1888-1889

NAME		ADDRESS	CITY	STATE
Wilson & Vaughn			Savannah	GA
Beauchamp*	C. E.		Tallapoosa	GA
Goodloe	W.		Valdosta	GA
Grubbs	J. A.		Waynesborough	GA
Stephens	H. H.		Waynesborough	GA
Haynes & White			Eagle Rock	ID
Johnson	William		Abingdon	IL
McConnell	F. B.		Albion	IL
Root	W. H.		Aledo	IL
Boyer	T. G.		Altamont	IL
Walker	G. H.		Altamont	IL
Crossman	C. L.		Alton	IL
Fortin*	Joseph		Alton	IL
Lewis	German		Amboy	IL
Shurtleff	Henry		Amboy	IL
Berger	Frederick		Anna	IL
Goodman*	J. W.		Apple River	IL
Moore	A. C.		Arcola	IL
Welsh	William		Ashton	IL
Dodge	S.		Assumption	IL
Sheahan	James		Astoria	IL
Browning	G. W.		Atlanta	IL
Ketchum	W. G.		Augusta	IL
Arcouet	Casimer		Aurora	IL
Pratt	De W. C.		Aurora	IL
Reiff	J. F.		Aurora	IL
Snook	V. H.		Aurora	IL
Taylor	S. B.		Aurora	IL
Christian	J.		Ava	IL
Benedict	W. W.		Barrington	IL
Burnham	E. R.		Barry	IL
Whitney	L. M.		Batavia	IL
Proctor	J. B.		Batchtown	IL
Ficken & Haines*			Baylis	IL
Schaeffer	W. L.		Beardstown	IL
Blurton	W. F.		Beecher City	IL
Crouch	W. T.		Belleville	IL
Shultz*	Mr. & Mrs.		Belvidere	IL
Smedley	J. E.		Belvidere	IL
Youndt	N. M.		Belvidere	IL

PHOTOGRAPHERS LISTED BY CITY/STATE IN THE UNITED STATES 1888-1889

NAME		ADDRESS	CITY	STATE
Hodge	L. F.		Bement	IL
Buchannan	J. G.		Benton	IL
Browing	G. W.		Bloomington	IL
Bush & Kadgehn			Bloomington	IL
Fenwick	Richard		Bloomington	IL
Garrett	T. P.		Bloomington	IL
Keeran	J. W.		Bloomington	IL
Nute	C. N.		Bloomington	IL
Tankersley	J. R.		Bloomington	IL
Luchtemey	Louis		Blue Island	IL
O'Hara	A.		Bowensburgh	IL
Stirrat*	Robert		Braceville	IL
Canfield	H. A.		Braidwood	IL
Ford	B. A.		Braidwood	IL
Griswold	T. F.		Braidwood	IL
Grover*	W. H.		Bridgeport	IL
Rice*	S. A.		Brighton	IL
Atkins	W. B.		Bunker Hill	IL
Alvord	E. D.		Bushwell	IL
Pierce	H. C.		Bushwell	IL
McIntire & Steele*			Cairo	IL
Phelps	A. O.		Cairo	IL
Allen	W. R.		Cambridge	IL
Wimermark & Field*			Cambridge	IL
Holden	C. W.		Camp Point	IL
Breath	E. H.		Canton	IL
Mangrum & Moran			Canton	IL
Seavey	William		Canton	IL
Hudson	Alinzar		Carbondale	IL
Stewart	J. G.		Carlinville	IL
James, Jr.	Thomas		Carlyle	IL
Bowen	J. C.		Carmi	IL
Willis	Abner		Carmi	IL
Beatty	J. W.		Carrollton	IL
Simpson	Crit		Carthage	IL
Ethelberry	William		Casey	IL
Evans	Z. W.		Centralia	IL
Gray	John C.		Centralia	IL
Kohn	Arnold		Centralia	IL
McKnight	Frank		Centralia	IL

PHOTOGRAPHERS LISTED BY CITY/STATE IN THE UNITED STATES 1888-1889

NAME		ADDRESS	CITY	STATE
Abernathy	Arthur		Champaign	IL
Holland	O. E.		Champaign	IL
Naughton	Thomas		Champaign	IL
Hall	A. H.		Chatsworth	IL
Kelly Bros.			Chenoa	IL
Smith	Thomas		Chester	IL
Abbott	C. A.	351 Lincoln	Chicago	IL
Acme Copying Co.		302 W. VanBuren	Chicago	IL
Ahern	John	175 Milwaukee	Chicago	IL
Ahlbon*	W. H.	335 W. Madison	Chicago	IL
Ahlborn	W. H.	335 W. Madison	Chicago	IL
Ames	A. E.	214 State	Chicago	IL
Ames & Co.	A. E.	3035 Indiana	Chicago	IL
Ansher	L.	57 W. Madison	Chicago	IL
Ansher*	Louis	835 S. Halsted	Chicago	IL
Anson	E.	46 W. Madison	Chicago	IL
Armor	A. H.	465 W. Indiana	Chicago	IL
Asthoff	Herman	237 N. Clark	Chicago	IL
Auberts	A. J.	305 North	Chicago	IL
Baird	J. H.	209 Wabash	Chicago	IL
Balatka Bros.		363 Division	Chicago	IL
Baldwin & Ames		55 Central Music Hall	Chicago	IL
Baldwin & Charles		2029 Wabash	Chicago	IL
Ball*	H. A.	333 W. 14th	Chicago	IL
Bassett*	G. T.		Chicago	IL
Bender	Louis	305 North	Chicago	IL
Bennett	C. E.	3915 Cottage Grove	Chicago	IL
Berlin Photographic Studio*			Chicago	IL
Bertrand	S. A.	149 Chicago	Chicago	IL
Bielefield	P. F.	169 Canalport	Chicago	IL
Bigden	F. A.	262 W. Madison	Chicago	IL
Bitter & Weston		148 State	Chicago	IL
Blanchard*	J. B.	57 W. Madison	Chicago	IL
Blumenshein	George	2826 State	Chicago	IL
Bodge	E. R.	330 E. Division	Chicago	IL
Borchers	A.	894 Sheffield	Chicago	IL
Boyd	S.	2176 Archer	Chicago	IL
Brand	E. L.	212 Wabash	Chicago	IL
Brown	W. S.	123 S. Halsted	Chicago	IL
Burt Studio		103 State	Chicago	IL

PHOTOGRAPHERS LISTED BY CITY/STATE IN THE UNITED STATES 1888-1889

NAME		ADDRESS	CITY	STATE
Busse*	R.	113 N. Halsted	Chicago	IL
Busse	Robert	165 W. Madison	Chicago	IL
Butkiewicz & Putrament		662 Noble	Chicago	IL
Canova Studios		241 Wabash	Chicago	IL
Charles & Hultgren		2029 Wabash	Chicago	IL
Chicago Art Publishing Co.		134 VanBuren	Chicago	IL
Chouinard	R. L.	775 S. Halsted	Chicago	IL
Clark	D. R.	2134 Michigan	Chicago	IL
Clement	E. L.	8-10 S. Peoria	Chicago	IL
Cooper	C. E.	631 W. Lake	Chicago	IL
Copelin	A. J. W.	237 Dearborn	Chicago	IL
Copelin Photographic	Studio	75 Madison	Chicago	IL
Cordingly	John	2106 Wabash	Chicago	IL
Coulter*	H. A.	134 E. Madison	Chicago	IL
Culver*	W. A.	134 E. Madison	Chicago	IL
Cunningham & Herbaugh*		57 W. Madison	Chicago	IL
Denison & Roberts		3907 Cottage Grove	Chicago	IL
Dippe	Henry	356 W. Chicago	Chicago	IL
Edgeworth	A. D.	157 S. Paulina	Chicago	IL
Edgeworth	Reuben	167 Blue Island	Chicago	IL
Evans		485 State	Chicago	IL
Evans	R.	207 S. Halsted	Chicago	IL
Felt	L. W.	215 Chicago	Chicago	IL
Fleischer	P.	249 Chicago	Chicago	IL
Fleischer*	Paul	245 N. Clark	Chicago	IL
Foster	W. E.	542 State	Chicago	IL
Fowler	Ed. L.	3105 Prairie	Chicago	IL
Friesleben	L. W.	3922 State	Chicago	IL
Fulsang	J.	2486 Archer	Chicago	IL
Garniere & Layton		3140 State	Chicago	IL
Garrity*	Misses &			
Woollett*	Mr.	430 N. Clark	Chicago	IL
Garvin	J. F.	1546 Wabash	Chicago	IL
Garvin*	J. F.	1230 State	Chicago	IL
Gehrig	J. W.	337 W. Madison	Chicago	IL
Gentile & Co.		81 State	Chicago	IL
Gentzel	A. H.	659 Lincoln	Chicago	IL
Gentzel*	A. H.	289 W. 12th	Chicago	IL
Victor & Co.	George	189 N. Clark	Chicago	IL
Gittings	J. H.	3432 Cottage Grove	Chicago	IL

PHOTOGRAPHERS LISTED BY CITY/STATE IN THE UNITED STATES 1888-1889

NAME		ADDRESS	CITY	STATE
Globe Novelty Co.		150 Dearborn	Chicago	IL
Goin	J. M.	101 W. Madison	Chicago	IL
Goldsmith Bros.			Chicago	IL
Goodell & Ganiere		299 W. Indiana	Chicago	IL
Graeff	Adolph	679 W. Lake	Chicago	IL
Greene	P. B.	342 W. Adams	Chicago	IL
Ham*	R. N.	357 W. Madison	Chicago	IL
Hanson	W. R.	884 Milwaukee	Chicago	IL
Harris	George A.	150 State	Chicago	IL
Harris & Co.*	George A.	148 State	Chicago	IL
Hartley	E. F.	309 W. Madison	Chicago	IL
Harvey	C. E.	3115 Indiana	Chicago	IL
Harvey & Lyles		271 Wabash	Chicago	IL
Harwick	E. B.	229 State	Chicago	IL
Hasenbein	H.	876 W. 21st	Chicago	IL
Heim	A.	876 W. 21st	Chicago	IL
Henshel	W. W.	3136 Cottage Grove	Chicago	IL
Henshel*	W. M., mgr	3136 Cottage Grove	Chicago	IL
Hesler	Alexander	99 State	Chicago	IL
Hilton	W. H .	7 Blue Island	Chicago	IL
Hirsch	William	245 Blue Island	Chicago	IL
Hobart	C.	134 E. Madison	Chicago	IL
Hough	J.	135 Chicago	Chicago	IL
Hough*	Joshua	125 E. Chicago	Chicago	IL
Huszah	O. H.	163 S. Halsted	Chicago	IL
Huszah	W. O.	1553 Wabash	Chicago	IL
Hutchinson	H. S.	149 22nd	Chicago	IL
Israel	S. G. & R. B.		Chicago	IL
Iverson*	H.	2176 Archer	Chicago	IL
Izard & Co.		229 State	Chicago	IL
Jacobson	O. C.	488 Milwaukee	Chicago	IL
Jaeger	Henry	302 S. Halsted	Chicago	IL
Jaeger*	H. J.	86 S. Halsted	Chicago	IL
Jaison	D.	237 Clark	Chicago	IL
Jestram	Henry	393 Blue Island	Chicago	IL
Johles	Robert	477 Milwaukee	Chicago	IL
Johnson & Co.		717 S. Halsted	Chicago	IL
Johnson	J. Scott	R 17, 134 Madison	Chicago	IL
Kanberg	J. J.	433 Division	Chicago	IL
Keeley*	H. C.	174 S. Halsted	Chicago	IL

PHOTOGRAPHERS LISTED BY CITY/STATE IN THE UNITED STATES 1888-1889

NAME		ADDRESS	CITY	STATE
Keeley	H. C.	1 Blue Island	Chicago	IL
Kelman & Spate*		305 E. Division	Chicago	IL
Kersting	H. C.	730 Milwaukee	Chicago	IL
Klein	George J.	206 N. Clark	Chicago	IL
Kooy	P.	90 N. Clark	Chicago	IL
Kraft*	L. A.	150 State	Chicago	IL
Kraft	L. A.	634 N. Clark	Chicago	IL
Kruse	August	255 North	Chicago	IL
Lambder	J. S.	95 E. Chicago	Chicago	IL
Larsen	Nicholas	465 W. Indiana	Chicago	IL
La Tour*	A. E.	249 Chicago	Chicago	IL
Le Bau	J. S.	167 Blue Island	Chicago	IL
Levin	Henry	430 N. Clark	Chicago	IL
Lewis	Augustus B.	306 Ogden	Chicago	IL
Lonergan	M. B.	3 N. Clark	Chicago	IL
Loomis	S. C.	357 W. Madison	Chicago	IL
Luplan	L.	169 Canalport	Chicago	IL
McDonald	G. H.	289 W. Madison	Chicago	IL
McLellan*	W. E.	363 E. Division	Chicago	IL
Malousek & Rubicek*		635 Blue Island	Chicago	IL
Markley & Son	T.	870 W. Madison	Chicago	IL
Martin	E. R.	296 S. Clark	Chicago	IL
Matousek	M.	635 Blue Island	Chicago	IL
Mauer*	Max	379 State	Chicago	IL
Mauer	Max	305 Division	Chicago	IL
Maul	Jacob	439 Milwaukee	Chicago	IL
Mehrle*	F. W.	345 W. Indiana	Chicago	IL
Melander & Bro.	L. M.	208 E. Ohio	Chicago	IL
Melander	S. P.	659 Sedgwick	Chicago	IL
Meyer	Adolph	c. Milwaukee & Ashland	Chicago	IL
Miller	Mrs. Jennie	157 Wabash	Chicago	IL
Mink	B. A.	715 S.Halsted	Chicago	IL
Mortensen	C. A.	173 W. Indiana	Chicago	IL
Mosher	C. D.	125 State	Chicago	IL
Myer	William	650 Milwaukee	Chicago	IL
Neibergall	Frederick	346 Larabee	Chicago	IL
Neidhardt*	G. E.	403 Larabee	Chicago	IL
Neidhardt	George E.	403 North	Chicago	IL
Neidhardt	H. F.	357 Milwaukee	Chicago	IL
Neidhardt*	H. F.	361 Milwaukee	Chicago	IL

PHOTOGRAPHERS LISTED BY CITY/STATE IN THE UNITED STATES 1888-1889

NAME		ADDRESS	CITY	STATE
Neidhardt	W.	984 Milwaukee	Chicago	IL
Nikodem*	A. M.	701 W. Madison	Chicago	IL
Nikodeur	Miss A. M.	701 Madison	Chicago	IL
Nye	W. A.	2228 Indiana	Chicago	IL
Olsen*	Charles	165 W. Madison	Chicago	IL
Orem	A. R.	717 S. Halsted	Chicago	IL
Orem*	A. R.	179 E. Chicago	Chicago	IL
Palmer	C. A.	207 S. Halsted	Chicago	IL
Panneberg	Amandus	219 North	Chicago	IL
Parr & Freeman*		299 W. Indiana	Chicago	IL
Parr*	J. S.	299 W. Indiana	Chicago	IL
Perry	Henry B.	3800 Cottage Grove	Chicago	IL
Perry & Varney*		3800 Cottage Grove	Chicago	IL
Peters	M. G.	3509 S. Halsted	Chicago	IL
Platz	Max	88 N. Clark	Chicago	IL
Rich	J. A.	95 Blue Island	Chicago	IL
Richards	R. B.	2826 State	Chicago	IL
Rider	B. L.	339 W. Madison	Chicago	IL
Robinson & Roe*		77 Clark	Chicago	IL
Robinson & Roe		79 Clark	Chicago	IL
Robinson	W. A.	631 W. Lake	Chicago	IL
Rocher	Henry	241 Wabash	Chicago	IL
Rose & Bassett*		103 State	Chicago	IL
Schmidt	L. N.	302 Milwaukee	Chicago	IL
Schmidt	Oscar	148 W. Randolph	Chicago	IL
Schneider	Peter	2135 Archer	Chicago	IL
Scholl	J. B.	547 S. Halsted	Chicago	IL
Scott	O. P.	2220 Indiana	Chicago	IL
Smith	Joshua	206 N. Clark	Chicago	IL
Sollitt	Thomas S.	2897 Archer	Chicago	IL
Sommer	C.	3810 State	Chicago	IL
Sommer*	Charles	3922 State	Chicago	IL
Stafford	Charles	3140 State	Chicago	IL
Starke & Thrall		60 Cass	Chicago	IL
Steffens	M. J.	2249 Cottage Grove	Chicago	IL
Stevens*	M. J.	108 Dearborn	Chicago	IL
Stevens	J. K.	55 McVicker's Theatre	Chicago	IL
Stone & Brooks		195 W. Indiana	Chicago	IL
Studley*	G. D.	46 W. Madison	Chicago	IL
Suessmmilch	F. V.	71 Washington	Chicago	IL

PHOTOGRAPHERS LISTED BY CITY/STATE IN THE UNITED STATES 1888-1889

NAME		ADDRESS	CITY	STATE
Taylor & Martin		81 State	Chicago	IL
Tohey	F. D.	145 22nd	Chicago	IL
Tomlinson	Anson	20 Claybourn	Chicago	IL
Tresselt	R.	984 Milwaukee	Chicago	IL
Urbano	Salvatore	1726 State	Chicago	IL
Vahlteich*	J.	292 North	Chicago	IL
Vahlteich	Julius	290 North	Chicago	IL
Von der Herd	F. D.	7 Blue Island	Chicago	IL
Vredenburg	Kelly	1013 W. Lake	Chicago	IL
Wahlstedt	Matilda	1 Blue Island	Chicago	IL
Wallace*	R. A.	154 Claybourn	Chicago	IL
Way	Fletcher	154 Claybourn	Chicago	IL
West	J. S.	96 Blue Island	Chicago	IL
Wilcox Bros		R45, 75 Madison	Chicago	IL
Wilson	J. B.	389 State	Chicago	IL
Wimermark	Mrs. A. H.	179 Chicago	Chicago	IL
Wingard	Frederick	173 W. Indiana	Chicago	IL
Wolf	J. P.	224 State	Chicago	IL
Young	George	220 Milwaukee	Chicago	IL
Young*	G. H.	136 Milwaukee	Chicago	IL
Baker*	H. J.		Chrisman	IL
Williams	W. C.		Clayton	IL
Wells	T. M.		Clinton	IL
Bosshard*	Gebhard		Cobden	IL
Pollock	David		Cobden	IL
Evans	G. E.		Collinsville	IL
Weible	E. T..		Columbia	IL
Rowe	Jesse		Cuba	IL
Cale	William		Dalson	IL
Boyce	Washington		Danville	IL
Lutes Bros			Danville	IL
Phillips	E. M.		Danville	IL
Phillips & Bergstresser			Danville	IL
Stone	M. T.		Danville	IL
Wells	W. H.		Danville	IL
Oleson*	J. O.		DeKalb	IL
Uleson	J. O.		DeKalb	IL
Haws	Mrs. Jennie		Decatur	IL
Piper	E. R.		Decatur	IL
Shiveley	E. W.		Decatur	IL

PHOTOGRAPHERS LISTED BY CITY/STATE IN THE UNITED STATES 1888-1889

NAME		ADDRESS	CITY	STATE
Krone*	Charles		Delavan	IL
Vosburgh	B. D.		Des Plaines	IL
Halstead	Joseph		Dixon	IL
McCune	Miles		Dixon	IL
Paris	R. A.		Dongola	IL
Thompson	J. R.		Dongola	IL
Dopp	J. C.		Du Quoin	IL
Wheatley	E. S.		Du Quoin	IL
Thorsen	John		Dundee	IL
Leach	A. L.		Dwight	IL
Walfrid*	Jonas		Dwight	IL
D'Lamatter	J. H.		Earlville	IL
Adams	R. F.		East St. Louis	IL
Cross	S. H.		Edwardsville	IL
Rundle*	Edward		Edwardsville	IL
Bissell	L. H.		Effingham	IL
Smith	L. F.		El Paso	IL
Adams	S. M.		Elgin	IL
Gerlach	C. S.		Elgin	IL
Platt	L. L.		Elgin	IL
Sherman	G. H.		Elgin	IL
Snow	Frank		Elgin	IL
Kolb	F. J.		Elizabeth	IL
Booth	S. L.		Elmwood	IL
Mendenhall	F. M.		Elmwood	IL
Van Patten	Emerson		Elmwood	IL
Smith	W. M.		Engelwood	IL
Moore	B. L.		Eureka	IL
Aikin	Charles		Evanston	IL
Stewart	H. F.		Evanston	IL
Tresize	W. F.		Fairbury	IL
Turnbull & Newton			Fairfield	IL
Barnes & White*			Farmer City	IL
Abbett	E. R.		Flora	IL
Heising	Fred		Frankfort Station	IL
Michaelis	Fred		Frankfort Station	IL
Kelly	J. C.		Freeburgh	IL
Allen	S. V.		Freeport	IL
Herlocker & Schaad			Freeport	IL
Kasten	William		Freeport	IL

PHOTOGRAPHERS LISTED BY CITY/STATE IN THE UNITED STATES 1888-1889

NAME		ADDRESS	CITY	STATE
Saul & Wareham			Freeport	IL
Thayer	O. B.		Freeport	IL
Barner	William		Galena	IL
Pooley	J. H.		Galena	IL
Barker	J. F.		Galesburgh	IL
Harrison	Thomas		Galesburgh	IL
Newberg	P. A.		Galesburgh	IL
Ney	Augustus		Galesburgh	IL
Emery	J. W.		Galva	IL
Weston*	B.		Galva	IL
Buell	J.		Geneseo	IL
Dubbs*	J. H.		Geneseo	IL
Kirkpatrick	W. L.		Geneseo	IL
Farley*	W. H.		Gibson City	IL
Jornes	F. W.		Girard	IL
Fahnestock	J. A.		Glasford	IL
Noel	C.		Grape Creek	IL
Butler	Elijah		Greenville	IL
Shields	H. H.		Greenville	IL
Clark	William		Griggsville	IL
Wendell	H.		Hampton	IL
Wilder*	W. W.		Harrisburg	IL
Parmley	C. H.		Harvard	IL
Hyder	Charles		Havana	IL
Abbott	C. E.		Henry	IL
Wright	Elias		Henry	IL
Jones	J. H.		Hillsborough	IL
Larrabee	F. H.		Hillsborough	IL
Luce	E. B.		Hinckley	IL
Pickerill	F. M.		Homer	IL
Hall	E. S.		Hoopeston	IL
Nidy & Zellar			Hutsonville	IL
Murphy			Ipava	IL
Morse	Andrew		Irving Park	IL
Clauser	W. H.		Jacksonville	IL
Clendenon & Nichols			Jacksonville	IL
Denton	J. W.		Jacksonville	IL
Humphrey	W. R.		Jacksonville	IL
Letton	J. A.		Jacksonville	IL
McKinnon & Kenneth			Jacksonville	IL

PHOTOGRAPHERS LISTED BY CITY/STATE IN THE UNITED STATES 1888-1889

NAME		ADDRESS	CITY	STATE
Gledhill	R. C.		Jerseyville	IL
Fay	W. D.		Joliet	IL
Gale	G. F.		Joliet	IL
Murr	Charles		Joliet	IL
Severn	Thomas		Joliet	IL
Westman	O. R.		Joliet	IL
Hotchkiss	Eugene		Kankakee	IL
Knowlton	Charles		Kankakee	IL
Voss	Charles		Kankakee	IL
Pardoe	H. W.		Keithsburgh	IL
Crowley & Frey			Kensington	IL
Johnson & Wilson			Kewanee	IL
Strong	L.		Kewanee	IL
Tyner	O. N.		Kinmundy	IL
Bryan	S. T.		Kirkwood	IL
Price	W. S.		La Fayette	IL
Libby	E. P.		La Harpe	IL
Gurrad	J. L.		La Salle	IL
Locke	W. A.		La Salle	IL
Forney	J. G.		Lacon	IL
Doolittle	A. P.		Lanark	IL
Ruschle	F. C.		Lanark	IL
Roberts	C. C.		Le Roy	IL
Lupton	John		Lebanon	IL
Anable	J. M.		Leland	IL
Wastermann	Otto		Lemont	IL
Harris	F.		Lena	IL
Tull	B. H.		Lena	IL
Taylor	C. H.		Lewistown	IL
Merrill	Stephen		Lexington	IL
Core	F. W.		Lincoln	IL
Tanley	W. S.		Lincoln	IL
Bickett	Hugh		Litchfield	IL
McManus	J. H.		Litchfield	IL
Richards	B. B.		Lockport	IL
Cleaver	John		Lovington	IL
Bennett	L. E.		McHenry	IL
Graites	H. W.		Macomb	IL
Patterson	Edgar		Macomb	IL
Philpot	Thomas		Macomb	IL

PHOTOGRAPHERS LISTED BY CITY/STATE IN THE UNITED STATES 1888-1889

NAME		ADDRESS	CITY	STATE
Cummingham	J. R.		Maquon	IL
Sherman	O. G.		Marengo	IL
Wilder	W. W.		Marion	IL
Arnold	C. R.		Marseilles	IL
Jenks*	J. M.		Marseilles	IL
Ring	S. T.		Marshall	IL
Snedeker	T. H. B.		Martinsville	IL
Miller	S. M.		Mason City	IL
Craycraft	A. B.		Mattoon	IL
Piatt	J. A.		Mattoon	IL
Young	R. W.		Mattoon	IL
Clark	J. W.		Mendota	IL
Clark & Son*	L. H.		Mendota	IL
Tansey	E. J.		Mendota	IL
Harris	N. J.		Meredosia	IL
Henderson	J. A.		Metropolis City	IL
Trostle	W. F.		Milford	IL
Plate	F.		Millstadt	IL
Hamrich	Wesley		Minonk	IL
Tice	C. E.		Minonk	IL
Lilly	T.		Mitchie	IL
Atkinson	C. W.		Moline	IL
Jones	T. M.		Moline	IL
Mangold	E. E.		Moline	IL
Miller	C. C.		Moline	IL
Porter*	Perez		Moline	IL
Denny	T. W.		Momence	IL
Nicol	John		Monmouth	IL
Root	Emerson		Monmouth	IL
Wildman	A. H.		Monticello	IL
Abbott	S. C.		Morris	IL
Crawford & Davis			Morris	IL
Griffing	W. W.		Morris	IL
Parker	W. L.		Morrison	IL
Sampson	Edward		Morrison	IL
Tilley	E. P.		Morrisonville	IL
Rockstead*	Andrew		Mount Carmel	IL
Whipple	S. M.		Mount Carmel	IL
Hoskings	J. M.		Mount Morris	IL
Duboce	M. A.		Mount Pulaski	IL

PHOTOGRAPHERS LISTED BY CITY/STATE IN THE UNITED STATES 1888-1889

NAME		ADDRESS	CITY	STATE
Grant	W. P.		Mount Sterling	IL
Hitchcock	James		Mount Vernon	IL
Tracy*	C. B.		Moweaqua	IL
Snodgrass	G. M.		Mulberry Grove	IL
Stewart	E. J.		Murphysborough	IL
Hohlweg	Louis		Naperville	IL
Kendig	A. C.		Naperville	IL
Standbrook	William		Nashville	IL
Williams	T. B.		New Boston	IL
Hammond	H.		New Windsor	IL
Maury	C. O.		Newton	IL
Steel	B. R.		Nokomis	IL
Davison	B.		Odin	IL
Burnett	Dryett		Olney	IL
Rush	Mrs. M. B.		Olney	IL
Lawhead	O. W.		Onarga	IL
Bulkley	J. A.		Oneida	IL
Curtis	C. L.		Oregon	IL
Wagner	A. H.		Oregon	IL
Osborn*	A. T.		Orion	IL
Bowman	W. E.		Ottawa	IL
Wheeler	W. S.		Ottawa	IL
Wilson	J. A.		Ottawa	IL
Tracy	C. B.		Pana	IL
Cashner	J. N.		Paris	IL
Davis	P. H.		Paris	IL
Martin	Jay		Paris	IL
Clark	W. S.		Paw Paw	IL
Bjorlund	Swamug		Paxton	IL
Noble	O. D.		Paxton	IL
Herves	George		Payson	IL
Witter	A. L.		Pecatonica	IL
Cole	H. H.		Pekin	IL
Sargent	M.		Pekin	IL
Carson*	A. M.		Peoria	IL
Erler	Max		Peoria	IL
Gray	Benjamin		Peoria	IL
Lasswell	G. F.		Peoria	IL
Loquist Bros.			Peoria	IL
Mills	Thomas		Peoria	IL

PHOTOGRAPHERS LISTED BY CITY/STATE IN THE UNITED STATES 1888-1889

NAME		ADDRESS	CITY	STATE
Myers	J. B.		Peoria	IL
Sawyer	Jesse		Peoria	IL
Smith	C. E.		Peoria	IL
Van Doelzen	J. A.		Peoria	IL
Elliott	S. D.		Perry	IL
Even	Joseph		Peru	IL
McCullough	C. S.		Petersburgh	IL
Ducobu	Gustav		Pickneyville	IL
Clark	L. W.		Pittsfield	IL
Obst	C. L.		Pittsfield	IL
Orr	C. E.		Plano	IL
Davison	J. A.		Polo	IL
Huntoon	R. C.		Pontiac	IL
Reed	N. H.		Pontiac	IL
Linnenschmidt*	H. E.		Port Byron	IL
Immke	H. W.		Princeton	IL
Masters	C. H.		Princeton	IL
Affolter	W. H.		Princeville	IL
Hadaway	Miss Julia		Prophetstown	IL
Chandler	Ellis		Quincy	IL
Long & Son	George		Quincy	IL
Reed	Mrs. W. A.		Quincy	IL
Ringgold	Mrs. J. H.		Quincy	IL
Rood, Jr.	W. D.		Quincy	IL
Scott	O. P.		Quincy	IL
Waide	H. M.		Quincy	IL
Warner	A. M.		Quincy	IL
Doran*	J. J. T.		Rantoul	IL
Webb	W. J.		Red Bud	IL
Lindsay	S. T.		Robinson	IL
Freeman	W. H.		Rochelle	IL
McCabe Bros.			Rock Island	IL
Rasmussen	Charles		Rock Island	IL
Sigmund	John		Rock Island	IL
Anderson	J. T.		Rockford	IL
Atchley	A. S.		Rockford	IL
Barnes	G. W.		Rockford	IL
Cook & Knowles			Rockford	IL
Erickson	Erich		Rockford	IL
Hakelier	Oscar		Rockford	IL

PHOTOGRAPHERS LISTED BY CITY/STATE IN THE UNITED STATES 1888-1889

NAME		ADDRESS	CITY	STATE
Hobart	J. A.		Rockford	IL
Medlar	J. B.		Rockford	IL
Risberg	J. O. P.		Rockford	IL
Mendenhall	J. B.		Roodhouse	IL
Koopman	H. R.		Roseland	IL
Lower	G. W.		Roseville	IL
Baird	J. A.		Rushville	IL
Bays	E. W.		Rushville	IL
Parker	J. W.		St. Charles	IL
Feltman	A. M.		Salem	IL
Evans	T. A.		Samoth	IL
Orr	C. E.		Sandwich	IL
Satterlee	A.		Sandwich	IL
Berker*	H. F.		Savanna	IL
Smith	C. O.		Saybrook	IL
Watson	S. A.		Seneca	IL
Carman*	I. D.		Shabbona	IL
Carman	J. D.		Shabbona	IL
Carroll	L. A.		Sheffield	IL
Morse	W. H.		Sheffield	IL
Austin	Honoria		Shelbyville	IL
Babb & Root			Shelbyville	IL
Launey	A. R.		Shelbyville	IL
Norton	E. B.		Shelbyville	IL
Ryan	D. J.		Shelbyville	IL
Brockway	A.		Sheldon	IL
Linder	C. W.		South Chicago	IL
Madsen*	Andrew		South Chicago	IL
Huebschmann	L. C. F.		Sparta	IL
Minner & Son	J. W.		Sparta	IL
Anderson	L. S.		Springfield	IL
Brittingham*	J. G.		Springfield	IL
Gardnier	C. W.		Springfield	IL
German	C. S.		Springfield	IL
Halliday & Kessberger			Springfield	IL
Hesse	Henry		Springfield	IL
Jorns	G. W.		Springfield	IL
Ketchum	M. D.		Springfield	IL
McNutty	Finley		Springfield	IL
Peaker	Thomas		Springfield	IL

PHOTOGRAPHERS LISTED BY CITY/STATE IN THE UNITED STATES 1888-1889

NAME	ADDRESS		CITY	STATE
Pietz & Houchens			Springfield	IL
Pittman	J. A. W.		Springfield	IL
Ryan	D. J.		Springfield	IL
Truesdell	W. F.		Springfield	IL
Coerver	John		Staunton	IL
Adams	J. A.		Sterling	IL
Greene	J. N.		Sterling	IL
Haynes	John		Sterling	IL
Houser	Mrs. E. F.		Sterling	IL
Lown	C. H.		Sterling	IL
Smith	C. F.		Sterling	IL
Lutes	C. M.		Stewardson	IL
Clark	L. W.		Streator	IL
Howland	E. H.		Streator	IL
Withers	E. H.		Streator	IL
Creech	A. S.		Sullivan	IL
Gosslee*	R. H.		Sullivan	IL
Ewing	H. H.		Sycamore	IL
Brua & Clark			Taylorville	IL
Burleigh	G. N.		Taylorville	IL
Thayer	L. R.		Tonica	IL
Van Osdell	G. C.		Toulon	IL
Boyce	D. N.		Tuscola	IL
Chase	M. E.		Urbana	IL
Read	W. F.		Vandalia	IL
Van Syckel	J. W.		Vermont	IL
Perkins	A. J.		Vienna	IL
Armstrong	J. W.		Virden	IL
McCullough	R. L.		Virden	IL
Mann	R. H.		Virginia	IL
Burress & Morlan			Walnut	IL
Chandler	E. C.		Walnut	IL
Anderson	J. T.		Warren	IL
Busec	S. L.		Warren	IL
Taylor	B. C.		Warsaw	IL
Goff*	George		Washburn	IL
Sharp*	W. O.		Washington	IL
Fults & Lafayette			Waterloo	IL
Hogle & Nims			Watseka	IL
Weaver	W. H.		Watseka	IL

PHOTOGRAPHERS LISTED BY CITY/STATE IN THE UNITED STATES 1888-1889

NAME	ADDRESS	CITY	STATE
Beard	H. A.	Waukegan	IL
Hook	R. W.	Waukegan	IL
Thompson	Mrs. Catherine	Waukegan	IL
Gates	C. L.	Waverly	IL
Boswell	A. C.	Wayne City	IL
Barrett	James	Wenona	IL
Suplau	Ludwig	Wheaton	IL
Morrow	O. A.	White Hall	IL
Mitchell	W. H.	Wilmington	IL
Merritt*	George	Winchester	IL
Copelin	T.	Winnetka	IL
Burbank	G. A.	Woodstock	IL
Meidlar	J. S.	Woodstock	IL
Pott*	Emil	Wright's Grove	IL
Mowry	C.	Wyanet	IL
Davis*	C. L.	Wyoming	IL
Hoff*	D. J.	Yorkville	IL
McKean	James	Anderson	IN
McKeon*	James	Anderson	IN
Hoff	J. B.	Angola	IN
Campbell	J. D.	Attica	IN
Henney	John A.	Attica	IN
Aber	J. F.	Auburn	IN
Walton	James N.	Aurora	IN
Gabler	George	Batesville	IN
Rogers	J. A.	Bedford	IN
Alison*	James D.	Bloomington	IN
Barnes	J. M.	Bloomington	IN
Summers	A. J.	Bloomington	IN
Harnish	George A.	Bluffton	IN
Wilkins	H. O.	Brazil	IN
Portenus	J. E.	Bremen	IN
Wells	A. F.	Bristol	IN
Hoffman	E.	Brookville	IN
Rounds	Benjamin H.	Cannelton	IN
Powell	J. W.	Charlestown	IN
Click	M. E.	Columbia City	IN
Jones	L. M.	Columbia City	IN
Coley & Tatman		Connersville	IN
Kellum	John	Connersville	IN

PHOTOGRAPHERS LISTED BY CITY/STATE IN THE UNITED STATES 1888-1889

NAME		ADDRESS	CITY	STATE
Gorham*	James E.		Covington	IN
Olds	F. A.		Covington	IN
Nicholson	John		Crawfordsville	IN
Hayward	W. H.		Crown Point	IN
Darwin	C. T.		Decatur	IN
Yeager, Jr.	L.		Decatur	IN
Ennis	John W.		Delphi	IN
Wolever	A.		Delphi	IN
Goff	Frank L.		Elkhart	IN
Jones	L. P.		Elkhart	IN
Douglass	S. W.		Evansville	IN
Ecker	J. M.		Evansville	IN
Feay	A. J.		Evansville	IN
Hunton	Frank N.		Evansville	IN
Schroeder	J. H.		Evansville	IN
Starr*	T. C.		Evansville	IN
Tharling	J. W.		Evansville	IN
Allen*	J. O.		Ft. Wayne	IN
Barrows	F. R.		Ft. Wayne	IN
Hoover	J. V.		Ft. Wayne	IN
Jones	Maurice L.		Ft. Wayne	IN
Mayers	Joseph M.		Ft. Wayne	IN
Salzmann	W.		Ft. Wayne	IN
Shoaff	John A.		Ft. Wayne	IN
Sommer	Carl		Ft. Wayne	IN
Thomlinson*	A.		Ft. Wayne	IN
Gamble	G. R.		Frankfort	IN
Heichert	L. V.		Frankfort	IN
Hicks	H. G.		Frankfort	IN
Smith & Bechtel*			Frankfort	IN
Hicks*	A. G.		Franklin	IN
Julian	C. H.		Fredericksburgh	IN
Dawdy	Andrew J.		Goshen	IN
Hower	William H.		Goshen	IN
Billingsley	George W.		Grandview	IN
Jones & Bower			Greencastle	IN
Spurgin	J. S.		Greencastle	IN
Webb*	Wilson T.		Greenfield	IN
Moberly	L.		Greensburgh	IN
Wallick	Joe		Hagerstown	IN

PHOTOGRAPHERS LISTED BY CITY/STATE IN THE UNITED STATES 1888-1889

NAME		ADDRESS	CITY	STATE
Rhine & Co.	Ithamar L.		Hartford City	IN
Bline	J. W.		Hartsville	IN
Schaub	J. T.		Hope	IN
Radobaugh	E. D.		Huntington	IN
Bishop	C.		Indianapolis	IN
Bowman*	H. M.		Indianapolis	IN
Braunberg*	M.		Indianapolis	IN
Brown	Albert		Indianapolis	IN
Brown	Charles		Indianapolis	IN
Bryant	D. C.		Indianapolis	IN
Buchanan	F. M.		Indianapolis	IN
Buchanan	H. N.		Indianapolis	IN
Cadwallader & Fearnaught			Indianapolis	IN
Clark	Daniel R.		Indianapolis	IN
Dodges	A. H.		Indianapolis	IN
Eisele	H.		Indianapolis	IN
Elliott	J. P.		Indianapolis	IN
Faries	T. C.		Indianapolis	IN
Fowler	Harry		Indianapolis	IN
Koehler	Gottfried		Indianapolis	IN
Lacey	Frank M.	Vance Block	Indianapolis	IN
McGaughey	C. O.		Indianapolis	IN
Miller*	J. E.		Indianapolis	IN
Pickerell	P.		Indianapolis	IN
Potter	W. H.		Indianapolis	IN
Potts	William B.		Indianapolis	IN
Rose	T. H.		Indianapolis	IN
Smith*	D.		Indianapolis	IN
Smith & Dryer			Indianapolis	IN
Wager	S. D.		Indianapolis	IN
Wilson	G.		Indianapolis	IN
Messmore	Isom		Jasper	IN
Finley	George W.		Jeffersonville	IN
Russell	William		Jeffersonville	IN
Cox	William H.		Kendallville	IN
Crofoot	J. E.		Kendallville	IN
Harnish	T. H.		Kentland	IN
Charles	Oliver		Knightstown	IN
Reed	Byron		Kokomo	IN
Strode	J. M.		Kokomo	IN

PHOTOGRAPHERS LISTED BY CITY/STATE IN THE UNITED STATES 1888-1889

NAME	ADDRESS	CITY	STATE
Wilson	F.	Kokomo	IN
Baldwin	J.	La Fayette	IN
Homrig	C. P.	La Fayette	IN
Phillips	S. D.	La Fayette	IN
Rising	Herman	La Fayette	IN
Wolever	P. W.	La Fayette	IN
Boyd	Cincinnatus	La Porte	IN
Bryant	John W.	La Porte	IN
Scott	William H.	La Porte	IN
Hissong	G. W.	Lagrange	IN
Shroy	J. A.	Lebanon	IN
Cornell & Bothwell		Ligonier	IN
Donaldson	Albert N.	Logansport	IN
Gripe*	David	Logansport	IN
Stevens	C. H.	Logansport	IN
Chandler*	J. H.	Madison	IN
Gorgas	J. R.	Madison	IN
Millar	H. C.	Madison	IN
Brown*	F. E.	Marion	IN
Hockett & Hartsook		Marion	IN
Thompson	Scott	Merom	IN
Hauser	G. E.	Michigan City	IN
Robinson	Edgar G.	Michigan City	IN
Smith	Lewis	Mishawaka	IN
Lighty Bros.		Monticello	IN
Jones	L. W.	Mount Vernon	IN
Martin*	J. R.	Mount Vernon	IN
Goodlander	M. D.	Muncie	IN
Robbins	N. L.	Muncie	IN
Buck	James W.	New Albany	IN
Heimberger & Son	C.	New Albany	IN
Kiser	J. B.	New Albany	IN
Taylor	Harry Morton	New Albany	IN
Wilson & Son	James A.	New Albany	IN
Albright	William H.	New Castle	IN
Harnish	O. A.	Noblesville	IN
Martin	J. J.	North Manchester	IN
Leas	J. O.	Peru	IN
Lentz Bros.		Peru	IN
Shelton	George B.	Peru	IN

PHOTOGRAPHERS LISTED BY CITY/STATE IN THE UNITED STATES 1888-1889

NAME		ADDRESS	CITY	STATE
Brady	J. M.		Petersburgh	IN
Haas	Albert		Petersburgh	IN
Tomlinson	Moses		Plainfield	IN
Biery	T.		Pleasant Lake	IN
Bradway Bros.			Richmond	IN
Reynolds*	M. B.		Richmond	IN
Ryder	D.		Richmond	IN
Stigleman	G. W.		Richmond	IN
Swaine	H. J.		Richmond	IN
Young	W. K.		Richmond	IN
Walton	D.		Rising Sun	IN
Gould	Robert		Rochester	IN
Moore & Bros.			Rochester	IN
Moore	Charles B.		Rochester	IN
Hunt	William		Rockville	IN
Sargent	A. J.		Rushville	IN
Stevens	H. S.		Rushville	IN
Goodrich	G. A.		Shelbyville	IN
Milleson	H. E.		Shelbyville	IN
Tatman	J. R.		Shelbyville	IN
Tatman & Son			Shelbyville	IN
Tatum	C. E.		Shelbyville	IN
Bonney	James		South Bend	IN
McDonald	Albert		South Bend	IN
Pool	E. E.		South Bend	IN
Smith	G.		South Bend	IN
Johnson	W. W.		Sullivan	IN
Hauser	Emil		Tell City	IN
Adams	John M.		Terre Haute	IN
Eppert	Charles		Terre Haute	IN
Henit	John B.		Terre Haute	IN
Staples	W. F.		Terre Haute	IN
Umber*	Udlemor		Terre Haute	IN
Wright	D. H.		Terre Haute	IN
Young	D. W.		Terre Haute	IN
Ennis	James W.		Trafalgar	IN
McLellan	J. W.		Valparaiso	IN
Mudge	M. M.		Valparaiso	IN
Whipple	Floyd M.		Valparaiso	IN
Whipple	Mrs. Galon		Valparaiso	IN

PHOTOGRAPHERS LISTED BY CITY/STATE IN THE UNITED STATES 1888-1889

NAME		ADDRESS	CITY	STATE
Walton	J. E.		Veray	IN
Dunn	J. H.		Vincennes	IN
Popp	E.		Vincennes	IN
Rawlins	W. J.		Vincennes	IN
Rogers	W. C.		Vincennes	IN
Souder*	J. W.		Vincennes	IN
McMahon	M. F.		Wabash	IN
Millice	H. C.		Warsaw	IN
Place	Frank		Warsaw	IN
Shoemaker	J. F.		Warsaw	IN
Hale	Mark L.		Winamac	IN
Summers	A. Y		Winamac	IN
Beck & Reese			Worthington	IN
Fowler	A.		Xenia	IN
Roosevelt & Frantz			Ackley	IA
Wilkinson	J. F.		Adair	IA
Swearingen & Zachariah			Adel	IA
Healy	A. A.		Afton	IA
Ralston	S. A.		Albia	IA
Nicaulin	J. F.		Algona	IA
Saunders	J. H.		Algona	IA
Mendenhall*	J. H.		Allerton	IA
Keith	S. F.		Alta	IA
Kamber	F. J.		Alton	IA
Cook	N. G.		Ames	IA
Morrison	Martin		Ames	IA
Littlefield	C. E.		Anamosa	IA
Miller	J. W.		Anamosa	IA
Mott	M. M.		Anamosa	IA
Egbert	W. P.		Atlantic	IA
McMullen	J. F.		Atlantic	IA
Harper	C. C.		Audubon	IA
Mendenhall	T. B.		Audubon	IA
Brendt Bros.			Avoca	IA
Coup	J. B.		Bedford	IA
Goldsberry	B. E.		Bedford	IA
Miles & Greenlee			Belle Plaine	IA
Streuser	M. J.		Bellevue	IA
Pigeon	Thomas		Belmond	IA
Delahunt	R. C.		Bertram	IA

PHOTOGRAPHERS LISTED BY CITY/STATE IN THE UNITED STATES 1888-1889

NAME		ADDRESS	CITY	STATE
Porter	Robert		Birmingham	IA
Huntington	H. H.		Blairstown	IA
Hughes Bros.			Blanchard	IA
Dunlap	F. A.		Bloomfield	IA
Head	F. D.		Bloomfield	IA
Henry	Levi		Bonaparte	IA
Harna	E.		Boone	IA
Martin	J. P.		Boone	IA
Green	L. H.		Brighton	IA
Bryan	S. T.		Burlington	IA
Lupton	O. L.		Burlington	IA
Monfort & Hill			Burlington	IA
Reynolds	J. H.		Burlington	IA
Ward	W. H.		Burr Oak	IA
Howard*	J. B.		Bush Creek	IA
Borlang	O. E.		Calmar	IA
Borlaug*	O. E.		Calmar	IA
Bohner	J. A.		Carrol	IA
Hoff	W. H.		Carrol	IA
Streuser	J. J.		Cascade	IA
Gilchrist	G. K.		Cedar Falls	IA
Lancaster Bros.			Cedar Falls	IA
Sorensen	Claus		Cedar Falls	IA
Buser	H. R.		Cedar Rapids	IA
Kilborn & Co.	W. F.		Cedar Rapids	IA
Swem	Mrs. Emeline		Cedar Rapids	IA
Wiggins	S. T.		Cedar Rapids	IA
Sawyer	G. L.		Central City	IA
Wales	T. L.		Center Ville	IA
Fairbanks	J. A.		Center Point	IA
Bridge	E. C.		Chariton	IA
Hiester*	H. T.		Chariton	IA
Watson	C. H.		Chariton	IA
Connor	G. P.		Charles City	IA
Mooney	Arthur		Charles City	IA
Miller	N. H.		Cherokee	IA
Wilson	J. C.		Cherokee	IA
Hurd & Son*	W. P.		Clarinda	IA
Park	O. H.		Clarinda	IA
Mather	H. S.		Clear Lake	IA

PHOTOGRAPHERS LISTED BY CITY/STATE IN THE UNITED STATES 1888-1889

NAME		ADDRESS	CITY	STATE
Setter	C.		Clermont	IA
Stetter*	C.		Clermont	IA
Ferguson	W. F.		Clinton	IA
Nichols	G. B.		Clinton	IA
Reed	J. H.		Clinton	IA
Temple & Co.	G. L.		Clinton	IA
Kindade Bros.*			Collins	IA
Gibboney	H. E.		Columbus Junction	IA
Oliver	E. W.		Columbus Junction	IA
Rogers	E. A.		Coon Rapids	IA
Proctor	Jefferson		Corning	IA
Flanders	C. M.		Corydon	IA
Hartshorn	J. G.		Corydon	IA
Wright	W. W.		Corydon	IA
Gorham	J. A.		Council Bluffs	IA
Luccock	C. D.		Council Bluffs	IA
Schmidt	Harry		Council Bluffs	IA
Shewaden	C. H.		Council Bluffs	IA
Bertrand	E. E.		Cresco	IA
McKay	A. L.		Cresco	IA
Reynolds	J. A.		Cresco	IA
Spurr	A. H.		Cresco	IA
Adams	Mrs. T. E.		Davenport	IA
Dahms*	Gustav		Davenport	IA
Hastings, White & Fischer			Davenport	IA
Huebinger Bros.			Davenport	IA
Rosmussen	J. C.		Davenport	IA
Schueler	John		Davenport	IA
Adams	Mrs. T. E.		Davis City	IA
Lindquist*	A. V.		Dayton	IA
Smith	Sylvester		De Witt	IA
Adams	A. W.		Decorah	IA
Reef	J. T.		Decorah	IA
Hoff	E. N.		Denison	IA
Trone	A. F.		Denison	IA
Arnold & Co.*			Des Moines	IA
Boyd	W. T.		Des Moines	IA
Davidson	T. M.		Des Moines	IA
Edinger	W. C.		Des Moines	IA
Freeborn	L. H.		Des Moines	IA

PHOTOGRAPHERS LISTED BY CITY/STATE IN THE UNITED STATES 1888-1889

NAME		ADDRESS	CITY	STATE
James	Thomas		Des Moines	IA
Little	H. N.		Des Moines	IA
Lounsbery	J. B.		Des Moines	IA
McLeisch	William		Des Moines	IA
Pearson & Nebit			Des Moines	IA
St. Clair	Alexander		Des Moines	IA
Belbrough	J.		Dubuque	IA
Jordan	H. A.		Dubuque	IA
Mackenzie	A. H.		Dubuque	IA
Morhiser	W. H.		Dubuque	IA
Root*	Samuel		Dubuque	IA
Waiteley	E. B.		Dunlap	IA
Weigel	Miss Mary		Dyersville	IA
Spurr*	E. W.		Dysart	IA
Jacobs	W. H.		Eagle Grove	IA
Howard	E. P.		Eldon	IA
Hudson	Edward		Eldora	IA
Kirby	Frank		Eldora	IA
Berger	J. N.		Elgin	IA
Bevair			Elgin	IA
Nichols	F. N.		Elkader	IA
Christensen	H. P.		Emmetsburgh	IA
Poock	C.		Essex	IA
Gilchrist	J. W.		Fairfield	IA
Hilbert	James		Fairfield	IA
Joseph	C. A.		Farley	IA
Goodenough	G. C.		Farmington	IA
Lucas*	W. J.		Farmington	IA
Orvis	J. R.		Fayette	IA
Carpenter	J. B.		Fonda	IA
Mowry	Cornelius		Fontanelle	IA
Reed	H. C.		Forest City	IA
Garrison	C. F.		Fort Dodge	IA
Gronemann	F. C.		Fort Dodge	IA
Dassau	Emil		Fort Madison	IA
O'Keefe	C. F.		Fort Madison	IA
Tewkesbury	J. R.		Fort Madison	IA
Seeverts	A.		Fremont	IA
Sandford	Gould		Garden Grove	IA
Thorpe	R. L.		Garwin	IA

PHOTOGRAPHERS LISTED BY CITY/STATE IN THE UNITED STATES 1888-1889

NAME		ADDRESS	CITY	STATE
Yeomans	O. L.		Gladbrook	IA
Tollman	T. W.		Glenwood	IA
Wallis	C. W.		Glenwood	IA
O'Donohue	Mrs. J. B.		Grand Junction	IA
Harvey	L. L.		Greene	IA
Ward*	G. A.		Greenfield	IA
Child	A. L.		Grinnell	IA
Stallings	W. F.		Grinnell	IA
Adams	G. H.		Griswold	IA
Reynolds	A. C.		Griswold	IA
Ford	E. A.		Grundy Center	IA
Houseman	J. H.		Grundy Center	IA
Rich	C. P.		Guthrie	IA
Smythe	James		Guttenberg	IA
Cowles	C. A.		Hamburg	IA
Phillips	M. F.		Hamburg	IA
Reagan	G. C.		Hampton	IA
Upson	D. D.		Hampton	IA
Dammand	R. P.		Harlan	IA
Fisher	C. U.		Harlan	IA
Lynn	E. A.		Hawarden	IA
Truax	John		Hazelton	IA
Muma	Charles		Holstein	IA
Kerberg	J. F.		Hull	IA
Parker	Damascus		Humboldt	IA
Flanders	C. M.		Humeston	IA
Blair	L. G.		Ida Grove	IA
Hansen	Neil		Ida Grove	IA
Smith	Mrs. Belle		Ida Grove	IA
Ensminger Bros.			Independence	IA
Phillips	L. H.		Independence	IA
Schooley	L. H.		Indianola	IA
Schooley*	Mrs. L. H.		Indianola	IA
Clinch	C. E.		Iowa City	IA
Elite Studio			Iowa City	IA
James	N. W.		Iowa City	IA
Townsend	T. W.		Iowa City	IA
Townsend	J. A.		Iowa Falls	IA
O'Donohue	J. B.		Jefferson	IA
Reynold	H. J.		Jefferson	IA

PHOTOGRAPHERS LISTED BY CITY/STATE IN THE UNITED STATES 1888-1889

NAME		ADDRESS	CITY	STATE
Beckley	Eli		Jesup	IA
Whitcomb	D. W.		Kellogg	IA
Gerhard*	W. P.		Keokuk	IA
Hassal	George		Keokuk	IA
Lobbrecht	G. J.		Keokuk	IA
Van Gricken	Samuel		Keokuk	IA
Fosnot	L. C.		Keosauqua	IA
Brinkley & Fry			Keota	IA
Holden & Brinkley*			Keota	IA
Ludewig	W. H.		Keystone	IA
Butler	C.		Kingsley	IA
Bittenbender	L. C.		Knoxville	IA
Reeder	James		Knoxville	IA
Thayer*	G. D.		Lake City	IA
Willard & Van Horn			Lake City	IA
Helgeson	T. J.		Lake Mills	IA
Kellett & wife*	T. A.		Laporte City	IA
Ward Bros.			Laporte City	IA
Dabb	R. I.		Le Mars	IA
Gosting	G. G.		Le Mars	IA
Fitzsimons	E. D.		Lehigh	IA
Joung*	E. S.		Leon	IA
Young	E. S.		Leon	IA
Crus	J. H.		Lineville	IA
Jacobs*	W. L.		Logan	IA
Leach*	J. H.		Logan	IA
Hall	G. S.		Lohrsville	IA
McNaught	John		Lothron	IA
Dale	D. E.		Lucas	IA
Fields & Son	William		Lyons	IA
O'Connor & Balcom			Lyons	IA
Farrington	Theodore		McGregor	IA
Elliott	H. S.		Madrid	IA
Elliott	John		Madrid	IA
Eaton	D. F.		Magnolia	IA
Dearborn	T. E.		Malvern	IA
Mills	C. B.		Manchester	IA
Walter	H. L.		Manchester	IA
Hansen	C. G.		Manning	IA
Williams	B. S.		Manson	IA

PHOTOGRAPHERS LISTED BY CITY/STATE IN THE UNITED STATES 1888-1889

NAME		ADDRESS	CITY	STATE
Brown*	H. F.		Mapleton	IA
Cundill	W. M.		Maquoketa	IA
Harvey	Mrs. H. P.		Maquoketa	IA
Cartwright	C. A.		Marengo	IA
Elliot	H. I.		Marion	IA
Waldron & Wilson			Marion	IA
Beverage	M. C.		Marshalltown	IA
Bonney	A. F.		Marshalltown	IA
Brown	T. A.		Marshalltown	IA
Jones	J. N.		Marshalltown	IA
Owens	H. A.		Marysville	IA
Bouton	C. H.		Mason City	IA
Kirk	H. P.		Mason City	IA
Busier	J. S.		Mechanicsville	IA
Baxter	M. D.		Melton	IA
Brown	L. P.		Michelville	IA
Yocum*	J. W.		Milo	IA
Brown	H. R.		Missouri Valley	IA
Morton	A. C.		Monona	IA
Hall	J. R.		Monroe	IA
Araah	Antheonia		Monticello	IA
Coyle	F. A.		Monticello	IA
Mazee	M. D.		Monticello	IA
Cloud	A. P.		Moulton	IA
Harper	C. L.		Mount Ayr	IA
Leisenring Bros.			Mount Pleasant	IA
McAdam Bros.			Mount Pleasant	IA
Buser	J. S.		Mount Vernon	IA
Owens Photo. Copy Co.			Mount Vernon	IA
Edwards	E. B.		Muscatine	IA
Owens	M. W.		Muscatine	IA
Phelps	J. P.		Muscatine	IA
Phelps & Phelps			Muscatine	IA
Beach	A. W.		Nashua	IA
Hamelton	G. C.		Nevada	IA
Goodhall	H. S.		New Hampton	IA
Gist	John		New Sharon	IA
Pardoe	H. W.		New Sharon	IA
Acme Portrait Co.*			Newton	IA
Kenney	A. L.		Newton	IA

PHOTOGRAPHERS LISTED BY CITY/STATE IN THE UNITED STATES 1888-1889

NAME		ADDRESS	CITY	STATE
Hubbard & Keys			Nora Springs	IA
Thompson	C. C.		Nora Springs	IA
Knudtson	J. O.		Northwood	IA
West	F. E.		Odebolt	IA
Soffer	F. F.		Ogden	IA
Stewart	Peter		Ogden	IA
Hillmann	C. C.		Olewein	IA
Schneider*	Phillip		Olewein	IA
Horner	Samuel		Onawa	IA
Spooner	E.		Onslow	IA
Weenink	H. D.		Orange City	IA
Samson & Corning			Osage	IA
Graves Bros.			Osceola	IA
Cammack	W. R.		Oskaloosa	IA
Duncan	W. A.		Oskaloosa	IA
Warrington	E. W.		Oskaloosa	IA
Oyloe	G. G.		Ossian	IA
Briggs & Co.	F. L.		Ottumwa	IA
Post	A. B.		Ottumwa	IA
Stopp	William		Ottumwa	IA
White & Hughes			Ottumwa	IA
Winn	J. M.		Ottumwa	IA
McManus	F. P.		Oxford	IA
Araah	Athonia		Oxford Junction	IA
Thompson	A. R.		Oxford Junction	IA
Dooley	C. O.		Panora	IA
Byerly	Orison		Parkersburg	IA
Renvers & Gesman			Pella	IA
Parker	Orne		Perry	IA
Stoops	L. M.		Perry	IA
Pummer	Monte		Pleasantville	IA
Beedy	F. N.		Postville	IA
Robaart	Jacob		Prairie City	IA
Blair*	W. F.		Randolph	IA
Moody	H. W.		Red Oak	IA
Van Alstine	C. W.		Red Oak	IA
Tice	N. J.		Redfield	IA
Staunton*	C. K.		Reinbeck	IA
Weatherby & Denison			Rock Valley	IA
Pierce	D. C.		Rockford	IA

PHOTOGRAPHERS LISTED BY CITY/STATE IN THE UNITED STATES 1888-1889

NAME		ADDRESS	CITY	STATE
Harris	James		Rolfe	IA
Esmay	John		Sabula	IA
Blair	W. E.		Sac City	IA
Williams*	C. D.		Sanborn	IA
Foster	H. C.		Shelby	IA
Williams	C. D. M.		Sheldon	IA
Apfel	Henry		Shell Rock	IA
Brewer	W. H.		Shenandoah	IA
Hamilton	J. B.		Shenandoah	IA
Carew	G. A.		Sibley	IA
Doolittle	H. G.		Sibley	IA
Tolman	T. W.		Sidney	IA
Beatty	William		Sigourney	IA
Anderson	C. M.		Sioux City	IA
Florence	C. W.		Sioux City	IA
Hamilton	J. H.		Sioux City	IA
Stamm	A. N.		Sioux City	IA
Severson	T. C.		Sioux Rapids	IA
Smith	N. W.		Sioux Rapids	IA
Rood	W. J.		Spencer	IA
Roblin	F. F.		Spirit Lake	IA
Shomber	A. J.		State Center	IA
Coman	G. S.		Storm Lake	IA
Torp	A. N.		Story City	IA
Gostin & Guerin			Strawberry Point	IA
Webb	J. F.		Strawberry Point	IA
Swartz	Adam		Stuart	IA
Kilbourn	J. E.		Tipton	IA
Hassal	A. J.		Toledo	IA
Moore	J. S.		Toledo	IA
Woolley	H. M.		Traer	IA
Waters	S. E.		Union	IA
Watters*	S. E.		Union	IA
Chatterton	H. D.		Villisca	IA
Fellows	E. G.		Vinton	IA
Macy	O. W.		Vinton	IA
Coyle*	J. H.		Walker	IA
Keller	H. D.		Wapello	IA
Armstrong	Samuel		Washington	IA
Black	A. C.		Washington	IA

PHOTOGRAPHERS LISTED BY CITY/STATE IN THE UNITED STATES 1888-1889

NAME		ADDRESS	CITY	STATE
Finney	S. B.		Washington	IA
Simmons, Latier & King			Waterloo	IA
Wilkins	C. E.		Waterloo	IA
Dunham	S. E.		Waucoma	IA
Dunlevy	J. M.		Waukon	IA
Huffmann & Barnard*			Waverly	IA
Pierce	N. E.		Waverly	IA
Clark	Lyman		Webster City	IA
Tounsend	Lill.		West Liberty	IA
Hawkes	M. E. H.		West Union	IA
Weehler	R. S.		What Cheer	IA
Wheeler*	R. S.		What Cheer	IA
Wise	S. H.		Wilton Junction	IA
Hyder	Ed.		Winterset	IA
Ware	G. A.		Winterset	IA
Hansbrough	J. A.		Abilene	KS
Levi*	Mrs. C. H.		Abilene	KS
Sexton	J. B.		Abilene	KS
Pallnoke	L.		Alma	KS
Imus	C. W.		Alton	KS
Mummy	Mrs. K. F.		Argonia	KS
Dresser	G. H.		Arkansas City	KS
Hill	Russell		Armstrong	KS
Fulker*	C.		Arcadia	KS
Martin Bros.			Ashland	KS
Butler*	D. S.		Atchison	KS
Conklin*	S. L.		Atchison	KS
Kleckner	M. A.		Atchison	KS
McLeod	D. M.		Atchison	KS
Stevenson*	R.		Atchison	KS
Crossman*	C. L.		Athony	KS
Hart	Willie		Athony	KS
Balding	L. W.		Augusta	KS
Willis	S.		Beattie	KS
Perronington & Son*			Bee	KS
Overstreet	W. S.		Belle Plaine	KS
Dobler Bros.			Beloit	KS
Greenwood	W. H.		Beloit	KS
Masters	W. H.		Blue Mounds	KS
Cranford	Charles		Brookville	KS

PHOTOGRAPHERS LISTED BY CITY/STATE IN THE UNITED STATES 1888-1889

NAME		ADDRESS	CITY	STATE
Trader	F. A.		Burlingame	KS
Coker	C. W.		Burlington	KS
Creese	M. P.		Burr Oak	KS
Hovey	Alvin		Burr Oak	KS
Cosand & Mosser			Caldwell	KS
Wehe	L. E.		Carbondale	KS
Foster & Creese			Cawker City	KS
Huckel	Joseph		Cawker City	KS
Allen*	F. W.		Chanute	KS
Shirley	Johnson O.		Chanute	KS
Wertz	J. C.		Chanute	KS
Miller	R. W.		Cherokee	KS
Loomis	F. C.		Cherry Vale	KS
Brach*	W. G.		Clay Center	KS
Howard	C. R.		Clay Center	KS
Howard	W. A.		Clay Center	KS
Taylor	B. F.		Clear Water	KS
Millard	Charles		Clifton	KS
King	J. R.		Clyde	KS
Bushnell	W. A.		Coffeyville	KS
Gaston & Co.*	J. B.		Coldwater	KS
Snyder*	George		Coldwater	KS
Johnson	J. M.		Columbus	KS
Mater	D. P.		Columbus	KS
Atherton	Mary		Concordia	KS
Linney & Tooley			Concordia	KS
Mulit	H. S.		Concordia	KS
Barnard & Johnson			Conway Springs	KS
Grove	Charles		Conway Springs	KS
Vetter	W. H.		Cottonwood Falls	KS
McMillan	G. A.		Council Grove	KS
Swanson	Harvey		Detroit	KS
Vancil & McDonald			Dodge City	KS
White*	W. S.		Douglas	KS
Adams*	C. E.		Downs	KS
Adams	Mrs. C. N.		El Dorado	KS
Kemp	Carl		El Dorado	KS
Stevenson	Edward		El Dorado	KS
Antle	Logan		Elk City	KS
Avenarius	G. A.		Ellsworth	KS

PHOTOGRAPHERS LISTED BY CITY/STATE IN THE UNITED STATES 1888-1889

NAME		ADDRESS	CITY	STATE
Brown	E. C.		Ellsworth	KS
Harden	A. B.		Emporia	KS
Page	L. S.		Emporia	KS
Rich & Co.	Miss D. B.		Emporia	KS
Waite	S. H.		Emporia	KS
Smith	L. W.		Enterprise	KS
Shively	S. L.		Erie	KS
Glines	W. B.		Eureka	KS
Howard	N. W.		Eureka	KS
Olin	Mrs. R. A.		Fall River	KS
Lee	F. W.		Florence	KS
Carden*	C. H.		Fort Scott	KS
Lean	Mrs. E. L.		Fort Scott	KS
Tressler	E. P.		Fort Scott	KS
Tressler	S. P.		Fort Scott	KS
Rice	B. T.		Frankford	KS
Loomis	D. A.		Fredonia	KS
Baker*	Miss C. E.		Galena	KS
Overstreet	Miss C. E.		Galena	KS
Rogers	W. S.		Garden City	KS
Farrow*	M. F.		Garnett	KS
McLain	William		Garnett	KS
Fickhardt*	W. R.		Gaylord	KS
Brown	H. M.		Girard	KS
Proctor	J. H.		Girard	KS
Sunderland	J. C.		Girard	KS
Ganisford	Mrs. Minerva		Great Bend	KS
Smith	Luke		Greenleaf	KS
Martin	W. J.		Greensburg	KS
Reeves	M. R.		Grenola	KS
Barnett	A. L.		Halstead	KS
Burgener	J. H.		Harper	KS
Wilson*	J. A.		Harper	KS
Voss	N. A.		Hays City	KS
Harmon	J. E.		Hiawatha	KS
Hickox	R. A.		Hiawatha	KS
Hoppe	E. D.		Holton	KS
Oakes & Ireland			Holton	KS
Bryant & Gilllingwater			Humboldt	KS
Harper	J. A.		Hutchinson	KS

PHOTOGRAPHERS LISTED BY CITY/STATE IN THE UNITED STATES 1888-1889

NAME		ADDRESS	CITY	STATE
Hirst	Samuel		Hutchinson	KS
McInturff	Andrew		Hutchinson	KS
Brown	A. L.		Independence	KS
Wright	William		Independence	KS
Pancoast	B. F.		Iola	KS
Christenson	Christ		Jamestown	KS
Flagg	B. A.		Junction City	KS
Wheeler	C. M.		Junction City	KS
Atkinson	George		Kansas City	KS
Brown	Harmon		Kansas City	KS
Carpenter	Marion		Kansas City	KS
Cheetham*	Edgar		Kansas City	KS
Gardiner	R. G.		Kansas City	KS
Gellie	Charles		Kansas City	KS
Malcolm*	Hugh		Kansas City	KS
Michell*	A. D.		Kansas City	KS
Parker & Co.*			Kansas City	KS
Ploetz*	Julius		Kansas City	KS
Scotford & Co.			Kansas City	KS
Thompson & Co.	D. P.		Kansas City	KS
Dallinds	J. S.		Kennekuk	KS
Derry	J. M.		Kingman	KS
Ioas & Parker*			Kingman	KS
Joas & Parker			Kingman	KS
Brumfeld	John		Kingsley	KS
Bradley	H. E.		Kirwin	KS
Young	J. A.		La Cygne	KS
Hargrave	J. J.		Larned	KS
Wheeler	D. N.		Larned	KS
Fix & Smith*			Lawrence	KS
Hamilton	A. C.		Lawrence	KS
Mettner	F. F.		Lawrence	KS
Shane	J. B.		Lawrence	KS
Bauer & Son	S.		Leavenworth	KS
Ferguson	J. H.		Leavenworth	KS
Haag	Joseph		Leavenworth	KS
Henry	E. E.		Leavenworth	KS
Mason	J. T.		Leavenworth	KS
Smith*	R. G.		Leavenworth	KS
George	Isaac		Lehigh	KS

PHOTOGRAPHERS LISTED BY CITY/STATE IN THE UNITED STATES 1888-1889

NAME		ADDRESS	CITY	STATE
Lemon	G. R.		Leon	KS
Vance*	M. C.		Leonardville	KS
Richardson	George		Logan	KS
Aplington	L. A.		Long Island	KS
Churchman	Henry		Longton	KS
Hupp	Phillips		Louisburgh	KS
Sellers*	J. M.		Ludell	KS
Ford	Harry		Lyndon	KS
Blaylock	J. W.		Lyons	KS
Shanafelt*	J. D.		Lyons	KS
Shanafeld	J. D.		Lyons	KS
Forell	Carl		McPherson	KS
Manning	E. J.		McPherson	KS
Wheeland	Mrs. Ross		McPherson	KS
Wheeland*	Mrs. Rosa		McPherson	KS
Porter	Mrs. M. A.		Madison	KS
Burgoyne	G.		Manhattan	KS
Hoop	S. W.		Manhattan	KS
Roberts	W. M.		Mankato	KS
Huston*	J. A.		Marion	KS
Hover	H. S.		Marysville	KS
Perkins	V. H.		Medicine Lodge	KS
Brace*	A. F.		Miltonvale	KS
Cole	H. G.		Minneapolis	KS
Hastings*	S. E.		Minneapolis	KS
McDonald	L. E.		Minneapolis	KS
Garner	Joseph		Moline	KS
Weld	D. S.		Mound City	KS
Heighton	Miss Libby		Mound Valley	KS
Howard	W. M.		Mulvane	KS
Hopp	H. H.		Neodesha	KS
Calhoun	Mrs. Ross		Ness City	KS
Bean*	R. T.		New Kiowa	KS
Windmayer & Co.*			New Kiowa	KS
Denton	B. F.		Newton	KS
Huddleston*	F. M.		Newton	KS
Tripp	F. D.		Newton	KS
McLaughlin	T. C.		Nickerson	KS
Ballard	M. O.		Nimrod	KS
Atherton	H. M.		North Topeka	KS

PHOTOGRAPHERS LISTED BY CITY/STATE IN THE UNITED STATES 1888-1889

NAME	ADDRESS	CITY	STATE
Freeman*	D. W. G.	North Topeka	KS
Bastian	Z. T.	Olathe	KS
Gebhart*	J. D.	Olathe	KS
Tyson	S. E.	Onago	KS
Slater	E. B.	Osage City	KS
Foreman	C. R.	Osage Mission	KS
Hill	Mrs. H. E.	Osage Mission	KS
Scott*	J. P.	Osage Mission	KS
Buell	O. W.	Osborne	KS
Rase	E. R.	Osborne	KS
Swank	William	Osborne	KS
Orsborne*	O. W.	Oswego	KS
Rase*	E. R.	Oswego	KS
Swank*	William	Oswego	KS
Barnes	J. H.	Ottawa	KS
Beekman	Fred.	Ottawa	KS
Corwin	E. H.	Ottawa	KS
Harris	C. L.	Ottawa	KS
Mathews & Reed		Ottawa	KS
Kent & Amburn*		Ottumwa	KS
Howard	W. S.	Paolo	KS
McMahon	Mrs. F. V.	Paolo	KS
Beck*	E. H.	Parsons	KS
Sipple	A. B.	Parsons	KS
Standiford	J. F.	Parsons	KS
Bishop & Buckley		Peabody	KS
Smith	E. W.	Pittsburgh	KS
Hampton	A. W.	Pleasonton	KS
Lyman & Son		Pomona	KS
Peterson	C.	Randolph	KS
Allen	J. H.	Russell	KS
Doolittle	R. C.	Sabetha	KS
Finley & Co.*	I. I.	St. Marys	KS
Holcomb	O.	Salina	KS
Hopkins	T. E.	Salina	KS
Jennings	Joseph	Scandia	KS
Jaquith	E. C.	Sedan	KS
Cottrell	D. H.	Seneca	KS
Shaff	J. S.	Seneca	KS
Hall	W. W.	Smith Center	KS

PHOTOGRAPHERS LISTED BY CITY/STATE IN THE UNITED STATES 1888-1889

NAME		ADDRESS	CITY	STATE
Cotton*	Enoch		Sterling	KS
Harens	C. V.		Sterling	KS
Atkinson*	A. T.		Thayer	KS
Aldridge	George	1013 N. Kansas	Topeka	KS
Atherton	M. M.		Topeka	KS
Downing	George		Topeka	KS
Griggs Bros.			Topeka	KS
Griggs	E. W.		Topeka	KS
Leonard & Martin			Topeka	KS
Leonard	J. H.	613 Kansas	Topeka	KS
Martin	H. T.	721 Kansas	Topeka	KS
Scott & Co.		602 N. Kansas	Topeka	KS
Snyder	C. J.		Topeka	KS
Snyder	R.	527 Kansas	Topeka	KS
Winney	M. A.	216 Kansas	Topeka	KS
Partlon	Mrs. L. A.		Toronto	KS
Hudson & Gard			Valley Center	KS
Shellaberger	G. G.		Valley Falls	KS
Workey	W. A.		Wakeeney	KS
Hammaker	J. D.		Wamego	KS
Glass*	C. G.		Washington	KS
Sproul	J. J.		Waterville	KS
Cooper	Thomas		Weir	KS
Davenport*	G. F.		Wellington	KS
Snell	E. B.		Wellington	KS
Zeller	W. E.		Wellington	KS
Vreeland & Bank			Westmoreland	KS
Hopkins*	C. E.		Wetmore	KS
Pusley			Wetmore	KS
Baldwin & Son			Wichita	KS
Enos & Co.	E. W.		Wichita	KS
Harden	A. W.		Wichita	KS
Mohler	J. W.		Wichita	KS
Rogers	W. S.		Wichita	KS
White	W. A.		Wilson	KS
Beck	Hezekiah		Winfield	KS
Kelly	M. F.		Winfield	KS
Rodocker	David		Winfield	KS
Babbitt	J. P.		Wyandotte	KS
Clute	E. E.		Wyandotte	KS

NAME		ADDRESS	CITY	STATE
Robinson	W. J.		Wyandotte	KS
Scanlon	Mrs. J. B.		Wyandotte	KS
Scott	A. B.		Xenia	KS
Shirley	S. R.		Yates Center	KS
Brush	L. N.		Bowling Green	KY
Shartle	H.		Bowling Green	KY
Simms	Nicholas		Central City	KY
McClain	J. W.		Columbia	KY
Morris	George W.		Cornishville	KY
Hoyer	H. C.		Covington	KY
Cox	W. H.		Cynthiana	KY
Fox	Ed. H.		Danville	KY
Hamilton*	J. K.		Frankfort	KY
Mattern	H. G.		Frankfort	KY
Bottomly	Thomas F.		Franklin	KY
Robertson	L. D.		Franklin	KY
Webb	Marion		Franklin	KY
Bottomly	Thomas F.		Glasgow	KY
Hardman	J. F.		Greenville	KY
Spillman	B. F.		Harrodsburg	KY
Hunton	F. N.		Henderson	KY
Roberts	A. G.		Henderson	KY
Campbell	H. S.		Hickman	KY
Bell	R. H.		Hodgensville	KY
Anderson	Clarence		Hopkinsville	KY
Anderson & Cheaney			Hopkinsville	KY
Butler	Robert G.		Lexington	KY
Johns	W. E.		Lexington	KY
Mullen	James		Lexington	KY
Bergmann	Caroline	204 W. Market	Louisville	KY
Bettison	N. Byron	323 4th	Louisville	KY
Brooks	Walter W.	748 E. Market	Louisville	KY
Carpenter & Chase		846 W. Market	Louisville	KY
Clemens	Mathias J.	336 Market	Louisville	KY
Craig*	Charles E.	637 Preston	Louisville	KY
Crosby	George E.	920 W. Market	Louisville	KY
Devenney	C. H.	267 W. Jefferson	Louisville	KY
Doerr	J. Henry	1202 W. Market	Louisville	KY
Elrod	J. C.	313 W. Jefferson	Louisville	KY
Garrity	Miss	307 4th	Louisville	KY

PHOTOGRAPHERS LISTED BY CITY/STATE IN THE UNITED STATES 1888-1889

NAME		ADDRESS	CITY	STATE
Gregory	J. M.	810 W. Market	Louisville	KY
Hays	E. William	924 1st	Louisville	KY
Husband	Harvey	613 W. Market	Louisville	KY
Klauber	Edward	332 4th	Louisville	KY
Roche	John L.	731 W. Market	Louisville	KY
Rue	A. B.	341 4th	Louisville	KY
Steinberg	Louis	216 W. Market	Louisville	KY
Stuber	W. G.	434 E. Market	Louisville	KY
Vander May	John S.	1409 ½ W. Market	Louisville	KY
Wybrandt	Frank	418 W. Market	Louisville	KY
Hardeman	L. E.		Madisonville	KY
Simpson & Wright			Mayfield	KY
Stevens & Trapp*			Maysville	KY
Brooks	E. A.		Morganfield	KY
Bryan	C. H.		Mount Sterling	KY
Carroll	J. P.		New Haven	KY
Cain	C. T.		Owensboro	KY
Mathis	George W.		Owensboro	KY
Morgan	W.		Paris	KY
Redmon	E. C.		Pine Knot	KY
Schlegel	Louis		Richmond	KY
Sandifer	J. M.		Somerset	KY
Jameson	J. W.		Stamping Ground	KY
Barr	Mike		Tompkinsville	KY
Barbour	J. S.		Williamstown	KY
Albert & Son	A.		Alexandria	LA
Lytte	A. D.		Baton Rouge	LA
Mealy	E. W.		Monroe	LA
Dubus	J.		New Iberia	LA
Adams*	Charles H.	111 Royal	New Orleans	LA
Adams	Charles H.	145 Canal	New Orleans	LA
Carriere	P. F.		New Orleans	LA
Clarke*	John H.	151 Canal	New Orleans	LA
Clarke	John H.	161 Canal	New Orleans	LA
Daliet & Bro.		33 Frenchman	New Orleans	LA
Decuir	J. A.	195 Canal	New Orleans	LA
Elkin	L.	163 ½ Poydras	New Orleans	LA
Elkins*	Mrs. Lotta	195 Canal	New Orleans	LA
Farrar	Mrs. Adele	284 Tulane	New Orleans	LA
Interguglielmi	Louis	227 Royal	New Orleans	LA

PHOTOGRAPHERS LISTED BY CITY/STATE IN THE UNITED STATES 1888-1889

NAME		ADDRESS	CITY	STATE
Jauchler*	Stephen	211 Orleans	New Orleans	LA
Kammer	Joseph H.	118 Pleasant	New Orleans	LA
Leitz	Mrs. Louisa	606 Magazine	New Orleans	LA
Lilienthal*	Theodore	32 Chartres	New Orleans	LA
Lilienthal	Theodore	137 Canal	New Orleans	LA
McClure	Marstela E.	192 ½ Camp	New Orleans	LA
Massicot	Eugene	Magazine	New Orleans	LA
Moses	Bernard	369 Dryades	New Orleans	LA
Moses	Gustave	92 Canal	New Orleans	LA
Prye*	Thomas	131 Poydras	New Orleans	LA
Pye	Thomas	131 Poydras	New Orleans	LA
Reyton	Miss Ada	147 Canal	New Orleans	LA
Robira	Louis	243 Royal	New Orleans	LA
Roth	Andrew	11 Frenchman	New Orleans	LA
Scoggins	James H.	163 Poydras	New Orleans	LA
Simon	Eugene	183 Canal	New Orleans	LA
Souby	Edward J.	113 Canal	New Orleans	LA
Washburn	W. W.	109 Canal	New Orleans	LA
Yenni	C. T.	113 Canal	New Orleans	LA
Perkins	John W.		Andover	ME
Ayer	G. O.		Augusta	ME
Hendel	J. S.		Augusta	ME
Shorey	C. E.		Augusta	ME
Dole	A. K.		Bangor	ME
Lansil	George		Bangor	ME
Marston	C. L.		Bangor	ME
Weston	F. C.		Bangor	ME
Hatch	A.		Bath	ME
Higgins	J. C.		Bath	ME
McFadden	A.		Bath	ME
Kilgore	H. L.		Belfast	ME
Tuttle	W. C.		Belfast	ME
White	Ed. N.		Belfast	ME
Hobbs	J. S.		Bethel	ME
Abbott	B.		Biddeford	ME
Gardner & Philbrick			Biddeford	ME
McLellan	R. R.		Biddeford	ME
Sawtell	E. E.		Biddeford	ME
Shaw	Arthur L.		Biddeford	ME
McDougall	F. H.		Booth Bay	ME

PHOTOGRAPHERS LISTED BY CITY/STATE IN THE UNITED STATES 1888-1889

NAME	ADDRESS	CITY	STATE
Cromwell	B. J.	Bowdoinhain	ME
Berry	E. M.	Bridgton	ME
Poor	C. G.	Brownfield	ME
Reed & Preble		Brunswick	ME
Pease	Mrs.	Bucksport	ME
McKay & Co.	H. D.	Calais	ME
Roberts & Betts		Calais	ME
Stoddard	F. A.	Calais	ME
Lane	W. V.	Camden	ME
Mills	H. A.	Camden	ME
Hau	E. W.	Caribou	ME
Larrabee	George A.	Carroll	ME
Osgood	T. B.	Damariscotta	ME
Powers	Peter	Deer Isle (Green's Landing)	ME
Fassett	A. G.	Dexter	ME
Dinsmore	Mrs. D. C.	Dover	ME
Morrison	J. T.	Dover	ME
Davis	Mrs. A.	East Corinth	ME
Loring	Davis	Eastport	ME
Bradley	B.	Eden	ME
Joy	B. F.	Ellsworth	ME
Osgood	Irving	Ellsworth	ME
Cook & Co.		Fairfield	ME
Starbird		Farmington	ME
Wallace	J. H.	Fort Fairfield	ME
Whitton	J. W.	Fort Fairfield	ME
Sumner	Charles	Foxcraft	ME
Coffin	Ira S.	Freeport	ME
Howe	Randolph	Fryeburg	ME
Cochran	J. H. & H. H.	Gardiner	ME
McIntosh	George F.	Gardiner	ME
Variel	J. S.	Gardiner	ME
Hunton	F. D.	Hallowell	ME
Flye	Winfeld W.	East Hiram	ME
Bryson	John	Houlton	ME
Estabrook*	I. S.	Houlton	ME
Estabrook	J. S.	Houlton	ME
Turner	J. C.	Isle Au Haut	ME
Wooster	Jno.	Jonesport	ME

PHOTOGRAPHERS LISTED BY CITY/STATE IN THE UNITED STATES 1888-1889

NAME		ADDRESS	CITY	STATE
Dean	W. P.		Katahdin Iron Works	ME
Gulney	Caleb S.		Kennebunk	ME
Lane	A. H.		Lee	ME
Curtis & Rose			Lewiston	ME
Larrock	H.		Lewiston	ME
Stanley	F. E.		Lewiston	ME
Tapley	Isaac S.		Lewiston	ME
Worthley	W. E. G.		Lewiston	ME
Philpot	Fred. C.		Limerick	ME
Hamblin	Alpheus L.		Lovell	ME
Bonney & Roberts			Machias	ME
Vose	E.		Machias	ME
Ingall	Z.		Madison	ME
Clements	C. F.		Milo	ME
Bridge	E. C.	Mechanic's Falls	Minot	ME
Hall	John L.		Monson	ME
Sherburne	F. H.		Monson	ME
Ingalls	Z. D.		New Vineyard	ME
Barton	C. J.		North Anson	ME
Hartwell	C. C.		North Vassalborough	ME
Libby	Minnie		Norway	ME
Swan & Cobb			Norway	ME
Robinson	G.		Oakland	ME
Goding	C. G.		Old Orchard	ME
Whittemore	A. J.		Old Orchard	ME
Buker	M. S.		Oldtown	ME
Chase	J. K.		Oxford	ME
Peters	L. H.		Patten	ME
Kelly	John		Perry	ME
Pratt	A. S.		Phillips	ME
Howe	W. H.		Pittsfield	ME
Mason	A. F.		Porter	ME
Fox	A. R. P.		Rezar Falls	ME
Armand*	E. F.		Portland	ME
Brown	G. E.	285 ½ Middle	Portland	ME
Davis	Alonzo S.	180 Middle	Portland	ME
Harris	H. V.	16 Market Sq.	Portland	ME
Hearn	C. W.	514 Congress	Portland	ME
Hearn*	Charles W.		Portland	ME
Heath & Smith*			Portland	ME

PHOTOGRAPHERS LISTED BY CITY/STATE IN THE UNITED STATES 1888-1889

NAME		ADDRESS	CITY	STATE
Jackson & Kenny		478 ½ Congress	Portland	ME
King	M. F.	482 Congress	Portland	ME
Lamson*	J. H.		Portland	ME
Lamson Studio		5 Temple	Portland	ME
Nason & Son*	J. H.		Portland	ME
Norton	H. Q.	276 Middle	Portland	ME
Peck	John M.		Portland	ME
Wright Studio		518 ½ Congress	Portland	ME
Sweet	J. A.	518 ½ Congress	Portland	ME
Estabrook	T. S.		Presque Isle	ME
Kimball	A. W.		Richmond	ME
Crockett	T. H.		Rockland	ME
Singhi	John F.		Rockland	ME
Smith	W. A.		Rockland	ME
Webber	W. L.		Saco	ME
Chandler	J. W.		St. Albans	ME
Osborn	L.		St. Albans	ME
McKechnye	E.		Sangerville	ME
Colson	Edgar A.		Searsport	ME
Veazie	J. H.		Sherman	ME
Conant	F. L.		Skowhegan	ME
Hawkes	N. S.		Skowhegan	ME
Sturtevant*	E. E., Crayon Artist		Skowhegan	ME
Sturtevant	E. F.		Skowhegan	ME
Gordon	E. M.		Solon	ME
Morse	Levi		Thomaston	ME
Emory & Bradbury		S. W. Harbor	Tremont	ME
Whitmore	J. W.		Waldoborough	ME
Parsons*	W. H.		Waterborough	ME
Carlton	C. G.		Waterville	ME
Flanagan	J. H.		Waterville	ME
Pitcher	Gideon		Waterville	ME
Vose & Son	S. S.		Waterville	ME
Healey	C. D.		Wells	ME
Day	F. O.		Wesley	ME
Day	George A.		Wesley	ME
Day	M. E.		Wesley	ME
Roberts	H. H.		Wesley	ME
Gustin	J. E.		West Brook	ME
Wheelden	G. R.		Winterport	ME

PHOTOGRAPHERS LISTED BY CITY/STATE IN THE UNITED STATES 1888-1889

NAME		ADDRESS	CITY	STATE
Hammond	C. E.		Winthrop	ME
Gooding	Charles G.		Yarmouth	ME
Brachrach & Bros.		327 W. Lexington	Baltimore	MD
Baltimore Photographic Co.		66 Lexington	Baltimore	MD
Beck	G. F.	327 S. Sharp	Baltimore	MD
Bendann	D.	28 E. Baltimore	Baltimore	MD
Betz, Jr.	John	417 N. Washington	Baltimore	MD
Blessing & Co.*		46 N. Charles	Baltimore	MD
Blessing & Co.		214 N. Charles	Baltimore	MD
Bowerman & Becker		605 E. Baltimore	Baltimore	MD
Buffham Bros.*		116 S. Broadway	Baltimore	MD
Buffham Bros.		5 W. Lexington	Baltimore	MD
Busey*	N. H.	24 N. Charles	Baltimore	MD
Busey	N. H.	112 N. Charles	Baltimore	MD
Chase	William M.	Eutaw	Baltimore	MD
Clinedinst	B. M.	216 N. Charles	Baltimore	MD
Clindiust*	B. M.	20 N. Charles	Baltimore	MD
Cover*	W. L.	560 W. Baltimore	Baltimore	MD
Cover	W. L.	754 W. Baltimore	Baltimore	MD
Cronhardt & Son	Henry	1412 E. Madison	Baltimore	MD
Cummins*	J. S.	7 N. Charles	Baltimore	MD
Cummins	J. S.	106 N. Charles	Baltimore	MD
Ernsberger	John D.	419 E. Baltimore	Baltimore	MD
Freeburger	Alexander	709 Light	Baltimore	MD
Getz	William	210 N. Charles	Baltimore	MD
Holyland*	J.	229 W. Baltimore	Baltimore	MD
Holyland	J.	3 W. Baltimore	Baltimore	MD
Leach*	C.	207 W. Biddle	Baltimore	MD
Leach	C.	19 E. Baltimore	Baltimore	MD
Lusby*	C. P.	91 W. Baltimore	Baltimore	MD
Lusby	C. P.	403 E. Baltimore	Baltimore	MD
Mason & Co.	H. M.	1519 E. Pratt	Baltimore	MD
Metzung	F. J.	472 W. Baltimore	Baltimore	MD
Mueller & Co.*		166 S. Broadway	Baltimore	MD
Mueller & Co.		515 Broadway	Baltimore	MD
Oberdallhoff*	W. H. S.	125 W. Baltimore	Baltimore	MD
Perkins*	H. L.	103 W. Baltimore	Baltimore	MD
Perkins	John W.	1316 Pennsylvania	Baltimore	MD
Pollock*	H.	44 Lexington	Baltimore	MD
Pollock	H.	9 E. Lexington	Baltimore	MD

PHOTOGRAPHERS LISTED BY CITY/STATE IN THE UNITED STATES 1888-1889

NAME		ADDRESS	CITY	STATE
Proctor	J. H.	409 N. Gay	Baltimore	MD
Quarterly*	C.	217 W. Baltimore	Baltimore	MD
Robinson*	M. L.	Eutaw & Lexington	Baltimore	MD
Robinson	Martin L. .	Eutaw	Baltimore	MD
Rooney*	F. A.	19 E. Baltimore	Baltimore	MD
Rooney*	J. H.	73 W. Baltimore	Baltimore	MD
Rooney	J. H.	417 E. Baltimore	Baltimore	MD
Rudolph	Ernest B.	646 W. Baltimore	Baltimore	MD
Russell & Co.		17 & 203 W. Lexington	Baltimore	MD
Schaefer*	J. H.	643 W. Baltimore	Baltimore	MD
Schaefer	J. H.	887 W. Baltimore	Baltimore	MD
Schutte	Henry B.	423 N. Washington	Baltimore	MD
Selander	Julius	1710 Eastern	Baltimore	MD
Shorey	W. F.	131 E. Baltimore	Baltimore	MD
Stahn*	M.	87 N. Gay	Baltimore	MD
Stahn	M.	229 N. Gay	Baltimore	MD
Towson & Proctor		163 N. Gay	Baltimore	MD
Trainor	J. M. D.	731 W. Baltimore	Baltimore	MD
Wagner	C. A.	65 W. Baltimore	Baltimore	MD
Wagner & Son*	F.	63 W. Baltimore	Baltimore	MD
Wagner & Sons	F.	427 E. Baltimore	Baltimore	MD
Walzi*	Richard	205 W. Baltimore	Baltimore	MD
Walzl	Richard	21 E. Baltimore	Baltimore	MD
Walzl	L.	157 S. Broadway	Baltimore	MD
Wilkes*	D. J.	125 W. Baltimore	Baltimore	MD
Wilkes	D. J.	211 E. Baltimore	Baltimore	MD
Wunder	Mary A.	217 N Eutaw	Baltimore	MD
Damelle	T. L.		Cumberland	MD
Berger	William A.		Frederick	MD
Byerly	J. Davis		Frederick	MD
Marken	J. R.		Frederick	MD
Wagoner	J. H.		Hagerstown	MD
Barry	A. L.		Port Deposit	MD
Reese	C. S.		Westminster	MD
Marsh	Levi		Adams	MA
Parsons	W. D.		Adams	MA
Morin	I. Noel		Amesburg	MA
Thompson	William C.		Amesburg	MA
Lovell	J. L.		Amherst	MA
Litchfield	Edward C.		Arlington	MA

PHOTOGRAPHERS LISTED BY CITY/STATE IN THE UNITED STATES 1888-1889

NAME		ADDRESS	CITY	STATE
Moore	G. W.		Athol	MA
Towne	Anna F.		Athol	MA
Emery	W. H.	Athol Center	Athol	MA
Ward	C. E.	North	Attleborough	MA
Burns	W. F.		Ayer	MA
Putnam	S. A.	Hyannis	Barnstable	MA
Hinckley	Frank W.		Barre	MA
Hodgman	Otis		Bedford	MA
Alley	Hiram F.		Beverly	MA
Alden	A. E.	63 Court	Boston	MA
Allen & Rowell		25 Winter	Boston	MA
Andrews	John D.	178 Washington	Boston	MA
Architectural Publishing Co.*		70 Kilby	Boston	MA
Astrom	Carl G.	7 State	Boston	MA
Ayer	George O.	74 Meridian	Boston	MA
Barentzen Photographic Parlors		11 Park Sq	Boston	MA
Beane	C. E.	2180 Washington	Boston	MA
Black & Co.	J. W.	333 Washington	Boston	MA
Bradley*	Alvin F.	18 Blue Hill	Boston	MA
Bradley	W. L.	14 Hanover	Boston	MA
Burnham	T. R.	725 Washington	Boston	MA
Bushby & McCurdy		521 Washington	Boston	MA
Chadband*	F. A.	330 Warren	Boston	MA
Chadband	F. A.	320 Warren	Boston	MA
Chickering*	Elmer	21 West	Boston	MA
Chickering*	W. E.	467 & 627 Washington	Boston	MA
Chickering	W. E.	467 Washington	Boston	MA
Conly	C. F.	465 Washington	Boston	MA
Coolidge	Baldwin	154 Tremont	Boston	MA
Cronin & Critcherson*		32 Hayward Place	Boston	MA
Cronin & Critcherson		33 Hayward Pl	Boston	MA
Dodge	George K.	646 Washington	Boston	MA
Dunshee & Co.	E. S.	3 Tremont Row	Boston	MA
Ellis	T. W.	120 Court	Boston	MA
Eoley*	Warren G.	6 Winter	Boston	MA
Fancy	J. A.	43 Winter	Boston	MA
Folsom	A. H.	48 Alleghany	Boston	MA
Foster	Charles H.	219 Hanover	Boston	MA
Freeman	G. W.	82 Main	Boston	MA
Fregeau	Lawrence	1607 Washington	Boston	MA

PHOTOGRAPHERS LISTED BY CITY/STATE IN THE UNITED STATES 1888-1889

NAME		ADDRESS	CITY	STATE
Gagne	E.	913 Washington	Boston	MA
Gertz	E. R.	105 Dorchester	Boston	MA
Gilchrist	George E.	24 Tremont Row	Boston	MA
Gillis	Frank E.	164 Leverett	Boston	MA
Glines	Arthur A.	6 Winter	Boston	MA
Gray	G. E.	1070 Tremont	Boston	MA
Haley	John F.	229 Atlantic	Boston	MA
Haley	John F.	Dover	Boston	MA
Haley	Joseph F.	249 Dover	Boston	MA
Haley	Joseph F.	Hanover	Boston	MA
Hall	I. Wilton	21 School	Boston	MA
Hardy	A. N.	493 Washington	Boston	MA
Hartford	F. A.	376 W. Broadway	Boston	MA
Hastings	George H.	147 Tremont	Boston	MA
Hatstat	A. J.	71 Cambridge	Boston	MA
Hawes	J. J.	19 Tremont Row	Boston	MA
Hill	C. G.	363 Washington	Boston	MA
Hill & Hazelton		24 Hanover	Boston	MA
Holland	H. F.	10 Temple Place	Boston	MA
Holmes Bros.		19 Main	Boston	MA
Holton	Eugene A.	8 Summer	Boston	MA
Jackson	Dwight N.	823 Washington	Boston	MA
Kimball	C.	140 Court	Boston	MA
King	C. H.	767 Washington	Boston	MA
Latto	J. C.	202 W. Broadway	Boston	MA
Leavitt & Sherman		145 A. Tremont	Boston	MA
Leavitt & Sherman		535 Washington	Boston	MA
Leddy	T. J.	1157 Tremont	Boston	MA
Litchfield	Charles M.	352 Washington	Boston	MA
McCormick	J. L.	22 Winter	Boston	MA
MacDonald & Co.	C. F.	2228 Washington	Boston	MA
Macorquodale	Hugh	171 Tremont	Boston	MA
Magras*	John	796 Washington	Boston	MA
Magras	John	196 Washington	Boston	MA
Marshall	Augustus	44 Boylston	Boston	MA
McCosker	T.	51 Washington	Boston	MA
McDowell	Alexander	46 Broadway Extension	Boston	MA
McGilvray*	Joseph	175 & 218 Dover	Boston	MA
McGilvray	Joseph	175 Dover	Boston	MA
Metcalf	Franklin	503 Washington	Boston	MA

PHOTOGRAPHERS LISTED BY CITY/STATE IN THE UNITED STATES 1888-1889

NAME		ADDRESS	CITY	STATE
Moloney	M.	35 Hanover	Boston	MA
Needham	F. J.	22 Tremont Row	Boston	MA
Notman*	James	99 Boylston	Boston	MA
Notman Photographic	Co.	3 Park	Boston	MA
Partridge	W. H.	2832 Washington	Boston	MA
Patten	J. D.	47 Hanover	Boston	MA
Peabody	Henry G.	52 Boylston	Boston	MA
Pepper	A. F.	1051 Tremont	Boston	MA
Photo-Etching Co.		299 Washington	Boston	MA
Pierce & Co.	William H.	352 Washington	Boston	MA
Plimpton	Arthur L.	7 Hawthorne	Boston	MA
Ritz	Ernest F.	58 Temple	Boston	MA
Shea	M. A.	194 ½ Hanover	Boston	MA
Sherman	Wilson S.	535 Washington	Boston	MA
Smith	Edward F.	22 Milk	Boston	MA
Smith*	H. G.	90 Studio Building	Boston	MA
Stebbins	N. L.	521 Washington	Boston	MA
Story	Augustus	3 Lewis	E. Boston	MA
Towne	W. L.	425 Washington	Boston	MA
Wardwell*	W. H.	1743 Washington	Boston	MA
Wardwell	W. H.	7143 Washington	Boston	MA
Warren	W. Shaw	41 Winter	Boston	MA
Whiting	G. W.	7 Tremont Row	Boston	MA
Wing & Co.	S.	120 Cambridge	Boston	MA
Wing & Co.	S.	478 Washington	Boston	MA
Wood	Fred J.	237 W. Canton	Boston	MA
Worden	N. R.	48 Winter	Boston	MA
Morse	Gardner S.		W. Boxford	MA
Robinson	H. N.		Bridgewater	MA
Bass	E. A.		Brockton	MA
Burrell	David T.		Brockton	MA
Caldwell	W. N.		Brockton	MA
Foy	C. W.		Brockton	MA
Stiff	Thomas P.		Brockton	MA
Bachs & Bros.	G. W.		Cambridgeport	MA
Barrett	Henry		E. Cambridgeport	MA
Butterfield	D. W.		Cambridgeport	MA
Morse	E. T.		Cambridgeport	MA
Pachs & Bros.*	G. W.		Cambridgeport	MA
Taylor	F. J.		Cambridgeport	MA

PHOTOGRAPHERS LISTED BY CITY/STATE IN THE UNITED STATES 1888-1889

NAME		ADDRESS	CITY	STATE
Whitney & Son			Cambridgeport	MA
Brown	C. E.		Chelsea	MA
Hayden	Mrs. Celia		Chelsea	MA
Taylor & Blair			Chelsea	MA
Ludwig	Frank		Chicopee	MA
Judd	H. M.		Chicopee Falls	MA
Boynton	J. J.		Clinton	MA
Helmold	Adolar		Clinton	MA
Kabley	Charles A.		Clinton	MA
Warren	Joseph W.		Cottage City	MA
Slater	A. C.		East Douglas	MA
Richardson	W. P.		Easthampton	MA
Williams	M. F.		North Easton	MA
Davis & Douglass			Fall River	MA
Gay	Mrs. Edwin F.		Fall River	MA
Jette	Joseph		Fall River	MA
Kellogg	H. W.		Fall River	MA
Suddad	John F.		Fall River	MA
Suddard*	John F.		Fall River	MA
Thibautt	Louis		Fall River	MA
Howard	E. E.		Fitchburg	MA
Kimball Bros.			Fitchburg	MA
Moulton	H. D.		Fitchburg	MA
Moulton	Joseph C.		Fitchburg	MA
Lewis	J. H.		Foxborough	MA
Stevens	Caleb A.		Foxborough	MA
Drake	H. S.		S. Framingham	MA
Sweet	J. L.		Framingham	MA
Reed	R. A.		Franklin	MA
Allen	Warren P.		Gardner	MA
Caswell Bros.			Gardner	MA
Batchelder*			Georgetown	MA
Adams	E.	120 Main	Gloucester	MA
Churchill	L. O.		Gloucester	MA
Katell	S. M.		Gloucester	MA
Lyon	T. D.		Gloucester	MA
White	Augustus A.		Gloucester	MA
Van Patten	W. H.		Great Barrington	MA
Popkins	Benjamin F.		Greenfield	MA
Briggs	S. M.		S. Hanson	MA

PHOTOGRAPHERS LISTED BY CITY/STATE IN THE UNITED STATES 1888-1889

NAME	ADDRESS	CITY	STATE
Cahoon	Clement A.	Harwich	MA
Kingsley	Lewis H.	Hatfield	MA
Anderson	A. W.	Haverhill	MA
Fowler	Edward P.	Haverhill	MA
Tennat	P. W.	Haverhill	MA
Vickey & Reed		Haverhill	MA
Vickery*	D. B.	Haverhill	MA
Butler	D. E.	Holyoke	MA
Cady	W. J.	Holyoke	MA
Demers & Son		Holyoke	MA
Goldsmith	Charles B.	Holyoke	MA
Labelle	E.	Holyoke	MA
Miles	W. B.	Holyoke	MA
Monty	John B. L.	Holyoke	MA
Burgess	Frank H.	Hopkinton	MA
Marean	W. C.	Hubbardston	MA
Sargent	F. V.	Hubbardston	MA
Lewis	Russell B.	Hudson	MA
Putnam	S. A.	Hyannis	MA
Barrett	W. H.	Hyde Park	MA
Beal	W. A.	Ipswich	MA
Dexter	George G.	Ipswich	MA
Bean	A. M.	Lawrence	MA
Hamor	A. B.	Lawrence	MA
Kenefick-Owen	A.	Lawrence	MA
Kenefick*	Owen A.	Lawrence	MA
Lawrence	C. A.	Lawrence	MA
Leck	George H.	Lawrence	MA
Russell	Frank	Lawrence	MA
Cutting	Chauncey P.	Lee	MA
Richardson	L. A.	Leominster	MA
Emerson	M. W.	Lowell	MA
Gilchrist	George C.	Lowell	MA
Hayden	M. M.	Lowell	MA
Kimball Photographic Art Studio		Lowell	MA
Loupret	N. J.	Lowell	MA
Marion	John S.	Lowell	MA
Morrill	Frank L.	Lowell	MA
Sanborn	Amos H.	Lowell	MA
Smith	Miss Costillia D.	Lowell	MA

PHOTOGRAPHERS LISTED BY CITY/STATE IN THE UNITED STATES 1888-1889

NAME		ADDRESS	CITY	STATE
Warren	O. H.		Lowell	MA
Woodside	W. E.		Lowell	MA
Bowers	W. T.		Lynn	MA
Cook	L. W.		Lynn	MA
Dewhurst	O. T.		Lynn	MA
Erickson	Frank C.		Lynn	MA
Lamson	Josiah		Lynn	MA
Sweetser	C. A.		Lynn	MA
Taggard	F. E.		Lynn	MA
Twist	Nathan H.		Lynn	MA
Wires	William H.		Lynn	MA
Burdick	H. R.		Malden	MA
Morrill	F. A.		Malden	MA
Page	F. R.		Malden	MA
Wilson	M. C.	76 Pleasant	Malden	MA
Allen	J. R.		Mansfield	MA
Albee	M. H.		Marlborough	MA
Kuhn	W. J.		Marlborough	MA
McKenney	A. S.		Marlborough	MA
Pratt	H. E.		Marlborough	MA
Richardson	J. C.		Marlborough	MA
Chandler	Martin		Marshfield	MA
Nelson	William B.		Mattapoisett	MA
Holmes	C. D.		Maynard	MA
Chamberlain	Ephraim		Medfield	MA
Treadwell	Albert		Medford	MA
Zert	William		Medford	MA
Putnam	George T.		Middleborough	MA
Beatty	Kate		Milford	MA
Gardner & Co.	A. C.		Milford	MA
Willis	E. L.		Milford	MA
Stewart	Frank		Millbury	MA
Chapman	George L.		Montague	MA
Freeman	Josiah		Nantucket	MA
Phillips	A.		Natick	MA
Woodhill	J. W.		Natick	MA
Benoit	A.		New Bedford	MA
Doane	Robert N. B.		New Bedford	MA
Gifford	Noah		New Bedford	MA
Hatch	Henry F.		New Bedford	MA

PHOTOGRAPHERS LISTED BY CITY/STATE IN THE UNITED STATES 1888-1889

NAME		ADDRESS	CITY	STATE
Hawes	William		New Bedford	MA
Knowles	Joseph C.		New Bedford	MA
Parlow	George F.		New Bedford	MA
Pierce & Bushnell			New Bedford	MA
Roberts	J. E.		New Bedford	MA
Smith	Henry		New Bedford	MA
Smith	Morris W. (Estate of)		New Bedford	MA
Taber & Co.	Charles		New Bedford	MA
Wolfenstein*	V.		New Bedford	MA
Wolsenstein	V.		New Bedford	MA
Chase	Ezra B.		Newburyport	MA
Chase	J. M.		Newburyport	MA
Macintosh	H. P.		Newburyport	MA
Reed	Selwin C.		Newburyport	MA
Glines*	Arthur A.		Newton	MA
Hurd*	Ernest W.		North Adams	MA
Ward*	H. D.		North Adams	MA
Work	Frank P.		North Brookfield	MA
Knowlton Bros.			Northampton	MA
Lovell	Charles O.		Northampton	MA
Schadee	Ferdinand Florence		Northampton	MA
Schillare	A. J.		Northampton	MA
Brigham	Joseph T.		Northfield	MA
Talbot	J. Warren		Norwood	MA
Thompson	C. P.		Orange	MA
Thompson	G. H.		Orange	MA
Wilcox	G. W.		Palmer	MA
Keith	Justin W.		Pelham	MA
Goss	E. L.		E. Pepperell	MA
Clark	Forester		Pittsfield	MA
Hollis	C. R.		Pittsfield	MA
Simmons	E. A.	74 North, Wollison Block	Pittsfield	MA
Watkins	Mr.	43 North	Pittsfield	MA
Watkins & Simmons*			Pittsfield	MA
Rogers	C. H.		Plymouth	MA
Skinner	F. A.		Plymouth	MA
Gifford	Fred A. H.		Provincetown	MA
Nickerson	G. H.		Provincetown	MA
Bussell	A. Frank		Quincy	MA
Dailey	E. V.		Rockland	MA

PHOTOGRAPHERS LISTED BY CITY/STATE IN THE UNITED STATES 1888-1889

NAME	ADDRESS		CITY	STATE
Bousley	Nathaniel C.		Salem	MA
Cross	A. B.		Salem	MA
Genest	Gedeon		Salem	MA
Gray	Warren A.		Salem	MA
Hussey	William A.		Salem	MA
Lefavour*	John S., (Landscape)		Salem	MA
Lefavour	John S.		Salem	MA
Peabody*	Edwin N. (Landscape)		Salem	MA
Peabody	Edwin N.		Salem	MA
Stamford	George E.		Salem	MA
Staniford*	George E.		Salem	MA
Taylor & Preston			Salem	MA
Wiston*	Samuel C.		Salem	MA
Wiston	Samuel C.		Salem	MA
Patch	Jonas K.		Shelburne Falls	MA
Freeman	B. F.		Somerville	MA
Keefe	Richard		Somerville	MA
Lamson & Co.			Somerville	MA
Sprague & Hathaway			Somerville	MA
Williams	James H.		S. Scituate	MA
Labonte	Soloman A.		Southbridge	MA
Lovell	George M.		Southbridge	MA
Hevy	L. N.		Spencer	MA
Jaynes	E. L.		Spencer	MA
Barnard	George C.	33 Goodrich	Springfield	MA
Bishop	S. J. & A. H.	380 Main	Springfield	MA
Brown	A. V.	380 Main	Springfield	MA
Bucholz	Herman	365 Main	Springfield	MA
Butler	W. S.	313 Main	Springfield	MA
Goldsmith & Co.	E. C.	374 Main	Springfield	MA
Hardy	F. W.	310 Main	Springfield	MA
Kittell	Charles		Springfield	MA
Laplant	Octave	Oak, I. O.	Springfield	MA
Laplant*	O.		Springfield	MA
Lazelle	Edward J.	358 Main	Springfield	MA
Mallory	J. H.	68 James	Springfield	MA
Miller	Walter M.		Springfield	MA
Moore & Co.	Chauncey L.	Republican Block	Springfield	MA
Moore	H. C.	Gill's Art Bldg	Springfield	MA
Ratelle	Charles	Worcester, I. O.	Springfield	MA

PHOTOGRAPHERS LISTED BY CITY/STATE IN THE UNITED STATES 1888-1889

NAME		ADDRESS	CITY	STATE
Edgecomb	J. E.		Stoneham	MA
Hunter Bros.			Taunton	MA
Munroe & Van Doorn			Taunton	MA
Woodward	J. A.		Taunton	MA
Smith	E. A. G.		Uxbridge	MA
Walker	W. C.		Uxbridge	MA
Thatcher	H.		Wakefield	MA
Percival	J. P.		Waltham	MA
Van Norman	George H.		Waltham	MA
Webster	W. A.	111 Moody	Waltham	MA
Dexter	J. C.		Ware	MA
Gleason	F. M.		Ware	MA
Carr	W. R.		Wareham	MA
Penfield	D. E.		Warren	MA
North	F. E.		Watertown	MA
Carr	E. S.		Webster	MA
Redman	George H.		Webster	MA
Smith	Charles A.		Webster	MA
Adams	C. A.		West Gardner	MA
Howard & Son	A.		West Gardner	MA
Nash	C. S.		Westborough	MA
Coleman	M. O. T.		Westfield	MA
Lemire	Henri		Westfield	MA
O'Flynn	T. F.		Weymouth	MA
Tirrell	G. W.		E. Weymouth	MA
Foye	C. E.		Whitman	MA
Rudolph	A.		Williamstown	MA
Smith	Hazen A.		Winchendon	MA
McLaughlin	James		Woburn	MA
Strout	Howard E.		Woburn	MA
Baker	J. H.	406 Main	Worcester	MA
Bennett*	A. C.		Worcester	MA
Blair	C. L.	44 Front	Worcester	MA
Blair & Son	R. H.	411 Main	Worcester	MA
Bullard	Mrs. S. G.	424 Main	Worcester	MA
Claflin	C. R. B.	377 Main	Worcester	MA
Clark	H.	352 Main	Worcester	MA
Daniels	A. F.	333 Main	Worcester	MA
Davis	A. E.	503 Main	Worcester	MA
Dupree	H.	239 Front	Worcester	MA

PHOTOGRAPHERS LISTED BY CITY/STATE IN THE UNITED STATES 1888-1889

NAME		ADDRESS	CITY	STATE
Everett	F. O.	393 Main	Worcester	MA
Fitton*	William H.		Worcester	MA
Flodin & Thyberg		411 Main	Worcester	MA
Gilmore Bros.*		204 Front	Worcester	MA
Gillmore	George W.	204 Main	Worcester	MA
Hanlon	T. F.	405 Main	Worcester	MA
Knight	J. H.	23 Washington Sq	Worcester	MA
Lawrence	Frank	492 Main	Worcester	MA
Reed	H. J.	581 Main	Worcester	MA
Rice	F. H.	311 Main	Worcester	MA
Rice	George M.	419 Main	Worcester	MA
Tucker	H. B.	397 Main	Worcester	MA
Underwood	George A.	326 Main	Worcester	MA
Chrisman	John		Adrian	MI
Fairbank	O. D.		Adrian	MI
Foster	J. A.		Adrian	MI
Kidney	W. F.		Adrian	MI
Ball	J. A.		Albion	MI
Graves	E. L.		Albion	MI
Lonsbury	G. W.		Allegan	MI
Porter	M. H.		Allegan	MI
Davidson	J. E.		Alma	MI
Lawson	A. J.		Alpena	MI
Haarer	John		Ann Arbor	MI
Dafoe	J. W.		Ann Arbor	MI
Gibson	J. J.		Ann Arbor	MI
Ravenaugh*	S. B.		Ann Arbor	MI
Speechly	Miss S. T.		Ann Arbor	MI
Story	D. D.		Ann Arbor	MI
Harcourt*	Myron		Baldwin	MI
*Misick	W. A.		Bancroft	MI
Northrup	L. L.		Bangor	MI
Barr & Hayter*			Battle Creek	MI
Battle Creek View Co.*			Battle Creek	MI
Hull & Son*			Battle Creek	MI
Miller	J. F.		Battle Creek	MI
Perry & Son	E. H.		Battle Creek	MI
Colburn	C. B.		Bay City	MI
Culver W. H.			Bay City	MI
Harman & Verner			Bay City	MI

PHOTOGRAPHERS LISTED BY CITY/STATE IN THE UNITED STATES 1888-1889

NAME		ADDRESS	CITY	STATE
Miller Bros.			Bay City	MI
Parker	C. W.		Bay City	MI
Sterling	G. F.		Bay City	MI
Markhain	John		Bellevue	MI
Coates	Alfred		Benton Harbor	MI
McCombe	Robert		Berrien Springs	MI
Chapman*	E. A.		Big Rapids	MI
Hobart	M. E.		Big Rapids	MI
Randall*	S. G.		Big Rapids	MI
Freeman	D. G.		Blissfield	MI
Mays*	Jacob		Blissfield	MI
Gough	George		Brockway Center	MI
Cathcart	Marvin		Buchanan	MI
Kerr	C. E.		Buchanan	MI
Reiterman	William		Burr Oak	MI
Anderson	John		Cadillac	MI
Newell*	A.		Cadillac	MI
Towle & Co.	H. R.		Cadillac	MI
Haefer	F. C.		Calumet	MI
Harper	T. J.		Camden	MI
Duck & Carlson			Caro	MI
Moor	M. V.		Carson City	MI
Maier	Jacob		Cass City	MI
Tainter	E. E.		Cassopolis	MI
Jones	W. H.		Cedar Springs	MI
Bradbeer	A. D.		Charlevoix	MI
Cheney & Christmas			Charlotte	MI
Fowler & Flower*			Charlotte	MI
Fowler	G. H.	S. Cochran	Charlotte	MI
Davidson	W. W.		Cheboygan	MI
Hoskins	C. A.		Cheboygan	MI
Wixson	G. S.		Cheboygan	MI
Shaver	E. E.		Chelsea	MI
Wrightson	Francis		Chesaning	MI
Nix & De Vogt			Clare	MI
Wright	John		Clifford	MI
Cornwall	C. T.		Coldwater	MI
Kleindinst	David		Coldwater	MI
Tiffany	C. E.		Coldwater	MI
Wolcott	C. S.		Coldwater	MI

PHOTOGRAPHERS LISTED BY CITY/STATE IN THE UNITED STATES 1888-1889

NAME		ADDRESS	CITY	STATE
Cornell	J. A.		Colon	MI
Swain	A. C.		Constantine	MI
Thurston	A. R.		Coopersville	MI
Cook *	F. E.		Corunna	MI
Prichard	C. F.		Decatur	MI
Abraham	A. W.		Detroit	MI
Aller*	Charles		Detroit	MI
Alvord	C. E.	244 Woodward	Detroit	MI
Arthur & Philbric		204 Woodward	Detroit	MI
Baker	C. R.	39 Monroe	Detroit	MI
Baker & Johnson*			Detroit	MI
Bardwell*	J. J.		Detroit	MI
Bardwell	Jex	115 Jefferson	Detroit	MI
Butler & Co.	A. C.	253 Woodward	Detroit	MI
Campbell	S. W.		Detroit	MI
De Lemas	Louis	134 Gratiot	Detroit	MI
Detroit Viewing Co.			Detroit	MI
Diehl & Co.	A. J.	246 Woodward	Detroit	MI
Earle	C. W.	53 & 55 Rowland	Detroit	MI
Eisenhardt	Constantine	204 Randolph	Detroit	MI
Emhuff	Joseph	154 Hastings	Detroit	MI
Farmer	C. W.	399 4th	Detroit	MI
Forster	J. S.		Detroit	MI
Forster & Son	John	178 Gratiot	Detroit	MI
Friend	Ferdinand		Detroit	MI
Hall & Son*	H. M.		Detroit	MI
Henri	J. R.	168 Bagg	Detroit	MI
Hill		47 & 48 Monroe	Detroit	MI
Holcombe & Aloord*			Detroit	MI
Holcombe	B. J.	222 Woodward	Detroit	MI
Howie	G. W.	145 Randolph	Detroit	MI
Hunter's Art Gallery		227 Jefferson	Detroit	MI
Imrie	H. N.	59 Monroe	Detroit	MI
Johnston	James	218 Michigan	Detroit	MI
Kiddle	Thomas	252 Michigan	Detroit	MI
Leonard*	C. W.		Detroit	MI
Levy	Charles	232 Woodward	Detroit	MI
Lutge	F. C.	53 Monroe	Detroit	MI
McMichael	A. G.	152 Woodward	Detroit	MI
Marratt, Jr. & Co.	William	274 Woodward	Detroit	MI

PHOTOGRAPHERS LISTED BY CITY/STATE IN THE UNITED STATES 1888-1889

NAME		ADDRESS	CITY	STATE
Marratt*	William		Detroit	MI
Massnick	O. H.	199 St. Aubin	Detroit	MI
Millard	C. A.	224 Woodward	Detroit	MI
Randall	C. C.	Madison	Detroit	MI
Salzmann*	William		Detroit	MI
Shattock	N. J.	175 Woodward	Detroit	MI
Shipley & Ladd		210-212 Woodward	Detroit	MI
Simonds	J. S.	214 Woodward	Detroit	MI
Smith	C. H.		Detroit	MI
Smith*	D. J.		Detroit	MI
Taylor	A. B.	41 Monroe	Detroit	MI
Tomlinson	F. N.	236 Woodward	Detroit	MI
Watson	J. E.		Detroit	MI
Weed	C. L.	120 Michigan	Detroit	MI
Clark	Andrew		Dexter	MI
Bailey	J. W.		Dowagiac	MI
Bigelow	H. S.		Dowagiac	MI
Angell	Daniel		East Saginaw	MI
Burdick	C. W.		East Saginaw	MI
Crouch	W. A.		East Saginaw	MI
Goodridge Bros.			East Saginaw	MI
McIntyre	D. J.		East Saginaw	MI
Macomber	A. D.		East Saginaw	MI
Smith	W. L.		East Saginaw	MI
Bradshaw	A. J.		East Tawas	MI
Ball	A. P.		Eaton Rapids	MI
Morey	L. F.		Edmore	MI
Thomas	J. A.		Edmore	MI
Wixson & McCourt			Escanabo	MI
Wolcott	N. E.		Escanabo	MI
Nix	T. F.		Evart	MI
Phipps	J. H.		Fentonville	MI
Boswell	William		Flint	MI
Foote	W. C.		Flint	MI
Foote	W. H.		Flint	MI
Forsythe & Hickok			Flint	MI
Jewell*	Daniel		Flint	MI
Lone	J. B.		Flint	MI
Call	Miss Mary		Flushing	MI
McMillen	Ephraim		Flushing	MI

PHOTOGRAPHERS LISTED BY CITY/STATE IN THE UNITED STATES 1888-1889

NAME		ADDRESS	CITY	STATE
Haight	E. M.		Fort Gratiot	MI
Cathcart	N. H.		Fowlerville	MI
Colburn	E. J.		Frankfort	MI
Fortune	E. W.		Fremont	MI
Brown	H. A.		Galesburgh	MI
Jacques	Joseph		Garden	MI
Ish	J. W.		Gaylord	MI
Egerton	George		Goodell's	MI
Baker	E. P.		Grand Haven	MI
Cass	William		Grand Haven	MI
Marvin	E. A.		Grand Ledge	MI
Barr	H. A.		Grand Rapids	MI
Barrows	J. G.		Grand Rapids	MI
Bayne	James		Grand Rapids	MI
Clark*	A. S.		Grand Rapids	MI
Goossen	N. B.		Grand Rapids	MI
Jackson	B. D.		Grand Rapids	MI
Merrill & Co.	C. L.		Grand Rapids	MI
Osborne	G. B.		Grand Rapids	MI
Perkins	T. B.		Grand Rapids	MI
Reynders, Jr.	P. C.		Grand Rapids	MI
Schelhous	Losen		Grand Rapids	MI
Schellhous*	Losen		Grand Rapids	MI
Wykes	Warren		Grand Rapids	MI
Bremen	Frederick		Greenville	MI
Morehouse	N. J.		Greenville	MI
Palethrope	Thomas		Greenville	MI
Ebert	Emery		Grind Stone City	MI
Haefer	F. C.		Hancock	MI
Pinter & Bro.	J.		Hancock	MI
Trumbull	L. J.		Harbor Springs	MI
Daley*	Jonas		Hart	MI
Whitney	A. B.		Hartford	MI
Ball	W. B.		Hastings	MI
Blocksom*	H. H.		Hastings	MI
Body	W.		Hillman	MI
Carson	W. H.		Hillsdale	MI
Cole	J. R.		Hillsdalc	MI
Burgess	A. M.		Holland	MI
Higgins	B. P.		Holland	MI

PHOTOGRAPHERS LISTED BY CITY/STATE IN THE UNITED STATES 1888-1889

NAME		ADDRESS	CITY	STATE
Judd*	J. E.		Holly	MI
Peppet	William		Homer	MI
Childs	B. F.		Houghton	MI
Menkee	Horace		Howard City	MI
Brown	M. & C.E.		Howell	MI
Jensen	N. P.		Howell	MI
Phinisey	T. W.		Howell	MI
Brown	F. D.		Hudson	MI
Slocum	D.		Hudsonville	MI
Haynes	Anson		Imlay City	MI
Clark	G. W.		Ionia	MI
Sharpsteen	S. A.		Ionia	MI
Vivian	N. J.		Iron Mountain	MI
Wagner	Hermann		Iron Mountain	MI
Childs	B.		Ishpeming	MI
Lidberg	Andrew		Ishpeming	MI
Lyon	E. W.		Ithaca	MI
Bailey	Robert		Jackson	MI
Barton	L. W.		Jackson	MI
Bigelow	L. W.		Jackson	MI
Cookingham	J. B.		Jackson	MI
Le Clear	A. A.		Jackson	MI
Paine	J. W.		Jackson	MI
Seymour	H. A.		Jackson	MI
Steele	H. A.		Jackson	MI
Underwood	Clarence		Jackson	MI
White*	W. S.		Jackson	MI
Cheney & Langdon			Jonesville	MI
Abbey	L. C.		Kalamazoo	MI
Johnson	C. F.		Kalamazoo	MI
Packard	C. C.		Kalamazoo	MI
Palmiter & Warrant			Kalamazoo	MI
Van Sickle & Adolphus			Kalamazoo	MI
Judd	W. H. E.		Kalkaska	MI
Skinner	Miss L. A.		Laingsburgh	MI
Conee	S. S.		Lake Linden	MI
Cassey & Whitney			Lansing	MI
Heath	L. F.		Lansing	MI
Leonard*	C. W.		Lansing	MI
Sweet	P. W.		Lansing	MI

PHOTOGRAPHERS LISTED BY CITY/STATE IN THE UNITED STATES 1888-1889

NAME		ADDRESS	CITY	STATE
Matson*	G. C.		Lapeer	MI
Watson	G. C.		Lapeer	MI
Webster	H. D.		Lapeer	MI
Allen	N. E.		Leslie	MI
McIntyre*	William		Lexington	MI
Clark*	W. H.		Litchfield	MI
Hiller	Milo		Lowell	MI
Smith	M. O.		Lowell	MI
Silver	F. C.		Ludington	MI
Judd	W. H. E.		Mancelona	MI
Davis	Samuel		Manchester	MI
Cawker*	Victor		Manistee	MI
Conat	C. W.		Manistee	MI
Hansen & Menke			Manistee	MI
Thornton	L. W.		Manistee	MI
Bake	E. P.		Maple Rapids	MI
Baker*	E. P.		Maple Rapids	MI
Clark	I. A.		Maple Rapids	MI
Myers	G. W.		Marcellus	MI
Courliss	William		Marine City	MI
Hager	J. S.		Marlette	MI
Childs	H. F.		Marquette	MI
Hook	W. E.		Marquette	MI
Mast	J. E.		Marshall	MI
Smith	S. B.		Marshall	MI
Van Slyke	C. W.		Mason	MI
Oberlin	G. W.		Mecosta	MI
Bassney	J. J.		Memphis	MI
Lonsbury*	H. E.		Mendon	MI
De Forest	D. A.		Menominee	MI
Herron & O'Donnell			Menominee	MI
Covelle	Mrs. F. A.		Middleville	MI
Coville*	Mrs. F. A.		Middleville	MI
Berryman	E. C.		Midland	MI
Bradley	H. N.		Midland	MI
Bissell	Edward		Milford	MI
Brown	J. M.		Milford	MI
Hill	J. G.		Monroe	MI
Marshall*	W. E.		Montague	MI
Converse	J. O.		Morenci	MI

PHOTOGRAPHERS LISTED BY CITY/STATE IN THE UNITED STATES 1888-1889

NAME		ADDRESS	CITY	STATE
Rock	Robert		Morenci	MI
Mintonye	John		Mount Clemens	MI
Schueller	Frederick		Mount Pleasant	MI
Smith	F. M.		Mount Pleasant	MI
McLaughlin	Miss P.		Muir	MI
Lawson	N. B.		Muskegon	MI
McComb	William		Muskegon	MI
Powe	T. W.		Muskegon	MI
Beebe & Feighner			Nashville	MI
Morrison*	F. P.		Nashville	MI
Wolcott & Hendricks			Nashville	MI
Gibbon*	H. F.		Negaunee	MI
Wolcott & Hendricks*			Negaunee	MI
Wolfe*	H. F.		Newaygo	MI
Densmore	Jay		Niles	MI
Franklin*	Edwin		Niles	MI
Ives	E. B.		Niles	MI
Brown	D. A.		North Branch	MI
Spencer	H. S.		North Port	MI
Devereaux	Albert		Olivet	MI
Chaplin*	Joseph		Ontonagon	MI
Bradshaw	A. J.		Oscoda	MI
Thaver	A. A.		Otsego	MI
Thayer*	A. A.		Otsego	MI
Merrill	W. E.		Ovid	MI
Beebe	W. S.		Owosso	MI
Dunham	Ephraim		Owosso	MI
Moore Bros.			Owosso	MI
Hodges	John		Paw Paw	MI
Prater	J. H.		Paw Paw	MI
Morrell Bros.			Pent Water	MI
Clark*	H. S.		Petoskey	MI
Flower	W. B.		Petoskey	MI
McInnis	H. C.		Petoskey	MI
Brigham	J. M.		Plainwell	MI
Moyer	D. C.		Plainwell	MI
Clegg & Parker*			Plymouth	MI
Bensen	J. H.		Pontiac	MI
Brummit	W. H.		Pontiac	MI
Eddington	C. G.		Pontiac	MI

PHOTOGRAPHERS LISTED BY CITY/STATE IN THE UNITED STATES 1888-1889

NAME		ADDRESS	CITY	STATE
Kittle	H. M.		Pontiac	MI
Barron	W. H.		Port Huron	MI
White	J. N.		Port Huron	MI
Showman	L. K.		Portland	MI
Marsh	W. C.		Quincy	MI
Rhodes	J. P.		Reading	MI
Atherton	F. P.		Reed City	MI
Nix	F. H.		Reed City	MI
Taylor	J. H.		Republic	MI
Stevens	G. L.		Richmond	MI
Stewart*	Robert		Richmond	MI
Austin	C. W.		Rockford	MI
Smith & Palmer			Romeo	MI
Butterworth	J. T.		Saginaw	MI
Smith	D. W.		Saginaw	MI
Smith*	Mrs. D. W.		Saginaw	MI
Smith	H. L.		St. Clair	MI
Westrick	J. C.		St. Clair	MI
Soper*	Allen		St. Ignace	MI
Marratt, Jr.	William		St. Johns	MI
Webster	J. C.		St. Johns	MI
Lesser	W. F.		St. Joseph	MI
Dawes	G. W.		St. Louis	MI
Sharpsteen	Elmer		St. Louis	MI
Oldfield*	T. M.		Sand Beach	MI
Carter	H. L.		Sand Lake	MI
Whalen*	A. J.		Saranac	MI
Mills*	W. H.		Saugatuck	MI
Rutherford	J.		Sault de St. Marie	MI
Woodward*	L. F.		Schoolcraft	MI
Dorrance	Charles		Scotts	MI
Bodey	Kate		Sherman	MI
Edwards	P. S.		South Haven	MI
Kinsman	W. E.		Sparta Center	MI
Chapman	I. O.		Stanton	MI
Chappell	Mrs. E. B.		Sturgis	MI
Brooks & Hicks			Tecumseh	MI
Brown*	M. P.		Tecumseh	MI
Hopkins*	C. A.		Tecumseh	MI
Brown	M. P.		Tekonsha	MI

PHOTOGRAPHERS LISTED BY CITY/STATE IN THE UNITED STATES 1888-1889

NAME		ADDRESS	CITY	STATE
Stark	W. L.		Tekonsha	MI
Hending	Daniel		Texas	MI
Churchill	Mrs. Susan		Three Oaks	MI
Udell	A. A.		Three Rivers	MI
McManus Bros.			Traverse City	MI
Holcomb*	G. W.		Union City	MI
Zimmerman	William		Unionville	MI
Batty	James		Utica	MI
Tibbitts	H. B.		Vassar	MI
Norton	H. M.		Vermontville	MI
Dorrance	C. E.		Vicksburgh	MI
Sessions	J. W.		Wayland	MI
Gorham	T. P.		Wayne	MI
Smith	E. J.		West Bay City	MI
Strong*	N. F.		Whitehall	MI
Skinner	N. C.		White Pigeon	MI
Philips	Chauncey		Williamstown	MI
Steele	W. A.		Williamstown	MI
Lewis & Gibson			Ypsilanti	MI
Stephenson	J. J.		Ypsilanti	MI
Waterman	G. E.		Ypsilanti	MI
Ver Lee	Isaac		Zeeland	MI
Thune & Folkedahl			Ada	MN
Faragher	T. J.		Adrian	MN
Fuller	J. A.		Albert Lea	MN
Halvorsen	J. R.		Albert Lea	MN
Trenham	N. J.		Alexandria	MN
Iler	F. M.		Amboy	MN
Bland	J. S.		Anoka	MN
Scott	S. W.		Ashby	MN
Haskins*	Nye		Ashton	MN
Hildahl	G. S.		Austin	MN
Slocum	Orville		Austin	MN
Older & Turner*			Barnesville	MN
Wetzel	Conrad		Barnesville	MN
Retallick	Chester		Battle Lake	MN
Hoiland	A. J.		Benson	MN
Fuller	C. E.		Birch Cooley	MN
Hill*	L. J.		Bird Island	MN

PHOTOGRAPHERS LISTED BY CITY/STATE IN THE UNITED STATES 1888-1889

NAME		ADDRESS	CITY	STATE
Tusdale	H. H.		Blooming Prairie	MN
More, Jr.	A. R.		Blue Earth City	MN
McColl	J. A.		Brainerd	MN
Robinson & Hopper			Brainerd	MN
Peterson	C.		Byron	MN
Saxe	Theodore		Caledonia	MN
Dahlen	H. P.		Cambridge	MN
Thornbladh	O. L.		Cannon River Falls	MN
Harris	H. E.		Carver	MN
Greeves & McFeeters*			Chaska	MN
Barnes	Isaac		Chatfield	MN
Whiting	Warren		Clitherall	MN
Johnson	Loren		Crookston	MN
Kertson	H. J.		Crookston	MN
Sandquist	J. J.		Dassel	MN
Coffin	W. J.		Delano	MN
Ryerson	R. D.		Detroit City	MN
Ayers	Ellis		Dodge Center	MN
Dahlquist	A. T.		Duluth	MN
Gaylord	P. B.		Duluth	MN
Lang	Charles		Duluth	MN
Schilling	W. P.		Duluth	MN
Thiel	Charles		Duluth	MN
Bigelow	G. H.		Elysian	MN
Stenberg	O. L.		Evansville	MN
Fouch	J. H.		Excelsior	MN
Townsend	H. L.		Fairmount	MN
Burnham	A. T.		Faribault	MN
Hummel & Hoerger			Faribault	MN
Peavey	Louis		Faribault	MN
Carr	A. B.		Farmington	MN
Dennison & Hardy			Fergus Falls	MN
Overland & Holand*			Fergus Falls	MN
Overland	Holand		Fergus Falls	MN
Williams	J. E.		Fergus Falls	MN
Kohnen	Arnold		Frazee City	MN
Hassan	Nelson		Glencoe	MN
Johnson	P. P.		Glenwood	MN
Steward	C. A.		Granite Falls	MN
Pixley*	S. E.		Hallock	MN

PHOTOGRAPHERS LISTED BY CITY/STATE IN THE UNITED STATES 1888-1889

NAME		ADDRESS	CITY	STATE
Rust	C. B.		Hastings	MN
Scott	A. A.		Hastings	MN
Berggren	P. A.		Hector	MN
Simmer	Mathias		Henderson	MN
Kelsey	Orrin		Hutchinson	MN
Wilson	G. A.		Janesville	MN
Gausemel	P. A.		Kenyon	MN
Jenson*	E. M.		Kerkhoven	MN
Roberts	A. C.		Lake Benton	MN
Wood	J. W.		Lake City	MN
Bergerson	W. O.		Lake Park	MN
Lucas*	W. P.		Larimore	MN
Ingalls	F. M.		Le Sueur	MN
Angell	C. L.		Litchfield	MN
Bacon	J. H.		Litchfield	MN
Neal	C. C.		Little Falls	MN
Smith	M. L.		Long Prairie	MN
Delling	G. W.		Madelia	MN
Bailer	S. J.		Mankato	MN
Davis	William		Mankato	MN
Eldridge & Price			Mankato	MN
Keen	George		Mankato	MN
Westphal	Hermann		Mankato	MN
McGandy	Joseph		Marshall	MN
Adams*	I. W.		Minneapolis	MN
Anderson	O. N.		Minneapolis	MN
Beal & Burt			Minneapolis	MN
Bishop Bros.			Minneapolis	MN
Borry & Co.*	J.		Minneapolis	MN
Brush	J. A.		Minneapolis	MN
Buck & Glaser			Minneapolis	MN
Burdick	O. C.		Minneapolis	MN
Chapin*	W. P.		Minneapolis	MN
Chase	W. H.		Minneapolis	MN
Dunham	M. M.		Minneapolis	MN
Farr	H. R.		Minneapolis	MN
Farr & Son			Minneapolis	MN
Flood*	G. W.		Minneapolis	MN
Floyd	G. W.		Minneapolis	MN
Jacoby	W. H.		Minneapolis	MN

PHOTOGRAPHERS LISTED BY CITY/STATE IN THE UNITED STATES 1888-1889

NAME	ADDRESS	CITY	STATE
Larson	Anton	Minneapolis	MN
Lewis	A. C.	Minneapolis	MN
McPhee*	Mrs. Catherine	Minneapolis	MN
Matter	William	Minneapolis	MN
Miller	W. R.	Minneapolis	MN
Moore & Friffiths*		Minneapolis	MN
Mowack	Michael	Minneapolis	MN
Nye	D. B.	Minneapolis	MN
Oleson	Mrs. J. H.	Minneapolis	MN
Oswald Bros.		Minneapolis	MN
Palmer	Frederick	Minneapolis	MN
Petterson	A. W.	Minneapolis	MN
Rich	J. E.	Minneapolis	MN
Roberts & Vanderwarker		Minneapolis	MN
Rugg	A. B.	Minneapolis	MN
Smith*	J. F.	Minneapolis	MN
Spatt*	F. R.	Minneapolis	MN
Stadon*	J. E.	Minneapolis	MN
Summerville*	M. L.	Minneapolis	MN
Vanderwarker & Nally		Minneapolis	MN
Brandmo & Lodgaard		Montevideo	MN
Olson & Anderson		Montevideo	MN
Kerman*	B. H.	Montgomery	MN
Nye	B. A.	Monticello	MN
Bigelow	A. M.	Moorhead	MN
Flaten	O. E.	Moorhead	MN
Elliott	R. F.	Morris	MN
Schoreder & Bargen		Mountain Lake	MN
Briggs	J. P.	Murdock	MN
Gay	Anton	New Ulum	MN
Seiter	E. E.	New Ulum	MN
Runions	L. F.	New York Mills	MN
James	E. N.	Northfield	MN
Sumner	I. E.	Northfield	MN
Lindahl	A. O.	Norwood	MN
Raymaker & Smith*		Ortonville	MN
Haskins	George	Osakis	MN
Chesley	G. W.	Owatonna	MN
Mueller*	Franklin	Owatonna	MN
Mueller & Franklin		Owatonna	MN

PHOTOGRAPHERS LISTED BY CITY/STATE IN THE UNITED STATES 1888-1889

NAME	ADDRESS	CITY	STATE
Lester	J. J.	Paynesville	MN
Howar*	J. S.	Pelican Rapids	MN
Wetzel, Jr.	Conrad	Perham	MN
Tanner	C. C.	Pipestone	MN
Saxe	Theodore	Plainview	MN
Sleyster	A. L.	Preston	MN
Hubbell	R. W.	Red Wing	MN
Kellogg	J. D.	Red Wing	MN
Phillips	John	Red Wing	MN
Crowell	E. S.	Rochester	MN
Easton	J. H. & Mrs. L. J. B.	Rochester	MN
Fowler	I. D.	Rochester	MN
Edwards	C. G.	Rushford	MN
Grossfield		Rushford	MN
Stebbins	A. W.	St. Charles	MN
Hill	E. S.	St. Cloud	MN
Hill	Joseph	St. Cloud	MN
Miller	W. R.	St. Cloud	MN
Walz	George	St. Cloud	MN
Palmer	J. W.	St. James	MN
Bramblett	W. R.	St. Paul	MN
Essery	R. W.	St. Paul	MN
Fredricks & Koester		St. Paul	MN
Gilmartin	F. J.	St. Paul	MN
Greanleaf	C. J.	St. Paul	MN
Hooker	A. E.	St. Paul	MN
Illingworth	W. H.	St. Paul	MN
Ingersoll	T. W.	St. Paul	MN
Lucas	J. H.	St. Paul	MN
Palmquist & Jurgens		St. Paul	MN
Pasel	O. C.	St. Paul	MN
Schlattman Bros.		St. Paul	MN
Swain	Allen	St. Paul	MN
Swem	T. M.	St. Paul	MN
Taylor	S. M.	St. Paul	MN
Weatherby	C. C.	St. Paul	MN
Zimmerman	C. A.	St. Paul	MN
Jacoby	H. J.	St. Peter	MN
Sarnblad	Charles	St. Peter	MN
Kertson & Curteau		Sank Center	MN

PHOTOGRAPHERS LISTED BY CITY/STATE IN THE UNITED STATES 1888-1889

NAME	ADDRESS	CITY	STATE
Lucas	G. L.	Sank Center	MN
Ashforth*	G. H.	Shakopee	MN
Palmer	W. H.	Shakopee	MN
Bangs	Dwight	Sleepy Eye	MN
Matsen	S. C.	Sleepy Eye	MN
Engel	Christian	Spring Grove	MN
Hoot	H. S. & J. W.	Spring Valley	MN
Stevens	J. A.	Spring Valley	MN
De Grush	F. H.	Stillwater	MN
Kuhn	J. M.	Stillwater	MN
Wiklund	Lamentz	Stillwater	MN
Sargent	S. C.	Taylor's Falls	MN
Van Blarcom	H.	Tower	MN
Carver	E. M.	Tracy	MN
Rhoades	D. C.	Verndale	MN
Stearns	E. E.	Wabasha	MN
Hoit	W. C.	Wadena	MN
Raimfield	Henry	Warren	MN
Manderfeld	Hubert	Waseca	MN
Christman	E. J.	Waterville	MN
Miller	R. E.	Waterville	MN
Rowe	C. G.	Waverly	MN
Bangs, Jr.	J. A.	Wells	MN
Handy*	C. F.	White Bear	MN
Sands, Jr.	J. A.	White Bear Falls	MN
Carlson	G. A.	Willmar	MN
Forsberg	J. C.	Willmar	MN
Perry*	E. F.	Windsor	MN
Barnes	William L.	Winona	MN
Brown & Eldridge		Winona	MN
Jones	A. C.	Winona	MN
Morgeneier	Robert	Winona	MN
Tenney	C. A.	Winona	MN
Buchan	E. F.	Worthington	MN
Cooledge	H. W.	Zumbrota	MN
Peck	G. G.	Zumbrota	MN
Henwood	A. R.	Aberdeen	MS
Page	Mary J.	Ackerman	MS
Archer	George W.	Baldwin	MS
Echard	W. C.	Columbus	MS

PHOTOGRAPHERS LISTED BY CITY/STATE IN THE UNITED STATES 1888-1889

NAME		ADDRESS	CITY	STATE
Rowsey	W. H.		Corinth	MS
Sullivan Bros.			Decatur	MS
Bell	C. G.		Greenville	MS
Robinson & Co.	J. T.		Holly Springs	MS
Pruitt	G. H.		Iuka	MS
Robinson	A. M.		Jackson	MS
Seutter & Co.	F.		Jackson	MS
Brookshire	W. C.		Meridian	MS
Norman	H. C.		Natchez	MS
Simmons	L. D.		Natchez	MS
Robinson & Co.	J. T.		Oxford	MS
Sullivan	Mrs. M. J.		Shubuta	MS
Blanks	A. L.		Vicksburg	MS
Fredericks	M. T.		Vicksburg	MS
Brook & Co.	W. T.		Water Valley	MS
Hardy	W. H. B.		Wesson	MS
Burnett	J. F.		West Point	MS
Stewart	J. R.		Williamsburgh	MS
City Art Gallery			Albany	MO
Forney	S. P.		Albany	MO
Burdge	Robert		Appleton City	MO
Sybarger	Noah		Ash Grove	MO
Duncan	Joseph		Aurora Springs	MO
Howland*	S. P.		Belton	MS
Harvey	S. H.		Berlin	MO
Papineau	Frank		Bethany	MO
Hixson	J. W.		Billings	MO
Catterlin	W. H.		Bolckow	MO
Racer	William		Bolivar	MO
Edwards	O. D.		Boonville	MO
Macurdy	J. C.		Boonville	MO
Meredith & Swap			Boonville	MO
Mitchell	Mrs. G. W.		Bowling Green	MO
McLaughlin	T. C.		Breckinridge	MO
Gardner	J. C.		Brookfield	MO
Senhart	R. D.		Brookfield	MO
Plumlee & Burkhard*			Brownsville	MO
Sharer	John		Brunswick	MO
Kendig	J. D.		Burlington Junction	MO
Stroud	J. T.		Burlington Junction	MO

PHOTOGRAPHERS LISTED BY CITY/STATE IN THE UNITED STATES 1888-1889

NAME		ADDRESS	CITY	STATE
Hagedorn	Charles		Butler	MO
Cooper	B. S.		California	MO
Hemingway	E. B.		Cameron	MO
Detwiler & Son			Canton	MO
Douglass*	W. H.		Cape Girardeau	MO
Wise*	E. W.		Cape Girardeau	MO
Heidel	Miss E.		Carrollton	MO
Newkam	F.		Carrollton	MO
Whiting's Art Gallery			Carrollton	MO
Castor & Bro.			Carthage	MO
Costello	J. K.		Carthage	MO
Roessler	E. E.		Carthage	MO
Kingsbury	William E.		Centralia	MO
McDaniel & Weathers*			Centralia	MO
Dunlap	William		Chillicothe	MO
Huffman	J. B.		Chillicothe	MO
Jones	R. H.		Clarence	MO
Baldwin & Co.	O. N.		Clarksville	MO
Corey	A. S.		Clinton	MO
Corey & Roberts			Clinton	MO
Tussey	J. C.		Clinton	MO
Thomas	Frank		Columbia	MO
Tobias	Henry		Columbia	MO
Mernnan & Engle*			Cosby	MO
Buel*	J. W.		Craig	MO
Caniff*	T. H.		Cross Timbers	MO
Perkins	W. C.		Cuba	MO
Rosedale	A. S.		De Soto	MO
Misick	G. W.		Doniphan	MO
Stump	W. H.		Eagleville	MO
Bryant & Zimmerman*			Edgerton	MO
Stapleton	Richard		East Lynne	MO
Manning	A. W.		Edina	MO
Moelk	C. F.		Edina	MO
Clark	J. T.		El Dorado	MO
Mahoney	C. C.		Ellenorah	MO
Dorsey*	W. A.		Everton	MO
Bidwell	G. W.		Farmersville	MO
Ratornez	G. A.		Farmington	MO
Fisher	Jacob		Fayette	MO

PHOTOGRAPHERS LISTED BY CITY/STATE IN THE UNITED STATES 1888-1889

NAME		ADDRESS	CITY	STATE
Macurdy	J. C.		Fayette	MO
Joseph	L. W.		Fordland	MO
Scanland	J. F.		Frankford	MO
Rhodes	J.		Fredericktown	MO
Godfrey	Peter		Fulton	MO
Wartleg	E. B.		Gallatin	MO
Bidwill	William		Galt	MO
Chiesman	E. D.		Galt	MO
Pennelle	R. W.		Glasgow	MO
Ware	Leonard		Glasgow	MO
Thompson	Orville		Glenwood	MO
McAhron	C. O.		Golden City	MO
De Vaux	E. S.		Gooch's Mill	MO
Needham	J. H.		Grant City	MO
Stephenson	C. A.		Greenfield	MO
Hare	T. H.		Hamilton	MO
Clark	D. L.		Hannibal	MO
Goodale*	C. M.		Hannibal	MO
Jackson	Calvin		Hannibal	MO
Fields & Daviess			Harrisonville	MO
Mumbrauer	R. C.		Hermann	MO
Peters	W. H.		Higginsville	MO
Buck Bros.			Holden	MO
Tompkins	E. P.		Holden	MO
Buck	F .A.		Hopkins	MO
Shearer	G. W.		Humphreys	MO
Croft	C. H.		Huntsville	MO
Ormsby	William		Independence	MO
Warnky	F. C.		Independence	MO
Watts	L. H.		Ironton	MO
Cropper	Samuel		Jamesport	MO
Suden	Gustav		Jefferson City	MO
Winans	Solomon		Jefferson City	MO
Seed	William		Jennings	MO
Randall	A. R.		Jericho	MO
Harden	A. B.		Joplin	MO
Houghton	J. & E.		Joplin	MO
Johnson	L. M.		Joplin	MO
Weyland	Jacob		Joplin	MO
Sansom	J. B.		Kahoka	MO

PHOTOGRAPHERS LISTED BY CITY/STATE IN THE UNITED STATES 1888-1889

NAME		ADDRESS	CITY	STATE
Atkinson*	George		Kansas City	MO
Beyer Portrait Co.		1713 Oak	Kansas City	MO
Brown	Harman		Kansas City	MO
Buckwater	Edward	618 Main	Kansas City	MO
Carpenter	Marion		Kansas City	MO
Gardner	R. G.		Kansas City	MO
Gili*	Charles		Kansas City	MO
Parker	J. T.		Kansas City	MO
Ploetz	Julius		Kansas City	MO
Pomeroy	Charles T.		Kansas City	MO
Ragan*	W. O.		Kansas City	MO
Rayan	W. O.		Kansas City	MO
Scotford & Co.	J. H.	715 Main	Kansas City	MO
Thomson & Co.	D. P.	610 Main	Kansas City	MO
Bryant	W. H.		King City	MO
Parcell	H. G.		Kirksville	MO
Phillips*	J. H.		Kirksville	MO
Tinsman	John		Kirksville	MO
Tull	G. W.		Kirksville	MO
Allen & Haines			La Plata	MO
Leggett*	A. W.		Lamar	MO
Swan	Harry		Lamar	MO
Taylor	C. R.		Lamar	MO
Farris	H. A.		Lancaster	MO
Barber & Son*			Lawson	MO
Bunn	J. W.		Lawson	MO
Guild	F. D.		Lebanon	MO
Duvall	J. H.		Lexington	MO
Martland	T. C.		Lexington	MO
Saunders & Son			Lexington	MO
Hicks	J. T.		Liberty	MO
Nix*	W. M.		Licking	MO
Reid	W. R.		Licking	MO
Tarter	G. W.		Linn	MO
Ross	J. B.		Linneus	MO
Hunter & Co.*			Lockwood	MO
Handsome	Pritchard		Louisiana	MO
Thomason & Leffler			Louisiana	MO
Henderson & Patterson			Macon	MO
Roswall	F. A.		Macon	MO

PHOTOGRAPHERS LISTED BY CITY/STATE IN THE UNITED STATES 1888-1889

NAME	ADDRESS	CITY	STATE
Neel*	J. C.	Madison	MO
Hale*	J. A.	Malden	MO
Hixson	J. W.	Marionville	MO
Johns & Son		Marshall	MO
Langan*	W. E.	Marshall	MO
McAtee*	P. H.	Marshall	MO
Stever	Miss Lizzie	Marshfield	MO
Byarlay	L. A.	Maryville	MO
Mendenhall	D. D.	Maryville	MO
Robinson*	W. J.	Maryville	MO
Johnson	L. W.	Maysville	MO
Simington	J. N.	Memphis	MO
Williams	O. H.	Memphis	MO
Graham	Richard	Mexico	MO
Head	J. G.	Mexico	MO
Rhodes	Bert	Milan	MO
Halstead	J. D.	Millard	MO
Devinney	B. F.	Moberly	MO
Edmiston	S. A.	Moberly	MO
Medcalf	E. B.	Monroe City	MO
Inglis	J. S.	Montgomery City	MO
Rainwater*	Terrel	Montrose	MO
Watts	D. B.	Montrose	MO
Bryan	Stockton	Mound City	MO
Decker	William	Mount Vernon	MO
Belts	J. W.	Neosho	MO
McKinzie & Mertins		Neosho	MO
Foster	C. E.	Nevada	MO
Guthrie*	J. A.	Nevada	MO
Harter	J. H.	Nevada	MO
Riley	J. P.	New Cambria	MO
Collier	G. L.	New Haven	MO
Cannon & Hayes		Norborne	MO
Martyr	C. J. J.	Norborne	MO
Byrne	T.	North Springfield	MO
Mathers	Miss E. L.	North Springfield	MO
Paul	J. P.	North Springfield	MO
Holmes	A. T.	Odessa	MO
Leffler*	Frank	Odessa	MO
Zook*	P. M.	Oregon	MO

PHOTOGRAPHERS LISTED BY CITY/STATE IN THE UNITED STATES 1888-1889

NAME		ADDRESS	CITY	STATE
Perkins	W. C.		Pacific	MO
Donnelly*	B. M.		Palmyra	MO
Stephens	W. J.		Palmyra	MO
Moss	J. T.		Paris	MO
Powers	T. C.		Perryville	MO
Duncan	William		Pierce City	MO
Bryant & Zimmerman			Plattsburgh	MO
Ainsworth	J. A.		Pleasant Hill	MO
Race	C. O.		Pleasant Hill	MO
Kennedy	W. H.		Poplar Bluff	MO
King	T. L.		Ponce de Leon	MO
Bearden	W. L.		Princton	MO
Morris	J. H.		Queen City	MO
Booth	H. M.		Rich Hill	MO
Langan Bros.			Richmond	MO
Phillips	J.		Ridgeway	MO
Rice	T. J.		Rockport	MO
Sparks	Oliver		Rockport	MO
Goolsbay	J. W.		Rockville	MO
Stonebrook & Brand*			Rockville	MO
Guild	W. J.		Rolla	MO
Goebel*	Rudolph		St. Charles	MO
Perkins*	W. C.		St. Clair	MO
Graham	J. W.		St. Joseph	MO
Harvey	George		St. Joseph	MO
Lozo	Alexander		St. Joseph	MO
Price*	D. A.		St. Joseph	MO
Saurman	J. S.		St. Joseph	MO
Smith	Abram		St. Joseph	MO
Sours Bros.			St. Joseph	MO
Uhlman	Rudolph		St. Joseph	MO
Austin & Bowers*			St. Joseph	MO
Beenck	P. H.	3727 N. Broadway	St. Louis	MO
Bell	E. H.	1427 Pine	St. Louis	MO
Belle Studio		716 Olive	St. Louis	MO
Benecke*	Robert		St. Louis	MO
Benecke	Theodore	4th S. E. c. Market	St. Louis	MO
Birig	George		St. Louis	MO
Boehl & Koenig		707 N. 4th	St. Louis	MO
Bosch			St. Louis	MO

NAME		ADDRESS	CITY	STATE
Bowers*	Rudolph		St. Louis	MO
Bozen	H. & F.		St. Louis	MO
Brimmer & Kalb		2 W. 4th	St. Louis	MO
Busche & Co.		901 N. 11th	St. Louis	MO
Cassilly	C. W.	421 Franklin	St. Louis	MO
Cassilly*	G. E.		St. Louis	MO
Cassilly*	J. H.		St. Louis	MO
Cassilly	Louisa	1266 S. Broadway	St. Louis	MO
Cramer	Gustavus		St. Louis	MO
Cuddy	S. B.	1103 Franklin	St. Louis	MO
Dippel	Louis A.	716 Olive	St. Louis	MO
Excelsior Copying House*			St. Louis	MO
Excelsior Portrait Co.*			St. Louis	MO
Fischer	J. W.	826 N. 9th	St. Louis	MO
Fox	A. J.	304 N. 6th	St. Louis	MO
Fragstein*	M. V.		St. Louis	MO
Franck & Swett*			St. Louis	MO
Genilli*			St. Louis	MO
Genelli, Hulbert Bros.		923 Olive	St. Louis	MO
Gross & Co.	Julius	1001 S. Broadway	St. Louis	MO
Guerin	F. W.	1534 S. Broadway	St. Louis	MO
Hagenstab	William J.	713 Chouteau	St. Louis	MO
Hammer	L. F.	1534 S.Broadway	St. Louis	MO
Hammers*	Fred		St. Louis	MO
Herwick*	W. M.		St. Louis	MO
Holborn	Henry	1631 Franklin	St. Louis	MO
Hulbert Bros.		923 Olive	St. Louis	MO
Klotter	Charles	906-912 N. 6th	St. Louis	MO
Klotter & Scherer*			St. Louis	MO
Kuhn Bros.		1628 Olive	St. Louis	MO
Leruez*	Arthur		St. Louis	MO
Linder	James A.	1747 N. Broadway	St. Louis	MO
Meier	C. F.	1406 S. Broadway	St. Louis	MO
New York Portrait Co.		1428 Franklin	St. Louis	MO
Norris	Joseph E.	2343 Olive	St. Louis	MO
Palmer	W. H.	208 S. 4th	St. Louis	MO
Parsons	F. R.	1407 Market	St. Louis	MO
Perry	Frank	607 Franklin	St. Louis	MO
Redheffer & Koch		419 N. Broadway	St. Louis	MO
Rino*	August		St. Louis	MO

PHOTOGRAPHERS LISTED BY CITY/STATE IN THE UNITED STATES 1888-1889

NAME		ADDRESS	CITY	STATE
Rino	Mrs. August	801 Franklin	St. Louis	MO
Rosch	J. E. & A. J.	1513-1515 Olive	St. Louis	MO
Saettele & Son*	F.		St. Louis	MO
Saettele*	Max (Estate of)		St. Louis	MO
Saettele	M. Lena	701 Franklin	St. Louis	MO
Schaefer	A. L.	1630 Franklin	St. Louis	MO
Schaefer	Henry C.	740 S. 4th	St. Louis	MO
Schaeffer*	A. L.		St. Louis	MO
Schaeffer*	H. C.		St. Louis	MO
Scherer	Martin	816 N. 6th	St. Louis	MO
Schneidt & Dippel			St. Louis	MO
Scholten	J. A.	920-922 Olive	St. Louis	MO
Setzer & Roth		1633 S. Broadway	St. Louis	MO
Strauss	Julius C.	1245-1247 Franklin	St. Louis	MO
Strauss Bros.*			St. Louis	MO
Swett & Co.	A. G.	1406 Franklin	St. Louis	MO
Taylor	D. D.	304 N. 7th	St. Louis	MO
Thomsen & Co.	B. E.	515 Locust	St. Louis	MO
Tonndorff	Charles H.	Choteau	St. Louis	MO
Voorhees*	Samuel		St. Louis	MO
Voorhees	S. M.	519 S. 4th	St. Louis	MO
White & Donnel*			St. Louis	MO
Wilson	C. D.	2407 S. Broadway	St. Louis	MO
Winkler	Otto M.	1114 Salisbury	St. Louis	MO
Neel	J. C.		Salem	MO
Snider	B. F.		Salem	MO
Davenport*	S. M.		Salisbury	MO
Kale	Mrs. L. R.		Sarcoxie	MO
Van Buskirk	M. L. & H.		Savannah	MO
Thompson	W. S.		Schell City	MO
Buffham	A. T.		Sedalia	MO
Latour	William		Sedalia	MO
Thomas	Frank		Sedalia	MO
Williams*	F. L.		Sedalia	MO
Williams*	T. J.		Seneca	MO
Dwight*	J. M.		Shelbina	MO
Bower*	M. B.		Slater	MO
Hildreth*	T. J.		Slater	MO
Ferguson*	G. W.		Springfield	MO
Potts*	W. B.		Springfield	MO

PHOTOGRAPHERS LISTED BY CITY/STATE IN THE UNITED STATES 1888-1889

NAME		ADDRESS	CITY	STATE
Sittler*	G. W.		Springfield	MO
Covey	E. J.		Stanberry	MO
Stempel	V. C.		Steelville	MO
Marian & Holmes			Stewartsville	MO
Berry	Marion		Sturgeon	MO
Ross	P. F.		Tipton	MO
Pritchard	D. W.		Tolona	MO
Peckham	C. E.		Trenton	MO
Brown	F. M.		Troy	MO
Fulkerson	Charles		Tuscumbia	MO
Shares*	O. P.		Union Star	MO
Ault & Clark			Unionville	MO
Stout	Thomas		Unionville	MO
Hinkel	A.		Warrensburgh	MO
Waddell & Johnson			Warrensburgh	MO
Parks	G. C.		Washington	MO
Linenschmidt	H. E.		Wellsville	MO
Carpenter	William		Weston	MO
Welton	C. W.		Willow Springs	MO
Huey	B. W.		Windsor	MO
Finch	W. B.		Billings	MO
Marsh	Daniel		Bozeman	MO
Dousseau	A. J.		Butte City	MT
Elliot	J. A.		Butte City	MT
Haupt			Butte City	MT
Hower & Hawes			Butte City	MT
Rutter	T. H.		Butte City	MT
Nesbit & Frew			Dillon	MT
Beckwith & Brown			Helena	MT
Bundy & Train			Helena	MT
Eckert	Mrs. M. A.		Helena	MT
Moriarty	J. M.		Helena	MT
Kahn	Leopald		Livingston	MT
Culver	W. H.		Maiden	MT
Huffman*	L. A.		Miles City	MT
Calfee	H. B.		Missoula	MT
Allen	A. T. H.		Townsend	MT
Wantz	James		White Sulphur Springs	MT
Delanoy	J. A.		Ainsworth	NE
Brokau	C. W.		Albion	NE

PHOTOGRAPHERS LISTED BY CITY/STATE IN THE UNITED STATES 1888-1889

NAME		ADDRESS	CITY	STATE
Madden	T. H.		Ashland	NE
Waltmire	N. J.		Ashland	NE
Sturdivant	J. B.		Atkinson	NE
Abbott	W. D.		Auburn	NE
Goss	Albert		Auburn	NE
Leon & Chapman			Aurora	NE
Vanlieu*	A. J.		Aurora	NE
Campbell	A. R.		Beatrice	NE
Case	F. R.		Beatrice	NE
Hough	E. H.		Beatrice	NE
Norton & Hawley			Beatrice	NE
Grover	F. A.		Bennett	NE
Harris	Charles H.		Blair	NE
Trimble	J. H.		Blair	NE
Steele	Frank		Blue Hill	NE
Datsman	P.		Blue Springs	NE
Kelly	I. P.		Broken Bow	NE
Kelley*	I. P.		Broken Bow	NE
Henry	J. W.		Cedar Rapids	NE
Stutsman	W. G.		Central City	NE
Haines	O. P.		Chadron	NE
Ross	A. J.		Chadron	NE
Woodworth	H. S.		Chapman	NE
Lundy	H. R.		Columbus	NE
McAllister	J. S.		Columbus	NE
Stearns	O. H.		Columbus	NE
Wiker	T. J.		Cortland	NE
Admire	C. A.		Cowles	NE
Turner	A. V.		Creighton	NE
Smith	A.		Crete	NE
Bailor	J. M.		Culbertson	NE
Partch	R. N.		Davenport	NE
Perry	O. H.		De Witt	NE
Staynor & Dahling			Edgar	NE
Bishop*	C. D.		Elwood	NE
Carnahan	G. E.		Fairbury	NE
Marcellus	P.		Fairbury	NE
Brown	G. A.		Fairfield	NE
Neihart	A. W.		Fairmont	NE
Hicks	E. J.		Falls City	NE

PHOTOGRAPHERS LISTED BY CITY/STATE IN THE UNITED STATES 1888-1889

NAME	ADDRESS		CITY	STATE
Oldroyd	L. K.		Falls City	NE
Hoffmeister	E.		Fremont	NE
Hull	A. C.		Fremont	NE
Briggs	J.		Friend	NE
Gregory	B. F.		Fullerton	NE
Sodreberg	Pont.		Geneva	NE
Bovee	W. L.		Gibbon	NE
Barling	Miss M.		Gordon	NE
Carson	C.		Gothenburg	NE
Moeller	J. R.		Grand Island	NE
Murphy	M.		Grand Island	NE
Heffner	H. C.		Guide Rock	NE
Leschinsky	J.		Harvard	NE
Churchill	G. O.		Hastings	NE
Nichols	E. P.		Hastings	NE
Townsends Bros.			Hastings	NE
Griffin	William		Hebron	NE
Wyatt	Mrs. M. J.		Holdredge	NE
Jacobsen*	J.		Hooper	NE
Mekels*	E.		Hooper	NE
Sellers	M. J.		Hubble	NE
Hughes	A. A.		Humboldt	NE
Barber	A.		Indianola	NE
Chenoweth	D. W.		Kearney	NE
Rowley Bros.			Kearney	NE
Andrews	H. L.		Lincoln	NE
Clements	E. G.		Lincoln	NE
Kelly & Co.			Lincoln	NE
Noble	H. E.		Lincoln	NE
Wallermire	P. C.		Lincoln	NE
Godkin	W. R.		Long Pine	NE
Nicholas	J. K.		Louisville	NE
Miller*	C. C.		Loup City	NE
Leach	E. A.		McCook	NE
Brinckman Bros.			Madison	NE
Swanson	C.		Mead	NE
McElhiney	H.		Nebraska City	NE
Neihart & Co.			Nebraska City	NE
Phillips	C. W.		Nebraska City	NE
Relfs	W. E.		Neligh	NE

PHOTOGRAPHERS LISTED BY CITY/STATE IN THE UNITED STATES 1888-1889

NAME		ADDRESS	CITY	STATE
Saxton	W.		Neligh	NE
Janousek	L.		Niobrara	NE
East	T.		North Loop	NE
Mathewson	T. C.		North Platte	NE
Anderson*	N. J.		Oakland	NE
Smith & Ayers			Odell	NE
Day	E. M.		Ogallala	NE
Currier*	F. E.		Omaha	NE
Eaton	E. L.		Omaha	NE
Gray	H. E.		Omaha	NE
Heyn	G.		Omaha	NE
Heyn	H.		Omaha	NE
Hughes	B. E.		Omaha	NE
Meyers*	A.		Omaha	NE
Nelson	O. R.		Omaha	NE
Rinehart	F. A.		Omaha	NE
Schwabe	H.		Omaha	NE
Tollman & Co.			Omaha	NE
Anderson*	W. A.		Ord	NE
Delglish Bros.*			Ord	NE
Brown	O. B.		Osceola	NE
Foster	J. C.		Pawnee City	NE
Mahan	W. H.		Pawnee City	NE
Abbott	W. D.		Peru	NE
Bentley*	A. L.		Pierce	NE
Johns*	H. C.		Plattsmouth	NE
Leonard	V. V.		Plattsmouth	NE
Wilson	B. A.		Plum Creek	NE
Mason	S. Rufus		Purple Crane	NE
Wikoff	A. W.		Rising City	NE
Cramer	J.		Rulo	NE
Henderson Bros.			St. Paul	NE
Hall*	H. G.		Schuyler	NE
Givens	W. D.		Seward	NE
Preston	H. C.		Seward	NE
Fling	J.		Shelby	NE
Harrington	J. H.		Sidney	NE
Armstead & Son*			South Bend	NE
Leon*	Thomas		Springfield	NE
Hathaway Bros.			Staplehurst	NE

PHOTOGRAPHERS LISTED BY CITY/STATE IN THE UNITED STATES 1888-1889

NAME		ADDRESS	CITY	STATE
Pickels	J. W.		Stella	NE
Wheeler	W. D.		Sterling	NE
Shultz	W. B.		Stromsburg	NE
Edny	James		Superior	NE
Linkskog & McCoy			Sutton	NE
Soderburg	P.		Sutton	NE
Foster	H. W.		Syracuse	NE
Bedell	S. W.		Talmage	NE
Forbes	John		Tecumseh	NE
Hover	W. M.		Tecumseh	NE
Parkinson	H. B.		Tecumseh	NE
Burneo	L.		Takamah	NE
Gebhard & Mendenhall*			Unadilla	NE
Croley	W. A.		Valentine	NE
Benton*	W. E.		Valparaiso	NE
Yoho & Bence*			Waco	NE
Anderson	U. J.		Wahoo	NE
Perky	Lenore		Wahoo	NE
Kortwright			Wayne	NE
Flower	W. A.		Weeping Water	NE
Langer	H.		West Point	NE
Butcher	S. D.		West Union	NE
Fike	G. W.		Wilber	NE
Campbell & Co.*	C. R.		Wisner	NE
Bischoff	C. S.		Wymore	NE
Hayden	J. A.		York	NE
Weller	L. A.		Austin	NV
Marston	C. A.		Carson City	NV
Peterson	C. E.		Carson City	NV
Monaco	Louis		Eureka	NV
Butler	E. P.		Reno	NV
Dunham & Kelsey			Reno	NV
Noe	J. S.		Virginia City	NV
Clement	F. M.		Berlin Falls	NH
Briggs	F. H.		Bristol	NH
Locke	J. T.		Canaan	NH
Drake	J. L.		Center Effingham	NH
Webster	J. F.		Center Harbor	NH
Busch	C. G.		Claremont	NH
Fisher	E. C.		Claremont	NH

PHOTOGRAPHERS LISTED BY CITY/STATE IN THE UNITED STATES 1888-1889

NAME		ADDRESS	CITY	STATE
Kenyon	F. H.		Claremont	NH
Rogers	Frank		Colebrook	NH
Bailey	H. C.		Concord	NH
Gillett Copying Co.			Concord	NH
Kimball	W. G. C.		Concord	NH
Moore	H. P.		Concord	NH
Brigham	E. T.		Dover	NH
Drew	A. P.		Dover	NH
Foss	F. H.		Dover	NH
Morse	S. G.		Exeter	NH
Shackford	A. W.		Farmington	NH
Hunt	C. L.		Franklin Falls	NH
Lodge	S. H.		Gilmanton	NH
Hobbs	C. H.		Gorham	NH
Deland	E. J.		Great Falls	NH
Taylor	A. Sylvester		Great Falls	NH
Martin	Allis		Greenville	NH
Clement	F. M.		Haverhill	NH
Lincoln	George W.		Hillsborough Bridge	NH
Fisher	A. F.		Hindsdale	NH
French	J. A.		Keene	NH
Stevens*	H. S. & G. E.		Keene	NH
Stevens	H. S.	30 Central Sq.	Keene	NH
White	E. M.		Keene	NH
Moon	T. C.		Laconia	NH
Tabbetts	G. H.		Laconia	NH
Tebbetts*	G. H.		Laconia	NH
Ward	E. D.		Lake Village	NH
Haseltine	J. P.		Lancaster	NH
Granger	H. P.		Lebanon	NH
Lewis	C. E.		Lebanon	NH
Hunt	M.		Lisbon	NH
Aldrich	George H.		Littleton	NH
Hall & Priest			Littleton	NH
Call	W. R.		Manchester	NH
Colby	L. W.		Manchester	NH
Desmarais	O.		Manchester	NH
Ellinwood	J. G.		Manchester	NH
Langley	Josiah T.		Manchester	NH
Piper	Stephen		Manchester	NH

PHOTOGRAPHERS LISTED BY CITY/STATE IN THE UNITED STATES 1888-1889

NAME		ADDRESS	CITY	STATE
Quint	S. D.		Manchester	NH
Rogers	Charles F.		Manchester	NH
Wallace	Henry C.		Manchester	NH
Shepard	Charles		Melvin Village	NH
Colby	C. H.		Meredith Village	NH
Hubbard	E. E.		Milford	NH
Austin	A. C.		Nashua	NH
Farley	A. D.		Nashua	NH
Gauthier	Joseph		Nashua	NH
Glenton	Frederick		Nashua	NH
Lindsey	Charles H.		Nashua	NH
Currier	Herman J.		New London	NH
Lewis	T. R.		New Market	NH
Brown	H. J.		Newport	NH
Pease	Nathan W.		North Conway	NH
Lamprey	M. S.		Penacook	NH
Wilson	L. E.		Peterborough	NH
Osgood	Henry W.		Pittsfield	NH
Heath	Harry		Plymouth	NH
Cook	O. H.		Portsmouth	NH
Davis Bros.			Portsmouth	NH
Newell	L. V.		Portsmouth	NH
Clarke	G. W.		Raymond	NH
Collins	I. A.		Rochester	NH
Swain	S.		Rochester	NH
Colby	James T.		Springfield	NH
Wilkins	Joseph W.		Suncook	NH
Moulton	F. J.		Tilton	NH
Harriman	M. C.		Warner	NH
Bugbee	F. E.		Wilton	NH
Murdock	W. N.		Woodstock	NH
Applegate & Sons	J. R.		Atlantic City	NJ
Bellis	Henry		Atlantic City	NJ
Burr	J. E.		Atlantic City	NJ
Chandler & Sheetz			Atlantic City	NJ
Enterekin Photographic Gallery			Atlantic City	NJ
Ewald & Bro.	J. E.		Atlantic City	NJ
Herks Photographic Gallery			Atlantic City	NJ
Hewitt	W. S.		Atlantic City	NJ
Paynter	William		Atlantic City	NJ

PHOTOGRAPHERS LISTED BY CITY/STATE IN THE UNITED STATES 1888-1889

NAME		ADDRESS	CITY	STATE
Phillips	Henry		Atlantic City	NJ
Rau & Kidd			Atlantic City	NJ
Ketchledge	P. D.		Belvidere	NJ
Phillips*	W. C.		Bordentown	NJ
Smith	J. E.		Bordentown	NJ
Service	W. E.		Bridgeton	NJ
Baker	Thomas		Burlington	NJ
Philadelphia Gallery			Burlington	NJ
Tichenor	G. W.		Burlington	NJ
Humphreys	A. H.		Camden	NJ
Hunt	E. J.		Camden	NJ
Sims	Andrew		Camden	NJ
Woodruff	L.		Camden	NJ
Long	William		Cape May	NJ
Eagle Gallery			Dover	NJ
Asnon	A. F.		Elizabeth	NJ
Dimmock	W. H.		Elizabeth	NJ
Hall	John		Elizabeth	NJ
Hill	W. H.		Elizabeth	NJ
Moore	H. L.		Elizabeth	NJ
Sunderlin	J. C.		Flemington	NJ
Cottrell	Frank		Freehold	NJ
Lockwood	F. C.		Freehold	NJ
Rush	E. W.		Glen Gardner	NJ
Snyder	F. H. F.		Gloucester	NJ
Williams	J. A.		Hackensack	NJ
Kenney	C. C.		Hackettstown	NJ
Harrold*	W. H.		Hammonton	NJ
Jones	J. W.		Hammonton	NJ
Dalrymple	J. P.		Hightstown	NJ
Breiner	William	252 Washington	Hoboken	NJ
De Lappotterie	Charles	140 Washington	Hoboken	NJ
Fichtl	Sigmund	46 Bloomfield	Hoboken	NJ
Lay	Herman N.	204 Washington	Hoboken	NJ
Nagel	Louis	192 Washington	Hoboken	NJ
Ayers	Edgar M.	269 Warren	Jersey City	NJ
Beals	Charles	654 Newark	Jersey City	NJ
Costello	Alfred B.	588 Newark	Jersey City	NJ
Gubelman	Theodore	79 Newark	Jersey City	NJ
Henkel	Charles A.	345 Palisade	Jersey City	NJ

PHOTOGRAPHERS LISTED BY CITY/STATE IN THE UNITED STATES 1888-1889

NAME		ADDRESS	CITY	STATE
Jones	William	40 Newark	Jersey City	NJ
Keim	John H.	40 Newark	Jersey City	NJ
Marvin	Henry R.	99 Montgomery	Jersey City	NJ
Rice	Phillip J.	87 Montgomery	Jersey City	NJ
Steiner	Julius H.	77 Newark	Jersey City	NJ
Burd	M. S.		Junction	NJ
Fritz	F. Z.		Lambertville	NJ
Tibbels	J. C.		Lambertville	NJ
Freeland	G. W.		Milford	NJ
Carpenter	D. W.		Millville	NJ
Taylor	C. W.		Morristown	NJ
Keeler	H. L.	37 Main	Mount Holly	NJ
Walker*	J. S.		Mount Holly	NJ
Walker*	P.		Mount Holly	NJ
Clark	David		New Brunswick	NJ
Dunn	F. P.		New Brunswick	NJ
Scott	J. C.		New Brunswick	NJ
Bennett	Jalet	793 Broad	Newark	NJ
Crane	T. F.	156 First	Newark	NJ
Creighton & Mix		653 Broad	Newark	NJ
De Camp	George W.	671 Broad	Newark	NJ
Friederich	H.	163 Springfield	Newark	NJ
Huff	F. L.	707 Broad	Newark	NJ
Jeush	W.	695 Broad	Newark	NJ
Kirk	Joseph	661 Broad	Newark	NJ
Loder	W. R.	773 Broad	Newark	NJ
Miller & Nichols*		1 Cedar	Newark	NJ
Price	Frank H.	925 Broad	Newark	NJ
Rache	Thomas J.	94 Washington	Newark	NJ
Schill	Ludwig	839 Broad	Newark	NJ
Schumacher	H.	186 William	Newark	NJ
Smith	J. Henry	769 Broad	Newark	NJ
Smith	J. Rennie	727 Broad	Newark	NJ
Swift	Jno. M.	480 Broad	Newark	NJ
Thein	Henry	476 Broad	Newark	NJ
Thielemann	J.	82 Springfield	Newark	NJ
Thomas & Co.		791 Broad	Newark	NJ
Wood	Henry T.	615 Broad	Newark	NJ
Longcor	Levi		Newton	NJ
Townley	A. C.		Newton	NJ

PHOTOGRAPHERS LISTED BY CITY/STATE IN THE UNITED STATES 1888-1889

NAME		ADDRESS	CITY	STATE
Benjamin & Sons	W. C.		Orange	NJ
Brady	H. J.		Orange	NJ
Handel	F. G.		Orange	NJ
Dennell*	J. J.		Passaic	NJ
Hillman Bros.			Passaic	NJ
Lamb*	R. B.		Passaic	NJ
Doremus	L. H.		Paterson	NJ
Howd	D. H.		Paterson	NJ
Kemp	J. M.		Paterson	NJ
Post	H. F.		Paterson	NJ
Reid	John		Paterson	NJ
Simpson	W. P.		Paterson	NJ
Speakers	I. G.		Paterson	NJ
Demarest & Staler*			Perth Amboy	NJ
Gillen	J. R.		Phillipsburgh	NJ
Allen	G. B.		Plainfield	NJ
Hunt & Fisher			Plainfield	NJ
Langhorne	F. C.		Plainfield	NJ
Thorn	G.		Plainfield	NJ
Williams	G. H.		Pleasantville	NJ
Pach	G. W.		Princeton	NJ
Rose	R. H.		Princeton	NJ
Stacy	J. G.		Rahway	NJ
White	A. H.		Red Bank	NJ
Breece	H. S.		Salem	NJ
Apgar	W. A.		Sommerville	NJ
Kelley	E. T.		Sommerville	NJ
McClure	W.		Toms River	NJ
Beer	A. G.		Trenton	NJ
Lovejoy	H. C.		Trenton	NJ
Pine	George		Trenton	NJ
Foster	Fred W.	115 Lewis	Union Hill	NJ
Telfer	James	120 ½ Hackensack Plank	Union Hill	NJ
Johnson	L. D.		Vineland	NJ
Waters	R. J.		Virginia City	NJ
Flannagan	H. H.		Woodstown	NJ
Armsbury	Stiles P.		Adams	NY
Johnson	Adelaide		Adams	NY
Hooker	F. S.		Addison	NY
Abbott	J. L.	91 N. Pearl	Albany	NY

PHOTOGRAPHERS LISTED BY CITY/STATE IN THE UNITED STATES 1888-1889

NAME		ADDRESS	CITY	STATE
Buenschhoff	A.	151 Central	Albany	NY
Byron	J. N.	50 S. Pearl	Albany	NY
Coates	James H.	82 Hudson	Albany	NY
Holmes	A. S.	66 State	Albany	NY
Horton	V. W.	15 N. Pearl	Albany	NY
McDonald	J. N.	520 Broadway	Albany	NY
McElroy	J. W.	67 S. Pearl	Albany	NY
Mosher	G. A.	444 Broadway	Albany	NY
Notman Photograph Co.		48 N. Pearl	Albany	NY
Payn*	C. S.	9 N. Pearl	Albany	NY
Rabinoau	C. S.	9 N. Pearl	Albany	NY
Sterry	E. S.	520 Broadway	Albany	NY
Veedor	A.	32 N. Pearl	Albany	NY
Waldbillig	A. F.	394 2nd	Albany	NY
Waldbillig*	A. F.	30 N. Pearl	Albany	NY
Wendorer	T. J.	51 State	Albany	NY
Wood	J. M.	496 Broadway	Albany	NY
Wood	W. W.	56 State	Albany	NY
Belden	A.		Albion	NY
McIntyre & Co.	A. C.		Alexandria Bay	NY
Saunders	Irving		Alfred Center	NY
Crocker	Abel B.		Allegany	NY
Hall	C. H.		Amenia	NY
Kibble	George		Amsterdam	NY
Searles	George W.		Amsterdam	NY
Carman	Charles		Andes	NY
Wealthy	John E.		Angola	NY
Churchill	C. E.		Arcade	NY
HIlls	Martin T.		Attica	NY
Barber & Co.	A. J.		Auburn	NY
Brown & Sellick			Auburn	NY
Bruce & Co.			Auburn	NY
Crayton	J. A.		Auburn	NY
Ernsberger	W. H.		Auburn	NY
French & Hoagland			Auburn	NY
Gibbs	George E.		Auburn	NY
Hoffman	G. W.		Auburn	NY
Hutchins	C. S.		Auburn	NY
Lindsley	H. B.		Auburn	NY
Seails	E. T.		Auburn	NY

PHOTOGRAPHERS LISTED BY CITY/STATE IN THE UNITED STATES 1888-1889

NAME		ADDRESS	CITY	STATE
Smart	O. M.		Auburn	NY
Spuyer	H. S.		Auburn	NY
Stevens	B.		Auburn	NY
Ten Eyck & Co.			Auburn	NY
Vail	K.		Auburn	NY
Van Valkenburg	Charles E.		Auburn	NY
Smith	Arthur H.		Avon	NY
North	A. M.		Bainbridge	NY
Wheeler	S. S.		Bainbridge	NY
Dunbar	Mrs. H. M.		Baldwinsville	NY
Arnold	T. J.		Ballston	NY
Maxon	E. H.		Ballston	NY
Houseknecht	P. B.		Batavia	NY
Cross	M. F.		Batavia	NY
Keis*	G.		Batavia	NY
Knight*	O. P.		Batavia	NY
Patrick*	John C.		Batavia	NY
Tallman	C. W.		Batavia	NY
Brooks	A. F.		Bath	NY
Davis, Jr.	S. H.		Berne	NY
Cobb	George N.		Binghampton	NY
Evans	L. R.		Binghampton	NY
Gilmore	Lowell		Binghampton	NY
Murphy	E.		Binghampton	NY
Osborn	Emerson		Binghampton	NY
Cudding	A. J.		Bolivar	NY
Baker	N. B.		Brockport	NY
Abrahams	David	273 Fulton	Brooklyn	NY
Bainbridge*	J. G.	291 Manhattan	Brooklyn	NY
Batterson	Lincoln S.	635 Third	Brooklyn	NY
Bickelman	O. Conrad	397 Grand	Brooklyn	NY
Biffar	Bernard T.	516 Broadway	Brooklyn	NY
Biffar	Henry W.	109 Bedford	Brooklyn	NY
Bijou Photo Studio		235 Fulton	Brooklyn	NY
Block	Benoit	179 Myrtle	Brooklyn	NY
Bock	Frederick	418 Fulton	Brooklyn	NY
Bolles	Charles E.	242 Fulton	Brooklyn	NY
Bowers	Berry F.	340 Fulton	Brooklyn	NY
Bowers*	William F.	340 Fulton	Brooklyn	NY
Bradfisch	Louis	227 Fulton	Brooklyn	NY

PHOTOGRAPHERS LISTED BY CITY/STATE IN THE UNITED STATES 1888-1889

NAME		ADDRESS	CITY	STATE
Brighton Photo Art. Co.		733 Fulton	Brooklyn	NY
Chapman & Co.		115 Bedford	Brooklyn	NY
Coe*	Theodore D.	331 Grand	Brooklyn	NY
Crawford	Jno. W.	543 Fulton	Brooklyn	NY
Douglas	Charles B.	55 Myrtle	Brooklyn	NY
Duryea*	C. W.	39 Greenpoint	Brooklyn	NY
Duryea	S. B.	253 Fulton	Brooklyn	NY
Dutton	William M.	1635 Atlantic	Brooklyn	NY
Ehm	Henry	566 Broadway	Brooklyn	NY
Ericsson	William	614 Fifth	Brooklyn	NY
Ericuis	Emil A.	130 Broadway	Brooklyn	NY
Farrach	John	31 Myrtle	Brooklyn	NY
Fredericks	Charles	672 Broadway	Brooklyn	NY
Galloway*	Robert	318 Fulton	Brooklyn	NY
Galloway & Co.		318-320 Fulton	Brooklyn	NY
Gardner & Co.		276 Fulton	Brooklyn	NY
Gorham	Edwin L.	103 S. Portland	Brooklyn	NY
Gross Bros.		176 Atlantic	Brooklyn	NY
Hall	Joseph	111 Fulton	Brooklyn	NY
Harding	Stephen T.	1666 Fulton	Brooklyn	NY
Hartman	Jay J.	231 Grand	Brooklyn	NY
Henigar	W. L.	437 Grand	Brooklyn	NY
Hicks	Lemuel S.	191 Grand	Brooklyn	NY
Holler	Henry	149 Ewen	Brooklyn	NY
Howson	William S.	957 Fulton	Brooklyn	NY
Hunter	William F.	243 Fulton	Brooklyn	NY
Jacobs	Alfred W.	204 Atlantic	Brooklyn	NY
Jenkins Bros.		1059 Green	Brooklyn	NY
Kane*	Thomas	459 Grand	Brooklyn	NY
Kempf	Charles L.	185 Myrtle	Brooklyn	NY
Kempf	Charles L.	627 Myrtle	Brooklyn	NY
Kopke	John	407 Fulton	Brooklyn	NY
Kosel*	W. E.	181 Myrtle	Brooklyn	NY
Leeds	G. W.	262 Columbia	Brooklyn	NY
Loud*	George W.	397 Bedford	Brooklyn	NY
Markham & Johnson		335 Washington	Brooklyn	NY
Newton	Samuel	451 Grand	Brooklyn	NY
Nightengale & Son		69 Carroll	Brooklyn	NY
Noll	Charles	597 Fifth	Brooklyn	NY
Palmeri	A.	691 Myrtle	Brooklyn	NY

PHOTOGRAPHERS LISTED BY CITY/STATE IN THE UNITED STATES 1888-1889

NAME		ADDRESS	CITY	STATE
Parshley	Frank	308 Fulton	Brooklyn	NY
Pearsall	Alva	615 Fulton	Brooklyn	NY
Pearsall	G. Frank E.	298 Fulton	Brooklyn	NY
Pendleton	W. S.	336 Fulton	Brooklyn	NY
Ramsdell	John	162 Court	Brooklyn	NY
Rawson	Charles S.	257 Fulton	Brooklyn	NY
Redmond*	James	162 Court	Brooklyn	NY
Reynolds	Charles C.	403 Grand	Brooklyn	NY
Richardson Bros.		107 Broadway	Brooklyn	NY
Richardson & Speh*		131 Broadway	Brooklyn	NY
Robotham	Bedford		Brooklyn	NY
Robotham*	Bedford	c. Broadway	Brooklyn	NY
Rosenger	Otto B.	55 Myrtle	Brooklyn	NY
Schwarzer*	H. G.	11 Union	Brooklyn	NY
Sheppard	Arthur	61 Myrtle	Brooklyn	NY
Silkworth	Amos W.	261 Manhattan	Brooklyn	NY
Smith	C. A. N.	397 Bedford	Brooklyn	NY
Smith	David H.	531 Fulton	Brooklyn	NY
Stevenson	Joshua	271 Broadway	Brooklyn	NY
Stoffregen	Alfred	133 Montrose	Brooklyn	NY
Swanell	Charles R.	483 Fulton	Brooklyn	NY
Taylor	Sanford A.	453 Fulton	Brooklyn	NY
United States Portrait Co.		311 Fulton	Brooklyn	NY
Van Houten	Arthur	461 Fulton	Brooklyn	NY
Wendel	William	91 Court	Brooklyn	NY
Werner	Otto	680 Broadway	Brooklyn	NY
Winder	Gustav	118 Myrtle	Brooklyn	NY
Wolt	Jacob	615 Broadway	Brooklyn	NY
Wunder	H.	722 Fulton	Brooklyn	NY
Zundel	Adolph	405 Broadway	Brooklyn	NY
Baker	W. J.	390 Main	Buffalo	NY
Bigden	C. W.	252 Main	Buffalo	NY
Bliss	H. L.	368 Main	Buffalo	NY
Dressel	G. A.	179 West	Buffalo	NY
Emerling	F.	193 Genesee	Buffalo	NY
Ginther	J.	329 Main	Buffalo	NY
Griffin	M.	446 Main	Buffalo	NY
Grinton	D.	191 Seneca	Buffalo	NY
Hillman	Adolph	539 Main	Buffalo	NY
Knight	W. M.	321 Main	Buffalo	NY

PHOTOGRAPHERS LISTED BY CITY/STATE IN THE UNITED STATES 1888-1889

NAME		ADDRESS	CITY	STATE
Levilly	L.	515 Main	Buffalo	NY
McMichael	H.	246 Main	Buffalo	NY
Murdock*	W. S.	359 Main	Buffalo	NY
Nims	C.	372 Genesee	Buffalo	NY
Paige	E. H.	53 Arcade Bldg.	Buffalo	NY
Potter	J. R.	323 Main	Buffalo	NY
Sickler	H. O.	39 Seneca	Buffalo	NY
Simon	A. W.	215 W. Tupper	Buffalo	NY
Simson	A.	456 Main	Buffalo	NY
Stuart	C. A.	186 Seneca	Buffalo	NY
Taft	O. A.	272 Main	Buffalo	NY
Torrey*	W. H.	154 Broadway	Buffalo	NY
White	W. W.	374 Seneca	Buffalo	NY
Wells	H. M.		Cambridge	NY
Dygert	S.		Canajoharie	NY
Gilman	J. Bryant		Canajoharie	NY
Crandall Bros.			Canandaigua	NY
Finley	Horace		Canandaigua	NY
Freeman	W. U.		Canandaigua	NY
Plank	Thomas J.		Canastota	NY
Stebbins	A. B.		Canisteo	NY
Hitchcock	J.		Canton	NY
Wells	Ernest G.		Canton	NY
Wel's*	Ernest G.		Canton	NY
Lewis	G. F.		Carthage	NY
Wasburn	G. L.		Castile	NY
Allen	Frank		Catskill	NY
Van Gorden	C. E.		Catskill	NY
Johnson	A. A.		Cazenovia	NY
Barney	J. R.		Champlain	NY
Reynolds	D. A.		Chatham Village	NY
Bendixen*	Emil		Chittenango	NY
Cook	A. L.		Cincinnatus	NY
Breslow	B.		Clayton	NY
Cooper	C. S.		Clyde	NY
Muth	J. R.		Clyde	NY
Hess	Louis		Cobleskill	NY
McGarry	Charles		Cohoes	NY
Meinerth Bros.			Cohoes	NY
New	John H.		Cohoes	NY

PHOTOGRAPHERS LISTED BY CITY/STATE IN THE UNITED STATES 1888-1889

NAME		ADDRESS	CITY	STATE
Cornell	Miss S. A.		Colden	NY
Bucher, Jr.	Herman	Box 116	College Point, L. I.	NY
Hunold	Frank	4th Ave.	College Point, L. I.	NY
Taylor*	Mrs. Richard		Coney Island	NY
Cooley	Alfred		Cooperstown	NY
Smith	W. G.		Cooperstown	NY
Lawton	D. G.		Corinth	NY
Dampf	John H.		Corning	NY
Gaynes	A. D.		Corning	NY
Jaynes & Bristol*			Corning	NY
Paye*	C. M.		Cortland	NY
Pruden & Jones			Cortland	NY
Selorer & Schutt			Cortland	NY
Johnson	E. M.		Crown Point	NY
Carroll	William		Cuba	NY
Benjamin	De Forrest		De Ruyter	NY
Farrington	Maurice		Delhi	NY
Brace	Fredrick		Dundee	NY
Clark	Damon P.		Dunkirk	NY
Gifford	B. R.		Dunkirk	NY
Hambelton & Potter			East Aurora	NY
Penton	C. E.		East Aurora	NY
Bullock	Seneca		East Durham	NY
Bailey	Elisha		Eden	NY
Davis	W. S.		Ellenville	NY
Tice	A. W.		Ellenville	NY
Thompson*	J. H.		Ellicottsville	NY
Hart	A. P.		Elmira	NY
Howe	C. J.		Elmira	NY
Larkin	John E.		Elmira	NY
Rowley	C. W.		Elmira	NY
Van Aken	E. M.		Elmira	NY
Vanakin*	E. M.		Elmira	NY
Whitley	J. H.		Elmira	NY
Porter	A. W.		Farmer Village	NY
Roe	Sylvester		Flushing	NY
Nims	William		Fort Edward	NY
Marshall	T.		Fort Plain	NY
Wentworth	W. D.		Fort Plain	NY
Wells	George		Franklin	NY

PHOTOGRAPHERS LISTED BY CITY/STATE IN THE UNITED STATES 1888-1889

NAME	ADDRESS		CITY	STATE
McNeill	Henry		Fredonia	NY
Pringle	Charles		Fredonia	NY
Saunders	Irving		Friendship	NY
Beals	H. C.		Fulton	NY
Merrill	J. C.		Geneseo	NY
Hinckley	A. S.		Geneva	NY
Wood	T. H.		Geneva	NY
Conkey	George W.		Glens Falls	NY
Lovejoy*	Charles I.		Glens Falls	NY
Lovejoy	Charles J.		Glens Falls	NY
Stoddard	S. R.		Glens Falls	NY
Scidmore	D.		Gloversville	NY
Cunningham	J. K.		Gouverneur	NY
Rhodes	A. S.		Gouverneur	NY
Weber	F. J.		Gowanda	NY
Barker	George B.		Granville	NY
Barler	Oliver K.		Granville	NY
Stoddard	H. H.		Granville	NY
Sullivan	Jeremiah F.		Greenbush	NY
Warner	A. W.		Greene	NY
Howard	George		Greenport	NY
Arnold	A.		Greenwich	NY
Nott	Edward S.		Hamburgh	NY
Hid	Henry I.		Hamilton	NY
Myers	Benjamin		Hancock	NY
Bedford	George O.		Haverstraw	NY
Wildey	O. H.		Homer	NY
Smith	S. B.		Honeoye	NY
Estabrook	E. R.		Hoosick Falls	NY
Beels	H. M.		Hornellsville	NY
Sutton	W. L.		Hornellsville	NY
Young	G. A.		Hornellsville	NY
Forshew	Frank		Hudson	NY
Beardsley	J.		Ithaca	NY
Eagles	Joseph D.		Ithaca	NY
Evans	Even		Ithaca	NY
Frear	W.		Ithaca	NY
Hanford*	J.		Ithaca	NY
Rubin	H.		Ithaca	NY
Rubin	Levy		Ithaca	NY

NAME		ADDRESS	CITY	STATE
Stanley	G. C.		Ithaca	NY
Camp	A. N.		Jamestown	NY
Jull	R. W.		Jamestown	NY
Monroe	C. H.		Jamestown	NY
Moore	J. R.		Jamestown	NY
North American Photo-Copying Co.			Jamestown	NY
Prudden*	D. E.		Jamestown	NY
Prudden & Dunihue			Jamestown	NY
Smith	James G.		Jamestown	NY
Hazer	W. H.		Johnstown	NY
Kibbe	W. H.		Johnstown	NY
Dygert	George H.		Jordan	NY
Folsom	Edward S.		Katonah	NY
Lewis	T. C.		Kingston	NY
McKown	George		Kingston	NY
Short	Lorenzo		Kingston	NY
Lamson	George L.		La Fargeville	NY
Harris	G. W.		Lancaster	NY
Allis	J. R.		Lansingburgh	NY
Drury	A. K.		Le Roy	NY
Graeff & Gardner			Liberty	NY
Whittaker	R. B.		Liberty	NY
Abbott	W. H.		Little Falls	NY
Boyer	W. H.		Little Falls	NY
Buttman	J. J.		Little Falls	NY
Keller & Jarvis			Little Falls	NY
Hopkins	G. P.		Lockport	NY
Montgomery	Joseph		Lockport	NY
Ranney	O. N.		Lockport	NY
Schurr*	Theodore P.		Lockport	NY
Smith	George M.		Lockport	NY
Carter	G. W.		Lowville	NY
Ravell	C. H.		Lyons	NY
Keesler	J. J.		Marathon	NY
Minard	William E.		Marathon	NY
Hedley	G. H.		Medina	NY
Stacy	C. A.		Medina	NY
Jessup	Edward		Middletown	NY
Milliken	William		Monticello	NY
McFarlin & Speck*			Moravia	NY

PHOTOGRAPHERS LISTED BY CITY/STATE IN THE UNITED STATES 1888-1889

NAME		ADDRESS	CITY	STATE
Speck	Col.		Moravia	NY
Stickney	L.		Morris	NY
Gorham	L. D.		Mount Kisco	NY
Marks	Robert		Mount Vernon	NY
Stivers	J. A.		Mount Vernon	NY
Crocker	J. L.		Naples	NY
Hennigar*	John W.		New Rochelle	NY
Acker	Victor	159 6th	New York City	NY
Adams Safford & Co.		48 Bond	New York City	NY
Allen	Jonathan	335 8th	New York City	NY
Alley & Bell		123 5th	New York City	NY
Alman	Louis	172 5th	New York City	NY
American Portrait Co.		13 Bible	New York City	NY
Anderson & Co.*	Daniel	785 Broadway	New York City	NY
Anderson	D. H.	785 Broadway	New York City	NY
Andrie	Charles	94 Chatham	New York City	NY
Arnold*	Charles D.	10 E 14th	New York City	NY
Arnold	Charles D.	25 E. 14th	New York City	NY
Arnow	Nathan	16 W. 14th	New York City	NY
Baag	Peter	1536 3rd	New York City	NY
Bach	Frederick	507 8th	New York City	NY
Bachman	Rudolph	1437 Broadway	New York City	NY
Bancroft	George W.	6 City Hall Place	New York City	NY
Banthoux	Emil	2 First	New York City	NY
Barcalow & Co.	R. G.	76 Bowery	New York City	NY
Barkman*	Charles G.	419 Broadway	New York City	NY
Barnett	George W.	2 New Chambers	New York City	NY
Beach & Shaw		125 Fulton	New York City	NY
Beal	Joshua H.	278 Pearl	New York City	NY
Becker & Co.		405 8th	New York City	NY
Benicsky	Sara	2 New Chambers	New York City	NY
Bennett	Alexander	420 3rd	New York City	NY
Bennett & Co.		1311 Broadway	New York City	NY
Biggart Solar Printing Co.		58 & 60 University Place	New York City	NY
Bogardus		348 6th	New York City	NY
Bogardus*		349 6th	New York City	NY
Bogardus	Abraham	872 Broadway	New York City	NY
Bogardus*	Edward W.	349 6th	New York City	NY
Bostwick	H. L.	98 6th	New York City	NY
Bouffier	Charles	4 New Chambers	New York City	NY

PHOTOGRAPHERS LISTED BY CITY/STATE IN THE UNITED STATES 1888-1889

NAME		ADDRESS	CITY	STATE
Bowers	Sereno A.	110 E. 125th	New York City	NY
Brasseur	Charles	123 Chambers	New York City	NY
Briggs*	Charles W.	311 8th	New York City	NY
Briggs & Davis		311 8th	New York City	NY
Brooklyn Photo-Enlarging co.		59 E. 9th	New York City	NY
Buhler	Otto	1434 3rd	New York City	NY
Bulkley*	Eli E.	2294 3rd	New York City	NY
Bulkley*	Eli E.	383 N. 3rd	New York City	NY
Bulkley	Eli E.	2294 3rd	New York City	NY
Bulkley	William M.	1132 N. 3rd	New York City	NY
Busse*	William M.	1132 N. 3rd	New York City	NY
Carroll	Joseph F.	192 E. 125th	New York City	NY
Carroll*	Lawrence	101 W 21st	New York City	NY
Carvalho	D. N.	291 Broadway	New York City	NY
Chapman	A.	756 Broadway	New York City	NY
Clauss	C. M.	61 Bond	New York City	NY
Coe	Norman L.	681 Broadway	New York City	NY
Cole*	James K.	832 Broadway	New York City	NY
Cole	James K.	34 W. 14th	New York City	NY
Cole	James K.	174 6th	New York City	NY
Cowan*	Henry	577 8th	New York City	NY
Cowan	Henry	181 8th	New York City	NY
Cowley	D. J.	34 W. 14th	New York City	NY
Cox*	George C.	826 Broadway	New York City	NY
Cox & Co.	C. C.	59 E. 12th	New York City	NY
Dana	Edward C.	63 W. 14th	New York City	NY
Davis	James P.	495 6th	New York City	NY
Davis*	Josphine E.	180 E. 121st	New York City	NY
Davis	Josephine E.	180 6th	New York City	NY
Davis	William A.	180 6th	New York City	NY
De Foro	Frank	19 Union Sq W.	New York City	NY
Decker	Philip I.	365 8th	New York City	NY
Dellac	Marcellin	54 W. 14th	New York City	NY
Denninger	Anson	93 E. Houston	New York City	NY
Dessaar	Fernando	551 8th	New York City	NY
Deyoung	Joseph B.	815 Broadway	New York City	NY
Dimmers	Kuno	388 Bowery	New York City	NY
Dimmers	Theodore G.	105 4th	New York City	NY
Dober	Daniels	27 Ave. A	New York City	NY
Doumet & De Ligarde		102 W. 18th	New York City	NY

PHOTOGRAPHERS LISTED BY CITY/STATE IN THE UNITED STATES 1888-1889

NAME		ADDRESS	CITY	STATE
Drummond	Alonzo J.	50 Fulton	New York City	NY
Duchochois	Peter C.	123 Chambers	New York City	NY
Dummer	Oscar	433 6th	New York City	NY
Dummer	Thomas G.	105 4th	New York City	NY
Dunne & Co.	A.	56 Reade	New York City	NY
Dupont Studio		110 E. 125th	New York City	NY
Duque	Francis	760 Broadway	New York City	NY
Duryea	William C.	201 6th	New York City	NY
Edsall	Frank	487 8th Ave	New York City	NY
Edsall*	Frank	248 W. 125th	New York City	NY
Ehrlich	Professor	160 E. 66th	New York City	NY
Eichler	George	13 Ave. A	New York City	NY
Eisenmann	Charles	18 W. 14th	New York City	NY
Eisermann*	Charles	229 Bowery	New York City	NY
Ely	William F.	756 Broadway	New York City	NY
Empire Photographic Studio		361 Canal	New York City	NY
Falk	Benjamin J.	949 Broadway	New York City	NY
Falk*	Benjamin J.	947 Broadway	New York City	NY
Favre	Leon	236 W. 44th	New York City	NY
Feeley	James R.	58 W. 23rd	New York City	NY
Feinberg & Koran		228 Bowery	New York City	NY
Ferry & Holtzman		132 Bowery	New York City	NY
Fielding	John H.	2196 3rd	New York City	NY
Finkenberg	Philip	10 Ave. B.	New York City	NY
Fredricks	Charles D.	770 Broadway	New York City	NY
Fricke	William	50 Bowery	New York City	NY
Galliker	Charles H.	509 8th	New York City	NY
Galloway*	Robert	779 Broadway	New York City	NY
Garber	Davis	747 Broadway	New York City	NY
Gardner	Edwin B.	200 W. 34th	New York City	NY
Gardner & Son	J. B.	147 Fulton	New York City	NY
Gates	Thomas	693 8th	New York City	NY
Gebhard	Julia	314 2nd	New York City	NY
Gesberger	Charles	264 ½ Bowery	New York City	NY
Gline	Andrew	794 3rd	New York City	NY
Gogler	Louis	350 Bowery	New York City	NY
Goldesman	Nachson	38 Bowery	New York City	NY
Goldesman*	Nachson	391 Canal	New York City	NY
Grimsehl	Herman	227 Bleecker	New York City	NY
Grotecloss	John H.	46 W. 14th	New York City	NY

PHOTOGRAPHERS LISTED BY CITY/STATE IN THE UNITED STATES 1888-1889

NAME		ADDRESS	CITY	STATE
Grotecloss	W. G.	138 E. 42nd	New York City	NY
Hagelstein Bros.		142 Bowery	New York City	NY
Hall & Son	George P.	157 Fulton	New York City	NY
Hammersley	Charles H.	109 8th	New York City	NY
Harbers	Gunther	354 Grand	New York City	NY
Hargrave & Gubelman		40 W. 23rd	New York City	NY
Hargrave & Gubelman*		38 W. 23rd	New York City	NY
Harris	Louis	124 Park Row	New York City	NY
Harrison	Washington	22 W. 4th	New York City	NY
Hatton	Clarence R.	419 Broadway	New York City	NY
Hawkes	A. T.	401 Canal	New York City	NY
Heffer	O. W.	872 Broadway	New York City	NY
Hegger	Frank	927 Broadway	New York City	NY
Hegger	Frank	1181 Broadway	New York City	NY
Heimburg	Charles H.	555 3rd	New York City	NY
Hennigar	Charles L.	180 E. 121st	New York City	NY
Hill Bros.		1216 Broadway	New York City	NY
Hill Bros.*		50 W. 14th	New York City	NY
Hill Photo. Co.		1227 Washington	New York City	NY
Hirshberg	Julius	150 2nd	New York City	NY
Howe & Co.		1557 Broadway	New York City	NY
Howe	Fredrick L.	58 W. 23rd	New York City	NY
Hull	Huber H.	381 Canal	New York City	NY
Hunter	John B.	229 Greenwich	New York City	NY
Hunter	John E.	551 N. 3rd	New York City	NY
Jaeger	G. J.	202 2nd	New York City	NY
Jaeger	Josephine	18 Ave. B.	New York City	NY
Jahn Bros.		760 Broadway	New York City	NY
James	Caroline B.	583 8th	New York City	NY
James*	Caroline B.	407 8th	New York City	NY
Johnson	H. Worthley	395 8th	New York City	NY
Johnson*	H. Worthley	205 6th	New York City	NY
Johnson & Lacombe		384 Bowery	New York City	NY
Jordan Photo-Art Gallery		419 Broadway	New York City	NY
Keim & Co.	G. W.	260 Bowery	New York City	NY
Kelley	James H.	832 Broadway	New York City	NY
Kelly	E. T.	767 Broadway	New York City	NY
Klein	Charles	481 1st	New York City	NY
Klein	Jacob	324 Grand	New York City	NY
Knowlton	Willis	335 4th	New York City	NY

PHOTOGRAPHERS LISTED BY CITY/STATE IN THE UNITED STATES 1888-1889

NAME		ADDRESS	CITY	STATE
Koester & Sievers		279 6th	New York City	NY
Kraft Bros.		390 Bowery	New York City	NY
Kraft	John F.	216 3rd	New York City	NY
Kuhlmann	Bruno	55 3rd	New York City	NY
Kurtz	William	6 E. 23rd	New York City	NY
Kurtz*	William	233 Broadway	New York City	NY
Kyle	Alexander	1316 3rd	New York City	NY
Langill & Darling		10 E. 14th	New York City	NY
Lednare	A. J.	249 6th	New York City	NY
Lewin	Otto	1296 3rd	New York City	NY
Lewis	Harriet H.	1216 Broadway	New York City	NY
Lewis*	Richard A.	160 Chatham	New York City	NY
Lichtenberger & Co.		183 Essex	New York City	NY
Lopez	Jose	16 W. 14th	New York City	NY
Ludovici	Julius	254 5th	New York City	NY
Ludovici*	Julius	152 5th	New York City	NY
McCaffrey	Patrick H.	139 E. 59th	New York City	NY
McNab	Francis P.	813 Broadway	New York City	NY
McQueen	Alfred G.	275 6th	New York City	NY
Mackey	Lawrence J.	418 Grand	New York City	NY
Mahler	Henry	547 8th	New York City	NY
Main	John F.	304 Lenox	New York City	NY
Matthews	Thomas R.	50 W. 14th	New York City	NY
Maxwell	Augustus	104 Chatham	New York City	NY
Maxwell	Joseph E.	202 Bowery	New York City	NY
Maxwell & Hobby*		136 Bowery	New York City	NY
Maxwell & Mansfield		186 Bowery	New York City	NY
Mercantile Photograph & Photo-Engraving Co.		218 Fulton	New York City	NY
Meuer	Max	252 Bowery	New York City	NY
Meuro & Co.		361 6th	New York City	NY
Meyer	Max	38 Bowery	New York City	NY
Micciullo & Co.		64 S. Washington	New York City	NY
Miller	Charles	60 Nassau	New York City	NY
Moffet & Co.		174 6th	New York City	NY
Monroe*	Harry D. S.	220 Bowery	New York City	NY
Monroe	Harry D. T.	180 E. 121st	New York City	NY
Mora	Jose M.	707 Broadway	New York City	NY
Moreno & Lopez		4 E. 14th	New York City	NY
Mueller	John G.	28 Ave. C.	New York City	NY

PHOTOGRAPHERS LISTED BY CITY/STATE IN THE UNITED STATES 1888-1889

NAME		ADDRESS	CITY	STATE
Mueller*	John G.	20 Ave. C.	New York City	NY
Muench	William	147 3rd	New York City	NY
Munich	C.	756 Broadway	New York City	NY
Naegeli	William A.	46 E. 14th	New York City	NY
National Crayon Portrait Co.		50 W. 14th	New York City	NY
Neale	William A.	102 W. 18th	New York City	NY
Neggesmith & Robinson		260 Bowery	New York City	NY
Newman & Co.		181 Essex	New York City	NY
Nichols & Handy		229 Mercer	New York City	NY
Nichols	John W.	840 Bowery	New York City	NY
Noll*	Charles	232 Bleecker	New York City	NY
Noll	Lawrence	232 Bleecker	New York City	NY
O'Dwyer	Joseph	413 Canal	New York City	NY
O'Dwyer*	Joseph	283 8th	New York City	NY
O'Neil	Hugh	31 Union Sq.	New York City	NY
O'Neil	James	177 E. 127th	New York City	NY
Ollivier	Horace M.	1162 Broadway	New York City	NY
Pach Bros.		841 Broadway	New York City	NY
Parkinson & Co.		29 W. 26th	New York City	NY
Parkinson*	Maurice D.	29 W. 26th	New York City	NY
Paxson	J.	65 E. 9th	New York City	NY
Perkinson	L. C.	176 E. 125th	New York City	NY
Perkinson	L. C.	2308 3rd	New York City	NY
Photo-Gravure Co.		853 Broadway	New York City	NY
Picken & Co.		79 Greenwich	New York City	NY
Pleasants	Bazil B.	735 Broadway	New York City	NY
Pollock	W. E.	196 Worth	New York City	NY
Purivance	William E.	115 Christopher	New York City	NY
Putnam	Franklin	481 Canal	New York City	NY
Quantrell	M. L. & E.	101 W. 15th	New York City	NY
Reilly	Thomas F.	249 6th	New York City	NY
Roberts	Benjamin W.	824 3rd	New York City	NY
Rockwood	George C.	17 Union Sq. W.	New York City	NY
Rupp	Christian	24 Ave. A	New York City	NY
Sarony	Napoleon	37 Union Sq. W.	New York City	NY
Saul	William H.	214 Bowery	New York City	NY
Schaidner	Charles B.	186 E. 124th	New York City	NY
Schoerry	Henry	143 E. 3rd	New York City	NY
Schoolof	William B.	415 E. 79th	New York City	NY
Schultze	Carl	17 Chatham Sq	New York City	NY

PHOTOGRAPHERS LISTED BY CITY/STATE IN THE UNITED STATES 1888-1889

NAME		ADDRESS	CITY	STATE
Schultze*	Carl	5 Chatham Sq.	New York City	NY
Schwind	William	1422 2nd	New York City	NY
Schwind, Jr.	William	27 Ave. A	New York City	NY
Schwind*	William	27 Ave. A.	New York City	NY
Selden	Harris	134 Park Row	New York City	NY
Shackell & Clauss		828 3rd	New York City	NY
Shettle	William M.	279 6th	New York City	NY
Shorrock	Ralph	19 Center	New York City	NY
Siebert	A. Z.	74 University Pl.	New York City	NY
Silver	W. W.	102 Fulton	New York City	NY
Silver*	William W.	102 Fulton	New York City	NY
Smith	Aaron	8 Bowery	New York City	NY
Smith	Catharine	840 Broadway	New York City	NY
Smith	Charles H.	302 Broadway	New York City	NY
Smith*	Charles H.	303 Broadway	New York City	NY
Smith	James W.	145 8th	New York City	NY
Spiess	William	13 Ave. A	New York City	NY
Stead	James U.	383 6th	New York City	NY
Steinhardt	Theodore	145 8th	New York City	NY
Steinhardt*	Theodore	183 8th	New York City	NY
Stengel	H.	710 Broadway	New York City	NY
Stevenson	John	200 E. 34th	New York City	NY
Terreforte	Juan M.	2148 3rd	New York City	NY
Terry	William	826 Broadway	New York City	NY
Thomas	Samuel A.	717 6th	New York City	NY
Throckmorton	Franklyn	363 Bowery	New York City	NY
Thwaites	Joseph	1 Chambers	New York City	NY
Ulrich	Fredrick	156 Bowery	New York City	NY
Vail	William F.	46 Vesey	New York City	NY
Van Dyke	Valentine	1234 3rd	New York City	NY
Vandyke	Ferdinand	509 8th	New York City	NY
Vaupel	Herman M.	989 3rd	New York City	NY
Von Fielitz		297 Bowery	New York City	NY
Waller	Fredrick	135 S. 5th	New York City	NY
Weinig & Schmidt	G.	388 Bowery	New York City	NY
Weismantel	William	242 4th	New York City	NY
Wilbur	Henry	46 W. 14th	New York City	NY
Wilhelm	Rudolph	1000 3rd	New York City	NY
Wilkie	James	163 8th	New York City	NY
Wilkie	Sarah	165 8th	New York City	NY

PHOTOGRAPHERS LISTED BY CITY/STATE IN THE UNITED STATES 1888-1889

NAME		ADDRESS	CITY	STATE
Williams & Co.	F. H.	985 Broadway	New York City	NY
Williams & Co.*	F. H.	683 Broadway	New York City	NY
Winslow	Nathan	294 Bowery	New York City	NY
Winslow	Nathan	381 Canal	New York City	NY
Winslow	Nathan	274 Grand	New York City	NY
Winslow*	Nathan	228 Bowery	New York City	NY
Wittkins	Bernard	116 Bowery	New York City	NY
Wood	John	208 Bowery	New York City	NY
Wood	Richard L.	401 Canal	New York City	NY
Wright	James	89 Fulton	New York City	NY
Wurst	Otto	180 6th	New York City	NY
Ziesik	Felix S.	365 Bowery	New York City	NY
Hennigar	John W.		New Rochelle	NY
Richards	S. S.		Newark	NY
Decker	P. J. & J. P.		Newburgh	NY
Peck	Abel		Newburgh	NY
Remmillard	A. B. E.		Newburgh	NY
Whiddit	W. W.		Newburgh	NY
Wood & Co.	T. E.		Newburgh	NY
Barker	George		Niagara Falls	NY
Bierstadt	C.		Niagara Falls	NY
Curtis	George E.		Niagara Falls	NY
Hendrickson	C. E.		Niagara Falls	NY
Jerauld & Co.	P. W.		Niagara Falls	NY
Neilson & Brundage			Niagara Falls	NY
Cornell & Wick			Norwich	NY
Hotchkiss	A. E.		Norwich	NY
Walrath	G. A.		Norwood	NY
Insley	Henry A.		Nyack	NY
Van Wagoner*	I. M.		Nyack	NY
Van Wagoner	J. M.		Nyack	NY
Crane	F. M.		Ogdensburg	NY
Dow	J. M.		Ogdensburg	NY
Winsor & Whipple			Olean	NY
Richardson	W. T.		Oneida	NY
Stewart & Toast			Oneida	NY
Winans	E. R.		Oneonta	NY
Young	P. R.		Oneonta	NY
Alford	B. F.		Oswego	NY
Austin	Samuel		Oswego	NY

PHOTOGRAPHERS LISTED BY CITY/STATE IN THE UNITED STATES 1888-1889

NAME		ADDRESS	CITY	STATE
Collins	E. M.		Oswego	NY
Jackson	John		Oswego	NY
McIntosh	W. H.		Oswego	NY
Nagle	J. R.		Oswego	NY
Nesbitt & Co.	H. R.		Oswego	NY
Flagg	Charles		Ovid	NY
Elton	George M.		Palmyra	NY
Hopkins	A. C.		Palmyra	NY
Edick	E. L.		Parish	NY
Cary	Frank		Penn Yan	NY
Smith*	H. N.		Penn Yan	NY
Smith	J. A.		Penn Yan	NY
Crocker	M. N.		Perry	NY
Lynd	J. A.		Perry	NY
Gokay	E. S.		Petersburgh	NY
Pardee	D.		Phelps	NY
Lane	Alonzo		Pike	NY
Baldwin	G. W.		Plattsburgh	NY
Bigelow	W. A.		Plattsburgh	NY
Howard	James		Plattsburgh	NY
Bigelow	W. H.		Port Henry	NY
Allerton	W. H.		Port Jervis	NY
Lundelius	August	184 Pike	Port Jervis	NY
Masterson*	E. P.		Port Jervis	NY
Sunderlins*	August		Port Jervis	NY
Kenyon	A. J.		Port Leyden	NY
Eaton	A. B.		Potsdam	NY
Murphy	J. W.		Potsdam	NY
Stone*	N. L.		Potsdam	NY
Stone & Sons	N. L.	58-60 Market	Potsdam	NY
Bedell	E.		Poughkeepsie	NY
Gallup	C. H.		Poughkeepsie	NY
Meadler	John W.		Poughkeepsie	NY
Millan	William		Poughkeepsie	NY
Schaeffer	C. E.		Poughkeepsie	NY
Vail Bros.			Poughkeepsie	NY
Avery*	R. S.		Pulaski	NY
Bayme	J. A.		Pulaski	NY
Dunwick	W. H.		Pulaski	NY
Taylor	J. W.		Randolph	NY

PHOTOGRAPHERS LISTED BY CITY/STATE IN THE UNITED STATES 1888-1889

NAME		ADDRESS	CITY	STATE
Haverly	P.		Rensselaervile	NY
Coumbe	J.		Rhinebeck	NY
Miner & Guivits			Richfield Springs	NY
Zeller	F. M.		Richfield Springs	NY
Downs*	Dana		Rivershead	NY
Bacon	F. W.			
	& G. W.	118 E. Main	Rochester	NY
Bowdish & Hoagland		94 Arcade	Rochester	NY
Brownell Mfg. Co.			Rochester	NY
Crossman	B. P.	150 State	Rochester	NY
Davis	C. H.	138 E. Main	Rochester	NY
Dumble	A. E.	44 State	Rochester	NY
Fox	J. M.		Rochester	NY
Furman	Robert H.	62 State	Rochester	NY
Godfrey	G. W.	146 E. Main	Rochester	NY
Gregg	S.	94 State	Rochester	NY
Hale	B. F.	150 State	Rochester	NY
Hovey's Sons	D.	74 Asylum	Rochester	NY
Kent*	John H.	24 State	Rochester	NY
Kent	John H.	243-247 State	Rochester	NY
Lehnkering	A. L.	208 E. Main	Rochester	NY
Miller	S.	156 State	Rochester	NY
Peart	F. T.	112 E. Main	Rochester	NY
Pomeroy	C. T.	30 E. Main	Rochester	NY
Punnett*	Milton B.		Rochester	NY
Schutter	E. D. H.	142 State	Rochester	NY
Sherman	Levi	40 State	Rochester	NY
Taylor	J. W.	152 E. Main	Rochester	NY
Walter	J. P.	742 N. Clinton	Rochester	NY
Wardlaw*	Samuel D.	16 State	Rochester	NY
Webster & Albee		175 Front	Rochester	NY
Williamson	E. R.	102 State	Rochester	NY
Brainerd	J. M.		Rome	NY
Hovey	J. S.		Rome	NY
Williams	J. W.		Rome	NY
Williamson	E. H.		Rome	NY
Auchmoody	D. J.		Rondout	NY
Buchmoody*	D. J.		Rondout	NY
Dintruff	J. H.		Rushville	NY
Blessing	J. H.		Salamanca	NY

PHOTOGRAPHERS LISTED BY CITY/STATE IN THE UNITED STATES 1888-1889

NAME		ADDRESS	CITY	STATE
Kinney	S. C.		Salem	NY
Baker	W. H.		Saratoga Springs	NY
Brown	Hugh J.		Saratoga Springs	NY
Record & Epler			Saratoga Springs	NY
Deyo	Phillip		Schoharie	NY
Pease	A. H.		Schuylersville	NY
Hale	J. E.		Seneca Falls	NY
Wentworth	H.		Sharon Springs	NY
Parker	H. R.		Sherburne	NY
Dunihue*	W. J.		Sinclairville	NY
Harris & Co.	Frank		Skaneateles	NY
Thornton	J. M. & S.		Skaneateles	NY
Pierce	Miss Ann		Springville	NY
Spaulding	S. E.		Springville	NY
Cornell	S. S.		Stamford	NY
Allgier	F. X.	8 Syracuse House Bl.	Syracuse	NY
Curtis	M. E.	62 S. Salina	Syracuse	NY
Curtiss	Nathan S.		Syracuse	NY
Doust	J. V.	24 E. Genesee	Syracuse	NY
Flint	F. C.	100 S. Salina	Syracuse	NY
Goodman	R. A.	60 S. Salina	Syracuse	NY
Parker	A. H.	46 N. Salina	Syracuse	NY
Ranger	W. V.	43 S. Salina	Syracuse	NY
Ryder	P. S.	72 S. Salina	Syracuse	NY
Winter	J. W.	Washington c. Salina	Syracuse	NY
Ahrens	Fredrick		Tarrytown	NY
Rogers	S.		Tarrytown	NY
Arnout	J. M.	River co. 4th	Troy	NY
Fox	G. S.	98 Congress	Troy	NY
Hardy & Van Arnum		390 River	Troy	NY
Holmes	A. S.	282 River	Troy	NY
Irwing	J.	13 2nd	Troy	NY
Lloyd	J. H.	44 3rd	Troy	NY
Magill	Z. F.	17 Keenan Bldg.	Troy	NY
Mowrey	W. C.	51 Boardman Bldg.	Troy	NY
Preston	W. C.	282 River	Troy	NY
Schroder	J. D.	308 River	Troy	NY
Spencer	K. W.		Union	NY
Abbott	R. R.		Union Springs	NY
De Voll & Co.			Utica	NY

PHOTOGRAPHERS LISTED BY CITY/STATE IN THE UNITED STATES 1888-1889

NAME		ADDRESS	CITY	STATE
Gutley	G. W.		Utica	NY
Mundy	L. C.		Utica	NY
North	W. C.		Utica	NY
Scofield	C. H.		Utica	NY
Williams	L. B.		Utica	NY
Wright	W. P.		Utica	NY
Young	C. P.		Utica	NY
Miller & Sprague*			Walton	NY
Sprague	F. L.		Walton	NY
Smith	Walter		Wappinger's Falls	NY
Hanigan	John O.		Warsaw	NY
Dougherty*	Henry J.		Waterloo	NY
Pullman	Charles		Waterloo	NY
Baldwin & Peck			Watertown	NY
Banta	J. C.		Watertown	NY
Gegoux	Theodore		Watertown	NY
Hart	C. S.		Watertown	NY
Hart	W. E.		Watertown	NY
Johnson Bros.			Watertown	NY
Minor	Guievits		Waterville	NY
Minor & Guievits*			Waterville	NY
Minor	T. L. R.		Waterville	NY
Crum & Son	R. D.		Watkins	NY
Gates	W. D.		Watkins	NY
Hillerman	Leonard		Watkins	NY
Hope	J. D.		Watkins	NY
Comstock	A. B.		Waverly	NY
Bendixen*	E.		Weedsport	NY
Rider	J. A.		Wellsville	NY
Wright	O. S.		Wellsville	NY
Talbot	F. T.		West Winfield	NY
Melven	L. B.		Westfield	NY
Adams	C. W.		Whitehall	NY
Brown	H. G.		Whitehall	NY
Foot	David		Wolcott	NY
Wright	George B.		Worcester	NY
Ahrens & Bro.	J.		Yonkers	NY
Wyer	Henry S.		Yonkers	NY
Browne	E. E.		Asheville	NC
Bamgartem	H.		Charlotte	NC

PHOTOGRAPHERS LISTED BY CITY/STATE IN THE UNITED STATES 1888-1889

NAME		ADDRESS	CITY	STATE
Van Ness	James H.		Charlotte	NC
Rochelle	C. W.		Durham	NC
Clark	David L.		High Point	NC
Skinner	T.		Kinston	NC
Gerock	Edward		New Berne	NC
Andrews	D. W.		Raleigh	NC
Swift	G. W.		Raleigh	NC
Watson	J. W.		Raleigh	NC
McArthur	W. E.		Shelby	NC
Gates	C. W.		Wilmington	NC
Winstead	F. M.		Wilson	NC
Harden	C. T.		Windsor	NC
Broadaway	J. S.		Winston	NC
Campbell	J. A.		Ada	OH
Gilbert	M. V.		Ada	OH
Boone & Co.	C. H.	185 Howard	Akron	OH
Battles	B. F.	106 E. Market	Akron	OH
Groesel Bros.	Howard		Akron	OH
Groesel Bros.*	Howard	SW corner Market	Akron	OH
Hitchcock	George	185 S. Howard	Akron	OH
Howard	E. J.	32 Arcade	Akron	OH
Kline Bros.	Exchange		Akron	OH
Malloy*	John W.	109 E. Market	Akron	OH
Saunders	A. Tresize	210 Fir	Akron	OH
Saunders Bros.*		141-143 S. Howard	Akron	OH
Snook	George J.	186 S. Howard	Akron	OH
Miller	Louis E.		Alliance	OH
Steffey	J. H.		Alliance	OH
Wonders	Lafe		Alliance	OH
Hubbard*	A. L.		Ashland	OH
Miller*	E. E.		Ashland	OH
Teeple	T.		Ashland	OH
Blakeslee & Moore			Ashtabula	OH
Way	F. B.		Ashtabula	OH
Addleman	B. T.		Athens	OH
Brannan	J. C.		Athens	OH
Barnes	William H.		Barnesville	OH
Vance	Handel		Barnesville	OH
Carter	R. R.		Basil	OH
Kline	J. A.		Batavia	OH

PHOTOGRAPHERS LISTED BY CITY/STATE IN THE UNITED STATES 1888-1889

NAME		ADDRESS	CITY	STATE
Speaker	E. R.		Beach City	OH
Dennison*	J. W.		Bedford	OH
Benson	Harvey		Bellaire	OH
Sellars	James W.		Bellaire	OH
Tappan	T. S.		Bellaire	OH
Koogle	Milton		Bellefontaine	OH
Milliken	J. J.		Bellefontaine	OH
Drake	B. W.		Belleville	OH
Gaugler & Heal			Bellevue	OH
Falor	A. C.		Berea	OH
Smedley	F. S.		Berea	OH
Frazee	A. R.		Bethel	OH
McCall	A. F.		Bethel	OH
Brown	Eva		Beverly	OH
Kratzer	J. W.		Blanchester	OH
Tripplett	W. A.		Bluffton	OH
Clark	R.		Bolivar	OH
Morrison	R. P.		Bowling Green	OH
Parker	J. T.		Bowling Green	OH
Lockhart	William H.		Bryan	OH
Brenner	Daniel		Bucyrus	OH
Dougherty	James		Bucyrus	OH
Moyer*	R. D.		Bucyrus	OH
Davis	Henry		Cadiz	OH
Carson	Arthur		Caldwell	OH
Brown	J. P.		Cambridge	OH
Mackey	Thomas M.		Cambridge	OH
McPeek*	John		Cambridge	OH
Strickmaker	John		Canal Dover	OH
Kunkler	B. P.		Canal Dover	OH
Courtney	S. V.	43 S. Market	Canton	OH
Geer	William F.	10 ½ Market	Canton	OH
Manly	George W.	19 E. 8th	Canton	OH
Prince	John H.	18 E. Tuscarawas	Canton	OH
Schenck	Philip	R21, Saxton Blk, 8th	Canton	OH
Knoder	H. F.		Cardington	OH
Zimmerman	J. F.		Carey	OH
Baxter	Port C.		Carrollton	OH
Gould*	J. W.		Carrollton	OH
Conley Bros.			Celina	OH

PHOTOGRAPHERS LISTED BY CITY/STATE IN THE UNITED STATES 1888-1889

NAME		ADDRESS	CITY	STATE
Higbee	E. R.		Chagrin Falls	OH
Shaw*	Thomas		Chagrin Falls	OH
Evick	Christ		Chillicothe	OH
Woodward*	George T.		Chillicothe	OH
Aldrich & Ludeke		600 McMillan	Walnut Hills, Cin.	OH
Arrico	Frank	146 W. 5th	Cincinnati	OH
Brownell	C. A.	196 W. 5th	Cincinnati	OH
Core & Co.*	E. B.	56 W. 5th	Cincinnati	OH
Core & Co.	F. B.	50 W. 5th	Cincinnati	OH
Correvont*	Frank	1030 Central	Cincinnati	OH
Correvont	Frank	1032 Central	Cincinnati	OH
Dettmer	John	402 Freeman	Cincinnati	OH
Dickinson*	Wellington	96 W. 5th	Cincinnati	OH
Fellison	O. F.	192 W. 5th	Cincinnati	OH
Firoe	J. W.	28 Emery Arcade	Cincinnati	OH
French	L. B.	405 Vine	Cincinnati	OH
Goins	J. M.	163 Race	Cincinnati	OH
Green	Josiah H.	Harrison Pike	Cincinnati	OH
Groomes	John W.	170 W. 5th	Cincinnati	OH
Hamilton & Co.	J. K.	5th & Plum	Cincinnati	OH
Henry	Frank	102 W. 5th	Cincinnati	OH
Howland*	C. W.	176 W. 4th	Cincinnati	OH
Howland	E. A.	427 Kemper	Cincinnati	OH
Keenan	N. E.	238 ½ Elm	Cincinnati	OH
Krogmann	Charles	2245 Spring Grove	Cumminsville, Cin.	OH
Krogman*	Charles H.	Spring Grove, 25th Ward	Cincinnati	OH
Krug	Simon	531 Vine	Cincinnati	OH
Krug*	Simon	Vine & 15th	Cincinnati	OH
Landy	James	208 W. 4th	Cincinnati	OH
Lindsey & Leighton*		Gilbert Ave.	Cincinnati	OH
McMillan & Co.	Q. A.	28 W. 4th	Cincinnati	OH
Marceau & Bellsmith		148 W. 5th	Cincinnati	OH
Martin	Charles W.	195 W. 5th	Cincinnati	OH
Meyer	J. H.	465 Vine	Cincinnati	OH
Mueller	H.	627 Central	Cincinnati	OH
Raffell*	T.	28 Arcade	Cincinnati	OH
Reiman	Joseph	842 Central	Cincinnati	OH
Reinhold	J. H.	449 Vine	Cincinnati	OH
Rombach & Groene		476 W. 4th	Cincinnati	OH
Schuster	George	489-491 W. 6th	Cincinnati	OH

PHOTOGRAPHERS LISTED BY CITY/STATE IN THE UNITED STATES 1888-1889

NAME		ADDRESS	CITY	STATE
Shaw	G. S.	7th & Race	Cincinnati	OH
Shaw*	G. S.	8th & Race	Cincinnati	OH
Skewes	J. D.	222 W. 5th	Cincinnati	OH
Slocum	A. T.	160 W. 5th	Cincinnati	OH
Smith	Aaron A.	402 Freeman	Cincinnati	OH
Thomas	A. S.	166 W. 5th	Cincinnati	OH
Titus	Frank M.	228 W. 5th	Cincinnati	OH
Van Loo	Leon	148 W. 4th	Cincinnati	OH
Waldack	Mrs. Charles	Vine & Liberty	Cincinnati	OH
Watson's		156 W. 4th	Cincinnati	OH
Weckman	J. P.	128 W. 5th	Cincinnati	OH
Weingartner	Leo	6th & Central	Cincinnati	OH
White*	G. William	475 Beech	Cincinnati	OH
Wilson	A. B.	22 ½ E. 4th	Cincinnati	OH
Zieverink	A.	Colerain & Marshall	Camp Washington	OH
Zutterling	Peter	503 Vine	Cincinnati	OH
Reed & Bock			Circleville	OH
Spencer	O. H.		Circleville	OH
Spencer	T. W.		Circleville	OH
Hall	S. A.		Clarington	OH
Bailey*	David C.	2566 Broadway	Cleveland	OH
Barge	John W.	249 Superior	Cleveland	OH
Becker Bros.		783 Lorain	Cleveland	OH
Beckwith & Son	M. E.	261 Pearl	Cleveland	OH
Bidde	Henry	75 Euclid	Cleveland	OH
Biddle*	Henry	75 Euclid	Cleveland	OH
Burkitt	C. W.	472 Pearl	Cleveland	OH
Chase	Harvey E.	2550 Broadway	Cleveland	OH
Copeland	J. H.	586 Pearl	Cleveland	OH
Crobaugh	Samuel	Congress	Cleveland	OH
Decker	E.	143 Euclid	Cleveland	OH
Decker & Wilber*		143 Euclid	Cleveland	OH
Dennison*	John	136 Ontario	Cleveland	OH
Dennison	William M.	647 Pearl	Cleveland	OH
Freedle & Bro.	J. W.	225 Superio	Cleveland	OH
Green	J. M.	209 Superior	Cleveland	OH
Gubin	Oscar	190 Ontario	Cleveland	OH
Gumbiuski	Leon	196 Ontario	Cleveland	OH
Hubbel	O. C.	649 Pearl	Cleveland	OH
Johnson	George G.	99 Euclid	Cleveland	OH

NAME		ADDRESS	CITY	STATE
Koestle Bros.		629 Lorain	Cleveland	OH
Korn Bernhardt		897 Pearl	Cleveland	OH
Krumhar & Co.	R. F.	548-550 Pearl	Cleveland	OH
Lawrence*	S. A.	1293 Lorain	Cleveland	OH
Liebich's Photographic Art Gallery		344 Ontario	Cleveland	OH
McLeod	N. E. A.	262 Pearl	Cleveland	OH
Nock	E. B.	148 Ontario	Cleveland	OH
Powelson	G. A.	17 Chester	Cleveland	OH
Reeves	Henry H.	1594 Hough	Cleveland	OH
Roberts & Brooks		130 Ontario	Cleveland	OH
Ryder*	J. F.	239 Superior	Cleveland	OH
Ryder	John H.	211 Superior	Cleveland	OH
Salen	Peter	131 Fulton	Cleveland	OH
Sheldon	Alfred	640 St. Clair	Cleveland	OH
Sprague	E. D.	374 Ontario	Cleveland	OH
Stiles	A. J.	533 Pearl	Cleveland	OH
Stone	Elbridge G.	652 St. Clair	Cleveland	OH
Sweeney	Thomas T.	R13, 307 Superior	Cleveland	OH
Udell	M. M.	13 Euclid	Cleveland	OH
Zeleny	A. L.	417 Woodland	Cleveland	OH
Brown	H. V.		Clyde	OH
Wiles	A. W.		Clyde	OH
Webb & Co.	John M.		Columbiana	OH
Baker	L. M.	Comstock's Opera House	Columbus	OH
Buckmyer	F. J.	69 S. High	Columbus	OH
Capital Gallery		222 S. High	Columbus	OH
Columbus Excelsior Copying House*		405 N. High	Columbus	OH
Dewey	George N.	177 N. High	Columbus	OH
Elliott	George R.	High & Main	Columbus	OH
Elliott	J. M.	95 S. High	Columbus	OH
French & Co.		102 S. High	Columbus	OH
Kuehner	Fred W.	High & Main	Columbus	OH
Mathew	Thomas	18 E. Broad	Columbus	OH
Neville	David S.	60 N. High	Columbus	OH
Pfeiffer	John A.	228 S. High	Columbus	OH
Price	W. A.	180 N. High	Columbus	OH
Urlin	George C.	216 S. High	Columbus	OH
Woodward	W. M.	180 N. High	Columbus	OH
Pitcher	H. P.		Conneaut	OH

PHOTOGRAPHERS LISTED BY CITY/STATE IN THE UNITED STATES 1888-1889

NAME		ADDRESS	CITY	STATE
Mortonson	Peter		Corning	OH
Coe	E. V.		Coshocton	OH
Hempsted	Charles		Coshocton	OH
Mathews	E. W.		Coshocton	OH
Townsend	William		Covington	OH
McIntire	J. H.		Crestline	OH
Rodecker	L. M.		Cumberland	OH
Shumway	H. L.		Cuyahoga Falls	OH
Appleton	J. M.	3rd & Jefferson	Dayton	OH
Bowersox	A. L.	2nd & Main	Dayton	OH
Bradley	Isaac	73 S. Terry	Dayton	OH
Bunker	H. P.	Jefferson	Dayton	OH
Cridland	F. W.	12 Main	Dayton	OH
Kaufmain*	Peter	Wayne SE c. McLain	Dayton	OH
Lalonrette	Mrs. H.	214 E. 5th	Dayton	OH
McCandless	W. H.	5th & Wayne	Dayton	OH
Miller	Charles H.	34 S. Main	Dayton	OH
Moler	George B.	Wayne & Van Buren	Dayton	OH
Neff	Joseph	6 E 3rd	Dayton	OH
Neff*	Joseph	7 E. 3rd	Dayton	OH
Wolfe	M.	106 S. Main	Dayton	OH
Denman	M. H.		Defiance	OH
Bodurtha	Charles H.		Delaware	OH
Ulrey	W.		Delaware	OH
Mathis	E. R.		Delphos	OH
Ream Bros.			Delphos	OH
Roloson	S. G.		Delphos	OH
Walker	O. A.		Delta	OH
Donaldson	Sol. I.		Dexter City	OH
Heffelman	O. B.		Doylestown	OH
Williams	B. L.		Doylestown	OH
Rineberger	L.		Dunkirk	OH
Atkinson Bros.			East Liverpool	OH
Border	Henry		East Liverpool	OH
Bower	Henry		East Liverpool	OH
Gould	A. R.		East Liverpool	OH
Cress	Mell		East Palestine	OH
Wickenden	J. N.		East Toledo	OH
Harlan	C. C.		Eaton	OH
Miley	J. H.		Eaton	OH

PHOTOGRAPHERS LISTED BY CITY/STATE IN THE UNITED STATES 1888-1889

NAME		ADDRESS	CITY	STATE
Slater	E.		Edgerton	OH
Palmer	Mrs. W. H.		Edon	OH
Park & Lee			Elyria	OH
Williams	S. H.		Elyria	OH
Houghton	R. R.		Felicity	OH
Crozior & Linaweaver			Findlay	OH
Nichols	A. H.		Findlay	OH
Zay	F. B.		Findlay	OH
Presler	Hiram		Forest	OH
Hoyt	J. S.		Fort Recovery	OH
Ball	James		Fostoria	OH
Gribble	Charles		Fostoria	OH
Slater	Joseph		Franklin	OH
Packard	W. D.		Frazeyburgh	OH
Credlebaugh*	T. L.		Fremont	OH
Grobe	R.		Fremont	OH
Pascoe	C. J.		Fremont	OH
Kindmark	E.		Galion	OH
Lobenthal	Lewis		Galion	OH
Reck	L. M.		Galion	OH
Curtis & Thompson			Gallipolis	OH
Fenner	W. J.		Gallipolis	OH
Woodworth	J. P.		Geneva	OH
Spencer	Francis A.		Georgetown	OH
Barnhart*	James		Germantown	OH
Kerns	N. A.		Girard	OH
Dulenbaugh	H. A.		Gordon	OH
Callihan			Grand Rapids	OH
Brown	H. V.		Green Spring	OH
Casselman	S. R.		Greenfield	OH
Price	E. J.		Greenfield	OH
Beem	R. D.		Greenville	OH
Harper	J.		Greenville	OH
Johnson	A. M.		Greenville	OH
Mote	E. V.		Greenville	OH
Leiter	Elmer E.		Hamilton	OH
Overpeck	L. C.		Hamilton	OH
Hammond	C. E.		Hampden	OH
Rogers	W. B.		Hattonia	OH
Elliott	H. G.		Hicksville	OH

PHOTOGRAPHERS LISTED BY CITY/STATE IN THE UNITED STATES 1888-1889

NAME		ADDRESS	CITY	STATE
Johnson	E.		Hicksville	OH
Downing	N. H.		Hillsborough	OH
Foulk	J. Z.		Hillsborough	OH
Barrette	Thornton		Ironton	OH
Hitt	C. P.		Ironton	OH
Cahoon	J. C.		Jackson	OH
Miller & Williams			Jackson	OH
Loomis	Milo A.		Jefferson	OH
Poister	F. E.		Kent	OH
Wark	James		Kent	OH
Davis	S.		Kenton	OH
Hays*	I. N.		Kenton	OH
Hays	J. N.		Kenton	OH
Shawd	J. R.		Kenton	OH
Winters Bros.			Kenton	OH
Borah	C. W.		Lancaster	OH
Fulton & Fureman			Lancaster	OH
Nutter	T. S.		Lancaster	OH
Osborne & May			Lancaster	OH
Wolfe	J. J.		Lancaster	OH
Finch	P. F.		Lebanon	OH
Patterson	George P.		Lebanon	OH
Heaton	H. F.		Lebanon	OH
Smith	N. W.		Leetonia	OH
Bowdle*	E. T.		Lewistown	OH
Colehase	William		Lewistown	OH
Lindsay & Leighton*			Lewistown	OH
Mock*	J. W.		Lewistown	OH
Trauss & Ebersole*			Lewistown	OH
Beery*	G. W.		Logan	OH
McLain	J. D.		Logan	OH
Tresize*	Samuel P.		Logan	OH
Sifrit & Coover			London	OH
Dideron	Joseph		Lorain	OH
Hinman	Frank C.		Loudonville	OH
Poff	J. H.		Loudonville	OH
Phillips	T. L.		Lowellville	OH
McKee	C. L.		Lucas	OH
Ayres	J. T.		McConnelsville	OH
Wetherell	Edwin		McConnelsville	OH

PHOTOGRAPHERS LISTED BY CITY/STATE IN THE UNITED STATES 1888-1889

NAME		ADDRESS	CITY	STATE
Gregory, Jr.	E. R.		Manchester	OH
Campbell & Camp		8 ½ N. Main	Mansfield	OH
Hawkins	J. A.	3 ½ N. Park	Mansfield	OH
Seiler	J. C.	59 ½ N. Main	Mansfield	OH
Cadawallader	J. D.		Marietta	OH
Reis	F. L.		Marietta	OH
Green	Nathaniel		Marion	OH
Moore	W. H.		Marion	OH
Prentice & Vail			Marion	OH
Enoch	Alexander C.		Martin's Ferry	OH
Cherrington	T. J.		Marysville	OH
Sidey	Thomas		Marysville	OH
Haring	Jacob C.		Massillon	OH
Schertzer	Leavitt L.		Massillon	OH
Mann	S. M.		Mechanicsburgh	OH
Hawkins	T. I.		Medina	OH
Mason	J. S.		Medina	OH
Clark	J. L.		Miamisburgh	OH
Runnels	J. L.		Middleport	OH
Slater	W. F.		Middletown	OH
Hall	R.		Millersburgh	OH
Tibbals	Fred B.		Millersburgh	OH
Carpenter	Dyer H.		Minerva	OH
Brown	Theo.		Mount Gilead	OH
Enoch	A. C.		Mount Pleasant	OH
Crowell	F. S.		Mount Vernon	OH
Elliott	A. B.		Mount Vernon	OH
Gardner & Son			Napoleon	OH
McDowell	Lee		Nelsonville	OH
Bowdle	C. M.		Nevada	OH
Frees	J. H.		Newcomerstown	OH
Horn	M. U.		Newcomerstown	OH
Boroman	H. G.		New Lexington	OH
Moore	George S.		New Lisbon	OH
Fuller	William		New London	OH
Strickmaker	Joseph N.		New Philadelphia	OH
Strickmaker	Philip		New Philadelphia	OH
Butterworth	Charles		New Vienna	OH
Chase	G. W.		Newark	OH
Connel & Murphy			Newark	OH

PHOTOGRAPHERS LISTED BY CITY/STATE IN THE UNITED STATES 1888-1889

NAME	ADDRESS	CITY	STATE
Pausch	O. M.	Newark	OH
Smith	Walter A.	Newark	OH
Tibbals	Lawrence J.	Niles	OH
Butt	George	Norwalk	OH
Edmondson	G. W.	Norwalk	OH
Foster	F. D.	Norwalk	OH
Kellogg	C. H.	Norwalk	OH
Platt	H. M.	Oberlin	OH
Upton	L. W.	Oberlin	OH
Shaw*	J. R.	Olmstead	OH
Harrington*	Neal P.	Orrville	OH
Arnold	S. C.	Ottawa	OH
Toler	J. C.	Ottawa	OH
Barnard	G. N.	Painesville	OH
Davis	D. R.	Painesville	OH
Yager	Leroy	Paulding	OH
Freash	F. B.	Philo	OH
Sweetman	F.	Pioneer	OH
Woodruff	W. C.	Pioneer	OH
Gale	C. A.	Piqua	OH
Thorn	J. R.	Piqua	OH
McPeek & Dutcher		Plainfield	OH
Waite	C. B.	Plymouth	OH
Curtis	W. B.	Pomeroy	OH
Feiger	E. F.	Pomeroy	OH
Newton	W. M.	Port Clinton	OH
Hathaway	John G.	Portsmouth	OH
Hull	H. B.	Portsmouth	OH
Lutz	J. N.	Portsmouth	OH
French*	Charles L.	Ravenna	OH
Oakley	John H.	Ravenna	OH
Thompson	Ada A.	Ravenna	OH
Watson	A.	Richwood	OH
Groomes	J. C.	Ripley	OH
Hale	O. C.	Ripley	OH
Dolph	O. A.	Rock Creek	OH
Ferron	John	St. Clairsville	OH
Kelsey	Will. H.	St. Marys	OH
Hewitt & Hewitt		Salem	OH
McDermott*	J. W.	Salem	OH

PHOTOGRAPHERS LISTED BY CITY/STATE IN THE UNITED STATES 1888-1889

NAME		ADDRESS	CITY	STATE
Parks	J. B.		Salem	OH
McFadden	J. J.		Salineville	OH
Bishop & Co.		Washington Row	Sandusky	OH
Gross	C. A.	232 Columbus	Sandusky	OH
Lloyd	J. M.		Sandusky	OH
Platt	A. C.	Water & Columbus	Sandusky	OH
Wetherell*	M. L.	224 Columbus	Sandusky	OH
McClannahan	W. H.		Shawnee	OH
Smith	F. H.		Shelby	OH
Van De Grift	C. W.		Sidney	OH
Widner	A. W.		Sidney	OH
Fulkerson	W. W.		Somerset	OH
Kent	Eugene		Sparta	OH
Bumgardner	J. A.	38 S. Market	Springfield	OH
Buckingham	W.	127 ½ W. Main	Springfield	OH
Calendar	H. W.	23 S. Limestone	Springfield	OH
Clark & Lewis		14 ½ E. Main	Springfield	OH
Cripps	O. N.	35 ½ W. Main	Springfield	OH
Cushman	W. S.	1 Arcade	Springfield	OH
French & Co.*	W. G.	19 E. Main	Springfield	OH
Gano	Richard M.	13 ½ E. Main	Springfield	OH
Hunster	Louie P.	13 ½ E. Main	Springfield	OH
Maxwell	James A.	21 ½ S. Market	Springfield	OH
Smith	J. E.	26 ½ S. Market	Springfield	OH
Vansickle	A. H.	40 E. Main	Springfield	OH
Fickes	John C.		Steubenville	OH
Filson & Son	D.		Steubenville	OH
Harry	A. S.		Steubenville	OH
Donaldson	George T.		Tiffin	OH
Frees	O. P.		Tiffin	OH
Miller	W. D.		Tiffin	OH
Pennington	Barclay		Tiffin	OH
Tunison & Son			Tiffin	OH
Alley	E. H.	91 Summit	Toledo	OH
Austin	Americus	108 Wakeman	Toledo	OH
Babcock	W. R.	235 Summit	Toledo	OH
Beck & Fields		207 Summit	Toledo	OH
Claflin	D. B.	183 Summit	Toledo	OH
Fields	George	57 Summit	Toledo	OH
Fitch*	M. W.	SW c. Beacon	Toledo	OH

PHOTOGRAPHERS LISTED BY CITY/STATE IN THE UNITED STATES 1888-1889

NAME		ADDRESS	CITY	STATE
Hughes	R. F.	32 Chamber of Commerce	Toledo	OH
Koella	John	Division	Toledo	OH
Lane	Amos	186 ½ Summit	Toledo	OH
Lenhart Bros.		330 Broadway	Toledo	OH
McKecknie & Oswald		197 Summit	Toledo	OH
Rockwood	J. M.	Cherry	Toledo	OH
Sessions & Kohne			Toledo	OH
Trost	F. J.	49 Summit	Toledo	OH
Van Loo	W. F.	149 Summit	Toledo	OH
Lawson	Elisha		Troy	OH
Schnell	C. A.		Troy	OH
Moye	J. C.		Uhrichsville	OH
Bevington & Stutz			Upper Sandusky	OH
McCahon	J.		Upper Sandusky	OH
Wickenden*	J. W.		Upper Sandusky	OH
Graham	F. P.		Urbana	OH
Wilhelmi	F. G.		Urbana	OH
Rank & Co.	J. F.		Van Wert	OH
Smith*	Isaiah		Van Wert	OH
Harris & Abell			Vermillion	OH
Clark	J. W.		Vinton	OH
Wolbach	T. D.		Wadsworth	OH
Potter	William E.		Wapakoneta	OH
Haines	Charles B.		Warren	OH
Holman	Charles		Warren	OH
Rice	Luther M.		Warren	OH
Snyder	C. S.		Washington Ct House	OH
Willet	W. F.		Washington Ct House	OH
Blackmann	F. G.		Wauseon	OH
Miller	E. P.		Waverly	OH
Rummel	A.		Waynesburgh	OH
Downing	J. J.		Waynesville	OH
Gilson	A. S.		Wellington	OH
Sheets	Frederick		Wellsville	OH
Crosier	George		West Richfield	OH
Oppenheimer*	Ben		West Union	OH
Butterworth	Charles		Wilmington	OH
Carroll	John		Wilmington	OH
Slack & Berry			Wilmington	OH
Skinner	J. A.		Woodsfield	OH

PHOTOGRAPHERS LISTED BY CITY/STATE IN THE UNITED STATES 1888-1889

NAME		ADDRESS	CITY	STATE
Brainerd*	Emma		Wooster	OH
Cochran	Will		Wooster	OH
Teeple	Mrs. J. S.		Wooster	OH
Foltz & Cochran*			Wooster	OH
Lewis	H. C.		Worthington	OH
Biddle	F. S.		Xenia	OH
Gratch	W. M.		Xenia	OH
Baird	J. B.	22 S. Phelps	Youngstown	OH
Baird*	J. R.	22 S. Phelps	Youngstown	OH
Blackburn & Webb		120 W. Federal	Youngstown	OH
Keck	Calvin	W. Federal	Youngstown	OH
Leroy & Terrill		45 N. Phelps	Youngstown	OH
Lauck	J. A.	112 Main	Zanesville	OH
Rich	S. A.	101 Main	Zanesville	OH
Rich	Mrs. S. A.	13 N. 5th	Zanesville	OH
Sedgwick	H. M.	133 Main	Zanesville	OH
Starke	W. G.	5th S. E. c. Main	Zanesville	OH
Sturgeon	William J.	200 Main	Zanesville	OH
Shanswood	John		Adam	OR
Shanswool*	John		Adam	OR
Crawford	J. C.		Albany	OR
Logan	Charles W.		Ashland	OR
Crow	S. B.		Astoria	OR
Shute & Co.			Astoria	OR
Moore	F.		Baker City	OR
Rey	Miss Josie		Baker City	OR
Venner	J. F.		Brownsville	OR
Hazeltine	G. I.		Canyon City	OR
Abell & Son			Corvallis	OR
De Groot	H.		Corvallis	OR
Ellis	M. D.		Dallas	OR
Hickathier	A.		Drain	OR
Hendee	D. H.		East Portland	OR
Yocum	A. M.		East Portland	OR
Bankins	Frank A.		Eugene City	OR
Winters	C. L.		Eugene City	OR
Everitt	E. F.		Grant's Pass	OR
Husbands	S.		Hood River	OR
Frost	G. B.		Independence	OR
Britt	Peter		Jacksonville	OR

PHOTOGRAPHERS LISTED BY CITY/STATE IN THE UNITED STATES 1888-1889

NAME		ADDRESS	CITY	STATE
Grobe	Jacob		Jacksonville	OR
Crow	J. W.		Knappa	OR
May	George W.		Lebanon	OR
Davidson	J.		Linkville	OR
Price	W. V.		McMinnville	OR
McMillan Bros.			Marshfield	OR
Kester	C. M.		Oregon City	OR
Abell & Son			Portland	OR
Davidson	I. G.		Portland	OR
Davies	George W.		Portland	OR
Judkins	S. B.		Portland	OR
Morse	C. C.		Portland	OR
Parrott	W. S.		Portland	OR
Patridge	E. J. & W. H.		Portland	OR
Russ	H. M.		Portland	OR
Thwaites	Joseph		Portland	OR
Towne & Moore			Portland	OR
Vantersell	A. S.		Portland	OR
Woodward & Co.	Clark		Portland	OR
Winters	C. L.		Prineville	OR
Oakes	Omega		Roseburgh	OR
Ward	T. C.		Roseburgh	OR
Johnson	William P.		Salem	OR
Pickerill	F. A.		Salem	OR
Shuster	H. S.		Salem	OR
Gilhousen	W. H.		The Dalles	OR
Partidge			The Dalles	OR
Jones Bros.			Union	OR
Freehoefer	F.		Adamstown	PA
Duncan	D.		Adamsville	PA
Aufrecht	G.		Allegheny	PA
Bricker & Corliss*			Allegheny	PA
Corliss	Edward J.		Allegheny	PA
Fielding	Paul		Allegheny	PA
Kirk	F. J.		Allegheny	PA
Kneeland	Charles		Allegheny	PA
Merriman	A. G.		Allegheny	PA
Nulf	O. E.	299 Beaver	Allegheny	PA
Pearson	J. R.		Allegheny	PA
Pfaff	Henry		Allegheny	PA

PHOTOGRAPHERS LISTED BY CITY/STATE IN THE UNITED STATES 1888-1889

NAME		ADDRESS	CITY	STATE
Shook	C. W.	196 Beaver	Allegheny	PA
Sonnenberg	H.	52 Federal	Allegheny	PA
Sonnenberg	J. E.		Allegheny	PA
Sperber	John		Allegheny	PA
Tomlinson*	Isaac		Allegheny	PA
Bachman & Co.*			Allentown	PA
Jeanes	E. D.		Allentown	PA
Lockman	Benjamin		Allentown	PA
Wertz	E. S.		Allentown	PA
Bishop Bros.			Altoona	PA
Bonine*	Robert A.		Altoona	PA
Daily	John		Altoona	PA
Wolfe	A. S.		Apollo	PA
Keon & Miller			Ashland	PA
Merriman	F. S.		Baker's Landing	PA
Hammerly	A. O.		Barnhart's Mills	PA
Chalfant	A. B.		Beaver Falls	PA
Kail*	W. H.		Beaver Falls	PA
Foltz	F. H.		Bedford	PA
Moore	J. W.		Bellefonte	PA
Blatt	C. G.		Bernville	PA
Broadt	J. F.		Berwick	PA
Eggert	H. B.		Bethlehem	PA
Gross	P. L.		Bethlehem	PA
Lochman*	C. L.		Bethlehem	PA
Lockman	C. L.		Bethlehem	PA
Reynolds	J. J.		Bigler	PA
Green	George M.		Blairsville	PA
Rosenstock	H.		Bloomsburgh	PA
Russell	Edward L.		Blossburgh	PA
Keystone Gallery			Braddock	PA
Detlor & Waddell			Bradford	PA
Latham	Charles		Bradford	PA
Robbins	Frank		Bradford	PA
West	Jacob		Bradford	PA
Bostwick	J. H.		Bristol	PA
Hall	E. Clark		Brookville	PA
Abrams & Son	J. R.		Brownsville	PA
Adamson	Samuel J.		Brownsville	PA
Thompson	A. M.		Brownsville	PA

PHOTOGRAPHERS LISTED BY CITY/STATE IN THE UNITED STATES 1888-1889

NAME		ADDRESS	CITY	STATE
Bagley	F. L.		Butler	PA
Bayley*	F. L.		Butler	PA
Criley	N. J.		Butler	PA
McDonnell	C. P.		Cambridgeborough	PA
Perry	W. E.		Canton	PA
Cramer	Adon C.		Carbondale	PA
Choate	J. N.		Carlisle	PA
Dinmon*	Henry		Carlisle	PA
Beck*	John C.		Carry	PA
Barbour	J. W.		Chambersburgh	PA
Bishop	Henry		Chambersburgh	PA
Sonders*	F. A.		Chambersburgh	PA
Souders	F. A.		Chambersburgh	PA
Bellis & Cummings			Chester	PA
Burland	C. S.		Chester	PA
Jeans	Joseph		Chester	PA
Kroneberger	F. A.		Chester	PA
Lewis	F. M.		Clarion	PA
Bottorf	J. K.		Clearfield	PA
Gibson	J. B.		Coatsville	PA
Whittling	Louis		Cochranton	PA
Newcomer	W. S.		Codorus	PA
Bailey	William		Columbia	PA
Howard	S. H.		Connellsville	PA
Kromer	Nicholas		Connellsville	PA
Porter	Byron		Connellsville	PA
Cope & Day			Conshohocken	PA
Beck	John C.	35 First Ave.	Corry	PA
Lyman	Mrs.		Corry	PA
Polder & Beck*			Corry	PA
Tice	A. W.		Corry	PA
Bliss	L. R.		Coudersport	PA
Forrest	S. D.		Covington	PA
Aubner	Calvin		Curllsville	PA
Moore & Duffey			Curwensville	PA
Smith	C. W.		Dalmatia	PA
Leisenring*	H. H.		?	PA
McMahon & Ireland*			?	PA
Graves	Jesse A.		Delaware Water Gap	PA
Brown*	A. W.		Delmont	PA

PHOTOGRAPHERS LISTED BY CITY/STATE IN THE UNITED STATES 1888-1889

NAME	ADDRESS		CITY	STATE
Billian	Benjamin		Doylestown	PA
Beard	A. S.		Du Bois	PA
Holmes & Davis			Du Bois	PA
Bell	A. S.		East Brady	PA
Greisemer	S.		East Greenville	PA
Primrose	George M.		East Stroudsburgh	PA
Brown	Charles		Easton	PA
Hoffmeir	S. B.		Easton	PA
Knecht	Frank		Easton	PA
Naramore	W. S.		Easton	PA
Stout	J. V.		Easton	PA
Sloan	F. J.		Eau Claire	PA
Van Dyke	W. H.		Edinborough	PA
Corell			Eldred	PA
Nicholas*	N. E.		Emporium	PA
Schreiver	J. B.		Emporium	PA
White	Etta P.		Emporium	PA
Bassett	F. J.		Erie	PA
Boepple	Charles		Erie	PA
Crowell & Son			Erie	PA
Keith	W. S.		Erie	PA
Morano	W. A.		Erie	PA
Ohlwiler	E. H.		Erie	PA
Pier	F. B.		Erie	PA
Weber Bros.			Erie	PA
Bruce & Fisher			Everett	PA
Stumm & Co.*	A. Y.		Farmingham	PA
Black	Isaiah		Franklin	PA
Jackson	J. O.		Franklin	PA
Wilt & Son			Franklin	PA
Kemp*	H.		Fredricksburgh	PA
Bricker	J. M.		Freeport	PA
Coffee	D. G.		Freeport	PA
Mimper	Levi		Gettysburg	PA
Tipton	W. H.		Gettysburg	PA
Kester*	Elias		Grampian Hills	PA
Hile	William		Greenburgh	PA
Low	Michael E.		Greenburgh	PA
Shadle	Isaac		Greenburgh	PA
Alter	David		Greencastle	PA

PHOTOGRAPHERS LISTED BY CITY/STATE IN THE UNITED STATES 1888-1889

NAME		ADDRESS	CITY	STATE
Meacham	C. T.		Greenville	PA
Lochman	W. J.		Hamburgh	PA
Frommeyer	David A.		Hanover	PA
Weaver	Peter S.		Hanover	PA
Burnite	D. C.		Harrisburgh	PA
Crystal*	D. S.		Harrisburgh	PA
Howard & Miller*			Harrisburgh	PA
Lemer	Le Rue		Harrisburgh	PA
Roshon	C. S.		Harrisburgh	PA
Schriver	C. C.		Harrisburgh	PA
Hensel	Londolph		Hawley	PA
Jellotson*	Nelson		Hawley	PA
Kellmer	Peter		Hazelton	PA
Proctor	E. C.		Hollidaysburgh	PA
White	E. F.		Hollidaysburgh	PA
Bodie	Joseph A.		Honesdale	PA
Evans	William M.		Houtzdale	PA
Bare	M. E.		Hummelstown	PA
Kline	Luther B.		Huntingdon	PA
Frey	Henry		Hyde Park	PA
Clark	Thomas B.		Indiana	PA
Tiffany	B. B.		Indiana	PA
Adams	J. M.		Irwin	PA
Gorman	W. H.		Jersey Shore	PA
Briber	Ed. L.		Johnstown	PA
Henninger	John H.		Johnstown	PA
Statler	George		Johnstown	PA
Gardner*	Levi		Kent	PA
Shadle	C. C.		Kittanning	PA
Walthers*	C. B.		Knox	PA
Dietrich	W. A.		Kutztown	PA
Snyder	C. W.		Kutztown	PA
Betz & Richards			Lancaster	PA
Cummings	Thomas		Lancaster	PA
Gill	W. L.		Lancaster	PA
Hubley	J. W.		Lancaster	PA
Inman	William M.		Lancaster	PA
Rote	J. E.		Lancaster	PA
Saylor	B. F.		Lancaster	PA
Smalling	J. J.		Lancaster	PA

PHOTOGRAPHERS LISTED BY CITY/STATE IN THE UNITED STATES 1888-1889

NAME	ADDRESS	CITY	STATE
Shadle	Amos	Latrobe	PA
Shadle	Edwin J.	Latrobe	PA
Groeff	J. W.	Lebanon	PA
Quinby*	F. J.	Lebanon	PA
Roshon	C. S.	Lebanon	PA
Cornelius	J. W.	Lewisburgh	PA
Ginter	W. M.	Lewisburgh	PA
Eaton	E. F.	Lewistown	PA
Smith	J. W.	Lewistown	PA
Kunkle*	Isaac	Liberty	PA
Stockton & Pitcher		Linesville	PA
Slaugenhaupt	H. T.	Littlestown	PA
Dorey	Charles	Lock Haven	PA
Floyd	J. W.	Lock Haven	PA
Woods	T. W.	Lock Haven	PA
Long	J. H.	Longville	PA
Gerdom	H. E.	Lykens	PA
Miller*	L. T.	Lykens	PA
McPherson	J. G.	McKeesport	PA
Momeyer	W. P. & M. B.	McKeesport	PA
Wagner*	M. C.	McKeesport	PA
Whitehead	W. H.	McKeesport	PA
Bowman	D. A.	Mahanoy	PA
Miller	W. D.	Manheim	PA
Spencer	Frank M.	Mansfield	PA
Dillinger	S. L.	Marietta	PA
Zelner	James	Mauch Chunk	PA
Dennington	C. J.	Meadville	PA
Dunn	J. D.	Meadville	PA
Fowler	A. R.	Meadville	PA
Martin*	A. A.	Meadville	PA
Boss	D. W.	Mechanicsburgh	PA
Pearson	W. B.	Mercer	PA
Armbrust	J. D.	Meyersdale	PA
Haus	James	Mifflinburgh	PA
Hess	Joseph	Mifflintown	PA
Johnson	L. K.	Mill Village	PA
Ripple Bros.		Milton	PA
Wheeland	W. P.	Milton	PA
Smith	William W.	Minersville	PA

PHOTOGRAPHERS LISTED BY CITY/STATE IN THE UNITED STATES 1888-1889

NAME		ADDRESS	CITY	STATE
Bayha	G. L.		Monongahela City	PA
Cooper	Robert F.		Monongahela City	PA
Doolittle	George W.		Montrose	PA
Talbot	Walter E.		Montrose	PA
Stauffer & Co.	A. N.		Mount Pleasant	PA
Mowry*	E. L.		Muncy	PA
Schell	George		Myerstown	PA
Pennepacker	C.		Nanticoke	PA
Barnes	J. C.		New Bethlehem	PA
Evens*	Winfield		New Brighton	PA
Noss	Henry		New Brighton	PA
Gellespie	S. M.		New Castle	PA
Gorrell*	S. C.		New Castle	PA
Phipps & Johnson			New Castle	PA
Cable	Jacob		Newport	PA
Randall	W. F.		Newtown	PA
Cope & Day*			Norristown	PA
Day	George W.	317 DeKalb	Norristown	PA
Fisher	S. R.		Norristown	PA
Lenzi	George A.		Norristown	PA
Saurman	O. S.		Norristown	PA
Stewart & Phear			North East	PA
Robbins	Frank		Oil City	PA
Sires	J. W.		Oil City	PA
McCormack	Alexander		Oxford	PA
George & Lelless			Parker's Landing	PA
Brown	H. W.		Penfield	PA
Cross	L. P.		Petrolia	PA
Applegate	James R.	256 N. 8th	Philadelphia	PA
Baumgardner & Helbling		3915 Lancaster	Philadelphia	PA
Beech*	Thomas J.	706 Chestnut	Philadelphia	PA
Bell	William	2330 Montgomery	Philadelphia	PA
Blaul	Louis	1937 Germantown	Philadelphia	PA
Blaul & Baumgardner*		3915 Lancaster	Philadelphia	PA
Breuker	John C.	722 Chestnut	Philadelphia	PA
Bride	Henry C.	1112 Hunter	Philadelphia	PA
Broadbent Bros.		1415 Chestnut	Philadelphia	PA
Bronson	James	4646 Germantown	Philadelphia	PA
Brown & Co.	Samuel W.	915 Sansom	Philadelphia	PA
Carroll	William	2640 South	Philadelphia	PA

PHOTOGRAPHERS LISTED BY CITY/STATE IN THE UNITED STATES 1888-1889

NAME		ADDRESS	CITY	STATE
Chandler & Scheetz		828 Arch	Philadelphia	PA
Chillman	Philip E.	914 Arch	Philadelphia	PA
Clemons	John R.	915 Sansom	Philadelphia	PA
Crossley	William	192 Hains	Germantown	PA
Crystal	David S.	21 School	Germantown	PA
De Morat*	Oliver B.	2 S. 8th	Philadelphia	PA
De Morte	Oliver B.	914 Chestnut	Philadelphia	PA
Draper	Edmund	1313 Columbia	Philadelphia	PA
Draper*	Edward	1313 Columbia	Philadelphia	PA
Dunshee	Edward S.	1330 Chestnut	Philadelphia	PA
Ehrlicher, Jr.	Henry	833 Arch	Philadelphia	PA
Entrekin	William G.	4384 Main	Philadelphia	PA
Erskine	Robert	138 N. 4th	Philadelphia	PA
Ewald Jr.	John A.	2145 Aramingo	Philadelphia	PA
Excelsior Portrait Co.		508 Arch	Philadelphia	PA
Fearn	William R.	120 S. 2nd	Philadelphia	PA
Fest	Paul	Wyoming	Germantown	PA
Gabriel	Herman C.	508 Arch	Philadelphia	PA
Gabriel*	Herman C.	1555 N. 4th	Philadelphia	PA
Garns & Co.	H. D.	526 S. 2nd	Philadelphia	PA
Gettie	John C.	2021 Frankfort	Philadelphia	PA
Gilbert & Bacon		820 Arch	Philadelphia	PA
Gilbert & Bacon		40 N. 8th	Philadelphia	PA
Greany	John T.	770 S. Broad	Philadelphia	PA
Greening	Louis A.	1800 N. Front	Philadelphia	PA
Grier Bros.		906 Arch	Philadelphia	PA
Gutekunst	Frederick	712 Arch	Philadelphia	PA
Haug	Robert R.	2743 Kensington	Philadelphia	PA
Hang*	Robert R.	2743 Kensington	Philadelphia	PA
Hemple	Sarah M.	1003 Spring Garden	Philadelphia	PA
Henrici	Henry	1157 S. Broad	Philadelphia	PA
Henrici & Brownworth		709 S. 2nd	Philadelphia	PA
Herschel	Gustav	611 Callowhill	Philadelphia	PA
Hinkle	David	4673 Germantown	Philadelphia	PA
Hodge & Huston		622 Arch	Philadelphia	PA
Holden	Alfred	2603 S. Walnut	Philadelphia	PA
Horning	Lewis	56-63 N. 8th	Philadelphia	PA
Hough	Edward B.	633 Arch	Philadelphia	PA
Hurst	John A.	1738 Ridge	Philadelphia	PA
Hurst*	John A.	1800 Ridge	Philadelphia	PA

PHOTOGRAPHERS LISTED BY CITY/STATE IN THE UNITED STATES 1888-1889

NAME		ADDRESS	CITY	STATE
Husted	Joseph F.	1344 Ridge	Philadelphia	PA
Jaeger	George	811 Arch	Philadelphia	PA
James	Charles H.	624 Arch	Philadelphia	PA
Johnson*	Edward J.	4209 Lancaster	Philadelphia	PA
Jones	Jacob	3313 Woodland	Philadelphia	PA
Jones*	Jacob	3311 Woodland	Philadelphia	PA
Keller	Henry S.	1431 Ridge	Philadelphia	PA
Kientzle	Alexander	733 Girard	Philadelphia	PA
Knecht	Charles F. A.	Ridge & Montgomery	Philadelphia	PA
Knecht*	Charles F. A.	Ridge and 25th	Philadelphia	PA
Kuebler, Jr.	William	1204 Chestnut	Philadelphia	PA
Kuser	William W.	1520 Market	Philadelphia	PA
Langdell	Gillis	1831 Lombard	Philadelphia	PA
Laughlin	John R.	3518 Market	Philadelphia	PA
Lee	James H.	4223 Frankford	Philadelphia	PA
Lee*	James H.	7th & Germantown	Philadelphia	PA
Leutwiler	John	937 S. 2nd	Philadelphia	PA
Lentwiler*	John	937 S. 2nd	Philadelphia	PA
Lock	William K.	602 1/2 Poplar	Philadelphia	PA
Long	William	1632 N. 13th	Philadelphia	PA
Lothrop	David	54 N. 9th	Philadelphia	PA
Loud Bros.		301 Market	Philadelphia	PA
Loud & Bros.*		508 N. 2nd	Philadelphia	PA
Lovejoy	Howard E.	500 S. 2nd	Philadelphia	PA
McIntire Bros .		1528 Ridge	Philadelphia	PA
McMullen	Samuel	1610 Page	Philadelphia	PA
Marsh & Co.	T. I.	829 Arch	Philadelphia	PA
Marshall	L. P.	1833 Ridge	Philadelphia	PA
Massey	Arthur G.	1109 Market	Philadelphia	PA
Meynen & Co.		540 Franklin	Philadelphia	PA
Miller & Co.	Albert	1725 Germantown	Philadelphia	PA
Moerk	Albert	1838 Callowhill	Philadelphia	PA
Myers	Abraham	2700 Palethrop	Philadelphia	PA
Myers*	Abraham	Lehigh & Palethorp	Philadelphia	PA
Newell & Son	R.	626 Arch	Philadelphia	PA
Newman	Adolph	228 N. 9th	Philadelphia	PA
Ortiz	P. N.	253 N. 9th	Philadelphia	PA
Parker	John J.	245 E. Orthodox	Frankford	PA
Parker*	John J.	Meadow & Cherry	Frankford	PA
Paullin	William T.	244 N. 8th	Philadelphia	PA

PHOTOGRAPHERS LISTED BY CITY/STATE IN THE UNITED STATES 1888-1889

NAME		ADDRESS	CITY	STATE
Paynter	William E.	Lehigh	Philadelphia	PA
Phillipi & Bro.	William	825 Arch	Philadelphia	PA
Phillips	Henry	2608 Frankford	Philadelphia	PA
Phillips	Henry C.	1206 Chestnut	Philadelphia	PA
Piper & Marcus		270 S. 2nd	Philadelphia	PA
Pirrong & Son		322 N. 2nd	Philadelphia	PA
Potter & Co.	G. C.	2 N. 13th	Philadelphia	PA
Pratt	Charles H.	727 S. Broad	Philadelphia	PA
Pratt*	Charles H.	1727 S. Broad	Philadelphia	PA
Rambo	R. L. C.	4080 Lancaster	Philadelphia	PA
Rau	George	930 Girard	Philadelphia	PA
Rehn & Clark		141 S. 5th	Philadelphia	PA
Reimer	Benjamin F.	613 N. 2nd	Philadelphia	PA
Rhoades		1800 Frankford	Philadelphia	PA
Richter & Co.	F. C.	1118 Passy'k	Philadelphia	PA
Rile & Co.		406 N. 10th	Philadelphia	PA
Rile & Kearns*		233 N. 8th	Philadelphia	PA
Rau	William H.	1324 Chestnut	Philadelphia	PA
Roberts	Martin	1943 Germantown	Philadelphia	PA
Roberts & Fellows*		1125 Chestnut	Philadelphia	PA
Rothengatter & Dillon		912 Arch	Philadelphia	PA
Rowland & Co.		2120 Callowhill	Philadelphia	PA
Santman	Conly T.	301 Girard	Philadelphia	PA
Sawyer	Llewellyn A.	159 N. 8th	Philadelphia	PA
Scannell & Co.	David	814 Arch	Philadelphia	PA
Schofield	John	4442 Frankford	Philadelphia	PA
Scholl	Emil	1632 Chestnut	Philadelphia	PA
Schreiber & Sons		819 Arch	Philadelphia	PA
Shane	William	1316 Girard	Philadelphia	PA
Shoemaker	William C.	602 ½ Poplar	Philadelphia	PA
Silver	Joseph P.	57 N. 8th	Philadelphia	PA
Sims & Sons		700 Arch	Philadelphia	PA
Sims & Sons*		203 Race	Philadelphia	PA
Smith	Henry F.	1800 Frankford	Philadelphia	PA
Smith & Miller		436 Walnut	Philadelphia	PA
Snyder	Adam W.	104 E. Girard	Philadelphia	PA
Snyder	B. Russell	1223 Woodbine	Philadelphia	PA
Snyder	Ralph F.	829 N. 5th	Philadelphia	PA
Snyder & Walton		227 Girard	Philadelphia	PA
Spieler	Jacob M.	722 Chestnut	Philadelphia	PA

PHOTOGRAPHERS LISTED BY CITY/STATE IN THE UNITED STATES 1888-1889

NAME		ADDRESS	CITY	STATE
Spencer*	John T.	616 E. Girard	Philadelphia	PA
Starr	Jesse	1320 Chestnut	Philadelphia	PA
Steinman	Jacob C.	504 S. 2nd	Philadelphia	PA
Street	Frank W.	1634 Chestnut	Philadelphia	PA
Sullivan	Charles M.	1705 South	Philadelphia	PA
Taylor	Benjamin F.	624 Arch	Philadelphia	PA
Taylor & Co.	W. Curtis	101 S. 13th	Philadelphia	PA
Taylor & Co.*	W. Curtis	1328 Chestnut	Philadelphia	PA
Tobin & Evans		725 Sansom	Philadelphia	PA
Trask	Albion K. F.	1210 Chestnut	Philadelphia	PA
Truscott	Charles	907 Filbert	Philadelphia	PA
Tryson	Harrison	1617 Spring Garden	Philadelphia	PA
Varnal	Mahabel B.	738 Spring Garden	Philadelphia	PA
Walker	Stephen J.	818 Arch	Philadelphia	PA
Webb	Henry A.	112 N. 9th	Philadelphia	PA
Werner & Co.		522 N. 2nd	Philadelphia	PA
Wieland	William D.	491 N. 3rd	Philadelphia	PA
Williams	De Witt C.	914 Arch	Philadelphia	PA
Wilson	Jeremiah F.	322 South	Philadelphia	PA
Wilson*	Jeremiah F.	324 South	Philadelphia	PA
Withers	William C.	2037 N. Front	Philadelphia	PA
Wyld	Frederick W.	1210 Columbia	Philadelphia	PA
Zorn	Philip	730 Spring Garden	Philadelphia	PA
Haines	Joseph		Phillipsburgh	PA
Channell	R. F.		Phoenixville	PA
Horning	J. M.		Phoenixville	PA
Shoemaker	W. L.		Phoenixville	PA
Ansbach	J. S.		Pillow	PA
Aunspach	W. S.		Pine Grove	PA
Alexander	J. B.	1930 Carson	Pittsburgh	PA
Aufrecht*	G.	66 Federal A.	Pittsburgh	PA
Barnes	John H.	2336 Carson	Pittsburgh	PA
Barnes*	John H.	2340 Carson	Pittsburgh	PA
Bower	Charles	6201 Penn	Pittsburgh	PA
Bower*	Charles	100 Collins	Pittsburgh	PA
Bricker & Corliss*		71 Federal A.	Pittsburgh	PA
Burke	Major	2514 Smallman	Pittsburgh	PA
Campbell	G. M.	38 S. 15th	Pittsburgh	PA
Dabbs	B. L. H.	602 Liberty	Pittsburgh	PA
Diehl	Albert	Wyoming	Pittsburgh	PA

PHOTOGRAPHERS LISTED BY CITY/STATE IN THE UNITED STATES 1888-1889

NAME		ADDRESS	CITY	STATE
Excelsior Art Portrait Co.		702 Smithfield	Pittsburgh	PA
Eureka Copying House		10 6th	Pittsburgh	PA
Fallert	Paul	1505 Carson	Pittsburgh	PA
Harger*	G. L.	514 Market, room 33	Pittsburgh	PA
Histed	E. W.	41 5th	Pittsburgh	PA
Iron City Photo Co.		99 5th	Pittsburgh	PA
Jessen	William	41 5th	Pittsburgh	PA
Kirk*	F. J.	196 Beaver	Pittsburgh	PA
Kneeland*	C.	143 Federal	Pittsburgh	PA
Kraeling*	B.	4016 Butler	Pittsburgh	PA
Lawyer*	J. H.	547 Smithfield	Pittsburgh	PA
Lawyer	R.	545 Smithfield	Pittsburgh	PA
Lawyer, Jr.	R.	6 6th	Pittsburgh	PA
Mahan	Davis	43 5th	Pittsburgh	PA
Mering	J. S.	505 5th	Pittsburgh	PA
Merriman*	A. R.	531 Smithfield	Pittsburgh	PA
Morris*	Joseph G.	16 Sixth	Pittsburgh	PA
Morris	S. D.	N. Canal & 11th	Pittsburgh	PA
Morrison	J. A.	505 5th	Pittsburgh	PA
Pearson	James R.	96 5th	Pittsburgh	PA
Pearson*	James R.	43 Federal	Pittsburgh	PA
Pfaff*	H.	82 Ohio	Pittsburgh	PA
Pittsburgh Bromide Co.		531 Smithfield	Pittsburgh	PA
Platts & Son	G. W.	36 & 65 5th	Pittsburgh	PA
Platts & Son*	G. W.	34 5th	Pittsburgh	PA
Robinson	S. M.	2-4 6th	Pittsburgh	PA
Russ	J. G.	104 5th	Pittsburgh	PA
Russ*	J. G.	204 5th	Pittsburgh	PA
Shipler & Co.		65 5th	Pittsburgh	PA
Sonnenberg*	H.	52 Federal	Pittsburgh	PA
Sonnenberg*	J. E.	120 Ohio	Pittsburgh	PA
Sperber*	J.	90-92 Federal	Pittsburgh	PA
Standard Copying Agency		36 6th	Pittsburgh	PA
Stanton Bros.		505 Forbes	Pittsburgh	PA
Stanton*	T. J. & D. W.	503 Forbes	Pittsburgh	PA
Thackeray & Kraeling		99 5th	Pittsburgh	PA
Trapp	J. B.	95 5th	Pittsburgh	PA
Trapp*	J. B.	20 5th	Pittsburgh	PA
Treganowan	Thomas	150 Wylie	Pittsburgh	PA
Truxell	J. H.	12 5th	Pittsburgh	PA

PHOTOGRAPHERS LISTED BY CITY/STATE IN THE UNITED STATES 1888-1889

NAME		ADDRESS	CITY	STATE
Miller	John W.		Pittstown	PA
Richards	L. Y.		Pittstown	PA
Beacham	James		Plymouth	PA
Durfee	E. O.		Port Allegany	PA
Andre & Dettra			Pottstown	PA
Lachman	I. S.		Pottstown	PA
Saurman	T. W.		Pottstown	PA
Taylor	Thomas		Pottstown	PA
Allen	A. M.		Pottsville	PA
Bretz	George M.		Pottsville	PA
Bretz*	Gill		Pottsville	PA
Lamont	Frank		Pottsville	PA
Greismer	T. P.		Quakertown	PA
Hafer	E. E.		Reading	PA
Lee	John		Reading	PA
Patton & Dietrich			Reading	PA
Strunk	J. D.		Reading	PA
Taylor	Charles A.		Reading	PA
Taylor & Morgan			Reading	PA
Bergstresser	J. B.		Renova	PA
Williams	J. C.		Reynoldsville	PA
Sharpnack	T.		Rice's Landing	PA
Landis	L. K.		Richland Station	PA
Harrling	J. C.		Ridgway	PA
Medlicott	T. S.		Rochester	PA
Strauch	H. W.		Rock	PA
Bridge*	H. W.		St. Mary's	PA
Portser	W. J.		Saltsburgh	PA
McIntyre	S. H.		Sandy Lake	PA
Deibert	H. S.		Schuylkill Haven	PA
McCutchin*	S. L.		Scottdale	PA
De Witt	M. M.		Scranton	PA
Easterline	J. W.		Scranton	PA
Frey	Henry		Scranton	PA
Hawley	N. D.		Scranton	PA
Jewell	Frank		Scranton	PA
Millard	D. B.		Scranton	PA
Owen	W. H.		Scranton	PA
Tillotson*	Nelson		Scranton	PA
Ulrich	R. L.		Selin's Grove	PA

PHOTOGRAPHERS LISTED BY CITY/STATE IN THE UNITED STATES 1888-1889

NAME		ADDRESS	CITY	STATE
Thomas	M.		Shamokin	PA
Dodd*	L. N.		Sharon	PA
Movies	S. D.		Sharpsburgh	PA
Anundson	Olaf		Sheffield	PA
Dockweiler*	M.		Shenandoah	PA
Hoffman	W. H.		Shenandoah	PA
Klugherz	Samuel		Shenandoah	PA
Graves	W. B.		Shinglehouse	PA
Beidle	H. F.		Shippensburgh	PA
Shadick	M. F.		Shunk	PA
Dengler	S. S.		Slatington	PA
Wassum	O. O.		Slatington	PA
Moses	Charles		Smethport	PA
Glenn	C. A.		Snow Shoe	PA
Welfley	W. H.		Somerset	PA
Ginter	David		Sunbury	PA
Hall	B. L.		Sunbury	PA
Ripple Bros.			Sunbury	PA
Harding	A. D.		Susquehanna	PA
Bailey	David		Tamaqua	PA
Carpenter	Marcus		Tionesta	PA
Goetchins	J. C.		Titusville	PA
Mathes	J. A.		Titusville	PA
Walker	W. W.		Titusville	PA
Bender	J. F.		Towanda	PA
Dayton	C. S.		Towanda	PA
Fisher	A. J.		Towanda	PA
Wood	J. G.		Towanda	PA
Gaertner	Sigmund		Tremont	PA
Beeles	H. M.		Troy	PA
Griffin	C. L.		Tunkhannock	PA
Burkholder	C. C.		Tyrone	PA
Harris*	Daniel		Tyrone	PA
Holtzinger	J. H.		Tyrone	PA
Werner	J. A.		Tyrone	PA
Carter	J. L.		Union City	PA
Hearn	J. P.		Union City	PA
Hadden	James		Uniontown	PA
Lingo	E. A.		Uniontown	PA
Moore	W. H.		Uniontown	PA

PHOTOGRAPHERS LISTED BY CITY/STATE IN THE UNITED STATES 1888-1889

NAME		ADDRESS	CITY	STATE
Bairstow	J. R.		Warren	PA
Bairstow	W. A.		Warren	PA
Kitchen	William		Warren	PA
Rogers & Son	J. H.	Wilson Bldg.	Washington	PA
Rogers*	Samuel G.		Washington	PA
Rothwell	J. W.		Washington	PA
Hagenbuch	H. W.		Watsontown	PA
McDonnell	C. A.		Wattsburgh	PA
Frederick	J. D.		Waynesboro	PA
Rogers & Son	J. H.		Waynesburgh	PA
Rogers & Guiher*			Waynesburgh	PA
Siveet	Charles A.		Wellsboro	PA
Beannor*	J.		West Bridgewater	PA
Marshall	E. S.		West Chester	PA
Taylor	T. W.		West Chester	PA
Moltz	T. M.		West Fairview	PA
Parshale	R. R.		Westfield	PA
Cary	C. H.		Wilkesbarre	PA
Collamer	G. W.		Wilkesbarre	PA
Cook	C. F.		Wilkesbarre	PA
Goodell	C. E.		Wilkesbarre	PA
Stearns	Lee		Wilkesbarre	PA
Sturdevant	A. T.		Wilkesbarre	PA
Sturdevant	E. K.		Wilkesbarre	PA
Dean & Cornwell			Williamsport	PA
Hess	Godfrey		Williamsport	PA
McCollin	A. W. T.		Williamsport	PA
Nice	R. Y.		Williamsport	PA
Stiltz	D. R.		Williamsport	PA
Stuart	Eugene		Williamsport	PA
Tinkbinder	J. A.		Williamsport	PA
Wright	R. L.		Williamsport	PA
Yarrington & Rappertte			Williamsport	PA
Fluck	Samuel B.		Woodbury	PA
Lowers	M.		Wood's Run	PA
Lloyd	J. H.		Wyalusing	PA
Buttoriff	Reuben H.		York	PA
Pentz	B. C.		York	PA
Swords & Pentz*			York	PA
Harman	H. J.		York-Sulphur Springs	PA

NAME		ADDRESS	CITY	STATE
Morton	H. Q.		Block Island	RI
Tretault	Edward		Centerville	RI
Aylesworth	John		East Greenwich	RI
Alman	Louis		Newport	RI
Child	Frank H.		Newport	RI
Davidson	William B.		Newport	RI
Holloway	Charles B.		Newport	RI
Leavitt	A. L.		Newport	RI
Ludovici	Julius		Newport	RI
Peckham	Leander A.		Newport	RI
Mills & Son	William		Olneyville	RI
Griggs	C. T.		Pascoag	RI
Bebby	Frederick		Pawtucket	RI
Eruscan Art Co.			Pawtucket	RI
Gurney	W. H.		Pawtucket	RI
Halloran Bros.			Pawtucket	RI
Ide	D. T.		Pawtucket	RI
Salisbury	Arnold F.		Pawtucket	RI
Aylesworth	John		Phenix	RI
Alden Photo Co.		62 Arcade	Providence	RI
Baker & Co.	L.	10 Weybosset	Providence	RI
Bodwell	Albert L.	37 Weybosset	Providence	RI
Brown	S. B.	243 Westminster	Providence	RI
Brownell	Alexander C.	90 Westminster	Providence	RI
Carlisle	George M.	199 Westminster	Providence	RI
Chase	Theodore F.	249 ½ Westminster	Providence	RI
Colman & Co.		283 Westminster	Providence	RI
Goodwin	James W.	59-65 Arcade	Providence	RI
Hacker Photo Co.		2 Moulton	Providence	RI
Heald Co.		159 Westminster	Providence	RI
Hodge	Arthur M.	16 Mitchell	Providence	RI
Horton Bros.		87 Westminster	Providence	RI
Hurd	Gustine L.	257 Westminster	Providence	RI
Jones	F. R.	357 Westminster	Providence	RI
McKenzie & Co.		19 Westminster	Providence	RI
Manchester Bros.		216 Fountain	Providence	RI
Morton	H. Q.	75 Westminster	Providence	RI
New York Photo Co.		174 Westminster	Providence	RI
Potter	William E.	171 Westminster	Providence	RI

PHOTOGRAPHERS LISTED BY CITY/STATE IN THE UNITED STATES 1888-1889

NAME		ADDRESS	CITY	STATE
Prior	John H.	81 Westminster	Providence	RI
Rose	P. H.	297 Westminster	Providence	RI
Shaal	Robert	202 Westminster	Providence	RI
Smith	F. Wheaton	33 Westminster	Providence	RI
Swindells	Arthur	1078 High	Providence	RI
Whiteman	H. W.	232 Westminster	Providence	RI
Hartford	George		River Point	RI
Fiske	Charles		Riverside	RI
Turnell	Joseph		Silver Spring	RI
Clarke	L. H.		Wakefield	RI
Atkins	Joseph		Warren	RI
Butler	G. W.		Westerly	RI
Schofield Bros.			Westerly	RI
Bennett	A. J.		Woonsocket	RI
Birtles	F. C.		Woonsocket	RI
Chamberlain	A. T.		Woonsocket	RI
Goddard	Emmerson		Woonsocket	RI
Masse	Theodore		Woonsocket	RI
Smith*	Edward A.		Woonsocket	RI
Hill*	E. T.		Abbeville	SC
Gunter	B. F.		Aiken	SC
Palmer	J. A.		Aiken	SC
Frambo*	W. L.		Bennettsville	SC
Alexander	W. S.		Camden	SC
Anderson's Studio		251 King	Charleston	SC
Cook	George L. V.	265 King	Charleston	SC
Howell	Frank A.	249 King	Charleston	SC
Leidloff	H.	269 King	Charleston	SC
Searles	H. C.	303 King	Charleston	SC
Baker & Johnson*			Chester	SC
Hennie & Bircher			Columbia	SC
Reckling	W. A.		Columbia	SC
Riser	A. M.		Columbia	SC
Glazener	J. R.		Easley	SC
Mims	R. H.		Edgefield	SC
Archer	William		Gaffney City	SC
Fitzgerald	J. C.		Greenville	SC
Langston	T. J.		Johnston	SC
Boggs	J. F.		Liberty	SC
Salter	J. Z.		Newberry	SC

PHOTOGRAPHERS LISTED BY CITY/STATE IN THE UNITED STATES 1888-1889

NAME		ADDRESS	CITY	STATE
Van Orsdells	C. M.		Orangeburgh	SC
Mouzon	S. C.		Spartanburgh	SC
Lewis	G. H.		Sumter	SC
Howard Bros.*			Westminster	SC
De Harradora	J. B.		Winnsborough	SC
McLain	T. B.		Yorkville	SC
Keyce	J. M.		Alamo	TN
Hodges Art Gallery			Bristol	TN
Smith	G. B.		Bristol	TN
Blake	E. F.		Chattanooga	TN
Clayton*	F. H.		Chattanooga	TN
Judd	A. W.		Chattanooga	TN
Lane	O. R.		Chattanooga	TN
Laue*	O. R.		Chattanooga	TN
Schmedling	Marcus E.		Chattanooga	TN
Stokes	D. S.		Chattanooga	TN
Dibble	H. E.		Clarksville	TN
McCormick	W. S.		Clarksville	TN
Judd	C. S.		Columbia	TN
Seavy	H. P.		Columbia	TN
Pinner	J. C.		Dyersburgh	TN
Rhine	G. C.		Gallatin	TN
McClintock & Harper			Jackson	TN
Keen	L. W.		Jonesborough	TN
Davis	G. S.		Knoxville	TN
Knaffe & Bros.			Knoxville	TN
Lindsey & Hodges			Knoxville	TN
McCrary & Branson			Knoxville	TN
Lively	W. S.		McMinnville	TN
Bingham & Hilliard			Memphis	TN
Blanks	A. L.		Memphis	TN
Gebhardt & Co.			Memphis	TN
Moyston	J. H.		Memphis	TN
Armstrong	W. E.		Nashville	TN
De Anguino & Son	Alex		Nashville	TN
Herstein	J.		Nashville	TN
Herstein & Mahon			Nashville	TN
Poole	R.		Nashville	TN
Schlier	T. M.		Nashville	TN
Thuss, Koelein & Giers			Nashville	TN

PHOTOGRAPHERS LISTED BY CITY/STATE IN THE UNITED STATES 1888-1889

NAME	ADDRESS	CITY	STATE
Miller	G. W.	Paris	TN
Miller & Jones		Paris	TN
Williams	C. C.	Somerville	TN
Tillett	James M.	Tullahoma	TN
Albritton & Ellison		Union City	TN
Lawrence	O. J.	Arlington	TX
Hill	Samuel B.	Austin	TX
Hillyer	Hamilton B.	Austin	TX
Marks	Harvey R.	Austin	TX
Schuwirth	George	Austin	TX
Cooper	F. P.	Belton	TX
Sink	D. P.	Calvert	TX
Casey	A. F.	Cisco	TX
Jefferson	R.	Clarendon	TX
Houser	J. K. P.	Clarksville	TX
Lindgreen	J. A.	Cleburne	TX
Smith	B. F.	Cleburne	TX
Hughes	W. F.	Colorado	TX
Wright	James L.	Comanche	TX
De Planque	Louis	Corpus Christi	TX
Cummings	M.	Corsicana	TX
Frey	E.	Corsicana	TX
Fay & Branling		Cuero	TX
Billows	A. R.	Dallas	TX
Webster	J. H.	Dallas	TX
Weatherington & Freeman		Decatur	TX
Foucar & Co.	E. L.	El Paso	TX
Parker	Francis	El Paso	TX
McKeon	J. T.	Ennis	TX
Robertson	W. N.	Ennis	TX
Caldwell	M.	Flatonia	TX
Daniel	J. E.	Fort Worth	TX
Rhine	G. C.	Fort Worth	TX
Swartz & Bro.	D. H.	Fort Worth	TX
Globen & Son		Gainesville	TX
Ingle	Mrs. Elizabeth	Gainesville	TX
Blessing	Samuel P.	Galveston	TX
Rose	P. H.	Galveston	TX
Clayton	J. F.	Groesbeck	TX
Crew	E.	Hempstead	TX

PHOTOGRAPHERS LISTED BY CITY/STATE IN THE UNITED STATES 1888-1889

NAME		ADDRESS	CITY	STATE
Wood	D. H.		Henderson	TX
Marable & Caldwell			Henrietta	TX
Antrey	George		Hico	TX
Ersley	P.		Hillsborough	TX
Dean	C. C.		Houston	TX
Wright	Charles J.		Houston	TX
Sloan	Mrs. W. W.		Jefferson	TX
Peterson	C.		La Grange	TX
Johnson	Ed		Ladonia	TX
Marshall	Samuel		Ladonia	TX
Cockrell	Thomas J.		Laredo	TX
Anthony	M.		Longview	TX
Freeman	Alfred		McKinney	TX
Brown	William		Marshall	TX
Arvin	A. J.		Mexia	TX
Eaves	J. & M.		Mount Pleasant	TX
Serdinko	J.		New Braunfels	TX
Lynn	Samuel		Paris	TX
Boyd	J. D.		Pittsburgh	TX
Stark	N. P.		Rosalie	TX
Ragsdale	M. C.		San Angelo	TX
Barr	D. P.		San Antonio	TX
Doerr	H. A.		San Antonio	TX
Savage	C. H.		San Antonio	TX
Johnson	Ed		Savoy	TX
Caradine	James N.		Sherman	TX
Carpenter	Thomas H.		Sherman	TX
Davidson	John N.		Sulphur Springs	TX
Whealdon	Joshua		Texarkana	TX
Shull	L. T.		Tyler	TX
Tegarden	G. A.		Tyler	TX
Jackson	W. D.		Waco	TX
Davenport	B. F.		Waxahachie	TX
Hemmings	Edward		Whitesborough	TX
Compton	Alma W.		Box Elder	UT
Gasberg	Jans C.		Brigham City	UT
Jensen	George		Ephraim	UT
Jensen	Martin		Ephraim	UT
Buys	William		Heber	UT
Willis	William		Heber	UT

PHOTOGRAPHERS LISTED BY CITY/STATE IN THE UNITED STATES 1888-1889

NAME		ADDRESS	CITY	STATE
Cardon	Thomas B.		Logan	UT
Kirkham*	Reuben		Logan	UT
Lewis	David		Logan	UT
Adams Bros.			Ogden City	UT
Stephens	J. O.		Ogden City	UT
White	A. D.		Ogden City	UT
Daniels, Jr.	T. E.		Provo City	UT
Nagely	Albert		Richfield	UT
Booth	James		St. George	UT
Carter	C. W.		Salt Lake City	UT
Fox & Symons			Salt Lake City	UT
Keeler	E. C.		Salt Lake City	UT
Newcomb	Marion W.		Salt Lake City	UT
Savage	Charles R.		Salt Lake City	UT
Cronning	J. P.		Scipio	UT
Young	Samuel		Willard	UT
Wilson	E. T.		Barton	VT
Blake	F. J.		Bellow's Falls	VT
Gokay	E. S.		Bennington	VT
Sipperly	W. H.		Bennington	VT
Brewster & Rogers			Bethel	VT
Allen	E. H.		Bradford	VT
Blanchard	W. T.		Braintree	VT
Parker	J. & G. L.		Brandon	VT
Smith*	S. S.		Brandon	VT
Howe & Son	C. L.		Brattleboro	VT
Proutty	Jason W.		Brattleboro	VT
Wyatt	Arthur B.		Brattleboro	VT
Dunton	E. H.		Bristol	VT
Smith	C. E.		Bristol	VT
Atwood	L. A.		Burlington	VT
Burlington Photo Co.			Burlington	VT
Brown	William J.		Burlington	VT
Ganvin & Bro.*	J. E.		Burlington	VT
Gauvin & Bro.			Burlington	VT
Hibbard	Charles P.		Burlington	VT
Wormell	E. O.		Burlington	VT
Bixby	M. J.		Castleton	VT
Pierce	A.		Cavendish	VT
Bixby	Hira L.		Chelsea	VT

PHOTOGRAPHERS LISTED BY CITY/STATE IN THE UNITED STATES 1888-1889

NAME	ADDRESS	CITY	STATE
Smith	S. S.	Chester	VT
Whitman	Mrs. M. E.	Chester	VT
Kittredge	F. K.	Danville	VT
West	W. E.	Derby Line	VT
Baker	W. W.	East Fairfield	VT
Kendall	O.	East Hardwick	VT
Kett	T. H.	Fairhaven	VT
Reynolds	E. E.	Fairhaven	VT
English	N. F.	Hartland	VT
Allen	M. W.	Jamaica	VT
Clark	E. C.	Jamaica	VT
Baker	G. W.	Johnson	VT
Merrill	N. L.	Johnson	VT
Baldwin	A. A.	Ludlow	VT
Bixby	M. A.	Ludlow	VT
Dunton	E. H.	Lyndonville	VT
Allen	H. S.	Manchester	VT
Chase	O. W.	Middlebury	VT
Dean	R. A.	Middlebury	VT
Berkely	George P.	Milton	VT
Smith	Joseph K.	Milton	VT
Blanchard	A. N.	Montpelier	VT
Corse	S. W.	Montpelier	VT
Harlow	A. C.	Montpelier	VT
Robinson	F. P.	Morrisville	VT
Hall	C. M.	Newport	VT
Stevens	H. N.	North Craftsbury	VT
Thayer	L. E.	North Craftsbury	VT
Lewis	H. H.	North Troy	VT
McIntosh	R. M.	Northfield	VT
Brown	C. L.	Peacham	VT
Rood	Frank M.	Poultney	VT
Crosier	Frank	Readsborough	VT
Wheeler	F. W.	Richford	VT
Baker	G. M.	Rutland	VT
Chandler	W. D.	St. Albans	VT
Smith	Rollin H.	St. Albans	VT
Clifford	D. A.	St. Johnsbury	VT
Haynes	T. C.	St. Johnsbury	VT
Shepherd	C. F.	St. Johnsbury	VT

PHOTOGRAPHERS LISTED BY CITY/STATE IN THE UNITED STATES 1888-1889

NAME	ADDRESS	CITY	STATE
Emery	G. H.	Saxton's River	VT
Nichols	C. W.	Saxton's River	VT
Perkins	A. D.	Saxton's River	VT
Taft	P. W.	Saxton's River	VT
Lamphere	E. C.	South Ryegate	VT
Hurd	William E.	South Shaftsbury	VT
Perrin	G. B.	Springfield	VT
Truax	L. B.	Swanton	VT
Hale	Herbert A.	Vergennes	VT
Cady	H. B.	Waitsfield	VT
Dow	James H.	Walden	VT
Cheney	C. B.	Waterbury	VT
Bracy	C. F.	Wells River	VT
Carl	E.	West Burke	VT
Carr*	E.	West Burke	VT
Kenney	H. J.	West Fairlee	VT
Hale	J. W.	West Randolph	VT
Sparhawk	L. T.	West Randolph	VT
Knowlton	G. E.	Windsor	VT
Langlois	E. T.	Winooski	VT
Gates	Edwin R.	Woodstock	VT
Pugh	C. A.	Blacksburgh	VA
Hemming	T. M.	Charlottesville	VA
Wampler	J. T.	Charlottesville	VA
Blunt	A. H.	Danville	VA
Frayser*	W. G. R.	Danville	VA
Trayser	W. G. R.	Danville	VA
Clary	James O. A.	Harrisonburgh	VA
Morrison	Hugh	Harrisonburgh	VA
Miley	M.	Lexington	VA
Smith	W. T.	Liberty	VA
Plecker	A. H.	Lynchburg	VA
Faber	J. J.	Norfolk	VA
Jeffers	J. E.	Norfolk	VA
Walter	Thomas	Norfolk	VA
Rockwell	J. E.	Petersburgh	VA
Campbell & Co.		Richmond	VA
Cook	G. S.	Richmond	VA
Davies	G. W.	Richmond	VA
Davies & Son	John W.	Richmond	VA

PHOTOGRAPHERS LISTED BY CITY/STATE IN THE UNITED STATES 1888-1889

NAME		ADDRESS	CITY	STATE
Powers	M. J.		Richmond	VA
Rees	C. R.		Richmond	VA
Wright & Co.			Richmond	VA
Maury	Charles L.		Salem	VA
Blackemore	B. A.		Staunton	VA
Wortham	J. D.		Winchester	VA
Bechtel	G. W.		Colfax	WA
Maxwell	J. D.		Dayton	WA
Clark	L. W.		Olympia	WA
Shanks	J. W.		Pomeroy	WA
McMurray	J. M.		Port Townsend	WA
Moore	George N.		Seattle	WA
Peiser	Theodore E.		Seattle	WA
Margo & Wunderlich			Spokane Falls	WA
Maxwell Bros.			Spokane Falls	WA
Margo	J. C.		Sprague	WA
Davidson	I. G.		Tacoma	WA
Jackson	W. P.		Tacoma	WA
King	E. C.		Tacoma	WA
Brodeck	H. H.		Walla Walla	WA
Winchester	F. E.		Walla Walla	WA
Farnsworth	W. E.		Buckhannon	WV
Besker & Fell			Charleston	WV
Castle*	F.		Charleston	WV
Gates	A. P.		Charleston	WV
Barrette*	T.		Clarksburg	WV
Houston	J.		Clarksburgh	WV
Hayes	P. M.		Coal Valley	WV
Foreman	Israel		Fairmont	WV
Foreman	Alexander		Grafton	WV
Hampton*	P. W.		Harper's Ferry	WV
Abbotts	D. E.		Huntington	WV
Eureka Photo Copying House			Huntington	WV
Kirk	George W.		Huntington	WV
Portmess	J. R.		Keyser	WV
Stewart	James L.		Mannington	WV
Hunter	P. C.		Martinsburg	WV
Rankin	R. J.		Martinsburg	WV
Protzman	Ed. C.		Morgantown	WV
Cadwallader*	J. D.		Parkersburg	WV

PHOTOGRAPHERS LISTED BY CITY/STATE IN THE UNITED STATES 1888-1889

NAME		ADDRESS	CITY	STATE
Loomis & Thompson			Parkersburg	WV
Ritter	J. F.		Parkersburg	WV
Wilde	J. F.		Piedmont	WV
Longlin	J. W.		Rowlesburg	WV
Loughlin*	J. W.		Rowlesburg	WV
Biggins	T. A.		Wheeling	WV
Brown	John		Wheeling	WV
Myles & Son			Wheeling	WV
Parsons	J. A. H.		Wheeling	WV
Plummer	F. W.		Wheeling	WV
Tappan & Co.			Wheeling	WV
Manville & McDonald			Ahnapee	WI
Gesel & Gerhard			Alma	WI
Baldwin*	O. K.		Amherst	WI
Morgan Bros.			Antigo	WI
Ballard	G. E.		Appleton	WI
Ballard*	M. T.		Appleton	WI
Blackburn	G. H.		Appleton	WI
De Guire	I. J.		Appleton	WI
Koonz	J. L.		Appleton	WI
Miller	J. C.		Appleton	WI
Seidmore	A.		Appleton	WI
Stimson	J. E. H.		Appleton	WI
Farrington	F. W.		Arcadia	WI
Wright	C. B.		Argyle	WI
Raitt	T. G.		Ashland	WI
Taylor*	B. H.		Ashland	WI
Whitesides	William		Ashland	WI
Dimmick	J. E.		Augusta	WI
Baer	Alfred		Baraboo	WI
Mould	T. J.		Baraboo	WI
Haynes	T. W. B.		Barron	WI
Silvernail	E. W.		Bayfield	WI
Horton	G. W.		Beaver Dam	WI
Veling	P.		Beaver Dam	WI
Weaver	O. F.		Beaver Dam	WI
Burpee	C. L.		Beloit	WI
Hurlburt*	G. H.		Beloit	WI
Churman	L. H.		Beloit	WI
Caldwell	F. M.		Berlin	WI

PHOTOGRAPHERS LISTED BY CITY/STATE IN THE UNITED STATES 1888-1889

NAME		ADDRESS	CITY	STATE
Holly	M. S.		Berlin	WI
Walcott	F. B.		Berlin	WI
Van Schaick	C. J.		Black River Falls	WI
Chambers	J. M.		Bloomington	WI
Anschultz	Leo		Boscobel	WI
Johnson	A. S.		Brandon	WI
Motzbanes	Joseph		Brillion	WI
Lucas	C. W.		Brodhead	WI
Wagner	J. A.		Burlington	WI
Sherman	Littleton		Cadott	WI
Weemink & Bros*	H. D.		Campbellsport	WI
Sander	F. W.		Cedarburgh	WI
Sauer	Albert		Cedarburgh	WI
Dake	J. R.		Centralia	WI
Harris	H.		Chetek	WI
Fadner	Henry		Chilton	WI
Allen	W. H.		Chippewa Falls	WI
Gallaher	J. B.		Chippewa Falls	WI
Spicer	C. A.		Clintonville	WI
Hasken	W. K.		Columbus	WI
Johnson	P. A.		Cumberland	WI
Clegg	Mrs. M. A.		Darlington	WI
Bowring	T. D.		De Pere	WI
Wilkens	C. E.		Delavan	WI
McElhose	E. H.		Dodgeville	WI
Parry	G. R.		Dodgeville	WI
Graves	T. K.		East Troy	WI
Bonnell	Frederick		Eau Claire	WI
Burns	M. W.		Eau Claire	WI
Faucett	E. E.		Eau Claire	WI
Merriman	O. G.		Eau Claire	WI
Preston	N. A.		Eau Claire	WI
Talmadge	Frank		Edgerton	WI
Hatch	A. E.		Elkhorn	WI
Bowen	G. M.		Elroy	WI
Williams	J. B.		Ettrick	WI
Beals	Ferris		Evansville	WI
Eskill	J. J.		Florence	WI
Buss	H. J.		Fond Du Lac	WI
Dillon	J. W.		Fond Du Lac	WI

PHOTOGRAPHERS LISTED BY CITY/STATE IN THE UNITED STATES 1888-1889

NAME		ADDRESS	CITY	STATE
Lang	C.		Fond Du Lac	WI
Lind	H. C.		Fond Du Lac	WI
Lind & Dittmar			Fond Du Lac	WI
McGowan	Maurice		Fond Du Lac	WI
McKenna	D. W.		Fond Du Lac	WI
Rogers	G. E.		Fond Du Lac	WI
Brissell	Mrs. E. C.		Fort Atkinson	WI
Carlisle	C. J. H.		Fort Howard	WI
Parkinson	L.		Fox Lake	WI
Paulus	Miss Annie		Fredonia	WI
McAdams	T. T.		Galesville	WI
Cramer	Joseph		Grafton	WI
Hebert	J. O.		Grand Rapids	WI
Lenz Bros.			Green Bay	WI
Miller & King			Green Bay	WI
Schneider	T. W.		Green Bay	WI
Sabin	J. B.		Hammond	WI
Sunderland	J. C.		Hartford	WI
Chapman	Henry		Hartland	WI
Goodrich*	H.		Highland	WI
Waegen	O. F.		Horicon	WI
Moss	T. F.		Hudson	WI
McElrose	R. D.		Humbird	WI
Glass	C. E.		Janesville	WI
Mead	Edwin		Janesville	WI
Rowley Bros.*			Janesville	WI
Tice & Donner			Janesville	WI
Turner	C. F.		Janesville	WI
Drew	H. B.		Jefferson	WI
Noyes	A. K.		Jefferson	WI
Crowns	J. H.		Kaukauna	WI
Lind	C. A.		Kaukauna	WI
Dittmar	C. F.		Kenosha	WI
La Marsh	Bernard		Kenosha	WI
Mathews	W. C.		Kewaskum	WI
Bennett	H. H.		Kilbourn City	WI
Andrews	A. F.		La Crosse	WI
Heath	H. C.		La Crosse	WI
McClelland	G. B.		La Crosse	WI
Mason	L. E.		La Crosse	WI

NAME		ADDRESS	CITY	STATE
Myers	Mrs. E. W.		La Crosse	WI
Mould	F. W.		La Crosse	WI
Pryor	W. A.		La Crosse	WI
Spettel	Clement		La Crosse	WI
Thompson	A. D.		La Crosse	WI
Bullock	John		Lake Geneva	WI
Drew	H. B.		Lake Mills	WI
Van de Wall	W. B.		Lancaster	WI
Nott	W. S.		Lodi	WI
Curtiss	E. R.		Madison	WI
Isaacs	A. C.		Madison	WI
Jones	N. P.		Madison	WI
Schubert	Joseph		Madison	WI
Thomas	J. K.		Madison	WI
Hentscher & Klingholz			Manitowoc	WI
Melendy & Packard			Manitowoc	WI
McIntyre	William		Maple Valley	WI
Bauder	G. W.		Marinette	WI
Hill	H. E.		Marinette	WI
Wolcott	U. E.		Marinette	WI
Jones*	L. M.		Markesan	WI
Bogrand	Peter		Marshfield	WI
James*	David		Marshfield	WI
Tucker	G. H.		Mauston	WI
Sunderland	W. F.		Mayville	WI
Zeit	Robert		Medford	WI
Bradley	G. W.		Menasha	WI
Long	J. T.		Menomonee	WI
Powell	J. E.		Menomonee	WI
Fuller	F. E.		Merrill	WI
Bunce	E. S.		Merrillon	WI
Coats	T. D.		Merrimack	WI
Burdick	E. H.		Milton	WI
Armstrong	W. A.	389 Broadway	Milwaukee	WI
Baltes	Frank E.	329 Grove	Milwaukee	WI
Bangs	E. D.	86 Wisconsin	Milwaukee	WI
Bishop	Frank, Jr.	99 Wisconsin	Milwaukee	WI
Brodesser*	Charles		Milwaukee	WI
Broich	Hugo	116-118 Grand	Milwaukee	WI
Brown	Joseph	136 Grand	Milwaukee	WI

PHOTOGRAPHERS LISTED BY CITY/STATE IN THE UNITED STATES 1888-1889

NAME		ADDRESS	CITY	STATE
Chadbourne*	G.		Milwaukee	WI
Conrad	Jacob	398 National	Milwaukee	WI
Feiker & Raab		1102 Walnut	Milwaukee	WI
Gomber	J. C.	229 Reed	Milwaukee	WI
Hagendoff	Louis	436 Milwaukee	Milwaukee	WI
Heeb	Adam	651 8th	Milwaukee	WI
Hercher	Henry	365 3rd	Milwaukee	WI
Jalass	H. V.	301 Prairie	Milwaukee	WI
Kastenholz*	John		Milwaukee	WI
Kirchhoff	Arthur	527-529 Chestnut	Milwaukee	WI
Kundler*	Gustav		Milwaukee	WI
Lecher	Paul	296 W. Water	Milwaukee	WI
Loops	Charles	758 12th	Milwaukcc	WI
McKenzie	Daniel N.	964 Kinnickinnie	Milwaukee	WI
Marvin*	E. D.		Milwaukee	WI
Meyer*	Mrs. L. M.		Milwaukee	WI
Miller	R. R.	276 5th	Milwaukee	WI
Milner	Alonzo W.	355 Reed	Milwaukee	WI
Mueller	H. J.	720 3rd	Milwaukee	WI
Neick	Henry J.	3rd and North	Milwaukee	WI
Penndorf	August	509 E. Water	Milwaukee	WI
Podoll	Gustav	333 3rd	Milwaukee	WI
Reimer & Katz		406 Milwaukee	Milwaukee	WI
Runkel	J. P.	469 3rd	Milwaukee	WI
Schroeder	Hugo	359 3rd	Milwaukee	WI
Stein	S. L.	310 State	Milwaukee	WI
Streit	F. W.	30 Juneau	Milwaukee	WI
Sutter	H. S.	128 Wisconsin	Milwaukee	WI
Torney & Co.		448 Mitchell	Milwaukee	WI
Voigt	C. F.	224 Grand	Milwaukee	WI
Vollert*	W. P.		Milwaukee	WI
Waurzyniakowiski*	M. J.		Milwaukee	WI
Weick*	H. J.		Milwaukee	WI
Wollensak	William	450 National	Milwaukee	WI
Jenkins & Hasking			Mineral Point	WI
Copeland & Greene			Monroe	WI
White*	H. J.		Montello	WI
Lane*	W. II.		Mount Horeb	WI
Bishop	G. W.		Necedah	WI
Ely & Meddins			Neenah	WI

PHOTOGRAPHERS LISTED BY CITY/STATE IN THE UNITED STATES 1888-1889

NAME		ADDRESS	CITY	STATE
Nelson	Elinor		Neenah	WI
Prebinson	Peter		Neenah	WI
Ennor	J. A.		Neillsville	WI
Kirklank & Schuster			Neillsville	WI
Ramsey	J. F.		New Lisbon	WI
Dawson	J. C.		New London	WI
Banister	Frank		New Richmond	WI
Childs	H. A.		New Richmond	WI
McGary	H. C.		Norwalk	WI
Lee	M. W.		Oconto	WI
Wilcox	G. W.		Oconto	WI
Munger*	D. G.		Oconomowoc	WI
Weller*	L. P.		Oconomowoc	WI
Reed*	F. H.		Omro	WI
Spettel	Clement		Onalaska	WI
Madison	Charles		Oshkosh	WI
Manzer	O. H.		Oshkosh	WI
Robinson	W. H. H.		Oshkosh	WI
Seibert & Wolff			Oshkosh	WI
Webster	W. F.		Oshkosh	WI
Yont	Alexander		Oshkosh	WI
Dawes	G. F.		Plainfield	WI
Nye	J. L.		Platteville	WI
Volquarto	C. H.		Plymouth	WI
Howard*	J. B.		Port Washington	WI
Perkins	O. R.		Portage	WI
Plumb	S. L.		Portage	WI
Ridgway	I. A.		Portage	WI
Butterfield	T. L.		Prairie du Chien	WI
Young	G. W.		Princeton	WI
Billings	E. T.	501 Main	Racine	WI
Leonard	P. F.	333 Main	Racine	WI
Mead	Edwin	506 6th	Racine	WI
Thomas	George C.	1219 College	Racine	WI
Turner	Charles F.	506 6th	Racine	WI
Bertlieb	William		Random Lake	WI
Kellogg	D. R.		Reedsburgh	WI
Nott	Charles		Rice Lake	WI
Hillman	W. J.		Richland Center	WI
Bush	G. C.		Rio	WI

PHOTOGRAPHERS LISTED BY CITY/STATE IN THE UNITED STATES 1888-1889

NAME		ADDRESS	CITY	STATE
Lockwood	Mrs. E. N.		Ripon	WI
Kellog	W. F.		River Falls	WI
Beck	A. A.		Sauk City	WI
Schaddle	P. J.		Sauk City	WI
Schadde*	P. J.		Sauk City	WI
Blackburn*	G. H.		Seymour	WI
Chamberlain	C. A.		Shawano	WI
Groh & Bro.	G. M.		Sheboygan	WI
Halbach	C. H.		Sheboygan	WI
Morgeneier	J. W.		Sheboygan	WI
Childs	H. L.		Shell Lake	WI
Chamberlin	H. B.		Shullsburgh	WI
Clegg	M. A.		Shullsburgh	WI
Gordon Bros.			Soldiers' Grove	WI
Beach	E. A.		Sparta	WI
Richardson Bros.			Sparta	WI
Skervis*	B. P.		Spring Geen	WI
Richardson	H. W.		Stevens' Point	WI
Huff	W. C.		Stevens' Point	WI
Fermann	W. A.		Stoughton	WI
Stoakes	T. A.		Sturgeon Bay	WI
Baldwin	W. D.		Superior	WI
Palmer	E. N.		Tomah	WI
Eastman	W. C.		Trempealeau	WI
Braun	John		Two Rivers	WI
Cook*	L. C.		Viola	WI
Losch*	D. W.		Viola	WI
Adlington & Chase			Viroqua	WI
Morgan	G. W.		Viroqua	WI
Drake	W. H.		Waterloo	WI
Fagan*	J. K.		Watertown	WI
Griffith	G. W.		Watertown	WI
May	J. B.		Watertown	WI
Rundlett	C. W.		Watertown	WI
Mann	W. G.		Waukesha	WI
Paige	E. H.		Waukesha	WI
Palmer	E. H.		Waupaca	WI
Warner*	Gustav		Waupaca	WI
Johnson	A. S.		Waupun	WI
Canfield	E. H.		Wausau	WI

PHOTOGRAPHERS LISTED BY CITY/STATE IN THE UNITED STATES 1888-1889

NAME		ADDRESS	CITY	STATE
Fleming	E. G.		Wausau	WI
Goff	F. L.		Wausau	WI
Lemke	Carl		Wausau	WI
Goetz	John		West Bend	WI
Lollin	Miss Mary		Weyauwega	WI
Goettel*	Philip		White Water	WI
Goodman	H. P.		White Water	WI
Winkle	Joseph		Wild Rose	WI
Brockway	S. B.		Winneconne	WI
Allen*	O. T. H	.	Buffalo	WY
Christopher*	C. E.		Cheyenne City	WY
Kirkland	C. D.		Cheyenne City	WY
Hartwell & Son			Laramie	WY
Heyn	L.		Laramie	WY

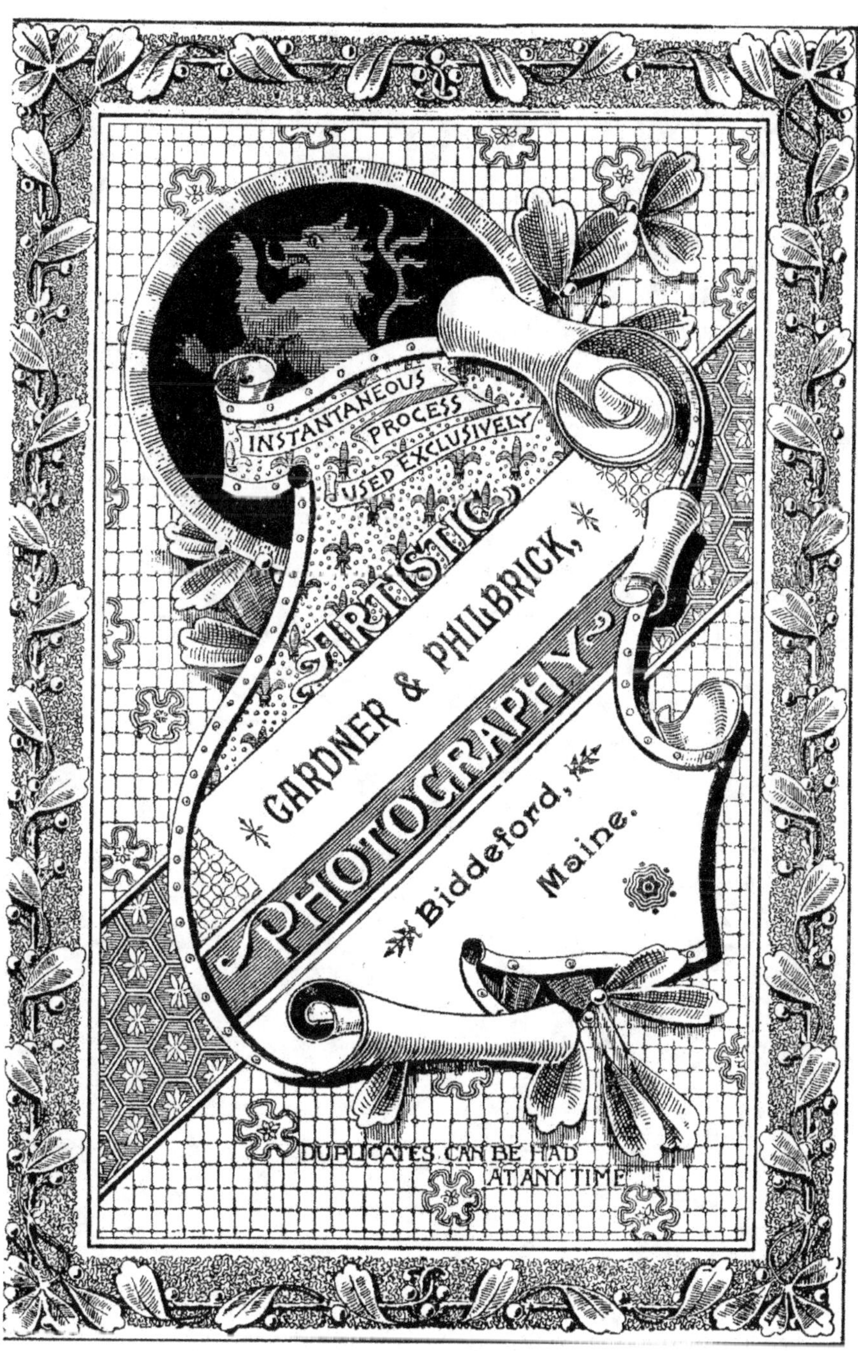
INSTANTANEOUS
PROCESS
USED EXCLUSIVELY
ARTISTIC
GARDNER & PHILBRICK,
PHOTOGRAPHY
Biddeford,
Maine.
DUPLICATES CAN BE HAD
AT ANY TIME

ALPHABETICAL LISTING OF PHOTOGRAPHERS IN CANADA IN 1889

NAME		ADDRESS	CITY	PROVINCE
Adams	T. G.	53 King	Toronto	ON
Adamson	W.		Lefroy	ON
Alexander & Co.			Toronto	ON
Archambault	H. E.	2202 Notre Dame	Montreal	PQ
Archambault	L. G. H.	1694 Notre Dame	Montreal	PQ
Arless & Co.	G.	261 St. James	Montreal	PQ
Armstrong	Thomas		Fergus	ON
Armstrong & Co.		83 St. Martin	Montreal	PQ
Arthur	Charles		Simcoe	ON
Arthur	J.		Chatham	ON
Ashelman	W. H.		Toronto	ON
Ashfield	James	98 Wellington	Ottawa	ON
Askew	A.		Oil Springs	ON
Askew	H.		Thorold	ON
Badgley	L.		Toronto	ON
Baird	David		Blenheim	ON
Balmer	Mrs. F.		Flesherton	ON
Banslaugh	A.		Brusscls	ON
Barber	D.		Listowell	ON
Barnes	J. A.		Mount Forest	ON
Barrand	A. T.		Barrie	ON
Barrett	August		Whithe	ON
Barrie	I. W.		Richmond	PQ
Barron	Jno.		Sarnia	ON
Barron	R.		Toronto	ON
Bassett	R. J.		Dresden	ON
Bauslaugh	T.		Paris	ON
Bayley & Murphy		167 Hollis	Halifax	NS
Beale	T. N.		Alliston	ON
Beaudet	William	15 ½ Gosford	Montreal	PQ
Becker	W. I.		New Hamburg	ON
Beckett	S. B.		Toronto	ON
Beckham	John		Hawkesbury	ON
Belanger	Louis	460 Sussex	Ottawa	ON
Bell	Jno.		Ailsa Craig	ON
Bell	John		Arnprior	ON
Bell & Son	W. P.		Kingston	ON
Belleau	N.	108 St. George	Quebec City	PQ
Benison	Jno.		Orillia	ON
Bennetts & Co.	I.		Winnipeg	MB

ALPHABETICAL LISTING OF PHOTOGRAPHERS IN CANADA IN 1889

NAME		ADDRESS	CITY	PROVINCE
Best	John	Main & McWilliams	Winnipeg	MB
Biddle	F.		Alliston	ON
Black	W. N.		Gananoque	ON
Bogart	W.	Box 121	New Market	ON
Boorne & May			Calgary	NWT
Bowman	Sol.		St. Clements	ON
Brault	P. E.		St. Johns	PQ
Brock & Co.			Brandon	NWT
Brock & Co.			Belleville	ON
Brockenshire	W. F.	Box 158	Wingham	ON
Brook	J. A.		Port Hope	ON
Brook	J. A.		Trenton	ON
Brooke	R. S.		Dundas	ON
Brouse	J. L.		Ingersoll	ON
Bruce	J.	118 King	Toronto	ON
Brule	Jacques	266 ½ St. Lawrence	Montreal	PQ
Bryce	J. F.	107 King W.	Toronto	ON
Bryce	J. W.		Belleville	ON
Burges	C. J.		Lakefield	ON
Burgess	J. H.		Almonte	ON
Burgess	W.		Guelph	ON
Burkett	J. W.	65 St. Jean	Quebec City	PQ
Burnham	E. W.		Cannington	ON
Bussiere	A.	11 Market Sq.	Montreal	PQ
Butler	J. S.		Chatham	ON
Buyers & Son	W.		Guelph	ON
Calcer	E.		Seaforth	ON
Calder	A.		Seaforth	ON
Campbell	A. L.		Alvinston	ON
Campbell	Alle		Stratford	ON
Campeau	Louis	1064 St. Lawrence	Montreal	PQ
Canuron	A. E.		Beaverton	ON
Carr	Mrs. R. E.		Winnipeg	MB
Carten	A. G.		Collingwood	ON
Castor	J. A.		Collingwood	ON
Caswell	S.		Palmerston	ON
Challmer	J. S.		Strathroy	ON
Chapman	J.	390 Richmond	London	ON
Chapman	Jno.		Kensington	ON
Charles	Thomas		St. Catherine's	ON

ALPHABETICAL LISTING OF PHOTOGRAPHERS IN CANADA IN 1889

NAME		ADDRESS	CITY	PROVINCE
Charron	B.		Mattawa	ON
Charron	William		Pembroke	ON
Clark	E. D.	23 Tiffany	Guelph	ON
Clark	J. A.		Omemee	ON
Cochran	C. S.	124 E. King	Hamilton	ON
Cohen	H.	227 Queen	Toronto	ON
Colville	Charles		Chesley	ON
Cook	J. B.	193 Yonge	Toronto	ON
Cook	J. F.		Port Arthur	ON
Cooper	F.	169 Dundas	London	ON
Cooper & Swift			Petrolia	ON
Cote	Ludger	220 Wolfe	Montreal	PQ
Coulter	H. A.		Ripley	ON
Coupland	T. P.		Winstead	ON
Craig	R. W.		Oshawa	ON
Craig	William		St. Catherine's	ON
Crawford	F.		Haliburton	ON
Creaig	William		Owen Sound	ON
Crealy	W.		Strathroy	ON
Cullis	Harry		Blyth	ON
Cumming	W. A.	242 St. James	Montreal	PQ
Cunningham	Alex.		Hamilton	ON
Dagenais	Henri	51 St. Vincent	Montreal	PQ
Dame	V. H.		Orangeville	ON
De Champlain	August		Ottawa	ON
Defliavrias	A. H.		Ottawa	ON
Degenais	J. A.	159 St. Lawrence	Montreal	PQ
Deirlamm	P.		Walkerton	ON
Derby	Charles		Vankleek Hill	ON
Desjardins	Charles T.		Sorel	PQ
Desmarais & Co.	L. E.	14 St. Lawrence	Montreal	PQ
Diamond	Charles C.		Granberg	ON
Dick	G. W.		Brantford	ON
Dixon	Mrs. J.	201 Yonge	Toronto	ON
Dixon	S. J.	78 Yonge	Toronto	ON
Dobereiner	F.		Guelph	ON
Doebereiner	P.		Caledonia	ON
Dorion & Delorme		140 Sparks	Ottawa	ON
Dorion & Delorme		569 Sussex	Ottawa	ON
Doyle	Ed		Toronto	ON

ALPHABETICAL LISTING OF PHOTOGRAPHERS IN CANADA IN 1889

NAME		ADDRESS	CITY	PROVINCE
Duffin & Co.	S.		Winnipeg	MB
Dufresne	P. H.		Toronto	ON
Dufresne	Ph.	615 Notre Dame	Montreal	PQ
Dukelow	Miss J.		Iroquois	ON
Dunham	Mrs. E.		Clifford	ON
Dunlop	William		Thornburg	ON
Early	G. G.		Peterborough	ON
Eckerson	N. G.		Hamilton	ON
Eddy	J. W.		London	ON
Eddy Bros.		214 Dundas	London	ON
Edwards	W. H.		St. Stephens	NB
Eggleston	R.	175 N. Hughson	Hamilton	ON
Eggman & Thompson			Norwich	ON
Elliott	William		Elora	ON
Ellis	J. A.		Lucan	ON
Ellison	T. A.		Eganville	ON
Emerson	Thomas		Caledonia	ON
England	Jno.		Niagara Falls South	ON
Erving	W. B.		Parkdale	ON
Esson	J.		Preston	ON
Fagen	John M.		Toronto	ON
Fanjoy	C. A.		Collingwood	ON
Farffeth	J. H.		London	ON
Farmer	William	35 King	Hamilton	ON
Farmer Bros.		8 King	Hamilton	ON
Farner	J. H.		Hamilton	ON
Farrell	Alexander		Perth	ON
Faster	J. W.		St. Thomas	ON
Faulkner	J. C.	13 Saulter	Toronto	ON
Fell	S. B.		Morrisburg	ON
Ferguson	A. W.		Prescott	ON
Feunell	Thomas		Gorrie	ON
Fick	T. A.		Laugton	ON
Fisher	Seb.		Elmira	ON
Fobey	W. B.		Tara	ON
Forester	George		Harriston	ON
Foster	H.		Clinton	ON
Foster & Boyley			Clinton	ON
Fowler	H.		Lindsay	ON
Fowler	W. H.		Mitchell	ON

ALPHABETICAL LISTING OF PHOTOGRAPHERS IN CANADA IN 1889

NAME		ADDRESS	CITY	PROVINCE
Fowler & Oliver			Lindsay	ON
Fraser	Gagen	79 W. King	Toronto	ON
Fulford	J. F.		Brighton	ON
Gagne	Mrs. E.	1823 St. Catherine	Montreal	PQ
Gagnon	P. M.	1507 St. Catherine	Montreal	PQ
Galaugher	A.		Mamora	ON
Gamble	Charles		Ridgetown	ON
Gamble	R. H.		Brockville	ON
Gamsby	W. S.		Orono	ON
Gardiner	W. H.	332 Yonge	Toronto	ON
Gardiner	William H.		Orangeville	ON
Gastonguay	Mrs. T.	115 St. Joseph	Quebec City	PQ
Gauthier	Theophile	173 McGill	Montreal	PQ
Gelmour	William A.		Almonte	ON
Gibson	Mrs. E. D.		Ottawa	ON
Gillespie	George		Shelburne	ON
Gould	William		Owen Sound	ON
Gray	John N.		St. Marys	ON
Green	A. S.		Port Elgin	ON
Green	P. H.		Peterborough	ON
Guguere	N. A.	68 Jacques Cartier	Montreal	PQ
Hadcock	M.		Alymer	ON
Hale	A. D.		St. Thomas	ON
Hall	Jno.		Wallaceburg	ON
Hall	T. S.		St. Barrington	ON
Hamill & Ball			Peterborough	ON
Hamilton	James		Collingwood	ON
Hamilton	James		Markdale	ON
Hanley	E. S.		Port Hope	ON
Harding	C. N.		Pembroke	ON
Head	T. B.		Paisley	ON
Hemstreet	G. A.		Milton	ON
Henderson	A.		Montreal	PQ
Henderson	Henry		Kingston	ON
Henry	R. H.		Bowmanville	ON
Hess	George		Zurich	ON
Hess	T. Y.		Picton	ON
Heubsweller	H.		Teeswater	ON
Higgins	W. W.		Trenton	ON
Hill	J. S.		St. Catherine's	ON

ALPHABETICAL LISTING OF PHOTOGRAPHERS IN CANADA IN 1889

NAME		ADDRESS	CITY	PROVINCE
Hines	William	107 E. King	Toronto	ON
Hodges	R. E.		Waterford	ON
Hogg	James		Meaford	ON
Holmes	George		Owen Sound	ON
Hood	A. M.		Stayner	ON
Hopkins	J. H.		St. Thomas	ON
Horsman	William		Chatham	ON
Huber	Alfred		Wellesley	ON
Huber	D. S.		Berlin	ON
Hugill	E. H.		Ingersoll	ON
Hulett	J. S.		Napanee	ON
Hunt	E. A.		Dutton	ON
Husband & Son			Fordwich	ON
Ions Bros.		82 ½ Sparks	Ottawa	ON
Jackson	Frank		Clinton	ON
Jackson	M. A.		Tweed	ON
Jackson	W. B.		Ayer	ON
Jarvis	S.	141 Sparks	Ottawa	ON
Johnson	E. L.		Lucknow	ON
Johnson	W. F.		Picton	ON
Jones	J. L.	42 Fabrique	Quebec City	PQ
Jones	W. L.		New Market	ON
Jones Bros.			Ottawa	ON
Kaake	Edwin		Wingham	ON
Kahr	W. H.		Georgetown	ON
Kearns	W. F.		Toronto	ON
Kiddle	Thomas		Wallaceburg	ON
Kilburn	M. D.		Coaticook	PQ
King & Young			Toronto	ON
Kinzie	George J.		Berlin	ON
Kirton	George		Woodstock	ON
Krupp	B. S.		Stratford	ON
Laflamme & Contant		1572 Notre Dame	Montreal	PQ
Lajoie	Mrs. Victorine	11 Chaboillez	Montreal	PQ
Lalonde	Noel C.	30 St. Lawrence	Montreal	PQ
Lambly	J. T.	105 Vitre	Montreal	PQ
Lane	R.	147 Yonge	Toronto	ON
Langdale	W.		Ayton	ON
Lapp	Charles		Harwood	ON
Larin	Henri	18 St. Lawrence	Montreal	PQ

ALPHABETICAL LISTING OF PHOTOGRAPHERS IN CANADA IN 1889

NAME		ADDRESS	CITY	PROVINCE
Lauer	Charles		Port Hope	ON
Lawes	Charles		Cobourg	ON
Le Gear	H. M.		Kincardine	ON
Le Maitre & Co.		324 Yonge	Toronto	ON
Leary	J.		St. Marys	ON
Lee	C. A.		Listowell	ON
Leet	W. R.		Danville	PQ
Leger	Damase	10-12 Murray	Ottawa	ON
Legget	J. R.		Parry Sound	ON
Lendrum	G. W.		Gananoque	ON
Leonard	William H.		Port Perry	ON
Lewis	C. L.		Oshawa	ON
Lewis	J. H.	110 W. Queen	Toronto	ON
Lezer	Danias		Ottawa	ON
Lindop	W. E.	31 Adelide W.	St. Thomas	ON
Lincrnois	J. E.	9 St. Jean	Quebec City	PQ
Loiselle & Co.	L. A.	St. Catherine & St. Andre	Montreal	PQ
Lord	G. A.		Uxbridge	ON
Ludbrook	A. A.		Verona	ON
Ludlow	R. L.		Burkes Falls	ON
Lyon & Co.	W. A.		Toronto	ON
Macrae	Alexander S.	127 Wellington	Toronto	ON
Madgett	T. H.		Welland	ON
Maguire	A. W.		Selkirk	ON
Maihn	P.		Montreal	PQ
Maitland	G. F.		Stratford	ON
Mandeville	Arthur	228 St. Lawrence	Montreal	PQ
Marr	George		Dresden	ON
Marshall	W. W.		Guelph	ON
Martial	Israel	546 Lagauchetiere	Montreal	PQ
Martin	George		Brussells	ON
Martin	Merritt	141 St. Peter	Montreal	PQ
Martin	Samuel		Kemptville	ON
Mason	Joseph		Wingham	ON
Matheson	E. C.		Toronto	ON
Mathews	M.		Wiarton	ON
Maynard	Mrs. R.		Victoria	BC
McAuley	C. W.		Montreal	PQ
McCaughrin	J. J.		Mono Road Station	ON
McCormick	Robert		Belleville	ON

ALPHABETICAL LISTING OF PHOTOGRAPHERS IN CANADA IN 1889

NAME		ADDRESS	CITY	PROVINCE
McDiarmid	A. E.		Dutton Station	ON
McFadden	William		Peterborough	ON
McIntyre & Co.	W. H.		Perth	ON
McMillan	D.		Dundas	ON
Menard	P. L.		L'Original	ON
Mertens	W. J.		Stouffville	ON
Metivier	Charles	469 Marianne	Montreal	PQ
Meyers	H. C.	274 W. Queen	Toronto	ON
Micklethwaite	F. W.	40 Jarvis	Toronto	ON
Miles	R. G.		Arnprior	ON
Moffat & Co.			Reufrew	ON
Moffet	W. H.		Palmerston	ON
Montining	M. A.	185 St. Joseph	Quebec City	PQ
Moodie	J. H.		Hamilton	ON
Moore	John		Smith's Falls	ON
Morrice	D.		Madoc	ON
Morrison	E.		Carleton Place	ON
Mundy	J. H.		Port Hope	ON
Murdoch	W. A.		Windsor	ON
Murray & Son			Brockville	ON
Nettleton	Thomas	2 Gain	Montreal	PQ
Newberg	Robert		Aurora	ON
Newcombe & Baird		237 Barrington	Halifax	NS
Norton	J. W.		St. Thomas	ON
Notman	William	39 George	Halifax	NS
Notman & Son	William	17 Bleury	Montreal	PQ
Nottman	William	54 Princess	St. John	NB
Noverre	J. H.	101 W. King	Toronto	ON
O'Brien	W. E.		Whitby	ON
Oliver	J. H.		Ingersoll	ON
Osgood	P. M.		Chapleau	ON
Pagent	W. P.		Beeton	ON
Palmer	E. J.		Toronto	ON
Park	Mrs. L.		Brampton	ON
Park & Co.			Brantford	ON
Parker	George F.		Yarmouth	NS
Parker	William		Windsor	ON
Parkins	F. W.		Seaforth	ON
Parks	J. G.	197 St. James	Montreal	PQ
Pecard	J.	281 St. Joseph	Quebec City	PQ

ALPHABETICAL LISTING OF PHOTOGRAPHERS IN CANADA IN 1889

NAME		ADDRESS	CITY	PROVINCE
Pemberton	W.		Uxbridge	ON
Pepper	W. F.		Lindsay	ON
Perkins	T. E.	293 Yonge	Toronto	ON
Perry	C. E.		Woodstock	ON
Perry	G. R.		Simcoe	ON
Phillips	E. S.		Hagersville	ON
Phillips	Mr.		Alymer	ON
Phippen	E. J.		Park Hill	ON
Photoglyptic Co.		77 King	Hamilton	ON
Pinssonnearet	P. F.		Three Rivers	PQ
Pittaway & Jarvis		117 Sparks	Ottawa	ON
Pollard	James		Tilsonburg	ON
Poole	E.		St. Catherine's	ON
Porteous	A. T.		Cornwall	ON
Porter	Thomas		Kingston	ON
Pound	C. F.		Port Perry	ON
Poweler	J. W.		Kingston	ON
Powell	E. H.		Dunnville	ON
Pratt	Mrs. E. S.		Parry Sound	ON
Query	Freres	10 St. Lambert	Montreal	PQ
Racette	E.	330 Notre Dame	Montreal	PQ
Rae	John M.		Sutton West	ON
Raith	William		Walters Falls	ON
Ramsey	J. G.		Toronto	ON
Rawe	G.		Brampton	ON
Ray	S. H.		Strathroy	ON
Reeves	W. C.		Barrie	ON
Reid & Young			Woodbridge	ON
Remington	Ed		Stratford	ON
Richardson	F. S.		Napanee	ON
Richmond	J. L.		Campbellford	ON
Riendeau	Charles	494 Laval	Montreal	PQ
Robson	G. B.		Petrolia	ON
Ross	J.	197 Hollis	Halifax	NS
Ross	J. A.		Calgary	NWT
Roy	H.	74 St. Joseph	Quebec City	PQ
Ruby	A. A.		Guelph	ON
Rughy	A. A.		Acton	ON
Russell	C. W.		Tottenham	ON
Sallows	R. R.		Goderich	ON

NAME		ADDRESS	CITY	PROVINCE
Sallows	R. S.		Goderich	ON
Sargent	Samuel Jr.		North Ridge	ON
Saucier	P. T.		Vankleek Hill	ON
Schneuker	C.		Berlin	ON
Scott	J. A.		Lindsay	ON
Scott & Hopkins			St. James	ON
Scott & Hopkins			St. Thomas	ON
Searle	G. W.		Brantford	ON
Seiler	George		Berlin	ON
Selley	J. M.		St. Thomas	ON
Selly	J. M.		Watford	ON
Senior	Charles		Exeter	ON
Senior	Charles	692 Yonge	Toronto	ON
Shannessy & Hall		258 Yonge	Toronto	ON
Shannon	Y.		Stratford	ON
Sheldon	H. K.		Kingston	ON
Sheldon & Davis			Kingston	ON
Sherk	W. B.		Drayton	ON
Simpson	H. E.	41 E. King	Toronto	ON
Simpson Bros.		357 Yonge	Toronto	ON
Slevis	F. G.		Ingersoll	ON
Smart	A.		Glencoe	ON
Smith	H. K.		Belleville	ON
Smith	H. K.		Brantford	ON
Smith	Harry		Mount Forest	ON
Smith	J. A.		Eganville	ON
Smith	R.		Mount Forest	ON
Smith	S. M.		Listowell	ON
Smith	S. W.		Jarvis	ON
Smith	T. H.		Galt	ON
Smith	Thomas		Guelph	ON
Snider	G. A.		Brantford	ON
Solomon	A.		Toronto	ON
Spinks	W. & R.		Woodstock	ON
Sproule	G. B.		Peterborough	ON
Staunton	E.	116 Yonge	Toronto	ON
Steele & Wing			Winnipeg	MB
Stephens	Jno.		Barrie	ON
Stewart	A. J.		Harriston	ON
Stewart	George	Lock Box 123	Goderich	ON

ALPHABETICAL LISTING OF PHOTOGRAPHERS IN CANADA IN 1889

NAME		ADDRESS	CITY	PROVINCE
Summerhayes & Walford		1 Bleury	Montreal	PQ
Sylvester	Jno.		Bobcaygeon	ON
Taggart & Co.	C. B.	Bank & Wellington	Ottawa	ON
Tait & Morrison			Bowmanville	ON
Talbot	C.		Gananoque	ON
Tarry	Robert		Durham	ON
Taylor	E. A.		London	ON
Taylor	T. B.		Watford	ON
Tegg	S. A.	71 W. King	Toronto	ON
Terry	D. H.		Amherstburg	ON
Thompson & Son		75 E. King	Toronto	ON
Thorn	J. S.		Sarnia	ON
Topley Studio		104 Sparks	Ottawa	ON
Toronto Lithographing		163 St. James	Montreal	PQ
Townsend	James		Almonte	ON
Treleaven	T. L.		Mount Forest	ON
Trickey	N. M.		West Winchester	ON
Trott	W. D.		Ridgetown	ON
True Press			London	ON
Trucman	Jno.		Gravcnhurst	ON
Trueman	R. H.		Brampton	ON
Tschinhart	P.		Neustadt	ON
Tschirhart	Miss H.		Mildmay	ON
Tueher	N. M.		West Winchester	ON
Uren	John		New Westminster	BC
Uren	R. F.		St. Catherines	ON
Valiquette	Mrs. Caroline	3 Fulford	Montreal	PQ
Vallee	L. P.	39 St. Jean	Quebec City	PQ
Vasey & Bland			Winnipeg	MB
Vodden	William		Hanover	ON
Wade	W. W.		Seaforth	ON
Walker	J. C.	Box 670	Brantford	ON
Walker	James		Galt	ON
Walker	W. J.		Chatham	ON
Wallis	J. D.	61 Sparks	Ottawa	ON
Walton	Miss M.		Chatham	ON
Wardwell	E.		Bracebridge	ON
Washburn	A. C.		Kincardine	ON
Weber	H. W.		Cornwall	ON
Weese	D. A.		Belleville	ON

ALPHABETICAL LISTING OF PHOTOGRAPHERS IN CANADA IN 1889

NAME		ADDRESS	CITY	PROVINCE
Weese	D. A.		Dunnville	ON
Weitzel	George		Elmira	ON
Welsh	Ed		Toronto	ON
Westlake	F. G.	394 Richmond	London	ON
Whiten	G. E.		Orillia	ON
Wigle	J. N.		Essex Centre	ON
Wildern	Adna		Vienna	ON
Willescroft	George		Paisley	ON
Williams	Newton		Bracebridge	ON
Williamson	Eli		Lindsay	ON
Williamson	J. C.		Cobourg	ON
Willis	G. E.		Carleton Place	ON
Wilson	George		St. Marys	ON
Wilson	J. W.		Waterloo	ON
Wilson & Crawford			Forest	ON
Witts	Charles		Deseronto	ON
Wright	H.		Rat Portage	ON
Wright	J. S.		Orillia	ON
Wymiss	Prof. R. S. A.		Brockville	ON
Yost	Levi		Elmira	ON
Young	J. H.		Woodbridge	ON
Young	Nelson		Bothwell	ON
Yuerg	George		Montreal	PQ
Zelensky	A.		Chatham	ON
Zybach	John		Niagara Falls South	ON

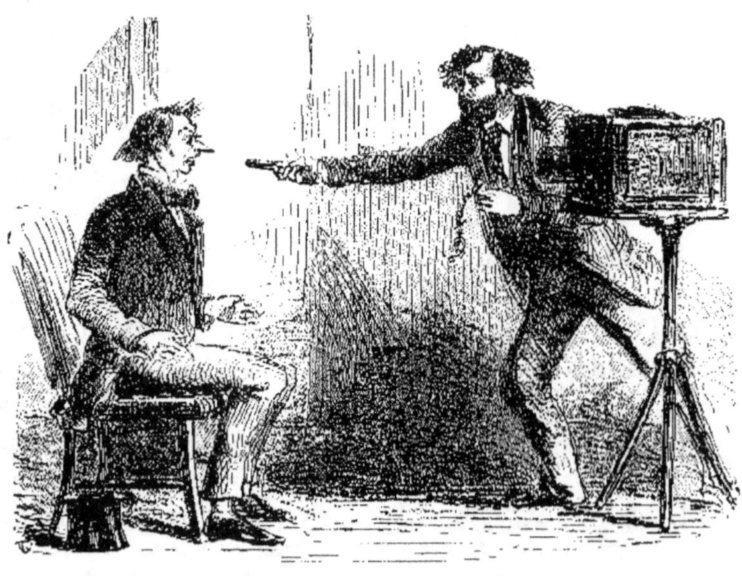

PROVINCIAL LIST OF PHOTOGRAPHERS IN CANADA IN 1889

NAME		ADDRESS	CITY	PROVINCE
Uren	John		New Westminster	BC
Maynard	Mrs. R.		Victoria	BC
Bennetts & Co.	I.		Winnipeg	MB
Best	John	Main & McWilliams	Winnipeg	MB
Carr	Mrs. R. E.		Winnipeg	MB
Duffin & Co.	S.		Winnipeg	MB
Steele & Wing			Winnipeg	MB
Vasey & Bland			Winnipeg	MB
Nottman	William	54 Princess	St. John	NB
Edwards	W. H.		St. Stephens	NB
Brock & Co.			Brandon	NWT
Boorne & May			Calgary	NWT
Ross	J. A.		Calgary	NWT
Bayley & Murphy		167 Hollis	Halifax	NS
Newcombe & Baird		237 Barrington	Halifax	NS
Notman	William	39 George	Halifax	NS
Ross	J.	197 Hollis	Halifax	NS
Parker	George F.		Yarmouth	NS
Rughy	A. A.		Acton	ON
Bell	Jno.		Ailsa Craig	ON
Beale	T. N.		Alliston	ON
Biddle	F.		Alliston	ON
Burgess	J. H.		Almonte	ON
Gelmour	William A.		Almonte	ON
Townsend	James		Almonte	ON
Campbell	A. L.		Alvinston	ON
Terry	D. H.		Amherstburg	ON
Bell	John		Arnprior	ON
Miles	R. G.		Arnprior	ON
Newberg	Robert		Aurora	ON
Jackson	W. B.		Ayer	ON
Hadcock	M.		Alymer	ON
Phillips	Mr.		Alymer	ON
Langdale	W.		Ayton	ON
Barrand	A. T.		Barrie	ON
Stephens	Jno.		Barrie	ON
Reeves	W. C.		Barrie	ON
Canuron	A. E.		Beaverton	ON
Pagent	W. P.		Beeton	ON

PROVINCIAL LIST OF PHOTOGRAPHERS IN CANADA IN 1889

NAME		ADDRESS	CITY	PROVINCE
Brock & Co.			Belleville	ON
Bryce	J. W.		Belleville	ON
McCormick	Robert		Belleville	ON
Smith	H. K.		Belleville	ON
Weese	D. A.		Belleville	ON
Huber	D. S.		Berlin	ON
Kinzie	George J.		Berlin	ON
Schneuker	C.		Berlin	ON
Seiler	George		Berlin	ON
Baird	David		Blenheim	ON
Cullis	Harry		Blyth	ON
Sylvester	Jno.		Bobcaygeon	ON
Young	Nelson		Bothwell	ON
Henry	R. H.		Bowmanville	ON
Tait & Morrison			Bowmanville	ON
Wardwell	E.		Bracebridge	ON
Williams	Newton		Bracebridge	ON
Rawe	G.		Brampton	ON
Trueman	R. H.		Brampton	ON
Park	Mrs. L.		Brampton	ON
Dick	G. W.		Brantford	ON
Park & Co.			Brantford	ON
Searle	G. W.		Brantford	ON
Smith	H. K.		Brantford	ON
Snider	G. A.		Brantford	ON
Walker	J. C.	Box 670	Brantford	ON
Fulford	J. F.		Brighton	ON
Gamble	R. H.		Brockville	ON
Murray & Son			Brockville	ON
Wymiss	Prof. R. S. A.		Brockville	ON
Banslaugh	A.		Brussells	ON
Martin	George		Brussells	ON
Ludlow	R. L.		Burkes Falls	ON
Doebereiner	P.		Caledonia	ON
Emerson	Thomas		Caledonia	ON
Richmond	J. L.		Campbellford	ON
Burnham	E. W.		Cannington	ON
Morrison	E.		Carleton Place	ON
Willis	G. E.		Carleton Place	ON

PROVINCIAL LIST OF PHOTOGRAPHERS IN CANADA IN 1889

NAME		ADDRESS	CITY	PROVINCE
Osgood	P. M.		Chapleau	ON
Arthur	J.		Chatham	ON
Butler	J. S.		Chatham	ON
Horsman	William		Chatham	ON
Walton	Miss M.		Chatham	ON
Walker	W. J.		Chatham	ON
Zelensky	A.		Chatham	ON
Colville	Charles		Chesley	ON
Dunham	Mrs. E.		Clifford	ON
Foster & Boyley			Clinton	ON
Foster	H.		Clinton	ON
Jackson	Frank		Clinton	ON
Lawes	Charles		Cobourg	ON
Williamson	J. C.		Cobourg	ON
Carten	A. G.		Collingwood	ON
Castor	J. A.		Collingwood	ON
Fanjoy	C. A.		Collingwood	ON
Hamilton	James		Collingwood	ON
Porteous	A. T.		Cornwall	ON
Weber	H. W.		Cornwall	ON
Witts	Charles		Deseronto	ON
Sherk	W. B.		Drayton	ON
Bassett	R. J.		Dresden	ON
Marr	George		Dresden	ON
Brooke	R. S.		Dundas	ON
McMillan	D.		Dundas	ON
Powell	E. H.		Dunnville	ON
Weese	D. A.		Dunnville	ON
Tarry	Robert		Durham	ON
Hunt	E. A.		Dutton	ON
McDiarmid	A. E.		Dutton Station	ON
Ellison	T. A.		Eganville	ON
Smith	J. A.		Eganville	ON
Fisher	Seb.		Elmira	ON
Weitzel	George		Elmira	ON
Yost	Levi		Elmira	ON
Elliott	William		Elora	ON
Wigle	J. N.		Essex Centre	ON
Senior	Charles		Exeter	ON

PROVINCIAL LIST OF PHOTOGRAPHERS IN CANADA IN 1889

NAME		ADDRESS	CITY	PROVINCE
Armstrong	Thomas		Fergus	ON
Balmer	Mrs. F.		Flesherton	ON
Husband & Son			Fordwich	ON
Wilson & Crawford			Forest	ON
Smith	T. H.		Galt	ON
Walker	James		Galt	ON
Black	W. N.		Gananoque	ON
Lendrum	G. W.		Gananoque	ON
Talbot	C.		Gananoque	ON
Kahr	W. H.		Georgetown	ON
Smart	A.		Glencoe	ON
Sallows	R. R.		Goderich	ON
Sallows	R. S.		Goderich	ON
Stewart	George	Lock Box 123	Goderich	ON
Feunell	Thomas		Gorrie	ON
Diamond	Charles C.		Granberg	ON
Trueman	Jno.		Gravenhurst	ON
Burgess	W.		Guelph	ON
Buyers & Son	W.		Guelph	ON
Clark	E. D.	23 Tiffany	Guelph	ON
Dobereiner	F.		Guelph	ON
Marshall	W. W.		Guelph	ON
Ruby	A. A.		Guelph	ON
Smith	Thomas		Guelph	ON
Phillips	E. S.		Hagersville	ON
Crawford	F.		Haliburton	ON
Cochran	C. S.	124 E. King	Hamilton	ON
Cunningham	Alex.		Hamilton	ON
Eckerson	N. G.		Hamilton	ON
Eggleston	R.	175 N. Hughson	Hamilton	ON
Farmer Bros.		8 King	Hamilton	ON
Farmer	William	35 King	Hamilton	ON
Farner	J. H.		Hamilton	ON
Moodie	J. H.		Hamilton	ON
Photoglyptic Co.		77 King	Hamilton	ON
Vodden	William		Hanover	ON
Forester	George		Harriston	ON
Stewart	A. J.		Harriston	ON
Lapp	Charles		Harwood	ON

PROVINCIAL LIST OF PHOTOGRAPHERS IN CANADA IN 1889

NAME		ADDRESS	CITY	PROVINCE
Beckham	John		Hawkesbury	ON
Brouse	J. L.		Ingersoll	ON
Hugill	E. H.		Ingersoll	ON
Oliver	J. H.		Ingersoll	ON
Slevis	F. G.		Ingersoll	ON
Dukelow	Miss J.		Iroquois	ON
Smith	S. W.		Jarvis	ON
Martin	Samuel		Kemptville	ON
Chapman	Jno.		Kensington	ON
Le Gear	H. M.		Kincardine	ON
Washburn	A. C.		Kincardine	ON
Bell & Son	W. P.		Kingston	ON
Henderson	Henry		Kingston	ON
Porter	Thomas		Kingston	ON
Poweler	J. W.		Kingston	ON
Sheldon & Davis			Kingston	ON
Sheldon	H. K.		Kingston	ON
Burges	C. J.		Lakefield	ON
Fick	T. A.		Laugton	ON
Adamson	W.		Lefroy	ON
Fowler & Oliver			Lindsay	ON
Fowler	H.		Lindsay	ON
Pepper	W. F.		Lindsay	ON
Scott	J. A.		Lindsay	ON
Williamson	Eli		Lindsay	ON
Barber	D.		Listowell	ON
Lee	C. A.		Listowell	ON
Smith	S. M.		Listowell	ON
Chapman	J.	390 Richmond	London	ON
Cooper	F.	169 Dundas	London	ON
Eddy	J. W.		London	ON
Eddy Bros.		214 Dundas	London	ON
Farffeth	J. H.		London	ON
Taylor	E. A.		London	ON
True Press			London	ON
Westlake	F. G.	394 Richmond	London	ON
Menard	P. L.		L'Original	ON
Ellis	J. A.		Lucan	ON
Johnson	E. L.		Lucknow	ON

PROVINCIAL LIST OF PHOTOGRAPHERS IN CANADA IN 1889

NAME		ADDRESS	CITY	PROVINCE
Morrice	D.		Madoc	ON
Galaugher	A.		Mamora	ON
Hamilton	James		Markdale	ON
Charron	B.		Mattawa	ON
Hogg	James		Meaford	ON
Tschirhart	Miss H.		Mildmay	ON
Hemstreet	G. A.		Milton	ON
Fowler	W. H.		Mitchell	ON
McCaughrin	J. J.		Mono Road Station	ON
Fell	S. B.		Morrisburg	ON
Barnes	J. A.		Mount Forest	ON
Smith	Harry		Mount Forest	ON
Smith	R.		Mount Forest	ON
Treleaven	T. L.		Mount Forest	ON
Hulett	J. S.		Napanee	ON
Richardson	F. S.		Napanee	ON
Tschinhart	P.		Neustadt	ON
Becker	W. I.		New Hamburg	ON
Bogart	W.	Box 121	New Market	ON
Jones	W. L.		New Market	ON
England	Jno.		Niagara Falls South	ON
Zybach	John		Niagara Falls South	ON
Sargent	Samuel Jr.		North Ridge	ON
Eggman & Thompson			Norwich	ON
Askew	A.		Oil Springs	ON
Clark	J. A.		Omemee	ON
Dame	V. H.		Orangeville	ON
Gardiner	William H.		Orangeville	ON
Benison	Jno.		Orillia	ON
Whiten	G. E.		Orillia	ON
Wright	J. S.		Orillia	ON
Gamsby	W. S.		Orono	ON
Craig	R. W.		Oshawa	ON
Lewis	C. L.		Oshawa	ON
Ashfield	James	98 Wellington	Ottawa	ON
Belanger	Louis	460 Sussex	Ottawa	ON
De Champlain	August		Ottawa	ON
Defliavrias	A. H.		Ottawa	ON
Dorion & Delorme		140 Sparks	Ottawa	ON

PROVINCIAL LIST OF PHOTOGRAPHERS IN CANADA IN 1889

NAME		ADDRESS	CITY	PROVINCE
Dorion & Delorme		569 Sussex	Ottawa	ON
Gibson	Mrs. E. D.		Ottawa	ON
Ions Bros.		82 1/2 Sparks	Ottawa	ON
Jarvis	S.	141 Sparks	Ottawa	ON
Jones Bros.			Ottawa	ON
Leger	Damase	10-12 Murray	Ottawa	ON
Lezer	Danias		Ottawa	ON
Pittaway & Jarvis		117 Sparks	Ottawa	ON
Taggart & Co.	C. B.	Bank & Wellington	Ottawa	ON
Topley Studio		104 Sparks	Ottawa	ON
Wallis	J. D.	61 Sparks	Ottawa	ON
Creaig	William		Owen Sound	ON
Gould	William		Owen Sound	ON
Holmes	George		Owen Sound	ON
Head	T. B.		Paisley	ON
Willescroft	George		Paisley	ON
Caswell	S.		Palmerston	ON
Moffet	W. H.		Palmerston	ON
Bauslaugh	T.		Paris	ON
Phippen	E. J.		Park Hill	ON
Erving	W. B.		Parkdale	ON
Legget	J. R.		Parry Sound	ON
Pratt	Mrs. E. S.		Parry Sound	ON
Charron	William		Pembroke	ON
Harding	C. N.		Pembroke	ON
Farrell	Alexander		Perth	ON
McIntyre & Co.	W. H.		Perth	ON
Early	G. G.		Peterborough	ON
Green	P. H.		Peterborough	ON
Hamill & Ball			Peterborough	ON
McFadden	William		Peterborough	ON
Sproule	G. B.		Peterborough	ON
Cooper & Swift			Petrolia	ON
Robson	G. B.		Petrolia	ON
Hess	T. Y.		Picton	ON
Johnson	W. F.		Picton	ON
Cook	J. F.		Port Arthur	ON
Green	A. S.		Port Elgin	ON
Brook	J. A.		Port Hope	ON

PROVINCIAL LIST OF PHOTOGRAPHERS IN CANADA IN 1889

NAME		ADDRESS	CITY	PROVINCE
Hanley	E. S.		Port Hope	ON
Lauer	Charles		Port Hope	ON
Mundy	J. H.		Port Hope	ON
Leonard	William H.		Port Perry	ON
Pound	C. F.		Port Perry	ON
Ferguson	A. W.		Prescott	ON
Esson	J.		Preston	ON
Wright	H.		Rat Portage	ON
Moffat & Co.			Reufrew	ON
Gamble	Charles		Ridgetown	ON
Trott	W. D.		Ridgetown	ON
Coulter	H. A.		Ripley	ON
Hall	T. S.		St. Barrington	ON
Charles	Thomas		St. Catherine's	ON
Craig	William		St. Catherine's	ON
Hill	J. S.		St. Catherine's	ON
Poole	E.		St. Catherine's	ON
Uren	R. F.		St. Catherine's	ON
Bowman	Sol.		St. Clements	ON
Scott & Hopkins			St. James	ON
Gray	John N.		St. Marys	ON
Leary	J.		St. Marys	ON
Wilson	George		St. Marys	ON
Faster	J. W.		St. Thomas	ON
Hale	A. D.		St. Thomas	ON
Hopkins	J. H.		St. Thomas	ON
Lindop	W. E.	31 Adelide W.	St. Thomas	ON
Norton	J. W.		St. Thomas	ON
Scott & Hopkins			St. Thomas	ON
Selley	J. M.		St. Thomas	ON
Barron	Jno.		Sarnia	ON
Thorn	J. S.		Sarnia	ON
Calcer	E.		Seaforth	ON
Calder	A.		Seaforth	ON
Parkins	F. W.		Seaforth	ON
Wade	W. W.		Seaforth	ON
Maguire	A. W.		Selkirk	ON
Gillespie	George		Shelburne	ON
Arthur	Charles		Simcoe	ON

PROVINCIAL LIST OF PHOTOGRAPHERS IN CANADA IN 1889

NAME		ADDRESS	CITY	PROVINCE
Perry	G. R.		Simcoe	ON
Moore	John		Smith's Falls	ON
Hood	A. M.		Stayner	ON
Mertens	W. J.		Stouffville	ON
Campbell	Alle		Stratford	ON
Krupp	B. S.		Stratford	ON
Maitland	G. F.		Stratford	ON
Remington	Ed		Stratford	ON
Shannon	Y.		Stratford	ON
Challmer	J. S.		Strathroy	ON
Crealy	W.		Strathroy	ON
Ray	S. H.		Strathroy	ON
Rae	John M.		Sutton West	ON
Fobey	W. B.		Tara	ON
Heubsweller	H.		Teeswater	ON
Dunlop	William		Thornburg	ON
Askew	II.		Thorold	ON
Pollard	James		Tilsonburg	ON
Adams	T. G.	53 King	Toronto	ON
Alexander & Co.			Toronto	ON
Ashelman	W. H.		Toronto	ON
Badgley	L.		Toronto	ON
Barron	R.		Toronto	ON
Beckett	S. B.		Toronto	ON
Bruce	J.	118 King	Toronto	ON
Bryce	J. F.	107 King W.	Toronto	ON
Cohen	H.	227 Queen	Toronto	ON
Cook	J. B.	193 Yonge	Toronto	ON
Dixon	Mrs. J.	201 Yonge	Toronto	ON
Dixon	S. J.	78 Yonge	Toronto	ON
Doyle	Ed		Toronto	ON
Dufresne	P. H.		Toronto	ON
Fagen	John M.		Toronto	ON
Faulkner	J. C.	13 Saulter	Toronto	ON
Fraser	Gagen	79 W. King	Toronto	ON
Gardiner	W. H.	332 Yonge	Toronto	ON
Hines	William	107 E. King	Toronto	ON
Kearns	W. F.		Toronto	ON
King & Young			Toronto	ON

PROVINCIAL LIST OF PHOTOGRAPHERS IN CANADA IN 1889

NAME		ADDRESS	CITY	PROVINCE
Lane	R.	147 Yonge	Toronto	ON
Le Maitre & Co.		324 Yonge	Toronto	ON
Lewis	J. H.	110 W. Queen	Toronto	ON
Lyon & Co.	W. A.		Toronto	ON
Macrae	Alexander S.	127 Wellington	Toronto	ON
Matheson	E. C.		Toronto	ON
Meyers	H. C.	274 W. Queen	Toronto	ON
Micklethwaite	F. W.	40 Jarvis	Toronto	ON
Noverre	J. H.	101 W. King	Toronto	ON
Palmer	E. J.		Toronto	ON
Perkins	T. E.	293 Yonge	Toronto	ON
Ramsey	J. G.		Toronto	ON
Senior	Charles	692 Yonge	Toronto	ON
Shannessy & Hall		258 Yonge	Toronto	ON
Simpson Bros.		357 Yonge	Toronto	ON
Simpson	H. E.	41 E. King	Toronto	ON
Staunton	E.	116 Yonge	Toronto	ON
Solomon	A.		Toronto	ON
Tegg	S. A.	71 W. King	Toronto	ON
Thompson & Son		75 E. King	Toronto	ON
Welsh	Ed		Toronto	ON
Russell	C. W.		Tottenham	ON
Brook	J. A.		Trenton	ON
Higgins	W. W.		Trenton	ON
Jackson	M. A.		Tweed	ON
Lord	G. A.		Uxbridge	ON
Pemberton	W.		Uxbridge	ON
Derby	Charles		Vankleek Hill	ON
Saucier	P. T.		Vankleek Hill	ON
Ludbrook	A. A.		Verona	ON
Wildern	Adna		Vienna	ON
Deirlamm	P.		Walkerton	ON
Hall	Jno.		Wallaceburg	ON
Kiddle	Thomas		Wallaceburg	ON
Raith	William		Walters Falls	ON
Hodges	R. E.		Waterford	ON
Wilson	J. W.		Waterloo	ON
Selly	J. M.		Watford	ON
Taylor	T. B.		Watford	ON

PROVINCIAL LIST OF PHOTOGRAPHERS IN CANADA IN 1889

NAME		ADDRESS	CITY	PROVINCE
Madgett	T. H.		Welland	ON
Huber	Alfred		Wellesley	ON
Trickey	N. M.		West Winchester	ON
Tueher	N. M.		West Winchester	ON
O'Brien	W. E.		Whitby	ON
Barrett	August		Whithe	ON
Mathews	M.		Wiarton	ON
Murdoch	W. A.		Windsor	ON
Parker	William		Windsor	ON
Brockenshire	W. F.	Box 158	Wingham	ON
Kaake	Edwin		Wingham	ON
Mason	Joseph		Wingham	ON
Coupland	T. P.		Winstead	ON
Reid & Young			Woodbridge	ON
Young	J. H.		Woodbridge	ON
Kirton	George		Woodstock	ON
Perry	C. E.		Woodstock	ON
Spinks	W. & R.		Woodstock	ON
Hess	George		Zurich	ON
Kilburn	M. D.		Coaticook	PQ
Leet	W. R.		Danville	PQ
Archambault	H. E.	2202 Notre Dame	Montreal	PQ
Archambault	L. G. H.	1694 Notre Dame	Montreal	PQ
Arless & Co.	G.	261 St. James	Montreal	PQ
Armstrong & Co.		83 St. Martin	Montreal	PQ
Beaudet	William	15 ½ Gosford	Montreal	PQ
Brule	Jacques	266 ½ St. Lawrence	Montreal	PQ
Bussiere	A.	11 Market Sq.	Montreal	PQ
Campeau	Louis	1064 St. Lawrence	Montreal	PQ
Cote	Ludger	220 Wolfe	Montreal	PQ
Cumming	W. A.	242 St. James	Montreal	PQ
Dagenais	Henri	51 St. Vincent	Montreal	PQ
Degenais	J. A.	159 St. Lawrence	Montreal	PQ
Desmarais & Co.	L. E.	14 St. Lawrence	Montreal	PQ
Dufresne	Ph.	615 Notre Dame	Montreal	PQ
Gagne	Mrs. E.	1823 St. Catherine	Montreal	PQ
Gagnon	P. M.	1507 St. Catherine	Montreal	PQ
Gauthier	Theophile	173 McGill	Montreal	PQ
Guguere	N. A.	68 Jacques Cartier	Montreal	PQ

PROVINCIAL LIST OF PHOTOGRAPHERS IN CANADA IN 1889

NAME		ADDRESS	CITY	PROVINCE
Henderson	A.		Montreal	PQ
Laflamme & Contant		1572 Notre Dame	Montreal	PQ
Lajoie	Mrs. Victorine	11 Chaboillez	Montreal	PQ
Lalonde	Noel C.	30 St. Lawrence	Montreal	PQ
Lambly	J. T.	105 Vitre	Montreal	PQ
Larin	Henri	18 St. Lawrence	Montreal	PQ
Loiselle & Co.	L. A.	St. Catherine & St. Andre	Montreal	PQ
McAuley	C. W.		Montreal	PQ
Maihn	P.		Montreal	PQ
Mandeville	Arthur	228 St. Lawrence	Montreal	PQ
Martial	Israel	546 Lagauchetiere	Montreal	PQ
Martin	Merritt	141 St. Peter	Montreal	PQ
Metivier	Charles	469 Marianne	Montreal	PQ
Nettleton	Thomas	2 Gain	Montreal	PQ
Notman & Son	William	17 Bleury	Montreal	PQ
Parks	J. G.	197 St. James	Montreal	PQ
Query	Freres	10 St. Lambert	Montreal	PQ
Racette	E.	330 Notre Dame	Montreal	PQ
Riendeau	Charles	494 Laval	Montreal	PQ
Summerhayes & Walford		1 Bleury	Montreal	PQ
Toronto Lithographing		163 St. James	Montreal	PQ
Valiquette	Mrs. Caroline	3 Fulford	Montreal	PQ
Yuerg	George		Montreal	PQ
Belleau	N.	108 St. George	Quebec City	PQ
Burkett	J. W.	65 St. Jean	Quebec City	PQ
Gastonguay	Mrs. T.	115 St. Joseph	Quebec City	PQ
Jones	J. L.	42 Fabrique	Quebec City	PQ
Linernois	J. E.	9 St. Jean	Quebec City	PQ
Montining	M. A.	185 St. Joseph	Quebec City	PQ
Pecard	J.	281 St. Joseph	Quebec City	PQ
Roy	H.	74 St. Joseph	Quebec City	PQ
Vallee	L. P.	39 St. Jean	Quebec City	PQ
Barrie	I. W.		Richmond	PQ
Brault	P. E.		St. Johns	PQ
Desjardins	Charles T.		Sorel	PQ
Pinssonnearet	P. F.		Three Rivers	PQ

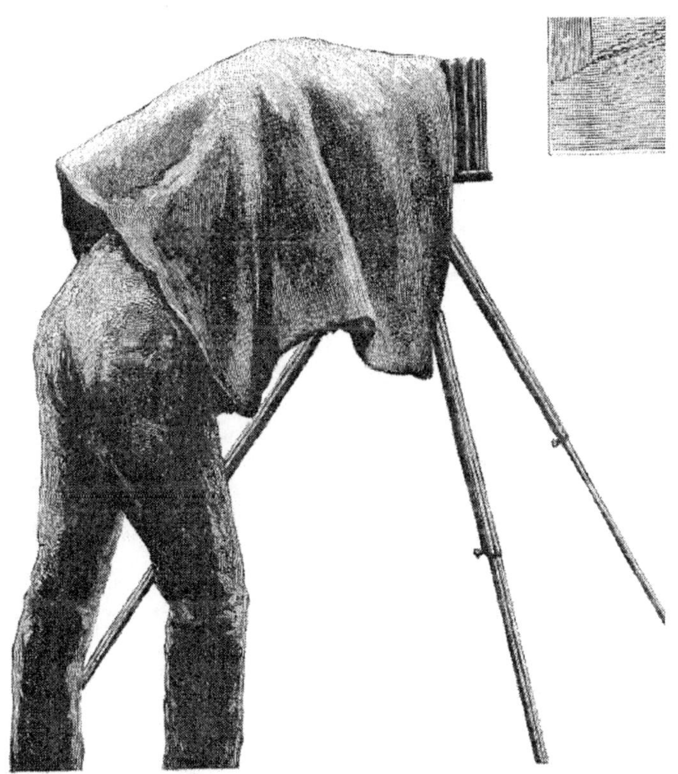

www.ingramcontent.com/pod-product-compliance
Lightning Source LLC
LaVergne TN
LVHW080019110826
845148LV00019B/971
9780788422638